A BIRD THAT FLIES WITH TWO WINGS

Kastom and state justice systems in Vanuatu

A BIRD THAT FLIES WITH TWO WINGS

Kastom and state justice systems in Vanuatu

Miranda Forsyth

ANU
THE AUSTRALIAN NATIONAL UNIVERSITY

E PRESS

ANU

E PRESS

Published by ANU E Press
The Australian National University
Canberra ACT 0200, Australia
Email: anuepress@anu.edu.au
This title is also available online at: http://epress.anu.edu.au/kastom _citation.html

---

National Library of Australia
Cataloguing-in-Publication entry

Author:	Forsyth, Miranda.
Title:	A bird that flies with two wings : the kastom and state justice systems in Vanuatu / Miranda Forsyth.
ISBN:	9781921536793 (pdf.) 9781921536786 (pbk.)
Subjects:	Law--Vanuatu.
	Customary law--Vanuatu.
	Vanuatu--Social life and customs.
	Vanuatu--Politics and government.
Dewey Number:	340.09595

Cover photo by Dan McGarry (imagicity.com)
Cover design by Teresa Prowse

The editors acknowledge with gratitude the financial support received from the Australian Research Council and the Pacific Ediorial Board of ANU E Press.

This book is dedicated to the late Chief Tom Kiri of Erromango, and other great chiefs of Vanuatu, past and present.

Miranda Forsyth is a senior lecturer in the law school of the University of the South Pacific, based in Port Vila, Vanuatu.

Table of Contents

Acknowledgments   ix

Foreword   xi

Prologue   xv

1. 'Igat fulap rod blong hem'   1

2. The possibilities and limitations of legal pluralism   29

3. Tradition and transformation in leadership structures and conflict-management mechanisms   61

4. Mat, kava, faol, pig, buluk, woman: the operation of the *kastom* system in Vanuatu today   95

5. The relationship between the state and *kastom* systems   139

6. The problems of the existing relationship between the state and *kastom* systems   175

7. A typology of relationships between state and non-state justice systems   201

8. A new method of legal pluralism   249

Bibliography   267

Acknowledgments

A large number of people have assisted me in producing this book and I am extremely grateful to all of them. Above all, I am especially thankful to Professor John Braithwaite, who has been the most inspiring, supportive, nurturing and kindly mentor it is possible to imagine. I am also extremely grateful to Dr Greg Rawlings and Dr Guy Powles, for their insightful comments and assistance, and for the support given to me by RegNet at The Australian National University. The time I spent working together with Professor Don Paterson was also richly rewarding due to his encyclopedic knowledge of Vanuatu, its legal system and its people. I would also like to thank all of the members of the judiciary, members of the legal profession, chiefs, community leaders and others who gave up their time to be interviewed by me, to those who housed and fed me when I travelled around Vanuatu and especially to those who read draft chapters and commented on them, or who took the time to listen to my ideas and respond to them. A very special thanks is due to the Vanuatu fieldworkers, members of the Young People's Project and the staff at the Vanuatu Cultural Centre, who assisted me with gathering data about the operation of the *kastom* system. My mother, stepmother, sister and friends were also enormously encouraging throughout the duration of this study and I am very grateful to them. In particular, I am grateful to Tom Clarke and Kendra Gates for their time spent proofreading and to Miguel Juston for his assistance with IT difficulties. Finally, I wish to thank my husband, Sebastien Lacrampe, for his unfailing support, encouragement and continuing interest in this project.

Foreword

Miranda Forsyth researched and wrote this book while teaching at the University of the South Pacific Law School in Vanuatu for the past six years. During this time, she acquired depth and breadth of knowledge of law and *kastom* in the South Pacific beyond Vanuatu from students who attended her classes from island societies all over the South Pacific. She also enjoys a broad network of indigenous and non-indigenous friends in Vanuatu who are deep thinkers and repositories of great learning about Melanesian *kastom*. All this combines with the sharpness of Miranda Forsyth's intellect to equip her to write an ambitious book such as *A Bird that Flies with Two Wings*.

One thing that impresses about the book is the wide-angle lens through which it views not just one island or language group of Vanuatu, but the whole, broad diversity and patterns of Vanuatu *kastom* and how that plurality interacts with the entire national criminal justice system of Vanuatu. That ambition has demanded impressively extensive fieldwork. There is no more important calling for social scientists born in Australia, like Miranda Forsyth, than to document and draw out the implications of the diversity of the cultures of the South Pacific. No part of the world has more linguistic and cultural plurality than Melanesia. As geographical mobility increases, almost everywhere in the world is becoming more culturally diverse than it used to be. At the same time, everywhere in the world is caught up in certain homogenising influences of globalisation. So there is special merit in ANU E Press concentrating its admirably open-access publishing on lessons from the most diverse part of the world on how it sustains that diversity while coping with globalisation that homogenises.

There are few more globalised institutions than criminal justice. Until a couple of centuries ago, very few societies had the distinction between criminal and civil law that was invented in Europe. Today every nation in the world recognises that distinction in its law. It was only in 1829 that Sir Robert Peel introduced the organisational innovation of a paramilitary organisation dedicated to crime control when he established the London Metropolitan Police. That institution has utterly globalised. There is no city in the world one can visit without seeing police in their almost invariably blue uniforms. Before Peel's Metropolitan Police, constables were generalist regulators of overwhelmingly civil law obligations.

My own view is that the globalising Peelian revolution in policing was a desirable and necessary thing for metropoles such as London, but not a good thing for village societies such as Vanuatu.[1] Vanuatu might be better served by regulatory generalist village constables rather more like the village constables of eighteenth-century England, America or France. One reason for this is apparent in Miranda Forsyth's work: village constables can get most of their work done by going with the grain of customary law, and this depends on rich local cultural knowledge more than police academy training in criminal law and its enforcement. At the same time, a degree of training in formal Western law can give the village constable a role as a check on customary abuses of power—for example, of husbands against wives. Miranda Forsyth's text is full of insight on formal law as a check and balance against the abuse of power by informal law, and vice versa.

This book also shows some of the ways in which the prison is a less than comfortable transplant from the North Atlantic to the South Pacific. While Vanuatu was not a penal colony, nearby Australia was a British penal colony and New Caledonia a French one. The colonies of the South Pacific were formed at the time of the great debate between the penitentiary and banishment to remote territory (transportation). Siberia was the only part of the world that was a bigger destination for transported European convicts than the South Pacific. The greatest intellectuals of the dominant powers of the transportation era—Bentham in England, de Toqueville in France—concluded that the penitentiary was a civilisationally superior innovation for inducing penitence, so transportation to the South Pacific ceased and instead prisons were built all over the Pacific. An irony was that the destination region had no history of building prisons, but a rich variety of traditions of banishment, including banishment across the ocean. Just as Vanuatu needs a Peelian police presence in its capital city, so it probably needs a prison there for some of those banished from or disaffected with village life, who migrate to survive on the edge of urban life. It is, however, harder to understand the justification for the literal carceral archipelago of lockups right across the South Pacific.

This book is a contribution to legal pluralism as a theoretical tradition—a profound and nuanced one. Readers of the book will acquire a richer understanding of the options for how state and non-state justice systems can productively and counterproductively interact. It turns out that most citizens of Vanuatu find some things that they like about their state and their non-state justice systems, and some things they don't like about both. This is the empirical foundation for the imaginative theoretical and policy analytical work Miranda Forsyth tackles in exploring options for synthesis, for different kinds of checks and balances between state and non-state law.

Myopically conservative political leaders in nations such as Australia often excoriate the idea of granting recognition to indigenous customary law by saying something like, 'We have one law that applies to all Australians.' Actually, we don't. If you belong to the tribe called stockbrokers, with its special initiation rituals and sacred meeting places, you are subject to special laws that do not apply to those forbidden from entering the sacred meeting places where stockbrokers conduct their rituals to call forth the bulls and ward off the bears that capitalists fear. As a stockbroker, you have little to fear from the criminal law that applies to all; your biggest fear, apart from the bear, is that the membership of the exchange will vote to banish you or suspend your membership for a period. Likewise if you are a doctor, one of the worst things that can happen to you is your professional college suspending your right to practice. Few matters of social protection in complex modern societies are as important as protecting us from dishonest or unprofessional financial brokers and doctors. Yet as a society we choose not to use the criminal law as the main defence against their predations. Multinational corporations have hugely significant private justice systems of a transnational reach that state justice systems cannot match. Even smaller organisations such as schools—private and public—have private justice systems. Hence, if one child criminally assaults another in the school playground, rarely will the police be called. The school will often mobilise its school anti-bullying policies and convene a gathering of affected students, teachers and parents to decide on a remedy or sanction.

Larger education institutions such as universities these days have their own private police; if an assault occurs in a lecture theatre, they will be called to manage the situation rather than the public police. In modern complex societies, according to Clifford Shearing, we move from one bubble of private security to another. We land at an airport and are protected by airport security; we stop at a shopping mall and are protected by mall security; we go to a workplace to be protected by workplace security; or to a nightclub protected by its security. The main role of the state police has become to look out for us when me move from one bubble of private security to another. This is the paradox of contemporary legal pluralism and why we have so much to learn from the sharper, more visible contests between state and non-state regulatory orders in a place such as Vanuatu. While globalisation in some ways—for example, Peelian police, prisons, courts—makes Vanuatu more like the West, in other ways globalisation is making the West more like Vanuatu, with the global proliferation of more and more private justice systems and private policing bubbles.

This book therefore does much more than simply instruct us in some important lessons in how law does and might work in Melanesia. It also contributes some remarkably clarifying thinking about different ways we might craft legally pluralist governance. It is possible for the strengths of formal law to cover weaknesses of customary law and vice versa. It is possible for one form of law to reinforce and enable the productive development of the other. Equally, it is possible for formal law to crush virtues of *kastom* and for *kastom* to crush virtues of formal law. Miranda Forsyth's thinking on these questions is much more systematic than anything that has gone before. It is a tour de force of criminal justice in Vanuatu and of the complexes of legal pluralist policy choice. This is also imaginative scholarship that takes us on a journey of enjoyable reading.

John Braithwaite
RegNet, College of Asia and the Pacific
The Australian National University

ENDNOTES

[1] Dinnen, Sinclair and Braithwaite, John 2009, 'Reinventing policing through the prism of the colonial *kiap*', *Policing and Society*.

Prologue

In 2001, I spent a year as a volunteer prosecutor in the Public Prosecutor's Office in Vanuatu, a small country in the South Pacific spread over approximately 83 inhabited and uninhabited islands. On one occasion, relatively soon after I had arrived, I went with some members of the Vanuatu Police Force to serve summonses in remote villages on one of the outer islands. We took a four-wheel drive and set out, following barely marked tracks, through the dense bush. From time to time, we arrived at villages consisting of leaf houses and surrounded by gardens used for subsistence agriculture, with perhaps only an odd yellow gumboot or an empty packet of rice lying around as a sign of modern life. On entering the village, we would announce why we had come and flourish a very white paper summons. Inevitably, the chief of the village would come to speak with us and explain in a bemused manner that the dispute that was the subject of the summons had been *'stretem long kastom finis'* (resolved in a customary manner already), often many months previously, and that everyone had forgotten about the conflict and had got on with their lives. The police were then in the unenviable position of having to explain that, nevertheless, the defendants would still have to attend court on the named day at the named time. Each time, the villagers would resignedly accept the summons and in return ply us with green coconuts and ripe pawpaw.

This excursion was the first time that I became aware of the indigenous system of conflict management (the *'kastom* system') in Vanuatu—a system that was unofficial and illegitimate in the eyes of the State, but that in effect was responsible for the maintenance of peace and harmony in most communities throughout Vanuatu. From time to time during that year, I came across other references to it: a complainant would tell me not to proceed with a case a few days before trial because the chiefs had dealt with it, or a defendant would plead in mitigation that he had already paid several pigs and fine mats in compensation to the victim's family. I occasionally heard intriguing references to *'kastom kots'* (customary courts) with written records of decisions and written laws. At the same time, I found myself working in an official system based on a Western model that seemed to suit the local circumstances like an old shirt several sizes too small—never fitting or working properly and constantly needing to be mended or 'strengthened', as the official development jargon put it.

When the year finished, I decided to investigate this *kastom* system of which I had had so many glimpses and hints, but had not been able to find discussed in any document or text. In particular, I wanted to discover what its real relationship with the state system was, and whether it was working, or whether the two systems were, as I suspected from the few times I had seen them involved in the same case, undermining and competing with each other. This book, therefore, investigates the problems and possibilities of plural legal orders through an in-depth study of the relationship between the state and *kastom* justice systems in Vanuatu.

To date, studies of conflict management and customary law in Vanuatu by legal scholars have been limited to an investigation of the state system. In addition, the response by the Vanuatu Government and donors to concerns about potential breakdowns of law and order has been to engage in projects designed to build the capacity of the state judicial, policing and penal institutions, ignoring entirely the *kastom* system. This book argues that there is a need to move away from such a state-centric approach, which has not led to a more stable, capable or legitimate justice system. Instead, the scope of capacity building and strengthening must be broadened to include *all* legal orders involved in conflict management, and must therefore include the *kastom* system.

There are three main advantages to such an approach. First, the *kastom* system is currently used to manage the majority of conflicts in rural and urban communities in Vanuatu. By ignoring it, the opportunity to develop a crucial mechanism for the maintenance of law and order is lost. Second, strengthening the state system without taking into account the *kastom* system can have the consequence of undermining *kastom*, thus weakening conflict management overall. Finally, developing a mutually supportive relationship and strong links with the *kastom* system is the best way for the State to enhance its legitimacy in the eyes of the ni-Vanuatu, who still tend to view the state system as foreign and imposed.

Adopting the wider approach just advocated, this book poses a series of highly specific questions about the operation of the *kastom* system and its relationship with the state system. In addition to investigating the current relationship between the state and *kastom* systems and its benefits and disadvantages, it poses normative questions about how a more constructive interaction between the two could be supported. It concludes that, despite the very different natures of the two systems, it *is* possible for them to work together in a mutually beneficial and supportive manner, but this requires changes to the structural relationship between them, as well as adaptations made within each system.

The focus of the analysis of the state system is the criminal justice system, rather than the state legal system as a whole, largely for reasons of manageability. Criminal justice was chosen because it is an area where there is considerable interaction between the two systems, and it is also where most ni-Vanuatu come into contact with the state system. The focus therefore allows for an analysis of an aspect of the state system that has some of the closest connections with the *kastom* system, and also the most relevance to the majority of ni-Vanuatu.[1]

The *kastom* system itself has not been split up into criminal and civil aspects because there is no traditional or current distinction between criminal law and civil law. The main areas that the *kastom* system deals with today are land disputes, issues relating to marriage and children, disputes over the payment of debts and failure to honour agreements and offences of some sort committed by one person against another. All of these are generally referred to as '*trabol*' (trouble) or '*raorao*' (a dispute). For example, for *kastom* purposes, there is no distinction between '*raorao blong graon*' (a land dispute) and '*raorao blong stilim woman*' (a dispute about adultery). In *kastom*, the overriding aim is to restore peace and harmony in the community, and therefore the distinction that is drawn in Western legal systems between punishment and compensation for criminal and civil matters does not apply. In conducting the study, however, the focus has been on those areas where the state criminal justice system and the *kastom* system interact and other areas, such as land disputes, are marginalised as far as possible.

The research in this book is based on five years of fieldwork in the *kastom* and state justice systems from 2002 to 2007. The primary research methodology was in-depth interviews with an extensive number of stakeholders from both systems. In total, 129 people were interviewed, from a variety of different groups, including: chiefs, police officers, members of the judiciary, prosecutors, lawyers, members of the provincial government, women's and youth organisations, cultural organisations, church officials and non-governmental organisations (NGOs). In addition, participant observation, documentary analysis and questionnaires were used. A final technique was the holding of a two-day conference that brought together chiefs, members of the judiciary, police and lawyers to discuss the issues raised in the study and to begin to take steps to formulate responses to them.[2] Much of the material gathered has never previously been recorded or commented on due to the previous focus by legal scholars on the use of substantive customary law by the *state* system and the consequent lack of attention paid to customary institutions and processes.

Chapter 1 of this book aims to orient the reader to present-day Vanuatu. It situates Vanuatu within Melanesia and explores the current cultural, social, political and legal setting through an examination of some of the most important divisions in Vanuatu society today: place (including land), language, politics, religion, gender and age. In doing so, it demonstrates that Vanuatu is a country accustomed to dealing with diversity and that a degree of fragmentation and lack of consistency and coherence throughout the country should not necessarily be seen as a sign of weakness or fragility. Rather, the ability of ni-Vanuatu to draw on diverse practices in all areas—religion, language, culture—is something that could be drawn on in developing a vibrant legal pluralism.

The next chapter sets up the theoretical framework within which the role of the *kastom* system and its relationship with the state system are analysed. It argues that legal pluralism is a more useful theory for this exercise than the positivist approach, which has previously been adopted by legal scholars examining customary law, as legal pluralism recognises that multiple forms of law may be present within any social field and that different forms of law can have different ranges of functions. Adopting a legal pluralist approach, the *kastom* system is recognised as a system of law existing semi-autonomously in the same social field as the state system. The chapter also discusses, however, some of the current limitations of legal pluralism—in particular, its current lack of concern with normative questions about what relationships between state and non-state justice systems could, and should, look like. Finally, the chapter draws together some threads that are used in later chapters to develop legal pluralism as a normative tool.

The next two chapters deal in detail with the operation of the *kastom* system. Chapter 3 is mostly historical and surveys the ethnography of Vanuatu since contact with Europeans to the present day, drawing out the main themes that relate to conflict management, the maintenance of law and order and leadership structures. The motifs elicited serve as an introductory framework within which the current debates over the role of the *kastom* system and chiefs can be more readily understood and appreciated. The fourth chapter explores the current operation of the *kastom* system. We see from the data that the *kastom* system is pervasive, diverse, mostly restorative, dynamic and focused on peace and harmony in the community more than on individual justice. In addition, there is considerable public support for its continuation, even among women, youth and key actors in the state justice system. It is, however, also at times discriminatory towards women and youth, biased, suffering from problems such as a lack of enforcement power and lack of respect, and is in need of checks on abuse of power by the chiefs who administer the system. The *kastom* system therefore, like the state system, is itself in need of strengthening and reform.

Chapter 5 then turns to considering the state system and its relationship with the *kastom* system. It does this through exploring various different institutions—the courts, police, the prosecution, the Public Solicitor, prisons and the National Council of Chiefs (the Malvatumauri)—their current capacity and the challenges they are facing, and the formal and informal relationship each institution has with the *kastom* system. Chapter 6 follows on from this by discussing the current problems with the relationship between the two systems and speculates why those problems exist. It does this largely through focusing on a case study. We see that the state system, based mainly on common law doctrines introduced during the colonial period, is geographically limited, under-resourced and viewed as foreign by a large proportion of the population. It is, however, generally respected and highly regarded for its independence. Currently, the state system does not formally recognise the *kastom* system and so the relationship between the two systems is an informal one whose specific form in any given place is determined largely by the particular individuals and histories involved. This has advantages in that it allows the relationship to be fluid, flexible and responsive to local circumstances, but there are many significant disadvantages as well. The main problems include: forum shopping; confusion, dispute and mutual irresponsibility about which system applies to a given case; a lack of clear pathways for moving matters between the two systems; double jeopardy; disempowerment and demoralisation by chiefs; and frustration by state officials and the wastage of state resources when cases are removed by the parties from the state system to be dealt with 'in *kastom*'. The two systems are therefore presently at best working in parallel and giving each other only limited assistance. More often, they compete with and undermine each other. Although very few ni-Vanuatu advocate abandoning the state system, the majority of the informants interviewed for this study feel that it needs to develop a far closer relationship with the *kastom* system to allow it to become more accessible, legitimate and culturally relevant. These findings suggest that what is needed in Vanuatu is structural reform that will allow the two systems to be mutually supportive and mutually accountable.

The last two chapters broaden the focus to explore the relationship between state and non-state systems in plural jurisdictions generally. Chapter 7 uses the insights generated through the empirical study of plural legal orders in Vanuatu and from a literature survey of 20 other jurisdictions to develop a typology of relationships that can exist between state and non-state justice systems. This typology is then used to develop a new method of *doing* legal pluralism in the final chapter. This new method allows a state to mould the form of legal pluralism in its jurisdiction by having regard to factors such as the strengths and weaknesses of the existing legal orders and their current relationship, the aims of the overall justice system, the extent to which the State is prepared to formally recognise the validity of the exercise of judicial power by a non-state system, whether the State is prepared to lend its coercive powers to a non-state system and how each system can recognise, regulate and adapt itself to the other. The question of what relationship between the state and *kastom* systems in Vanuatu would work best is therefore answered by providing a general methodology that can be used more widely to realise the potential of multiple legal orders.

ENDNOTES

[1] Of course, some non-criminal domains of state law are of little interest in *kastom*. Vanuatu *kastom* cares little about patent or international trade law. To that extent, the analysis of this thesis becomes less central in these domains. It is, however, hard to think of any aspect of law, including these two, where there is not some interaction. The customary laws of intellectual property rights are of burgeoning interest and Vanuatu villages do follow certain norms when they (occasionally) indulge in overseas trade.

[2] Forsyth, Miranda 2006a, *Report on the Vanuatu Judiciary Conference 2006: The relationship between the* kastom *and state justice systems*, University of the South Pacific, <http://paclii.org.vu/vu/2006_jud_conf_report.html>

1. *'Igat fulap rod blong hem'*

Vanuatu is situated geographically in Melanesia, an area of the world that has seen a recent succession of violent conflicts, deteriorating law and order and failing or fragile states.[1] The extent to which Vanuatu is at risk of going down the same road is a matter of some controversy, but it certainly shares some common Melanesian characteristics: a weak state, considerable poverty,[2] ethnic tensions, high youth unemployment in urban areas, poor governance, an exploding population and significant socioeconomic change.[3] The focus of this chapter concerns another shared Melanesian characteristic: diversity.[4] Using this theme, the current cultural, social and political setting to the study is explored through an examination of some of the most important pluralities in Vanuatu society today: place (including land), language, politics, religion, gender and age. This background contextualises the different challenges facing the Vanuatu legal system today and explains the various constraints within which any reform proposal must be moulded, as well as demonstrating the major causes of conflict and forces of change within society. It also highlights the advantages of such a plural society, demonstrating that ni-Vanuatu are used to dealing with difference and mediating between different approaches to the same issues, whether it be *kastom*, languages or beliefs. In later chapters, it will be suggested that this strength could be built on when considering the path forward for the relationship between plural legal orders. Finally, this background is provided following the advice of Shah that 'law must be studied as an aspect of the total culture of a people'.[5] First, however, this chapter provides a framework with a brief synopsis of some of the major events in Vanuatu's history.

Brief history of Vanuatu

The Austronesians—ancestors of the ni-Vanuatu—almost certainly came to Vanuatu from South-East Asia more than 3000 years ago in large ocean-going canoes.[6] Over time, further waves of immigrants came[7] and, as late as 1000 years ago, some Polynesian-speaking peoples also settled on the islands of the archipelago.[8]

The first Europeans to visit the archipelago were Spanish, French and English explorers in the seventeenth and eighteenth centuries,[9] followed by whalers in the 1820s and traders exploiting the islands for sandalwood, sea cucumber and indentured labour. The sandalwood trade continued from 1838 until 1865 when it was largely depleted.[10] The labour trade between Vanuatu and New Caledonia started in 1857 and had extended to Fiji and Queensland by 1863.[11] The trade, known as 'blackbirding', ended only in 1904 and it is estimated that between 40 000 and 61 000 ni-Vanuatu went to work in Queensland during that time.[12] The other early arrivals to the archipelago were the missionaries, who were not deterred by the cannibalistic practices in the southern islands.[13] The Presbyterian missionaries arrived first and, by 1856, many of the islands were well on the way to adopting Christianity.[14] The Anglicans and Catholics arrived later, positioning themselves in those areas where the Presbyterians had not yet secured a foothold. European settlers, mostly from England and France, began arriving from 1865 and establishing plantations, especially in the central and southern islands.[15]

As a result of pressure for annexation from French and British missionaries and settlers, the Condominium was created in 1906.[16] Under the Condominium, the British and the French jointly and equally ruled what was then known as the New Hebrides. The protocol[17] that provided the legal basis for the Condominium authorised the Condominium Administration to make joint laws for certain matters, and also empowered the two governments to establish their own bureaucracies governed by respective French and British laws for other matters, such as police forces, currencies, hospitals and schools.[18] The Condominium was almost uniformly condemned and was a constant source of ridicule. A new French Resident Commissioner was welcomed in 1913 with the following introduction:

> We had brought our magnificent colony, fully organised, to the mother country: she did not want it…For lack of something better and by reason of our ineffectual diplomacy, we were led into this constitution in disarray, this political monstrosity, this undertaking struck with death and sterility. I mean the Anglo-French Condominium.[19]

Calls for independence began in the mid-1960s, sparked by disputes over the system of land ownership under the Condominium, which conflicted with Melanesian customary land ownership. Before independence, two groupings of political parties emerged: the English-speaking pro-independence movement that became the Vanua'aku Pati and a number of French-speaking parties opposed to immediate independence. Independence was achieved on 30 July 1980, largely without bloodshed, except in the case of Santo, where there was a breakaway separatist movement known as 'Nagriamel' under the leadership of the charismatic Jimmy Stevens,[20] which was eventually quashed with the help of forces from Papua New Guinea.[21]

This chapter now turns to an exploration of the many pluralities in Vanuatu today.

Place

There are different aspects to the sense of place that ni-Vanuatu draw on to articulate sources of distinction between themselves. The two most significant of these are the phenomenon of 'islandism' and the urban–rural divide. Another is the issue of land ownership—a major source of conflict in Vanuatu today.

Islandism

The population of Vanuatu is spread over 65 inhabited islands[22] and today home islands provide one of the most salient senses of identity among ni-Vanuatu,[23] especially in urban areas.[24] People therefore often identify themselves with phrases such as *'Mi wan man Tanna'*, *'Mi wan man Ambae'* (I am a person from Tanna, I am a person from Ambae). This phenomenon, known as islandism, has important ramifications for almost every sphere of life.

One of the obvious consequences is the limited sense of nationalism that has developed and is perhaps now even decreasing after the excitement of decolonisation more than 20 years ago. Rousseau, an anthropologist working mainly in Port Vila in 2001–02, argues that today many people see the state government as a remote concept with little impact on their lives,[25] whereas 'island-based identity continues to be a powerful social norm that operates as [an] organisational factor in areas such as residence, ritual, recreation, exchange and the exercise of authority'.[26] Even politicians cannot afford to focus too much on national policies, as their electorates require them to focus on local concerns such as local development and access to funds in order to gain and keep office.[27]

Another ramification of islandism is the strong sense that people must look after people from their own community in government, business and social obligations.[28] It is often expected that when someone attains a position of power they will use the position to benefit the people from their island, before having regard to the interests of the society as a whole. Such attitudes affect the development of a meritocracy.[29] A specific example is the police force, where participants in a workshop recently cited the *'wantok'* system of officers of the same island or province favouring their own people for promotions as one of the issues affecting the effectiveness of the police force.[30] Islandism is also potentially problematic for the state criminal justice system, founded as it is on the values of independence, fairness and equality of treatment. For example, it creates difficulties with the use of lay people as tribunal members due to the perception that a person will always favour someone from his or her own island in resolving or judging a dispute. It is, however, also important to consider White's observation that although such ties can be seen as 'difficult to reconcile with western ideas of good governance…[they do] provide a high degree of stability in local communities'.[31]

A further consequence of islandism is that people are often 'labelled' according to which island they are from, particularly in 'mixed' areas, such as the towns and provincial centres, where people from many islands live together. For example, there is the perception in many islands that people from the island of Tanna are violent and troublemakers ('*stronghed*') and if a crime is committed it is often *'man Tanna'* to whom the finger of accusation points. Similarly, there is a belief that *'man Ambrym'* are to be feared as they have the power to use black magic to cause sickness and death.[32] Recently, there were two serious incidents caused in large part by these features of islandism. In 2006, there was a series of brawls and high tension in Luganville resulting from an East Santo chief being assaulted 'as payback' for a previous incident involving a man from Paama.[33] Then in early 2007 three men were killed and at least 10 houses burnt in clashes involving men from Ambrym and Tanna arising from allegations of the use of black magic by the former against the latter.[34]

There are many observers of Melanesia who are fearful that the ethnic diversity of Vanuatu could precipitate the kind of civil unrest that has recently been seen in other Melanesian countries such as Fiji, Solomon Islands and Papua New Guinea.[35] For example, the *Security in Melanesia* report presented to the Forum Regional Security Committee in May 2001 suggested that Vanuatu's cultural diversity was a potential cause of ethnic tension, especially in urban areas with large squatter settlements.[36] Morgan, however, argues that the 'sheer regional and ethnic diversity of Port Vila's 8,000 teenage and adult males…represents one of the main safeguards against serious inter-group conflict or collective conflict against the government'.[37] In regards to large-scale conflict, some comfort can be drawn from the fact that there are considerable differences between the issues of ethnic diversity in Vanuatu and those in Fiji and Solomon Islands, where there are two major ethnic groupings in conflict. In regard to small-scale conflict, however, islandism continues to be a significant cause of friction, and only time will tell whether it will dissipate as a result of increasing intermarriage or accelerate due to increasing competition over scarce resources such as land and employment. The two recent events just discussed have, however, made the forecast in this area gloomier than was previously the case.

The urban–rural divide: which one is the 'easy life'?

Another significant division today based on place is between urban and rural populations. There are two urban centres in Vanuatu: Port Vila, the national capital on the island of Efate, with a population of roughly 30 000; and Luganville, with a population of almost 11 000, on the geographically largest island, Santo.[38] Urban migration began in the late 1960s and early 1970s when factors such as the diversification of the urban economy, expansion of the civil service, the rise of tourism and the collapse of the price of copra meant that coming to town was the only way to earn a cash income. This pattern was strengthened by independence and the further centralisation of the economy. Today, there are still very few opportunities to participate in the cash economy in rural areas.[39] As a result, the urban population growth is currently 4.2 per cent compared with the national growth of 2.2 per cent, and 21.5 per cent of the population resides in the two towns.[40]

A new but significant phenomenon is that people are increasingly living in the growing 'settlements' inside and outside of town. These are crowded squatter communities where people from different islands live in houses patched together with corrugated iron and scrap materials, often without water, electricity or sanitation.[41] Storey notes that such peri-urban areas have emerged as critical sites of conflict in the urban Pacific and terms them 'grey areas' of 'negotiated territory', overtly urban but 'still rural, for municipal councils are kept at arm's length, the state frequently has limited legitimacy and village-based structures of leadership and social organisation often continue'.[42] Many observers have commented on the rise of criminal activities in the settlements. For example, Miles states that the urbanisation movement 'has spawned, particularly among the semi-educated young, crime, delinquency, unemployment, alcoholism and a breakdown in chiefly authority'.[43]

In contrast, approximately 80 per cent of the population lives as subsistence farmers in rural areas.[44] Due to the distances between the islands and the sporadic and expensive nature of transport, rural areas are often isolated from urban areas and central government. People living in rural areas are less likely to send their children to school, are less highly educated and are less likely to be employed in salary-earning work.[45] As rural people participate very little in the cash economy at present, there is a growing disparity between rural and urban cash income distribution and access to goods and services such as police, health, education, electricity and telecommunications.[46] In the rural areas, however, most people have their own food gardens and access to clean water. As discussed below, there is a good deal of debate about which of the two provides the *'isi laef'* (easy life).

There is a major difference between the impact of globalisation in urban and rural areas. In the two urban centres there is considerable Western influence, although most people maintain significant links to their land and community and adhere in various ways to traditional customs and ways of life. A research project into young people living in Port Vila in 1997–98 found that more than 60 per cent of the young people interviewed had passed through or experienced some kind of *kastom* activity and that *kastom* and vernacular languages were still very important aspects of their lives.[47] In rural areas, the extent of Western influence varies and in some remote areas of the country it is still possible to find people living entirely un-Westernised lives and living in traditional 'leaf houses', although today even in the most remote places people are starting to find ways to send their children to school.

The relationship between people living in town and on their home islands is a complex one. Historically, the trend was for 'circular mobility' as people would come to town for short periods and then go back to their home islands.[48] This pattern, however, appears to be changing as people are staying in town for longer and longer periods. In a study of young people living in Port Vila in 1997–98, it was found that approximately 50.5 per cent had been born in town or had lived there for a number of years with their parents and a substantial number (27.7 per cent) had never been back to their home island.[49] Rousseau comments that by the late 1980s, 'the idea of permanent residence in Vila was being accepted in academic literature'.[50] Even permanent residents, however, locate their identity in their home island rather than developing an urban identity: in five years of living here, I have never heard anyone identify themselves as '*man Vila*'. Many communities in Vila are formed along the lines of island identity, although Vila as a whole is 'mixed' in that there is no one island group that dominates.[51] Moreover, the lines of *kastom* authority in the various communities in Vila often follow home islands rather than geographical arrangements.[52]

It is common for urban dwellers to idealise their home island and present it as a place of relaxation and abundance, where one has only to wander into the garden and pick fruit and eat it, rather than work hard to pay for it as in town.[53] Town is, however, also seen by rural dwellers as being the source of the *isi laef*, a place of opportunity, where cash is readily available, there is freedom from continuous physical toil and youth can escape from the authority of their elders.[54] Town is also regarded as a place where women in particular are freer, especially in regard to choosing their own partners.[55] These two stereotyped images of the *isi laef* contain the seeds of many conflicts between urban and rural communities.

One of the major issues to have arisen between those who live in town and their home islands is the right for chiefs to force people to go back to the island. Urbanisation places considerable strain on the family and community networks in urban areas that are called on to support the migrants from the islands. For example, it is not uncommon for extended families living in overcrowded houses to have to take 'shifts' for the beds. Further, although many migrate for the purposes of finding work, not all are successful. Some turn to petty crime or just become generally disruptive through alcohol, kava or cannabis abuse. In such situations, pressure is put on chiefs in Vila to organise to send people back to the island. This situation also arises when women have run away to town to escape their husbands or an arranged marriage and their families contact the chiefs in town to demand they send them back. Article 5 of the Constitution, however, guarantees everybody freedom of movement and there is a common perception that chiefs who send people back to the island against their will are breaching this provision, causing them to complain that the State is unsuccessful at stopping the increase in urban crime but that they are being prevented from addressing the situation themselves.[56] This issue will be discussed further in Chapter 6.

Land

Land has always been central to ni-Vanuatu, providing food, a place to live and a sense of identity.[57] Discussions about land in Vanuatu often refer to the spiritual bond between people and the land and often the land is characterised as being the 'mother' of the ni-Vanuatu. A recent report into land in Vanuatu states:

> Land to ni-Vanuatu is everything they have, it embodies their link to their past, their present and their future. It contains everything they do in life…ni-Vanuatu see land as sacred and as a part of themselves, it is not seen as [a] mere commodity that can be used and then dispensed with.[58]

Today, however, land additionally provides the possibility for exploitation in order to participate in the cash economy. With the growing population, it is becoming a limited resource subjected to competing pressures. The Director of Lands recently stated that people were no longer seeing land as their mother, rather as 'something to get cash from'.[59] Henckel comments that the 'tension between these diametrically opposed paradigms is unlikely to be resolved any time soon'.[60]

At independence, all land that had been appropriated by foreigners was returned to 'the indigenous custom owners and their descendants'.[61] The constitution provides that 'rules of custom shall form the basis of ownership and use of land' (Article 74). This is, however, problematic, as Farran explains:

> There is no single system of customary land tenure in Vanuatu, but diversity, made increasingly complicated by the movement of people, intermarriage and changes in custom itself. In some parts of Vanuatu land rights pass patrilineally, elsewhere they pass matrilineally. At the same time individual ownership is not unknown, even in custom, although generally ownership is communal, although the unit of communal ownership will vary.[62]

Today disputes over land are one of the most significant sources of conflict and as yet no satisfactory way of resolving them has been established. Traditionally, such disputes have been resolved in *kastom*, but as Jowitt argues, 'custom is increasingly failing to resolve issues as uses for land are changing. People are no longer as willing to accept the legitimacy of custom settlements when settlements are not in their favour.'[63] At independence, the island courts were initially charged with the resolution of land disputes, with appeals going directly to the Supreme Court. This system, however, led to an enormous backlog of cases as 100 per cent of cases were appealed.[64] To try to overcome these problems, the *Customary Land Tribunal Act* was passed in December 2001, introducing a system of Customary Land Tribunals (CLTs) throughout the country to enable all cases involving land disputes to be dealt with at a local level—village, area and island—rather than through the state courts.[65] Two reviews of the CLT program in 2005, however, found that there were considerable problems with the tribunals, including a lack of ownership by the people of the process, lack of awareness and understanding of the CLTs, lack of proper support for the CLTs and for their implementation and, consequently, a lack of establishment of CLTs throughout the country.[66] To date, however, no actions have been taken with respect to the recommendations outlined in the reports and land continues to be an explosive issue.

Language

There are two significant levels to the pluralities in Vanuatu based on language. The first is a plurality of vernacular languages, of which there are currently about 105[67]—the highest concentration of different languages per head of any country in the world.[68] Lindstrom argues that such linguistic diversity cannot be explained on the basis of social isolation, as more and more evidence is being uncovered to show that in fact people are linked within economic and communicative grids. Rather, the diversity has been created and protected by what Lindstrom refers to as 'traditional cultural policies'.[69] The division of communities by language is another aspect of the division by place and provides a further sense of identity without, however, generating much conflict or difficulty.

This is largely because the problem of communication where a number of languages are spoken has been solved by the development of Bislama, a pidgin with a vocabulary of predominantly English origin (although there are also words from vernacular languages and French).[70] It was first established in the European trading stations around the mid-1800s and was then developed further by the ni-Vanuatu workers in the sugar plantations in Queensland, who needed to communicate with others from different islands and who then returned home to teach the new language to their communities.[71] Bislama, the only national language, is today the most widely spoken of the three official languages, followed by English and then French.[72] Unlike many of the other issues discussed in this chapter, Bislama is a uniting factor in Vanuatu. Bolton comments:

> Lindy Allen sees the acceptance of Bislama by the ni-Vanuatu themselves as crucial to the achievement of Independence, and attributes that acceptance to the translation of the New Testament. I myself see the use of Bislama on the radio as even more crucial to the process of wider identification, which led to and flowed from the Independence movement.[73]

The other plurality in regard to languages is the anglophone/francophone split, which generates significant conflict. The missionaries originated the split through the particular churches they represented: the Anglican and Presbyterian churches were mainly English and the Catholic Church predominantly French. These divisions were consolidated by the colonial administration, which separated education (and many other systems) into British and French control, producing the system that continues today of anglophone and francophone schools (70 per cent and 28.5 per cent, respectively).[74] A 1997 report by Vanuatu to the UN Committee on the Rights of the Child states:

> The two former colonial regimes while in power established three systems of government (British, French and Condominium) as well as three courts of law and, among other areas, two health and education systems. The Vanuatu Government had to struggle to put in place only one system and is still struggling in some areas, such as in education.[75]

This division was accentuated by the process of decolonisation in which the French and the indigenous francophone population resisted independence, while the anglophone parties pushed for it, creating a political split along anglophone/francophone lines, which is still extant today.[76] One positive consequence of this division from the perspective of this study is that during the colonial period the ni-Vanuatu became adept at mediating between the French and British systems.

Politics

Vanuatu is a democratic country with a 52-member Parliament elected to four-year terms by universal adult suffrage. In addition to the national government, there are six provincial councils. These are, however, under-resourced and badly coordinated with the central government.[77] There are numerous divisions within the political context in Vanuatu: between the parties, within the parties and even between the politicians and the electorate. As Rousseau states, '*Politik* is viewed as [an] essentially divisive phenomenon.'[78]

Political instability is endemic in Vanuatu; motions of no confidence regularly lead to the overthrow of governments and there is continual reshuffling of the political parties. Currently, 11 different political parties and nine independents form the government. In the past eight years there have been three national elections[79] and the government also changed at the end of 1998 after a change in coalition; in 1999, when the then Prime Minister resigned in order to avoid a vote of no confidence; in 2001, after a vote of no confidence; in 2003, after a change of coalition; and then again in December 2004 after a motion of no confidence in the then Prime Minister. Morgan states:

> A situation has arisen in which both opposition and government coalitions are intrinsically frail. Failure to provide desirable positions to coalition members can result in loss of government. Even the slightest

shift in power in parliament can initiate a complete reorganisation of ruling coalitions.[80]

Even at the local level there is considerable fragmentation of political parties. For example, in 2005, four different political parties were involved in signing two different memorandums of agreement just to appoint the Lord Mayor of Port Vila.[81] Such instability makes real reforms difficult to achieve, as political leaders are constantly thinking of how to ensure their own positions, making them reluctant to introduce any contentious legislation or even provide any coherent policy.

A further significant political division is between the leaders and the people they are elected to represent. The introduction of democracy is recent: Vanuatu celebrated its twenty-fifth year of independence in 2005. Before independence, authority was either exercised by force by the two colonial powers or was traditional and achieved its legitimacy through belief in the sanctity of traditions, *kastom* and obedience to community leaders, as discussed further in Chapter 3. At independence, there was a sudden shift to a different type of authority and a different, legal-rational basis of legitimacy.[82] Given the swiftness of this transition, it is perhaps no surprise that there is considerable ambivalence in the population towards the government. The popular view of politicians is shown in this speech by a 'minister' in a play by a local theatre company:

> It's a funny thing this democracy. People vote us in, never ask what we do. They never read the laws we make. They just blame us when they don't get what they want...To get back in, we have to give our supporters money...and to get all the money you need...you have to...find ways of stealing it. People think if they vote for you, you have to keep paying them back. Pay for every funeral, every marriage.[83]

This distrust of politicians is compounded by the involvement of various high-ranking members of the government in corruption,[84] as well as the failure of successive governments to provide adequate services. The prevailing view of politicians seems to be that it does not matter who is voted in, '*oli stap bisi nomo fulumap poket traoses blong olgeta*' (all they do is to try to line their own pockets). Transparency International states:

> Instability is a long-term feature of politics in Vanuatu, and is perceived to arise because of the abuse of power for personal advantage by individual members of parliament. It is common for members to cross the floor of parliament because a new party can offer more personal benefits than their old one. Legitimate reasons for crossing the floor, such as fundamental disagreements about policy, are rarely the motive for such defections.[85]

Unless there are significant reforms made,[86] it seems likely that disenchantment by the electorate and further fragmentation by the political parties will continue to be significant features of politics in Vanuatu.[87]

Religion and denomination

Missionaries arrived in Vanuatu in the nineteenth century and today more than 90 per cent of the population is Christian.[88] The churches play a central role in most communities and are involved in many aspects of peoples' lives—from education to sports training and counselling to dispute settlement. As Mortensen states, the 'churches' place in state-creation in Melanesia is critical, and often more important than civil government in remote areas where government has little presence and provides no services'.[89] There are two aspects of religion relevant to the current discussion: one displaying a tolerant approach, the other characterised by division. The tolerant approach has developed between Christianity and *kastom*, while there is often division between the different Christian denominations within the country.

As discussed further in Chapter 3, the relationship between *kastom* and Christianity has changed considerably over time. Initially, there was considerable antipathy towards *kastom* practices by the missionaries, who commonly made the distinction between the darkness of heathenism and the light of the Gospel.[90] The practitioners of the *kastom* religion, an animist-based religion, were also overtly hostile to the new church, and cannibalism of the missionaries was frequent in the early days of proselytising. Over time, however, many of the established churches became more accommodating towards *kastom*, allowing their congregations to engage in *kastom* practices such as dances and pig killing.[91] In addition, regardless of the official attitude of the Church, many ni-Vanuatu accepted Christianity while maintaining their belief in *kastom* ideas such as ancestral ghosts, *tabus* and the power of sorcerers.[92] For example, one respondent commented that a *kastom* reconciliation in which pigs were killed was based on the principle of 'Christian love' and that '*blad blong pig wasem sin blong man* [pig's blood washes man's sins]'.[93] Hess observes that in Vanua Lava some Christians believe that 'paradise' or the Christian 'heaven' is the same place as where the dead go according to *kastom*.[94]

At independence, there was a clear attempt to tie Christianity and *kastom* together. The preamble to the Constitution states that the Constitution is 'founded on traditional Melanesian values, faith in God and Christian principles'. The 'Father of Independence', Walter Lini, declared that 'God and custom must be the sail and steering paddle of our canoe'.[95] Although it could not be said that *kastom* and Christianity are harmonised today, there is recognition that both have a role in shaping the spiritual foundation of the country.[96] This is illustrated by the prevalence of the practice of opening and closing *kastom* meetings with a prayer—a practice remarked on with surprise by one anthropologist, who explained that she had assumed 'that people would see Christianity and *kastom* as in some way opposed to each other'.[97] She recalled that one *kastom* meeting she attended was closed with a prayer in which it was said that '*kastom* comes from you, Jesus'.[98] The relationship between Christianity and *kastom* is also shown in the development of some indigenous groups of Christians, such as the Melanesian Brotherhood, who to a certain extent blend *kastom* practices and Christianity.[99] A further example of the Church and *kastom* working together was recounted to me by one respondent as follows:

> If a deacon or elder or even a pastor commits a crime or creates a problem he must go to the *nakamal* to talk. The chief must give him a fine or punishment. At this time he must leave his position in the church. When he has paid his fine then he will be permitted to take up his work in the church again. [My translation]

She concluded by saying in relation to *kastom* and religion that '*tufala samting hemi mixup* [these two things are interwoven]'.[100]

The above discussion demonstrates the possibility of tolerance and acceptance between different belief systems, but religion also causes considerable conflict in Vanuatu today. The root of this division is the proliferation of Christian denominations that are introduced into, and develop within, the country. Today there are at least 19 different denominations of Christianity[101] in Vanuatu, and often six or seven denominations in one small village. This often precipitates conflict, such as an incident in 2006 on the island of Atchin involving tension between Catholics and Adventists over a festival celebrating the Virgin Mary.[102] The introduction of more new denominations into small communities is also often a significant cause of conflict.[103] As a result, many chiefs seek to limit the different religions that are permitted in their village, despite the fact that such actions appear to breach the constitutional right to freedom of religion. For example, the Malvatumauri's *Kastom Polisi* provides: 'Section 1: Malvatumauri policy is that everyone must be careful of admitting new religions in that we are a small population and they divide the people.'[104]

Somewhat surprisingly, there has as been only one reported case where the issue of freedom of religion has arisen. The case of *Marango vs Natmatsaro* arose from an attempt by the Seventh-Day Adventist Church to establish itself on an island that had previously had just the Anglican Church.[105] The chiefs opposed the new church, claiming that it would cause division in the community, and a representative of the church took the matter to court, seeking declarations that their constitutional rights had been breached. The case went backwards and forwards between the Magistrate's Court and the Supreme Court and eventually the matter was struck out for want of cause of action, as the defendant admitted that the plaintiff was entitled to practice and exercise his religious beliefs.[106]

The issue also arose in the legislative context, with the introduction of the *Religious Bodies (Registration) Act 1995*, which required all religious bodies in Vanuatu to register with the government. The act was advocated by the Vanuatu Council of Churches (the body that represented established churches), however, it met with considerable disapproval and was repealed in 1997. The same issues arise in this context as for the right to freedom of movement: to what extent should an individual's rights be limited in the interests of maintaining peace and harmony in the community? This question is particularly difficult because it pits a *kastom*-based communal outlook against a state-based individualistic one.

Gender

Legally, men and women are equal in Vanuatu.[107] Vanuatu is a signatory to the *Convention on the Elimination of All Forms of Discrimination Against Women*, and the promotion of the equal participation of women in domestic, local and national affairs has been part of the government's development plan since independence.[108] The Vanuatu National Council of Women was established in 1980 to provide a forum for women's issues and in 1992 the Vanuatu Women's Centre was established to assist victims of violence.[109] There is also a Department of Women's Affairs, which is responsible for programs to promote gender equality.[110]

In reality, however, there is an enormous division among ni-Vanuatu based on gender.[111] Men are overwhelmingly the heads of households,[112] are twice as likely as women to be in paid employment[113] and hold the majority of positions of power.[114] A report commissioned by the Department of Women's Affairs entitled *Gender, Kastom and Domestic Violence* notes that today 'there is a significant marginalization of women from pertinent discussions and decisions on areas of social and economic development, governance and human rights at community and national levels'.[115] It concludes that 'Vanuatu as a nation has, through its international obligations, put policies and programs [in place] and spent much money achieving equality, but little has changed'.[116]

Two of the most pressing issues for women today, in addition to lack of participation in leadership roles and public life generally, are domestic violence and the fact that women bear the burden of the majority of the housework, child raising and often the work of growing the family's food as well. In relation to domestic violence, the report states that '[i]t is a very commonly held view in Vanuatu today that domestic violence is an acceptable aspect of marriage or cohabitation', and that '[m]ost men and (even some women) seem to think that a woman is part of the man's property and that he can do what he wishes with her'.[117] The prevalence of domestic violence is illustrated by this extract from the script of a play by a local theatre group:

> Theresa: Everyone has to get married sometime, Louisa...
>
> Louisa: You want me to be like you? Get beaten all the time for nothing? That's not going to happen to me!
>
> Theresa: You think you're so much better than everybody else, don't you?
>
> Louisa: I don't! But I don't want to marry a man who will beat me. I don't!
>
> Theresa: Ah! All men do it! You'll just have to get used to it!
>
> Louisa: Oh...Theresa! [She starts to cry.]
>
> Theresa: Look it's not so bad. Women are made to suffer. We bear children in pain. We can take a few slaps from our husbands.[118]

The report shows that many men justify their right to beat their wives on two main grounds: *kastom* and religion.[119] On the *kastom* ground, men explain that *kastom* permits them to beat their wife and also that once they have paid the bride price—a practice that is pervasive across the country—they are entitled to beat her.[120] A local female poet expressed her view of the bride price as follows:

> Braed praes i mekem mi fil olsem wan spid bot
> O trak blong oli pem
> I mekem ol famili blong mi i gridi
> Mo oli wantem wan bigfala praes moa
> I mekem ol tambu mo ol tumbuna blong mi oli kros
> Taem mi no save bonem wan pikinini blong boe blong olgeta
> I mekem man blong mi i ting se mi mas obei
> *Long hem evri taem.* [121]

> [Bride price makes me feel like I am a motorboat or a truck that someone buys, it makes my family greedy and wanting a bigger price; it makes my parents-in-law angry if I am barren or do not produce a son and it makes my husband think that I must always obey him.]

Men also commonly use religion as a justification to beat their wives, arguing that the Bible gives them this right and that as men were created before women the man is the boss.[122] The chiefs and the church leaders who were interviewed in this study, however, maintained that *kastom* and the Church respectively were against violence and promoted peace and love within a family.[123] Other researchers have also reported such conflicting messages. Moldofsky noted that although the President of the National Council of Chiefs told her that *kastom* did not give men the right to beat their wives, his own daughter said to her, 'It's my husband's right to hit me when I don't do something he says.'[124]

This demonstrates that either there are some fundamental communication breakdowns between chiefs and church leaders and their communities or that the chiefs and church leaders are not being entirely honest in their answers. From the research I have carried out, the explanation seems to be that men are using whatever justification they can find and are not listening too hard when the Church and chiefs try to tell them they have misinterpreted a teaching. The extent to which chiefs and church leaders try to change these beliefs no doubt varies considerably as well. There are certainly chiefs who are outspoken in their beliefs that women should obey their husbands and remain out of public life. For example, a highly placed Port Vila chief and former president stated in the local paper that it was against Vanuatu *kastom* for women to put themselves forward as presidential candidates.[125] Other research also supports the view that some chiefs help to support the disempowerment and subordination of women. As will be discussed later, jurisdiction over cases involving violence against women is a major area of contestation between the state and *kastom* systems. There are, however, also many chiefs who support women and who actively try to limit the amount of domestic violence in their community.

The other significant issue for women in Vanuatu today is the vast amount of domestic labour they are expected to do. In 2002, a historian reported that '[t]he male leaders [of a particular area]…said that the men are lazy and do as little work as possible; they endorsed the ironic reproachful boast of several women that "women work, men talk"'.[126] My research also largely confirmed this: on one memorable occasion, I was sitting in a village in Erromango talking with a chief and I remarked to him that the village was very clean. He pointed to some women laboriously sweeping the red earth with brooms made from coconut-leaf spines and he said to me with absolute conviction that when the women woke up the first thing they thought about was sweeping! Tor and Toka's report concludes that 'Vanuatu women are practically enslaved, just as the men had been enslaved by planters and black-birders in the 18th century'.[127]

Whenever issues such as lack of participation in public life and leadership roles, the unequal sharing of domestic burdens and domestic violence arise, the explanation often given is that a woman's role is based on *kastom*. Consequently, it is implied, to challenge this role is to challenge the very foundation on which the society has been built. In the report, the authors challenge such arguments.[128] Through their research, they sought to demonstrate that traditionally women were valued and respected, had more independence than today and lived lives that were not dictated by their husbands. They argued that traditionally women were leaders and participated in the socioeconomic and political development of their community.[129] They attribute the decline of the participation of women in public life and her relegation to the home under the authority of her husband to the teachings of the missionaries and to the introduction of Western ideas, stating:

> Contemporary custom has not been favourable to the women of Vanuatu. It is rather more restrictive, coloured by modes of contemporary and foreign culture and Christian phenomena that serve to downgrade women's role in the community, and ultimately the nation.[130]

This view is supported by Jolly, who argues:

> The male domination inherent in the ancestral culture has been challenged but also in some ways intensified through its relation to colonial pressure. This has generated the strange paradox whereby men both mediate and monopolize modernity, and struggle to keep women apart from it. This self-conscious need to 'hold women tight' becomes not just an internal imperative but part of the resistant relation to external pressures.[131]

While the findings of Tor and Toka's report are certainly an important reminder that the position of women today is not necessarily reflective of the way they have traditionally been treated, they should also be treated with some caution. Historically, the treatment of women varied considerably from island to island and while in the northern islands it might have been that women did possess leadership roles, the same cannot be said of the islands in the south, particularly Tanna.

Thus, while the role of women is formally equal to men, in reality today there is a considerable division between them. This division generates conflict, especially in the context of the huge socioeconomic changes taking place in which the issue of women's rights is often used as a forum in which conflicting ideas about engagement with Western values and principles and *kastom* are fought out.[132] Tor and Toka's report represents a fascinating new development in this area. It shows that women are attempting to use *kastom* as a tool to assert their rights in much the same way as men have in the recent past used *kastom* as a tool to subjugate women.

Age

Today youth in Vanuatu make up a significant percentage of the population, with 45 per cent of the population less than fifteen years of age.[133] A sharp distinction is drawn, however, between youth and adults. Traditionally, and to a large extent even today, until they reach adulthood young people are expected to follow the directions of their family and community leaders and are often denied a voice in decision-making processes. In 1997, Vanuatu's report to the UN Committee on the Rights of the Child stated, 'Traditionally, the children of Vanuatu do not express their views freely.'[134] This approach applies even in relation to personal matters such as marriage. While today the number of 'love' marriages is increasing, there are still a considerable number of arranged marriages. Not all youth are opposed to arranged marriages, but a significant number blame their marital troubles on the fact that they were forced to be married, and young men and women regularly run away to urban areas to escape arranged marriages.[135] One interviewee in Tor and Toka's report tragically stated, 'My partner and I do these [acts of physical violence] because she was never my girlfriend. My parents and families forced me to marry her. That is why our married life will always have violence. When we are ready to die, that is when the violence will end.'[136]

Youth are also expected to obey their elders in many other aspects of life. This is illustrated by a case collected for this study in which a young boy from Tanna complained to the village council that his father had beaten him so much that 'blad i ron [blood ran]'. The father's defence was that he had beaten the boy because the boy went to sing with his friends rather than preparing his father's kava in the afternoon. Preparing kava in Tanna is an onerous task for the youth, who must thoroughly masticate the hard roots of the kava plant so that it can be mixed with water and drunk. The village council held that the boy had disobeyed his father and must pay him a fine and that every afternoon he must return to his house to prepare his father's kava.

The other significant issues facing youth are unemployment—particularly in urban areas—lack of educational opportunities, involvement in petty crime and alcohol and substance abuse. Unemployment is a problem for every sector of the population but particularly for youth, who have higher rates of unemployment and receive even less remuneration than others.[137] There is a major problem with educational opportunities in Vanuatu resulting from the lack of free education, even at primary level, and the lack of adequate places even for those who can afford the fees. As a result, currently more than 60 per cent of young people do not go to secondary school and a significant number do not finish primary school.[138]

Young people are also notoriously involved in criminal activities, often resulting from the lack of employment and other opportunities in town. Morgan and McLeod note that the 'preponderance of young people facing court reflects the systemic inability of national and provincial governments, and the private sector, to provide opportunities for young people'.[139] It is frequently said that Vanuatu's young people pose a significant threat to the country's stability, especially in urban areas[140] where there are high numbers of young people committing crimes and overburdening the legal system. Young people also engage in substance abuse—mainly kava and alcohol, but cannabis is a growing problem.[141] Kava and alcohol have been linked to domestic violence, family disruption and breakdown and accidents.[142]

In recognition of young people's lack of voice, the Young People's Project (YPP) was established under the auspices of the Vanuatu Cultural Centre in 1997. This project engaged in a range of research into issues affecting young people in Vanuatu and produced a report, *Young People Speak*, and a film, *Kilim Taem*, to accompany the report. One of the important findings of the research was that many young people preferred to have issues concerning their involvement in offences addressed through *kastom* rather than through the courts. The project report stated:

> Young people frequently mentioned that they would prefer to pass through traditional channels to resolve their problems with family or with the law when they are involved in some kind of trouble. One reason for this is that when they pass through *kastom* channels they are not left with a police record that will ruin their chances for future employment. Another reason…is that they don't always understand the white man's court system and they find the police are often brutal in their dealings with them.[143]

As a result of this finding, the Juvenile Justice Project (JJP) was established in 1998–99, which had as one of its five main objectives to 'identify the strategy and mechanisms needed to develop and provide an alternative system which effectively negotiates and incorporates *kastom* and western legal conceptions of justice to respond in a positive way to the situation of young offenders in Vanuatu'.[144] The final activity planned was the presentation of the report of the JJP to a national summit meeting on juvenile justice, which was to spend five days developing a national plan of action for dealing with juvenile offenders. It appears, however, that the project suffered from a number of problems that severely affected its ability to meet its objectives. There were numerous difficulties with the research methodology; the final report was not finished by the time of the national summit;[145] and the summit itself was 'dominated by chiefs, young people's voices were hardly heard'.[146] The set of recommendations produced by the national summit—recommending among other things that an act be drafted to empower *kastom* law and empower chiefs to implement *kastom* law, and that only chiefs should be able to say which cases should go to the state courts—was heavily criticised by many prominent NGOs in Vila.[147] A meeting was held to discuss these criticisms but there was no clear conclusion, although there was unanimity that *kastom* existed and was used and that there was a need for some form of integration and formalisation between it and state law.[148]

There is also little accommodation of juveniles by the state justice system. There is no legislation providing for special procedures to be followed by the police, prosecutors and courts when dealing with juvenile offenders and suspects, with the result that youth are processed in the same way as adults, giving no protection against police brutality or making allowances for their intimidation by the courts.[149] UNICEF found that currently the 'laws are outdated and do not adequately protect children from abuse of power'.[150] The sole concession to juveniles is a provision in the Penal Code providing that no person under sixteen years of age shall be sentenced to imprisonment unless no other method of punishment is appropriate (Section 38[1]) and that where this occurs it should be in a special establishment (Section 38[2]).

In reality, however, there are no special establishments for juveniles and so courts that wish to make a custodial order for juveniles are compelled to sentence them to imprisonment in the main jails where there is no way to segregate the youth from the other prisoners. In practice, children under sixteen years of age are rarely sent to prison, but there have been cases in which they have been.[151] Other problems facing juveniles in the state justice system are a lack of awareness of their rights in dealing with the police, lack of an appropriate complaints mechanism against police, lack of legal representation, lack of clear guidelines as to when parents or guardians are required to be present, lack of separate or appropriate detention facilities for juveniles and no structured form of pre-trial diversion.[152] These factors raise a considerable question mark over the findings of the JJP concerning the preference of youth to be dealt with by chiefs rather than the state justice system. It is possible that if the state system were reformed to more adequately meet the needs of youth and protect them from police brutality, this might meet their concerns just as well as empowering the chiefs.

Conclusion

This chapter has shown that in Vanuatu today there are many levels of plurality. The President recently stated, 'We are like 100 nations inside one country.'[153] What remains controversial is the extent to which this diversity operates as a source of instability, and what the response to it should be. In the context of Solomon Islands, White observes that the diversity of the region is often identified as a primary source of instability and 'the most commonly proposed solution is to strengthen central government as a means of holding the forces of disintegration together'.[154] Similar observations could be made about Vanuatu. White goes on to point out, however, that if a local perspective is adopted, rather than one that reads conflict from an outside perspective, one is 'more likely to hear about *legitimizing or empowering the local* than about strengthening the institutions of the (central) state'.[155] This book similarly views plurality as not necessarily equating with 'disunity, division and dispute'.[156] Rather, it explores the possibility of harnessing the strengths that are associated with pluralism—such as grassroots legitimacy, flexibility and easy adaptation to local circumstances—in the context of a plurality of legal orders.

The preceding discussion has shown two successful examples of relationships between pluralities in society that do not involve domination by one of the other. The first is that between Christianity and *kastom*—a relationship that has changed from one of mutual hostility to one of mutual tolerance and acceptance. Elements of each are found in the other, such as the examples of the prayers in the *nakamal* and the use of the chiefs to discipline church leaders discussed above. Further, it appears that many people are able to move between the two, taking the benefits that each is able to provide, without the need to either confront or reconcile the fundamental differences of approach of each system. This suggests one possible model for the relationship between *kastom* and the state justice system, whereby the two systems continue to exist in their own forms but with mutual attitudes of tolerance and acceptance of the role that each plays in society. The example of Christianity/*kastom* suggests that if such an attitude exists then elements of the two systems will naturally come to be adopted by the other. Further, it does not appear necessary to completely rationalise the differences of approach of the two systems before they can have a workable and mutually beneficial relationship.

A different solution has developed in response to the plurality of vernacular languages in Vanuatu: the creation of a new language, Bislama, which can be learnt and understood by all. This development has been wildly successful, enabling the people who speak 105 vernacular languages and two introduced languages to communicate with each other with ease. During my fieldwork, I was constantly amazed at how I could arrive in the middle of a remote village and sit down with an old chief under a mango tree and instantly be able to communicate. Bislama thus provides a different model for the relationship between *kastom* and the state justice system—that of the creation of a hybrid system.

The final point to emerge from this chapter with direct relevance to this study is that *kastom* is very much alive in Vanuatu today. This is shown in a number of ways: the extent to which *kastom* practices are still followed in urban areas; the way communities in town are still organised around the chiefs from their home islands; the fact that youth report significant involvement in *kastom* practices and their preference for chiefs to resolve their problems rather than state courts; and finally, the fact that women are starting to use *kastom* as a tool for achieving a greater role in public life and freedom from domestic violence, as demonstrated by Tor and Toka's report. The continuing power of *kastom* in Vanuatu has also been documented in many other contexts. For example, Morgan and McLeod comment that many ni-Vanuatu attribute the limited magnitude of contemporary conflicts to the continuing valence of 'traditional' modes of dispute resolution, particularly chiefly intervention.[157] The positive way in which *kastom* is viewed by the majority of the population and the current strength of the chiefly system demonstrated in later chapters are factors that set Vanuatu apart from many of the other countries in the 'arc of instability' and should be capitalised on in the development of the legal system. This simple fact seems to be widely accepted. The difficulty lies in how to do it, and this question is the subject of the remaining chapters of this study.

ENDNOTES

[1] For example, the crisis in Bougainville, coups in Fiji (in 1987, 2000 and 2006), the conflict in Solomon Islands between 1998 and 2003, which prompted military intervention by Australia, and continuing conflict in Timor Leste and West Papua. An Australian journalist recently described Melanesia as 'a huge disaster' (Sheridan, Greg 2006, 'Melanesia a huge disaster', *The Australian* [Sydney, Australia], 20 April 2006, viewed 20 April 2006 <http://www.theaustralian.com.au>).

[2] Vanuatu is ranked the third-poorest country in the Pacific and in 1995 was accorded UN Least-Developed Country status on account of its relatively low income, human resource weakness and high degree of economic vulnerability. The Human Poverty Index ranks Vanuatu number 49, and it is ranked 119 on the UNDP Global Human Development Index (United Nations 2006, *Human Development Report 2006*, United Nations Development Program, <http://hdr.undp.org/hdr2006/statistics/countries/data_sheets/cty_ds_VUT.html>). See also Henckel, Timo 2006, 'Vanuatu's economy: is the glass half empty or half full?', *Pacific Economic Bulletin*, vol. 21, no. 3, pp. 8–10.

[3] For a discussion of other factors, see Morgan, Michael and McLeod, Abby 2007, 'An incomplete arc: analysing the potential for violent conflict in the Republic of Vanuatu', *Pacific Affairs*, vol. 80, no. 1, p. 67.

[4] Sillitoe states that Melanesia is one of the most varied regions, in almost every sense, on Earth (Sillitoe, Paul 1998, *An Introduction to the Anthropology of Melanesia: Culture and tradition*, p. 1). Although history and environment clearly play a part in the creation of such diversity, it is becoming increasingly well recognised that even in matters such as language, ni-Vanuatu actively create divisions between themselves, perpetuating difference. See, for example, Lindstrom, Lamont 1994, 'Traditional cultural policy in Melanesia', in Lamont Lindstrom and Geoffrey M. White (eds), *Culture, Kastom, Tradition: Developing cultural policy in Melanesia*, p. 68; Jolly, Margaret 1994, *Women of the Place*: Kastom, *colonialism and gender in Vanuatu*, pp. 252–3. Indeed, it can be said that it is largely *through* creating differences between themselves that ni-Vanuatu define their own identity. Although this is true to an extent in every society, it is pervasive and fundamental in Vanuatu. One reason suggested for this behaviour is that in small-scale societies it is necessary to create distinctions between people in order to generate interest. If everyone is the same and can engage in every activity and have access to all the knowledge then life would be far duller than if there are differences between people regulating what they can do and know (Bolton, Lissant 2005, Respect in Vanuatu, Paper presented at the Friends of the Vanuatu Museum Talks Series, Port Vila, Vanuatu, 22 November 2005).

[5] Shah, Prakash 2005, *Legal Pluralism in Conflict: Coping with cultural diversity in law*.

[6] Bedford, Stuart 1996, *Pieces of the Vanuatu Puzzle*, pp. 3, 259; MacClancy, Jeremy 2002, *To Kill a Bird with Two Stones: A short history of Vanuatu*, p. 18.

[7] See Gorecki, Paul 1996, 'The original colonisation of Vanuatu', in Joel Bonnemaison et al. (eds), *Arts of Vanuatu*; Lynch, John 1998, *Pacific Languages: An introduction*, pp. 51–4.

[8] Bonnemaison, Joel 1996, 'Graded societies and societies based on title: forms and rites of traditional political power in Vanuatu', in Joel Bonnemaison et al. (eds), *Arts of Vanuatu*, p. 212; Tryon, Darrell 1996, 'Dialect chaining and the use of geographical space', in Joel Bonnemaison et al. (eds), *Arts of Vanuatu*, p. 170.

[9] Vanuatu was first 'discovered' by Pedro Fernandez de Quiros in 1606 and charted by Captain James Cook in 1774. For a description of de Quiros's experiences, see Bonnemaison, Joel 1994, *The Tree and the Canoe: History and ethnogeography of Tanna*, pp. 1–22.

[10] MacClancy, *To Kill a Bird with Two Stones*, p. 25. See also Wawn, William 1973, *The South Sea Islanders and the Queensland Labour Trade*.

[11] Shineberg, D. 1966, 'The sandalwood trade in Melanesian economics, 1841–65', *Journal of Pacific History*, vol. 1, p. 129.

[12] Philibert, Jean-Marc 1981, 'Living under two flags', in Michael Allen (ed.), *Vanuatu: Politics, economics and ritual in island Melanesia*, p. 317. There are differences of opinion as to whether workers were kidnapped or went voluntarily. The Queensland Government Royal Inquiry in 1869 found that in the majority of cases the 'natives' quite freely volunteered to go.

[13] Reverend John Williams of the London Missionary Society introduced the Gospel to the archipelago, placing three Samoan catechists on Tanna in November 1839 and sailing on to nearby Erromango, where he was killed and eaten by the local inhabitants. See Proctor, J. H. 1999, 'Scottish missionaries and the governance of the New Hebrides', *Journal of Church and State*, vol. 41, no. 2, p. 349. See also Rodman, Margaret 1987, *Masters of Tradition*, pp. 15–18; Jacomb, Edward 1914, *France and England in the New Hebrides: The Anglo French condominium*, pp. 179–82.

[14] Proctor, 'Scottish missionaries and the governance of the New Hebrides'. Jacomb (*France and England in the New Hebrides*, p. 28) records that in 1914, '[i]t is calculated that some two-thirds of the total population has come under mission influence'.

[15] MacClancy, *To Kill a Bird with Two Stones*, pp. 58–68.

[16] For a description of the negotiations preceding the creation of the Condominium, see Scarr, Deryck 1967, *Fragments of Empire: A history of the Western Pacific High Commission 1877–1914*, pp. 218–27.

[17] The *Protocol Respecting the New Hebrides* was signed in 1914 by Britain and France and ratified in 1922. It superseded the Anglo-French convention of 1906, which had established the Condominium of the New Hebrides in that year.

[18] Rodman, Margaret 2001, *Houses Far From Home: British colonial space in the New Hebrides*, ch. 1.

[19] Le Neo-Hebridais, December 1913, in Bonnemaison, *The Tree and the Canoe*, 94.

[20] Nagriamel, manipulated by American and French interests, proclaimed itself an independent state. See Kolig, Eric 1981, 'Custom or foreign influence: the paradox of Santo, Vanuatu', *Pacific Perspective*, vol. 10, no. 1, p. 60.

[21] Beasant, John 1984, *The Santo Rebellion: An imperial reckoning*; Shears, Richard 1980, *The Coconut War: The crisis on Espiritu Santo*.

[22] National Statistics Office 2000, *The 1999 Vanuatu National Population and Housing Census*, p. 16.

[23] Miles, William 1998, *Bridging Mental Boundaries in a Postcolonial Microcosm: Identity and development in Vanuatu*, p. 78; Douglas, Bronwen 2002, 'Christian citizens: women and negotiations of modernity in Vanuatu', *The Contemporary Pacific*, vol. 14, no. 1, p. 17.

[24] Within the islands, the typical settlement structure is small hamlets rather than large villages, and a variety of forces means that each area carefully guards its own culture and traditions, with people identifying with their local community rather than as belonging to the island as a whole.

[25] Rousseau, Benedicta 2004, The achievement of simultaneity: *kastom* in contemporary Vanuatu, PhD thesis, University of Cambridge, p. 74.

[26] Ibid., p. 104.

[27] Morgan states: 'Members of parliament are increasingly expected to provide access to resources and "development" funds. Indeed all members of parliament act as central nodes in networks of distribution and exchange focussed on access to state resources. In turn, this generates incredible pressure for members of parliament to provide for their constituents.' See Morgan, Michael 2004, 'Political fragmentation and the policy environment in Vanuatu, 1980–2004', *Pacific Economic Bulletin*, vol. 19, no. 3, p. 45.

[28] See, for example, the report by the Ombudsman of Vanuatu, which deals with the granting of land leases by a former Minister of Lands to himself, family members and members of his community: Ombudsman of Vanuatu 1999, *Granting of leases by the former Minister of Lands Mr Paul Telukluk to himself, family members and wantoks*, VUOM 6, <http://www.paclii.org.vu>

[29] A study in 1997–98 found that young people identified islandism as one of the obstacles that prevented them from finding work even when they had good qualifications. See Mitchell, Jean 1998, *Young People Speak: A report on the Vanuatu Young Peoples' Project—April 1997 to June 1998*, Vanuatu Cultural Centre, p. 31.

[30] Taurakoto, Michael 2005, *Good Governance, Education, Advocacy and Training Project Report*, Wan Smol Bag Theatre, p. 23. Such systems of patronage are found around Melanesia, such as the '*wantok*' system in Papua New Guinea, and there is a live debate about the extent to which this is a valid traditional practice or corruption. See, for example, Huffer, Elise 2005, 'Governance, corruption and ethics in the Pacific', *The Contemporary Pacific*, vol. 17, no. 1, p. 118.

[31] White, Geoffrey 2006, *Indigenous governance in Melanesia*, Research Paper, State Society and Governance in Melanesia Research Paper Series, The Australian National University, <http://rspas.anu.edu.au/melanesia/research.php>, p. 1.

[32] For a detailed description of black magic in Vanuatu and its treatment by the state criminal justice system, see Forsyth, Miranda 2006b, 'Sorcery and the criminal law in Vanuatu', *LawAsia*, p. 1.

[33] Garae, Len 2006, 'Police arrest five in tense Luganville', *Vanuatu Daily Post* (Port Vila), 4 August 2006, p. 1.

[34] 'Two confirmed dead in Ambrym and Tanna clash', *Vanuatu Daily Post* (Port Vila), 5 March 2007, p. 1. See also Willie, Royson 2007a, 'Armed police arrest over 100', *Vanuatu Daily Post* (Port Vila), 6 March 2007, p. 1.

[35] Morgan, Michael 2006, 'Vanuatu 2001–2004: political will and the containment of unrest', in Chris Griffin and Dennis Rumley (eds), *Australia's Arc of Instability*, p. 222.

[36] Quoted in ibid., p. 222.

[37] Ibid., p. 222.

[38] National Statistics Office, *The 1999 Vanuatu National Population and Housing Census*, p. 16.

[39] The migration of people to urban areas is a common phenomenon throughout the Pacific and it is predicted that within the next two generations more Pacific islanders will live in or near cities than in rural environments. See Storey, Donovan 2005, *Urban governance in Pacific island countries: advancing an overdue agenda*, Discussion Paper 2005/7, State, Society and Governance in Melanesia Discussion Paper Series, The Australian National University, <http://rspas.anu.edu.au/melanesia/discussion.php>, p. 3.

[40] National Statistics Office, *The 1999 Vanuatu National Population and Housing Census*, p. 16.

[41] Mitchell, Jean 2000, 'Violence as continuity: violence as rupture—narratives from an urban settlement in Vanuatu', in Sinclair Dinnen and Allison Ley (eds), *Reflections on Violence in Melanesia*, pp. 191–2.

[42] Storey, *Urban governance in Pacific island countries*, p. 3.

[43] Miles, *Bridging Mental Boundaries in a Postcolonial Microcosm*, p. 160.

[44] The National Statistics Office (*The 1999 Vanuatu National Population and Housing Census*, p. 16) puts it at 78.5 per cent.

[45] Ibid., pp. 22, 36.

[46] In 2002, a UN report noted: 'There are specific issues relating to the increased migration from rural to urban areas, with the unemployed poor and squatter settlements of urban areas also facing problems of inadequate housing, poor infrastructure and a lack of access to adequate water and sanitation services. Limited employment opportunities in urban areas, particularly among the youth, have also led to an increase in social problems such as theft, domestic violence and alcohol abuse.' See United Nations 2002, *Vanuatu: United Nations Development Assistance Framework (2003–2007)*, Office of the United Nations Resident Coordinator, p. 1 (on file with the author).

[47] Mitchell, *Young People Speak*, p. 18.

[48] Rousseau, The achievement of simultaneity, p. 101; Mitchell, 'Violence as continuity', pp. 192–3.

[49] Mitchell, 'Violence as continuity', p. iv.

[50] Rousseau, The achievement of simultaneity, pp. 102–3.

[51] Ibid., pp. 106–7.

[52] In her research in Vila, Rousseau (ibid., p. 127) found that only one out of the 93 interviewees said they did not have a chief where they lived, and 80 per cent of the respondents indicated that this chief exercised authority over a general island population rather than a geographically bounded one in terms of place of residence in town.

[53] Mitchell, 'Violence as continuity', pp. 192–3.

[54] Ibid., p. 192.

[55] There are many people in town who will not go back to their islands due to the fear that they will be forced into an arranged marriage.

[56] See, for example, 'Ol Jif blong Ambrym oli askem kompensesen mo depotsesen blong Franco long gavman', *The Independent* (Port Vila), 22 April 2007, p. 5; Vieroroa 2007, 'Freedom of movement clause', *Your Letters, Vanuatu Daily Post* (Port Vila), 26 March 2007, p. 7. See also Wirrick, Parkinson 2008, 'Restricting the freedom of movement in Vanuatu: custom in conflict with human rights', *Journal of South Pacific Law*, vol. 12, no. 1, viewed 12 November 2008, <http://paclii.org.vu/journals/fJSPL/vol1no1/>

[57] See, for example, Bolton, Lissant 1999, 'Women, place and practice in Vanuatu: a view from Ambae', *Oceania*, vol. 70, no. 1, p. 43.

[58] Simo, Joel 2005, *Report of the National Review of the Customary Land Tribunal Program in Vanuatu*, Vanuatu Cultural Centre, p. iv.

59 Russell Nari, Director-General of the Department of Lands and Natural Resources (Author's notes from conference presentation delivered at The Vanuatu Update, Port Vila, Tuesday, 14 November 2006).

60 Henckel, Timo 2006, 'Vanuatu's economy: is the glass half empty or half full?', *Pacific Economic Bulletin*, vol. 21, no. 3, p. 13.

61 *Constitution of the Republic of Vanuatu*, Article 73.

62 Farran, Sue 2002, 'Land in Vanuatu: moving forwards looking backwards', *Revue Juridique Polynesienne*, vol. 2, p. 214.

63 Jowitt, Anita 2004, 'Indigenous land grievances, customary land disputes and restorative justice', *Journal of South Pacific Law*, vol. 8, no. 2, <http://paclii.org.vu/journals/fJSPL/index.shtml>

64 Ibid.

65 See ibid. for further discussion of the Customary Land Tribunals. The act provides that where there is a dispute about customary land in a village, a party to the dispute may notify the principal chief of the village, who is required to appoint three people (which may include himself) knowledgeable in the custom of the area in which the land is situated to hear the dispute. An appeal from the decision of such a tribunal may be made to the council of chiefs of the custom area, who are to appoint a tribunal of three people knowledgeable in the custom of that custom area to hear the appeal. An appeal from a decision of the area land tribunal may be made to the island council of chiefs, who are to appoint a tribunal of five people knowledgeable in the custom of the area in which the land is situated to hear the appeal. A decision by the island land tribunal is final. No person who has an interest in the land in dispute is able to act as an adjudicator in a land tribunal at any level. Each tribunal is serviced by a secretary, who is also required to be independent, but does not take part in the decision making of the tribunal. No lawyer may take part in the proceedings of the tribunals.

66 Mavromatis, Geoff et al. 2005, *Implementation of the* Customary Land Tribunal Act No 7, 2001; Simo, *Report of the National Review of the Customary Land Tribunal Program in Vanuatu.*

67 Lynch, John and Crowley, Terry 2001, *Languages of Vanuatu: A new survey and bibliography*, p. 1.

68 National Statistics Office 2002, *Statistical Yearbook of Vanuatu*, p. 14.

69 Lindstrom, 'Traditional cultural policy in Melanesia', p. 68.

70 Crowley, Terry 2004, *Bislama Reference Grammar*, pp. 5–6; Charpentier, Jean-Michel 2002, in Brian Bresnihan and Keith Woodward (eds), *Tufala Gavman: Reminiscences from the Anglo-French condominium of the New Hebrides*, p. 155.

71 Crowley, *Bislama Reference Grammar*, pp. 4–5. See also Crowley, Terry 1990, *Beach-la-Mar to Bislama: The emergence of a national language in Vanuatu.*

72 *Constitution of the Republic of Vanuatu*, Article 3.

73 Bolton, 'Women, place and practice in Vanuatu', p. 51.

74 National Statistics Office, *The 1999 Vanuatu National Population and Housing Census*, p. 24.

75 Government of Vanuatu 1997, *Initial Report to the Committee on the Rights of the Child*, State Party Report, CRC/C/28/Add.8, <http://www.unhchr.ch/tbs/doc.nsf/(Symbol)/d29c5df777ac4b59802565240055b862?Opendocument>, p. 204.

76 Morgan, 'Political fragmentation and the policy environment in Vanuatu, 1980–2004'; Miles, *Bridging Mental Boundaries in a Postcolonial Microcosm*, p. 61; Jupp, James and Sawer, Marian 1982, 'Colonial and post-independence politics: Vanuatu', in R. J. May and Hank Nelson (eds), *Melanesia: Beyond diversity*, pp. 550–2.

77 For a discussion of the establishment of these councils, see Premdas, Ralph and Steeves, Jeff 1984, *Decentralisation and political change in Melanesia: Papua New Guinea, the Solomon Islands, and Vanuatu*, Working Paper No. 3, South Pacific Forum Working Papers Series, p. 53; Ghai, Yash 1985, 'Vanuatu', in Peter Larmour and R. Qalo (eds), *Decentralisation in the South Pacific*.

78 Rousseau, The achievement of simultaneity, p. 72.

79 In 1998, 2002 and 2004.

80 Morgan, 'Political fragmentation and the policy environment in Vanuatu, 1980–2004', p. 42. See also Morgan, Michael 2005, *Cultures of dominance: institutional and cultural influences on parliamentary politics in Melanesia*, Discussion Paper 2005/2, State, Society and Governance in Melanesia Research Paper Series, The Australian National University, <http://rspas.anu.edu.au/melanesia/research.php>, p. 1; Ambrose, David 1997, 'Vanuatu politics—two into one won't go', *Pacific Economic Bulletin*, vol. 12, no. 2, p. 121; Van Trease, Howard 1995, *Melanesian Politics: Stael blong Vanuatu.*

[81] Vurobaravu, Fred 2005, 'VP given mayor in new arrangement', *Vanuatu Daily Post* (Port Vila), 11 November 2005, p. 1.

[82] Weber states that legal-rational legitimacy is 'where the claim to legitimacy is based on a belief in the legality of normative rules and the right to those elevated to authority to issue commands under such rules. Obedience is owed to a legally established and impersonal order, and so office holders are obeyed only by virtue of the formal legality of their commands.' See Reagan, A. 1992, 'Constitutionalism, legitimacy and the judiciary', in R. James and I. Fraser (eds), *Legal Issues in Developing Society*, p. 17. See also Boege, Volker et al. 2008, *States emerging from hybrid political orders—Pacific experiences*, The Australian Centre for Peace and Conflict Studies *Online Occasional Papers Series*, vol. 11, viewed 12 November 2008, <http://www.uq.edu.au/acpacs/publications>, pp. 17–18.

[83] Jo Dorras, *Human Rights and Democracy Play*, Play script (on file with the author).

[84] Such as the forging of government guarantees by the former Prime Minister Barak Sope, discussed in Chapter 5. See also the plethora of Ombudsman reports at <http://paclii.org.vu/vu/ombudsman/>

[85] Jowitt, Anita 2005, 'Vanuatu', in Transparency International, *Global Corruption Report*, <http://www.transparency.org/publications/gcr/download_gcr/download_gcr_2005>, p. 216.

[86] For example, in 2007, the President intended to hold a summit to discuss the possibility of moving to a presidential system that might offer more stability.

[87] Interestingly, the negative perception of politics is currently being capitalised on by chiefs who are eager to contrast the images of greedy politicians with the wise and experienced chief who rules his community according to the rules of *kastom*. It remains to be seen whether this bid for power will be undermined by the increasing involvement of chiefs in politics. For example, it was reported that a number of chiefs presented themselves for the municipal elections in 2005. This was met by outrage by the Port Vila Council of Chiefs, who reportedly wanted to 'expel their colleagues standing in the municipal elections'. See 'Municipal elections: from chiefly to municipal council?', *The Independent* (Port Vila), 30 October 2005, p. 1.

[88] National Statistics Office, *The 1999 Vanuatu National Population and Housing Census*, p. 20. Interestingly, in the last census, 6 per cent of the population put 'custom' as their religion.

[89] Mortensen, Reid 2001, 'A voyage in God's canoe: law and religion in Melanesia', *Current Legal Issues*, vol. 4, p. 528.

[90] Bolton, Lissant 1998, Praying for the revival of *kastom*: women and Christianity in the Vanuatu cultural centre, Paper presented at the Women, Christians, Citizens: Being female in Melanesia today Conference, Sorrento, Victoria, 1998. Even today people commonly refer to the light of Christianity. For example, in a recent newspaper article, an MP stated that 'I feel that as leaders we must remind cultural authorities that in 1845 missionaries brought light to the people of Efate'. See Lini, Lora 2007, 'MP Kalsakau condemns black magic', *Vanuatu Daily Post* (Port Vila), 8 March 2007, p. 1.

[91] Douglas, Bronwen 2005, Christian custom and the Church as structures in 'weak states' in Melanesia, Paper presented at the Civil Society, Religion and Global Governance: Paradigms of power and persuasion Conference, Canberra, Australia, 2005, p. 4.

[92] Mortensen, 'A voyage in God's canoe', p. 511; Hume, Lynne 1986, 'Church and custom on Maewo, Vanuatu', *Oceania*, vol. 56, p. 304; Tonkinson, Robert 1982, 'Vanuatu values: a changing symbiosis', in R. J. May and Hank Nelson (eds), *Melanesia: Beyond diversity*, p. 73.

[93] Interview with a man from Erromango (Erromango, 18 May 2004). Such an approach is common across Melanesia, as is demonstrated by Mortensen ('A voyage in God's canoe'), who comments that Melanesia is 'noted for the continuing belief of its indigenous beliefs and practices' while also being among the world's most Christianised regions.

[94] Hess, Sabine 2006, 'Strathern's Melanesian "dividual" and the Christian "individual": a perspective from Vanua Lava, Vanuatu', *Oceania*, vol. 76, no. 3, p. 293.

[95] Lini, Walter 1980, *Beyond Pandemonium: From the New Hebrides to Vanuatu*, p. 62. This approach was not accepted by the entire population as was shown by the fact that the only two rebellions to have occurred in Vanuatu were both based on *kastom* religious movements: *Nagriamel* on Santo and the John Frum Cargo Cult on Tanna.

[96] Bronwyn Douglas argues that '[h]owever incompatible Christianity and *kastom* might seem to traditionalists, secular romantics, and Christian fundamentalists, their coalescence in nationalist rhetoric discloses just how profoundly Christianity has been indigenized'. See Douglas, Christian custom and the Church as structures in 'weak states' in Melanesia, p. 4.

[97] Bolton, Praying for the revival of *kastom*.

[98] Ibid.

[99] The Brotherhood, which originated in Solomon Islands, is part of the Anglican Church. For an excellent introduction to the Brotherhood, see Carter, Richard 2006, *In Search of the Lost*. Much of its work in Vila appears to involve visiting communities to uncover the sources of sorcery that are causing various ills in the community. For example, in 2007, when the wife of a well-known pastor died, the community members asked the Melanesian Brotherhood for help. According to the local newspaper, 'It was reported that the "Tasiu" as they are also known visited the families and other mourners and after praying confirmed that the woman's death was caused by black magic used by certain people from the community' ('The roots of the man Tanna/man Ambrym row', *The Independent* [Port Vila], 11 March 2007, p. 3).

[100] See also Tonkinson, 'Vanuatu values', pp. 84–8.

[101] The National Statistics Office (*Statistical Yearbook of Vanuatu*, p. 12) lists eight major denominations (Presbyterian, Anglican, Catholic, Seventh-Day Adventist, Church of Christ, Assemblies of God, Neil Thomas Ministries and Apostolic), but I am aware of many others: Jehovah's Witnesses, Mormons, Pentecostal, Revival, Reform (a splinter group from the Seventh-Day Adventist Church), the Healing Ministry, Christ's Church (different to Church of Christ), the Church of Living Waters, Church of the Covenant and Sandy Ministries. In addition, there are followers of the Baha'i faith and Muslims. It was even recently reported that a representative from the 'Promised Land' cult, whose main objective, in addition to worshipping God, was unifying Christian motorbike clubs, had gone to the remote islands in the Banks and Torres Groups looking for converts! See 'Premiers contacts entre Les Iles Banks/Torres et le ministere du culte "Terre Promise"', *The Vanuatu Independent* (Port Vila), 3–9 June 2007, p. 11.

[102] 'Confrontation religieuse a Atchin', *The Independent* (Port Vila), 5 November 2006, p. 3.

[103] This is often due to the issue of tithes. In most churches, tithes are collected in order to pay for the priest and other expenses of the church. When new churches come along and take new members away from the existing churches, this increases the pressure on the members that remain to pay higher tithes, leading to resentment against the new church.

[104] Malvatumauri 1994, 'Kastom polisi blong Malvatumauri', in Geoffrey M. White and Lamont Lindstrom (eds), *Culture, Kastom, Tradition: Developing cultural policy in Melanesia*, p. 229.

[105] *Marango vs Natmatsaro* (2002, VUSC 33, <http//:paclii.org.vu>). See also *Teonea vs Kaupule and Falekaupule* (unreported, High Court of Tuvalu, October 2005), in which the court took a very interesting approach to the issue of the relationship between fundamental rights and custom.

[106] *Marango vs Chief Natmatsaru and Maraki Navata Council of Chiefs* (2002, VUSC 33, <http://paclii.org.vu>).

[107] The *Constitution of the Republic of Vanuatu* (Article 5) provides that all people are entitled to fundamental freedoms without discrimination based on sex and to equal treatment under the law.

[108] Tor, Roselyn and Toka, Anthea 2004, *Gender, Kastom and Domestic Violence: A research on the historical trend, extent and impact of domestic violence in Vanuatu*, Department of Women's Affairs, p. 58.

[109] Today, the Vanuatu National Council of Women has representatives in all six provinces and the two municipalities and area councils throughout the country, and the Vanuatu Women's Centre also has subgroups throughout the islands.

[110] See Douglas ('Christian citizens', p. 20), who discusses these two organisations in detail.

[111] Malloch, Margaret and Kaloran, Morris 2006, A report on equity and women in Vanuatu, Paper presented at the Conference After 26 Years: Collaborative research in Vanuatu since independence, Port Vila, Vanuatu, 2006.

[112] Some 87 per cent, according to the 1999 Census (National Statistics Office, *The 1999 Vanuatu National Population and Housing Census*, p. 27).

[113] Ibid., p. 35.

[114] Since independence, only four women have been elected to Parliament.

[115] Tor and Toka, *Gender, Kastom and Domestic Violence*, p. 9.

[116] Ibid., p. 63.

[117] Ibid., pp. 39–40.

[118] Jo Dorras, *Louisa*, Play script (on file with the author).

[119] Tor and Toka, *Gender, Kastom and Domestic Violence*.

[120] The Malvatumauri originally 'set' the bride price as 80 000 vatu; however, this was officially overturned in 2006, and the new policy was that all *kastom* payments should not be made in cash.

121 Masing, Helen 1991, 'Braed praes', in Vanuatu National Council of Women (ed.), *Who Will Carry the Bag?*, p. 12.

122 Tor and Toka, *Gender, Kastom and Domestic Violence*, p. 39.

123 Ibid., pp. 41–2.

124 Moldofsky, L. 2001, *A Place in the Sun*, Time International, viewed 12 March 2007, <http://www.time.com/time/pacific/magazine/20010820/woman.html>

125 Tor and Toka, *Gender, Kastom and Domestic Violence*, p. 27.

126 Douglas, 'Christian citizens', p. 12. Note also a recent study that found that '[i]t was evident in the research that many young women are required to work far harder than their brothers' (Mitchell, *Young People Speak*, p. 32).

127 Tor and Toka, *Gender, Kastom and Domestic Violence*, p. 15.

128 Ibid.

129 Ibid., p. 25.

130 Ibid., p. 15.

131 Jolly, *Women of the Place*, p. 257.

132 Jolly, Margaret 1997, 'Woman–nation–state in Vanuatu: women as signs and subjects in the discourses of *kastom*, modernity and Christianity', in Ton Otto and Nicholas Thomas (eds), *Narratives of Nation in the South Pacific*.

133 Henckel, 'Vanuatu's economy', p. 10.

134 Government of Vanuatu, *Initial Report to the Committee on the Rights of the Child*, p. 112.

135 This was vividly portrayed in the Wan Smol Bag film *Eniwan iluk Rose?*. It is also supported by the findings from the Workshop on Governing for the Future: Young People and Vanuatu's Governance Agenda. See Morgan, Michael 2001, *Conference Report of the Governance for the Future: Young people and Vanuatu's governance agenda conference*, p. 4.

136 Tor and Toka, *Gender, Kastom and Domestic Violence*, p. 45. See also p. 34 of this report for another tragic tale.

137 Mitchell, *Young People Speak*, p. 29.

138 Ibid., p. 26. This study found that only 47 per cent of the urban youth interviewed had attained class six or less.

139 Morgan and McLeod, 'An incomplete arc', p. 12.

140 Ibid., p. 12.

141 For example, a local newspaper recently reported that '[m]arijuana cultivation and use is already a problem for the country since it is cultivated in nearly all the main islands of the country. Young people particularly are vulnerable to the use of the drugs as there are already cases in Port Vila where young people have been affected mentally as a result of taking in too much of the drugs, which is [sic] easily accessed on the streets.' See Willie, Royson 2007, 'Vt77m worth of Melip marijuana finally destroyed', *Vanuatu Daily Post* (Port Vila), 9 May 2007, p. 1.

142 A recent study found that '[m]any ni-Vanuatu urban youth are trying to cope with having little power and dominance stemming from living with poverty, unemployment, lack of adequate finances for personal use or to help out family members, uncertainty about their future, land inheritance disputes, black magic, not being heard and relationship problems. Many become frustrated and try to become powerful by being violent and aggressive while some become severely depressed. Many break into homes, drink alcohol or kava and *"kilim taem"* negatively.' See Hughes, Desma 2004, *Masculinity, Mental Health and Violence in Vanuatu Youth*, University of the South Pacific, p. 11.

143 Mitchell, *Young People Speak*, p. 21.

144 Rousseau, Benedicta 2003, *The Report of the Juvenile Justice Project: A resource on juvenile justice and kastom law in Vanuatu*, Vanuatu Cultural Centre, p. 1.

145 In fact, the staff of the project left as their contracts ran out and before completing the report, which was completed only in 2001. See Rousseau, The achievement of simultaneity, p. 180.

146 Morgan, *Conference Report of the Governance for the Future*, p. 2.

147 Rousseau, The achievement of simultaneity, p. 111.

148 Ibid., p. 180. Since the collapse of the JJP there have been no new developments in this area; the YPP itself operates only intermittently as it is entirely dependent on donor funding. Currently, the most outspoken voice for youth is the Wan Smol Bag Theatre Company, which produces a range of plays,

musicals and videos concerned with issues affecting youth and regularly tours the country, holding workshops in rural and urban communities to discuss the issues arising from the dramas.

[149] Other countries in the South Pacific region have started to introduce specialised juvenile justice legislation, such as the *Juveniles Act* (Cap 56) in Fiji and the *Young Offenders Act 2007* in Samoa.

[150] Super, Gail 2000, *A Needs Assessment of Juvenile Justice Issues in Fiji and Vanuatu*, UNICEF, p. 28.

[151] For example, in 2003, a twelve year old was jailed for five months in Santo Prison. See Ombudsman of Vanuatu 2003, *Detention of a 12 year old child in Santo Prison*, VUOM 2, <http://www.paclii.org.vu> See also Super, *A Needs Assessment of Juvenile Justice Issues in Fiji and Vanuatu*, p. 33.

[152] Ombudsman of Vanuatu, *Detention of a 12 year old child in Santo Prison*.

[153] Culliwick, Jonas 2007, 'Sessivi Vila burns', *Vanuatu Daily Post* (Port Vila), 11 March 2007, p. 1.

[154] White, *Indigenous governance in Melanesia*, p. 7.

[155] Ibid.

[156] Ibid.

[157] Morgan and McLeod, 'An incomplete arc', p. 68.

2. The possibilities and limitations of legal pluralism

The existence of normative legal systems operating independently or semi-independently from the State, such as the *kastom* system in Vanuatu, is an empirical reality in almost every decolonised country in the world.[1] Despite their prevalent nature,[2] however, and the growing official and academic recognition of their existence, there is currently no widely accepted theoretical position for analysing the relationships between such legal systems, or between such systems and the State. This chapter discusses three possible theoretical approaches—legal positivism, legal anthropology and legal pluralism—and the possibilities and limitations of each for answering the questions posed in this study. It argues that although a legal pluralist approach is the most useful in analysing empirical questions about the operation of non-state legal systems, neither it nor the other two approaches is of much assistance in answering the normative questions this study poses about improving the relationship between the *kastom* and state systems in Vanuatu.[3] The last two chapters take this analysis further by proposing a new methodology to fill the theoretical lacuna identified in this chapter.

There is a terminological issue that needs to be dealt with initially as there is no agreed terminology in this field. There have been numerous suggestions about what to call normative orders existing outside the State, including customary law, non-state justice systems, non-state legal fields, dispute-resolution systems, rule systems, folk law, informal justice, collective justice, popular justice and vigilantism. The difficulty arises from the fact that the terminology employed directly raises some of the central dilemmas in the field: are we just talking about a set of substantive norms or of processes as well? (The use of the terms 'customary law' and 'folk law', for example, can be taken as referring uniquely to legal norms.) Are these normative orders or fields really 'law'? Is a legal order broader than the mere resolution of disputes? These questions are discussed further below, but for present purposes the term 'non-state justice systems' is used. Although the focus of this study is conflict management in the context of law and order, rather than 'justice' as a whole, many of the other authors referred to do not limit their discussion to conflict management. The term non-state justice systems is also the one that is used most widely in the aid and development literature dealing with these issues, and is wide enough to cover non-state institutions as well as substantive norms.

The positivist approach

General principles

Questions of how to deal with a plurality of legal systems first came to the fore during the time of European imperialist expansion and colonialism. The British policy of indigenous sovereignty, often referred to as 'indirect rule', required colonisers to consider issues about what law was applicable to govern indigenous peoples, as well as which law would govern the relations between indigenous people and colonisers.[4] At the time these questions arose, the dominant legal theory was legal positivism, or analytical positivism. The central tenet of this theory, as expounded by one of its main nineteenth-century authors, John Austin, was that all law was the command of the sovereign. From this central principle, a number of consequences flowed, the most important of which in the context of non-state justice systems was that lawyers should confine themselves to the study of law and if societies did not have rules laid down by a sovereign or political superior then it followed that they did not have law.

Twentieth-century positivists modified the strict nineteenth-century approach in some respects, making special provision for systems of customary law. For example, Hart posited a dual system of rules: primary rules constituted the normative order in simple societies; secondary rules, characteristic of more advanced societies, specified the manner in which the primary rules could be ascertained, changed and applied. While Hart conceded that a society might exist that had only primary rules, he believed that these alone did not constitute a legal system and would need to be supplemented by secondary rules to take 'the step from the "pre-legal" into the legal world'.[5]

Positivism in Melanesia

Melanesia is a region where issues relating to non-state justice systems have always been on the agenda—during the colonial period and after independence of the countries of the region—although, significantly, such terminology has not previously been used to describe the issue. Rather, the debate has been couched in terms of the 'recognition' and 'integration' of 'customary law', putting the emphasis on customary norms rather than processes and on the appropriate action of the State towards customary law. Given such a choice of terminology, it is no surprise that the approach that has been adopted in the body of Pacific jurisprudence concerned with the relationship between introduced and customary law has been one of 'weak' legal pluralism, where the State recognises customary norms but not customary institutions. As discussed below (under 'Theoretical issues'), in many ways such an approach belongs in the legal positivism tradition rather than legal pluralism.[6]

The positivist approach taken by the colonial administrators and later by legislators of the independent states is shown clearly in the structures of the legal systems developed during these two periods. During colonisation, customary law was seen as being transient and the pluralist legal system a temporary state of affairs that would eventually be moulded into a universal national legal system. At independence, this goal was often incorporated in the new leaders' plans for the State.[7] Thus, new constitutions such as that of Vanuatu were drafted on the basis of a single, rather than a plural, system of law, with customary law incorporated to the extent that it did not conflict with other sources of law.[8] Vaai, summarising the situation in the South Pacific, states that '[i]ndependence, however, saw the establishment of new constitutional systems that were inevitably in accordance with Western ideologies and law'.[9] In fact, Westermark comments that, since the advent of independence, the external imposition of legal systems has in some ways increased, as 'the new nations frequently stress legal uniformity as a key to nation-building'.[10]

From an academic perspective, there has been a significant body of work generated by what Narokobi terms 'the search for a Melanesian Jurisprudence'.[11] The irony of the fact that since independence the legal systems of the region continue to follow the path laid down by the imperialist government has understandably generated a lot of questioning and thought on the part of lawyers, and occasionally anthropologists, working within the legal system. The majority of the legal academic literature on this issue has, however, been concerned with describing the legislative framework for the incorporation of customary law in countries in the South Pacific region and then analysing the various reasons why in fact there has been so little incorporation of customary law into the state system.[12] Stewart states:

> [T]he task of contemporary legal scholars is seen as interpreting the customary law which evolved in the colonial state courts in the light of contemporary legislation and supreme court practice. It is not concerned with understanding the contemporary social context despite the fact that the people's customs and practices are constantly evolving outside the framework of court decisions and interpretations.[13]

In other words, the approach adopted is essentially positivist, because it seeks to find ways for the state system to 'recognise' or 'integrate' customary law. Such an approach proceeds from the standpoint that it is only once the state legal system has accepted customary law that it can be considered 'law'. This is demonstrated by Zorn and Corrin Care's comment that '[t]he ultimate irony of customary law is that although state law must recognise and apply custom in order to make itself a part of the culture, state law cannot use custom without turning it into something else'.[14] As a result, there has been little consideration of institutions that are not officially constituted or recognised by state law.[15]

Even those such as Aleck who advocate 'new' approaches in fact still remain inside a state-centralist conception of law. Aleck argues that there are any number of factors to explain the current failure of Pacific courts and legislatures 'to bring about the development of "a new, culturally sensitive...jurisprudence which blend[s] customary law and institutions with modern Western law and institutions in an appropriate mix"'.[16] He suggests that the answer is for judges, lawyers and legal educators to recognise and act on the fact that 'the common law tradition itself is best understood, employed and developed when it is regarded fundamentally as a system of customary law'.[17] Such an analysis again belabours the idea that it is up to the state institutions to incorporate customary law and that this can be done through the State's own processes—an essentially positivist approach.

The adoption of this approach in Melanesia has had a number of consequences. First, it cannot really be said that the issue of non-state justice systems has in fact been addressed, because in order to address such issues there first needs to be some recognition that non-state justice systems exist, and such recognition as we have seen is not possible within a positivist paradigm. For example, at the beginning of this study not a single legal work referred in more than a passing way to the operation of the *kastom* system in Vanuatu. Second, the focus of most legal scholars dealing with customary law in the South Pacific has been on customary norms because, as Sack points out, 'positive law has no difficulty in dealing with even the most exotic forms of substantive foreign law', whereas 'foreign legal institutions, methods, processes and values are a different matter'.[18] The main focus of law reform in this area has therefore been to develop 'choice of law' rules to assist the courts to determine whether customary or 'formal' law should be recognised and applied in a given case.[19]

The legal anthropological approach

Anthropological jurisprudence, which first developed as a specialised discipline in the nineteenth century, has challenged many of the paradigms of the positivist view of law and, most relevantly for this study, has produced the various theories of legal pluralism, discussed separately below under 'The legal pluralist approach'. This section discusses its other major contributions to the study of non-state justice systems and also highlights its current limitations.

Initially, the evolutionist school dominated legal anthropology.[20] It was believed widely that all societies passed through clear and inescapable stages of development, distinguished by increasing complexity, and this was extended to include stages of legal development. Various legal systems were studied and compared with the aim of charting a general evolutionary direction, from a primitive to a civilised state.[21] The ethnocentric bias was such that Western European states represented the highest stage of development—a belief that was very convenient for the imperialistic policies of the European powers.[22]

Since the late nineteenth and twentieth centuries, there have been three separate periods in the development of the field of legal anthropology.[23] The first was the publication of the major empirical monographs before the 1960s that were mainly ahistorical, ethnographic descriptions of a single ethnic group and were concerned with seeking to understand whether all societies had law or its equivalent. A small number of monographs, including Maine's *Ancient Law* (1861), Malinowski's *Crime and Custom in a Savage Society* (1967) and Llewelyn and Hoebel's *The Cheyenne Way* (1941), provided the baseline for the discipline.[24] These monographs set the general framework for the methods of research that continue to be employed. Malinowski's work led the movement 'out of the armchair into the village', insisting that some legal phenomena could be understood by direct observation in the field. Before him, most scholars had relied for their material on the accounts of travellers, missionaries and colonial administrators.[25] Malinowski looked at the 'sociological realities' and the 'cultural mechanisms' acting to enforce law and demonstrated the variety of different forces that operated to maintain peace in the Trobriand Islands, including factors such as the cohesive force of relationships of reciprocal obligation.[26] He stated:

> In looking for 'law' and legal forces, we shall try merely to discover and analyse all the rules conceived and acted upon as binding forces, and to classify the rules according to the manner in which they are made valid. We shall see that by an inductive examination of facts, carried out without any preconceived idea or ready-made definition, we shall be enabled to arrive at a satisfactory classification of the norms and rules of a primitive community, at a clear distinction of primitive law from other forms of custom, and at a new, dynamic conception of the social organisation of savages.[27]

Following such works, the ethnocentric notion of evolutionism was criticised and writers turned their attention to the diversity of legal systems rather than their unity and to analysing them within their own terms rather than with reference to a notional universal standard.

With the exception of Malinowski, the other works during this period considered law primarily as a framework rather than as a process. Humphreys observes that '[t]hrough the influence of Durkheim on Radcliffe-Brown, it became a fundamental tenet of...anthropology from the 1920s to the 1950s that the anthropologist's task was to discover the "rules" governing the structure of the society' under study.[28] The influence of such beliefs is so strong that even today what Moore describes as the 'venerable debate' on the topic of the complex place of norms in customary systems continues.[29] Generally, however, later lawyers and anthropologists disagreed with such a focus on norms, stressing that law in traditional societies consisted of processes as well as norms. For example, Sack argues that 'Melanesian law does not express itself in obligatory norms but in the actual social organisation of the people'.[30] Narokobi similarly pointed out that in classical Melanesia, law was not a specialist discipline, but rather 'an integral part of the way in which people went about various tasks in a community'.[31] He comments that the emphasis 'was not on the law or the rule or the norm but on how to settle the conflict'.[32] In the African context as well, Moore writes that '[i]t is fairly well agreed that in many (most) African settings there was much that operated in the "resolution" of disputes other than a system of norms'.[33]

These early ethnographies were critical in establishing methodological approaches to the study of non-state justice systems. *The Cheyenne Way* [34] was 'the first systematic anthropological attempt to study law by a careful analysis of "trouble-cases"'[35] —namely, looking at disputes and inquiring into 'what the trouble was and what was done about it'. The data produced by this method were found to have been the most revealing in exposing the nature of law in Cheyenne society. The 'case method' approach has continued to be a standard method of research and is used in this study, particularly in Chapter 6. Max Gluckman,[36] Philip Gulliver[37] and Paul Bohannan[38] produced important studies during this era. Such studies were essentially critical ethnographic descriptions of non-European societies.

In the mid-1960s, there was then a shift towards the study of dispute settlement and of law as a process, in which the study of substantive rules and concepts was subordinated to the analysis of procedures, strategies and processes. Malinowski, who was already questioning the assumption that 'savages' invariably followed the 'rules', had foreshadowed this shift.[39] Malinowski's work thus gave rise to a new epistemological base in legal anthropology—namely, 'processual analysis', which studied the processes involved in the settlement of disputes. This contrasted with the prevailing idea of normative analysis that was based on the idea that law consisted, in essence, of a number of written and explicit norms and was often presented in codified form.[40] Humphreys identifies two ideas behind this shift: the first is 'that social change and areas of potential instability can be best understood and identified by focussing on disputes for evidence of changing norms, areas of ambiguity in social relationships and attempts to control change'.[41] The other idea is demonstrating that the basic principles used to investigate and adjudicate disputes in developed and less developed societies are similar.[42] Snyder observed that the studies in this period were limited because they did not acknowledge the profound social and economic changes that were occurring as a result of the colonisation process.[43]

The third period is the move since the mid-1970s towards the gradual elaboration of a plurality of approaches and more explicit concern with theory and attention to the role of the State. In the 1980s, anthropologists came to feel that 'the ethnographic case-study methodology of dispute processes was too narrow a canvas of analysis'.[44] It was argued that local disputes needed to be analysed within their socioeconomic and historical context.[45] Further, the case method was also criticised by some postmodernists, who claimed that 'the choice of the case as the unit of analysis shifts attention away from routine compliance with law and toward deviant and otherwise extraordinary behaviour, away from concord and to conflict'.[46] There were two responses to this. First, as discussed below, under the term 'legal pluralism', a debate arose as to how to conceptualise local processes and norms within the wider context of state laws and domination. The second response involved a 'critique of the atemporal quality of case studies of dispute processes and their Durkheimian understanding of dispute settlement as "social control"'.[47]

The preceding discussion demonstrates that legal anthropology has made a number of useful contributions to answering the specific questions this study is concerned with: first in research methods and second in emphasising certain aspects of the legal system that legal scholars tend to overlook, including the numerous modes of conflict management outside the courts and the general social context of the law.[48] At present, however, legal anthropology is limited in a number of respects. First, as Zorn points out, during the period legal anthropology has developed, 'law and anthropology have proceeded from different premises and have embraced different goals'.[49] She further explains that '[a]nthropology's primary aim is accurate description; the pre-eminent aim of law...is prescription'.[50] As a result, there is little general comparative work or theorising about the universal basis of norms or legal institutions in contemporary legal anthropology.[51] For example, Franz von Benda-Beckmann argues that it is rare in legal anthropology to have systematic comparisons of legal systems.[52] Second, with the significant exception of the development of the theory of legal pluralism, discussed below, legal anthropology has been in a period of stagnation and largely devoid of theoretical innovation in the past 20 years.[53] Riles therefore commented that in the 1980s legal anthropologists suffered a 'crisis of identity' and saw a waning of interest in their methods and subject matter.[54] She explains that

> practitioners of legal anthropology now pessimistically perceive the possibilities of their discipline. Likewise, although it is now increasingly fashionable for lawyers to turn outside their discipline for grand insights, they do so with increasing wariness. The image of what anthropology might have to offer, the totally new insight, the epistemology-bursting perspective, never seems fulfilled.[55]

In addition, legal anthropologists seem currently to be turning their attention away from their traditional focus of analysing the intersections between indigenous and European law, to analysing non-colonised societies such as Europe,[56] and also the United States.[57]

The legal pluralist approach

General principles

While definitions of legal pluralism abound, most would generally agree with Rouland's definition that it is the multiplicity of forms of law present within any social field.[58] Griffiths, one of the key developers of the theory, defines a situation of legal pluralism as

> one in which law and legal institutions are not all subsumable within one 'system' but have their sources in the self-regulatory activities which may support, complement, ignore or frustrate one another, so that the 'law' which is actually effective on the 'ground floor' of society is the result of enormously complex and usually in practice unpredictable patterns of competition, interaction, negotiation, isolationism and the like.[59]

One of the central arguments of the legal pluralists is that there exists a state of legal pluralism in virtually every society.[60] Sack takes this one step further, arguing that legal pluralism implies an ideological stance: that it sees the 'plurality as a positive force to be utilised—and controlled—rather than eliminated'.[61] Santos, however, argues that 'there is nothing inherently good, progressive, or emancipatory about "legal pluralism"'.[62]

Legal pluralism thus starts from the rejection of what Griffiths calls 'the ideology of legal centralism', by which he means the positivist notion that law necessarily is the law of the State, is uniform and exclusive and is administered by state institutions.[63] Legal pluralists have criticised the model of legal centralism on three main bases: the concept of 'law as universal across time and space'; its monopolistic claim to 'state power over the recognition, legitimacy and validity of law'; and the State's 'claims to integrity, coherence and uniformity'.[64]

The most widely used conception of plural legal systems is Moore's notion of the semi-autonomous social field.[65] Moore defines the semi-autonomous social field as one that 'has rule-making capacities, and the means to induce or coerce compliance; but it is simultaneously set in a larger social matrix which can, and does, affect and invade it, sometimes at the invitation of persons inside it, sometimes at its own instance'.[66] The boundaries of the field are defined by a processual characteristic: 'the fact that it can generate rules and coerce or induce compliance to them.'[67] Moore's concept of semi-autonomous social fields is an important development in the theory of legal pluralism because, in emphasising the lack of autonomy, it draws attention to the fact that different legal orders exist in relation to each other and hence affect the way that each is able to operate. Moore also demonstrates that studying the operation of semi-autonomous social fields assists in understanding how legal change is really effected, rather than, for example, merely relying on assumptions that a particular piece of legislation will have a desired effect.[68] The concept of semi-autonomous social fields also permits us to develop hypotheses concerning the relationships between the different spheres. Merry notes:

> Research in the 1980s emphasizes the way state law penetrates and restructures other normative orders through symbols and through direct coercion and, at the same time, the way non-state normative orders resist and circumvent penetration or even capture and use the symbolic capital of state law.[69]

Westermark expands on Moore's concept of semi-autonomous social fields by explaining that it can be analysed as an 'interactional approach' towards viewing the relationship between state law and indigenous law.[70] Such an approach, while recognising that in some instances 'imposed law extinguishes all local autonomy', also stresses that 'we cannot assume subjugation and exploitation as inevitable consequences'.[71] Applying such an approach to the village courts in Agarabi, Papua New Guinea, he demonstrates how they have generated their own set of rules and procedures, as have other village courts. He therefore stresses that while we must be aware of the potential domination of national legal institutions operating at the local level, we must not be blind to what Levi-Strauss describes as *bricolage*: 'people's capacity to select bits and pieces of the systems intellectuals build and recombine them for their own purposes in their own way.'[72]

While the concept of semi-autonomous social fields has been widely accepted, it has also been subject to some criticism. Woodman argues that in virtually all writings about legal pluralism it is assumed that the constituent elements of the legally plural world—the 'legal orders', 'legal systems' or 'social fields'—are 'reasonably well identified by their own visible characteristics'.[73] Woodman denies, however, the possibility that a map of legally pluralistic situations can be drawn because it is not clear who belongs to every social field and who does not, or even which law will be applied in which situation.[74] He also rejects Vanderlinden's argument that legal pluralism must be seen from the viewpoint of the individual subject of law, stating that the 'flight to the individual perhaps goes too far'.[75] Woodman proposes instead that we look at laws in terms of a 'population' and refer to the 'legal mechanisms' involved.[76] While Woodman's main argument—that the edges of each plural order are bound to be fuzzy and to have a merging tendency—is certainly valid and important to bear in mind, it is difficult to see how these problems with the concept of semi-autonomous social fields are overcome by replacing the words 'field' or 'system' or 'order' with 'population'.

There is some debate about the extent to which legal pluralism as a doctrine is well accepted. Riles talks about the 'universal fact' of legal pluralism that 'is so commonly accepted that it can be assumed'[77] and Griffiths claims that the ideology of legal centralism has been defeated and legal pluralism is now generally accepted as being 'the new paradigm'.[78] Woodman[79] and Harris,[80] however, query this claim. Hughes notes that 'within so-called Western societies, legal pluralism has not developed much beyond a marginal critique'[81] and Franz von Benda-Beckmann also comments that the majority of legal academics certainly do not really use the concept, and even among legal sociologists 'its use is rather the exception than the rule'.[82] A more nuanced view is provided by Roberts, who comments that while some of the general tenets of the legal pluralists are widely accepted—such as the heterogeneity of the normative domain and the criticism of the State's monopolistic claims to systemic qualities—beyond this, 'consensus is more difficult'.[83] A possible reason for this is the current disagreement about a number of theoretical issues, to which we now turn.

Theoretical issues

Legal pluralists have devoted recent decades to intense debates about a number of related issues: whether or not there is anything that differentiates a 'legal' system from a non-legal form of normative ordering; whether setting a meaning of 'law' is a useful exercise; whether there is a fundamental difference between state and non-state normative orders; and whether or not it is possible to have a situation of legal pluralism within a state system.[84] Franz von Benda-Beckmann therefore notes that '[b]eyond the threshold of the yes or no to legal pluralism, there is little uniformity in the conceptualisation of law, or legal pluralism, about the relations between such plurality and social organisation and interaction'.[85] These debates will be discussed together with their relevance to the application of the theory of legal pluralism to answering the specific questions with which this study is concerned.

What's in a name?[86]

Defining the boundary between non-state law and similar non-legal social phenomena has been a continuing problem for legal pluralists.[87] von Benda-Beckmann goes so far as to argue that the attempt to arrive at a definition of law for anthropological purposes 'still resembles a battlefield'.[88] Moreover, not only has no consensus emerged on what, if anything, differentiates a 'legal' system from a non-legal form of normative ordering, there is a division of opinion as to whether or not attempting to formulate such a definition is possible or even useful.

Under a positivist approach to law, the question 'What is law?' is answered in terms that take some centralised state organisation for granted and consider the presence of rules, courts or sanctions as essential.[89] For example, Roberts has recently argued that '[o]verall, I am left with the sense that it is very difficult to specify in a convincing way a secure grounding for "law" if we try to shake it free from particular forms historically associated with the state'.[90] Legal pluralists, however, claim that non-state legal structures exist, raising the problem of how to distinguish law from other forms of social ordering. The question then becomes whether or not all forms of social control are law or whether there are some other criteria that can be pointed to that distinguish the legal from the non-legal. One of the reasons why this is such a contentious issue is the legitimising power of the label of 'law'. As Tamanaha observes, today, 'law has an almost unmatched symbolic prestige, rivalled in influence only by science. It carries connotations of right, certainty and power.'[91]

In order to define law as a specific type of social control, most earlier legal anthropologists focused on the sanctions following deviance from the norm. In such a model, legal norms are only those whose violation results in a sanction enforced by an institution with authority over the parties involved.[92] Hoebel therefore contends that '[a] social norm is legal if its neglect or infraction is regularly met, in threat or in fact, by the application of physical force by an individual or possessing the socially recognised privilege of so acting'.[93]

Such definitions have, however, been criticised on the basis that '[t]hough the formal legal institutions may enjoy a near monopoly on the legitimate use of force, they cannot be said to have a monopoly of any kind on the other various forms of effective coercion or effective inducement'.[94] Recent attempts to amend Hoebel's definition have tried to grapple with this problem. For example, Frame and Benton propose the following definition: '[a] social norm is legal if its neglect or infraction is regularly met, in threat or in fact, by the application of physical force *or the imposition of serious social disadvantage* by an individual or group *or agency* possessing the socially recognised privilege of so acting.'[95]

Another definition is proposed by Griffiths, who employs Moore's concept of semi-autonomous social fields and defines law as 'the self-regulation of a "semi-autonomous social field"'.[96] He acknowledges that such regulation can be regarded as 'more or less "legal" according to the degree to which it is differentiated from the rest of the activities in the field and delegated to specialized functionaries'.[97] Unfortunately, he fails to explain *why* this should be the case, and his argument that these factors cause something to be 'more legal' seems to undermine his entire argument that state law is no more 'law' than other forms of normative ordering. Other definitions of law abound[98] —some so broad they are criticised as running 'the risk of including all forms of social control'.[99] Consequently, as Merry notes, 'The literature in this field has not yet clearly demarcated a boundary between normative orders that can and cannot be called law.'[100]

The failure of legal pluralists to agree on a definition of law has led to two reactions. The first, advocated by Tamanaha, who launched the most significant attack on what he referred to as the 'precociously successful doctrine' of legal pluralism in 1993, was that such a failure was fatal to the concept of legal pluralism.[101] He argued that although legal pluralism was one of the dominant concepts in the field of legal anthropology, it was 'constructed upon an unstable analytical foundation which will ultimately lead to its demise'.[102] He contends that the concept of law should be reserved for state law, as there is an empirical distinction between state law and other forms of social ordering. Further, calling normative orders other than state law 'law' is ethnocentric and obscures the fundamental differences in form, structure and effective sanctioning between state law and other normative orders.[103] Later, he modified this position, although he still contended that 'having this unresolved issue at its very core places the notion of legal pluralism on a tenuous footing'.[104] Woodman, who has been one of the few to deal with Tamanaha's arguments, criticises this approach, noting that 'the distinction between state law as doctrine and non-state law as social ordering is no more than a distinction of relative emphasis in the sources of information most readily available, not an ontological divide'.[105]

The second approach to the failure of legal pluralists to agree on a definition of law is to argue that in fact such a definition is not essential to the concept of legal pluralism.[106] Woodman's response to the issue of how to define law is therefore that we must accept that all social control is part of the subject matter of legal pluralism and that 'law covers a continuum which runs from the clearest forms of state law through to the vaguest form of informal social control'.[107] Merry similarly argues that '[d]efining the essence of law or custom is less valuable than situating these concepts in particular sets of relations between particular legal orders in particular historical contexts'.[108]   Humphreys comments:

> [W]e cannot draw precise definitional lines round 'law' but are dealing with a complex of ideas and institutions in which demarcation lines vary over time and between one group and another...and that rules of law and legal arguments are formulated, approved and cited in specific historical circumstances.[109]

Santos also refers to the fact that the debate has become 'increasingly perceived as sterile'.[110] Sack takes this approach to the furthest extreme, arguing that 'the main responsibility of law, including legal theory, is not analytical clarity and consistency but the performance of practical social tasks'.[111] Not all legal pluralists, however, are content to leave the definition of law undefined in this way. von Benda-Beckmann, for example, argues that more conceptual clarity is desirable.[112]

One way around this problem that has been proposed, ironically, by von Benda-Beckmann and Tamanaha is to recognise that there might be many different definitions of law depending on who is asking the question and why they are asking it. Franz von Benda-Beckmann[113] therefore advocates asking the more fundamental, theoretical questions 'What is it we want to compare and why do we want to compare it?' before focusing on the potential terminological problems.[114] Twining has most recently also adopted this approach, suggesting that we make 'the context and purposes of the inquiry supply criteria for distinguishing "legal" from other normative orders'.[115] Tamanaha argues that it is not necessary to 'construct a social scientific conception of law' before we can use legal pluralism.[116] Rather, we should treat as law what people in various social groups treat as law.[117]

In relation to the present study, the suggestion of these three authors can be followed, obviating the need to formulate a universal definition of 'law'. The problem this book investigates is the relationship between two mechanisms that are used within a country to manage conflicts. This therefore becomes the focus and the question as to whether such a mechanism is 'legal' or merely normative is not crucial to the analysis.

Is state law fundamentally different to non-state law?

The second major, and related, issue in legal pluralism is whether there is a fundamental difference between state law and non-state law. As Fitzpatrick observes, the relationship of legal pluralism to the State and to state law has been highly ambivalent. Some of its adherents attribute the State no special pre-eminence, leaving 'an unstructured and promiscuous plurality', while others 'reduce or subordinate plurality to some putative totality, usually the state or state law'.[118] Sack comments that this problem arises from the fact that legal pluralism makes sense only if it is assumed that one form of law is not objectively superior to all others in every respect.[119] He also observes,[120] however, that we cannot assume all forms of law to be equally valuable either, concluding that 'it is easy to see that a legal pluralist must also be some kind of relativist; it is more difficult to establish what this implies'.[121]

The idea that there is a fundamental difference between state law and non-state law has been termed a centralist approach.[122] Proponents of such a view often maintain that the empirical reality of the extensive power and influence of the State should not be ignored. For example, Zorn argues that legal pluralism's 'refusal to recognize that the state does have powers unavailable to other institutions…makes history impenetrable and denies the importance of power relationships. The reduction of society to chaos makes everything accidental and removes the ability to extract meaning from social events.'[123]

Merry similarly argues that state law should be seen as fundamentally different 'in that it exercises the coercive power of the state and monopolizes the symbolic power associated with state authorities'.[124] She also acknowledges that the State impacts ideologically on other legal orders because it acts as a framework for their practice.[125] In the context of grappling with the classification of global law as 'law', Roberts has recently argued that 'the growth of law and an ideology of legalism is most plausibly linked to the understandings and practices associated with the processes of centralisation that led ultimately to the formation and proliferation of the nation state'.[126]

The competing approach, termed the diffusive approach, is that law does not need the State to function, nor does it enjoy any particular relationship with the State. Proponents of this view, such as Griffiths[127] and von Benda-Beckmann, criticise the centralist approach as using the ideology of legal centralism. von Benda-Beckmann argues, therefore, in relation to Merry's comments, that she 'does not really move away from legal centralism because the predisposition to think of all legal ordering as rooted in state law is based on this fundamental difference'.[128] Fitzpatrick observes that legal pluralist scholars have tended to assume the ultimate domination of the State.[129] He notes, however, that the problem with the diffusive view is that it does not accord state law 'the original efficacy that, on occasion, it manifestly has'.[130] Further, he observes that treating all legal orders equally does not take into account the possibility of conflict between legal orders or the consequent overarching status state law might assume.[131]

Fitzpatrick argues that in fact both approaches are not inherently opposed, but rather reflect mutual elements of a wider process. He contends that state law does take identity by deriving support from other social forms and would thus appear to be one form among many, but that 'in the constitution and maintenance of its identity, state law stands in opposition to and in asserted domination over social forms that support it'.[132]

The solution to resolving this question for the purposes of the present study is similar to the solution proposed for the answer to the question of 'What is law?'. Whether or not there is a difference between state and non-state normative orders, and whether such a question is important, must be resolved in the context in which the question is being asked. If the question is whether state and non-state normative orders are equally legitimate, the question can be answered in one way. If, however, the question is whether state and non-state normative orders have the same resources available to them, the question can be answered in a very different way. When comparing two different normative orders, it is essential to draw distinctions between them in terms of their respective strengths, weaknesses, fields of influence and susceptibility to change. This applies whether or not one of the normative orders is the State. As Rouland notes, '[W]hether one applauds or bemoans the fact, states exist and are unlikely to disappear: the nature and importance of the state will not emerge from an over-critical attitude.'[133] For the purposes of this study, the approach adopted is to acknowledge the importance of the state system without privileging it over a non-state system unless there is a valid contextual reason to do so.[134]

Is it possible to have a situation of legal pluralism within a state system?

The final continuing theoretical issue among legal pluralists is whether legal pluralism can exist within the state system. There is a distinction commonly drawn by legal pluralists between 'weak' or 'state' or 'juridical' legal pluralism and 'deep', 'strong' or 'new' legal pluralism. While different definitions of the two exist, it can be said that deep legal pluralism involves the coexistence of legal orders with different sources of authority, whereas in weak legal pluralism there are two or more bodies of norms that have the same source of authority.[135]

Today there is a live debate as to whether or not 'weak' pluralism is also legal pluralism. The main protagonist in this debate is Griffiths, who argues that only deep pluralism is 'real' legal pluralism.[136] In criticising previous legal pluralist theories for their tendency towards legal centralism or statism, Griffiths argues that weak legal pluralism is only a facade, as it in fact serves the interests of the State. This is because the State determines the role these semi-autonomous bodies will play and also because it delegates to them only a subordinate role. For this reason, Griffiths argues that the recognition of customary law by the State is weak legal pluralism and in fact supports the ideology of legal centralism.[137] Woodman disagrees with Griffiths' argument, saying that weak (or, as he calls it, 'state') legal pluralism *is* a form of legal pluralism, although he acknowledges it can be distinguished from deep legal pluralism.[138]

These different approaches are discussed further below. For the purposes of this study, the question of whether weak pluralism is a pluralist or a positivist doctrine is not crucial.[139] What is important is recognising the distinction between the two approaches—one being concerned with institutions and processes and the other with substantive norms—as this has significant repercussions for answering the questions posed in this study. As Griffiths observes, '[T]hese two perspectives give rise to different strategies for dealing with customary law in a transnational world, namely whether to work for recognition of customary law within the state national legal system, or whether to claim recognition for it outside this system.'[140]

The framing of the research questions and the methodology chosen to answer them are therefore based on a deep legal pluralist approach, whereas previous studies in this area have adopted a weak or state pluralist approach. In the event, the final two chapters of this study demonstrate that once we start asking specific questions about the nature of the relationship between legal systems, and the pathways that should exist between them, the distinctions between deep and weak legal pluralism in practice become less clear.[141]

The possibilities and limitations of legal pluralism for Melanesia

It is clear from the above discussion that the theory of legal pluralism has enormous potential relevance to the study of the *kastom* system and non-state justice systems in general. This section first discusses the possibilities that it opens up, and the lessons that can be drawn from the existing literature, for the present study, and then turns to discussing the current limitations of the theory. Finally, a way forward is foreshadowed and subsequently developed in Chapters 7 and 8.

The possibilities of legal pluralism

The major contribution of legal pluralism to this book is that it facilitates the investigation of non-state justice systems by establishing them as a legitimate field of study and by providing many of the tools and terminology to do so. It therefore has considerable heuristic value in describing and analysing complex empirical situations such as are addressed in this study.[142] Legal pluralism offers a radically different approach to the positivist orientation adopted by scholars in Melanesia for addressing issues arising from the introduction of Western legal systems into a social field in which indigenous legal orders persist. As discussed above, previous approaches have focused on the way the state legal system could integrate customary norms within its existing framework. Not only has such an approach failed to date to produce the development of a 'Melanesian jurisprudence' by the state courts, it significantly limits the inquiry in sustaining the State as the sole repository of power.

Second, the literature also demonstrates that the focus of issues concerning legal pluralism should be structural in nature. Fitzpatrick is one of the first authors to suggest a focus on structure, observing:

> If legal pluralism is ever to transcend the perpetual surprise at this own re-discovery, it must confront structuring elements of unity, or at least cohesion, beyond the diversity it reflects. Yet it has to do this without, as is so often done, subordinating diversity to some abrupt totality—usually conceived in the literature as a formal or functional dominance of the state.[143]

Unfortunately, he does not develop this idea further, although his implied warning about avoiding the dominance of the State is an important one.[144] Similarly, Greenhouse argues that although current studies continue to treat dispute settlement in general as an internal group function, a group's *external* relationships are crucial to an understanding of its ability to resolve disputes. She analyses a number of anthropological studies and demonstrates that a mediator's effectiveness is enhanced by gestures towards other available forms of authority, his or her relationship to them and his or her ability to mobilise them rhetorically.[145] She notes:

> In situations where courts are available (accessible), disputants' invocations of explicit norms in effect assert that their arguments will have validity 'higher up' the judicial ladder; they are a claim to future success in an escalated conflict. Mediators' invocations of explicit norms carry the dual message of their own authority via their identification with the sources of power in society and an implicit threat to abandon the case to the courts if the disputants fail to come to terms.[146]

Greenhouse argues that 'the way in which a jural community perceives its access to wider systems of authority has, potentially, a profound impact on the efficacy of mediators in containing and resolving disputes'.[147] These comments suggest that seeking to understand the nature of the links between one semi-autonomous social field and another and their position in relation to each other is of the utmost importance—an important lesson for this study.[148]

The third important contribution of legal pluralism to this study is the recent emphasis that has been given to the importance of observing adaptation and transformation of plural legal orders, and particularly the influence that they have on each other.[149] Keebet and Franz von Benda-Beckman argue that '[u]nder conditions of legal pluralism elements of one legal order may change under the influence of another legal order, and new, hybrid, or syncretic legal forms may emerge and become institutionalised, replacing or modifying earlier legal forms'.[150]

They contend that 'such transformation processes are an integral part of legal pluralism' and point out that '[t]he trends are not uni-directional'. Svesson describes such processes of continuous interaction as '*interlegality*', arguing that 'it is the continual flow of legal perceptions, the dynamic force of pluralistic arrangement, that reshapes state law to better accommodate the cultural distinctiveness of indigenous people'.[151] Santos similarly draws attention to the 'porous' nature of the boundaries between different legal orders with 'dense' interactions, arguing that in such conditions 'each one loses its "pure", "autonomous" identity and can only be defined in relation to the legal constellation of which it is a part'.[152] A related point is made by Webber, who argues that the normative relationship between the colonists and aboriginal peoples in Canada was the result of mutual adaptation and that the structure of the relationship 'was formed as much from compromises on the ground as from abstract principles of justice'.[153] He also draws attention to the importance of not minimising the 'relations of power' when considering the development of normative regimes between different legal systems.[154] In addition, it has recently been suggested that external influences, such as globalisation and political change, affect power relationships and local constellations of legal ordering, as well as the legal understandings of former periods, be those colonial, socialist or other.[155]

The current limitations of legal pluralism

Legal pluralism has therefore been shown to be potentially very helpful in addressing cognitive-type questions about how plural legal systems operate in practice in any given jurisdiction. It does not, however, currently have a great deal to offer in relation to answering normative questions about how plural legal systems could best relate to each other[156] or other issues involving what Woodman calls 'planned pluralism'.[157] This type of inquiry involves asking such questions as 'How can we try to ensure that the different legal orders that exist in any particular jurisdiction operate in a way that maximises their ability to cross-fertilise, support and enrich each other, rather than to undermine and conflict with each other?' The fact that legal pluralism does not currently greatly assist in addressing such questions is possibly one reason why to date it has been largely overlooked by development agencies such as the World Bank and the United Kingdom's Department for International Development, which have recently started to become involved in the development and reform of non-state systems.[158]

There are three factors that have contributed to inhibiting the development of legal pluralism into a useful theory in the context of practical law reform. First, in the past decade or so, despite having made such large advances early on, legal pluralism has fallen into a theoretical morass out of which it appears unable to drag itself. Rather than moving the theory forward to develop clearer analytical and comparative frameworks for studying concrete non-state justice systems and their relationships, it has become embroiled in the sorts of internal theoretical debates discussed above, thus reducing its practical relevance. Consequently, as Twining argues:

> [D]iscussions of this broader 'new legal pluralism' became bogged down in obsessive and largely unproductive debates about the definition of 'law'…This is an increasingly important area in which theory has so far provided very little help to detailed research…Although it has produced some excellent specific studies, it continues to struggle with the problem of constructing an adequate theoretical framework.[159]

In this regard, it is noteworthy that a number of legal pluralists state explicitly that the theory ends up advocating immobility. Merry notes therefore that 'pluralism, just as deconstruction, ultimately ends in immobilisation, since if everything is complex and variable, just as if everything is a matter of interpretation, how can one say anything'.[160] Griffiths' assertion that legal pluralism involves 'an unsystematic collage of inconsistent and overlapping parts' and his frequent portrayal of anyone who suggests introducing some order into such a system by considering what attitude the State should take towards non-state legal systems as a 'statist' or 'legal centralist' is also not conducive to the idea of law reform.[161] Rouland argues that Griffiths' theory causes one to wonder 'whether in forcing the state and law further and further apart, we will not be driven up a theoretical blind alley'.[162] Even Sack, who approaches the question of legal pluralism as a lawyer, rather than an anthropologist, despite arguing that 'the aim of legal pluralism is…a situation where different forms of law cooperate, each performing the task or tasks for which it is best suited and in a way which maximises its potential',[163] ultimately also fails to provide any pragmatic solutions, concluding that 'the legal pluralist can, *qua* pluralist, do almost nothing constructive'.[164] Hughes similarly observes that legal pluralism appears to be an incomplete theory that offers a critique of the State but does not advance an alternative approach.[165]

The second factor limiting legal pluralism's relevance to law reform is its political nature. It is clear that the relationship between the State and other legal systems is at the heart of the debates about legal pluralism.[166] This is because law making and enforcing are two of the core functions of a State, arising from what certain political theorists term the 'social contract' between members of society and the State.[167] Hughes makes this relationship explicit, noting that '[l]egal pluralist argument…seems fundamentally to challenge our thinking about the state, if also its relationship to law, so it is a branch of political theory'.[168] He observes that in traditional societies themselves—once the heartland of legal pluralist research—there has been a strengthening of legal positivism, rather than a move towards a legal pluralist paradigm. This is seen to be due to new governing elites seeking out rapid development, international financing, structural reform and rapid assimilation to the liberal capitalist model of the State.[169] Rouland also draws attention to the fact that acting on legal pluralism is likely to encroach on state power, which is problematic because 'not all states are totalitarian, but they all contain the seeds of totalitarianism, since it is part of the underlying logic of the state to try to weaken, or even do away with, any authority that rivals its own'.[170] Ottley and Zorn argue that one reason why the legal system has failed to incorporate customary law in Papua New Guinea is the belief by state institutions that a customary legal system constitutes a threat to them and to the system of legislation and case law that reinforces the authority and legitimacy of the State.[171] They explain that

> [b]y monopolizing the law and its processes, the state reifies itself. Customary law, then, is viewed by the government, whether or not correctly, as a direct attack upon the legitimacy of the state. The

government and the propertied classes that the state protects believe that by taking force into their own hands and solving disputes using their own methods, clans are, in effect, communicating to the state that it is not needed and that its monopolies over basic areas of social control are not needed.[172]

Finally, and most relevantly for our purposes, the theory has had limited relevance for law reform because the material produced has tended to be largely descriptive rather than normative,[173] and limited to one site of study,[174] meaning that it has not been comparative, thus inhibiting the development of overarching theories that could be used in a law reform context.[175] As Snyder comments:

> Partly as a consequence of its relative unconcern for law and its emphasis on disputes and process, much recent legal anthropological writing would appear incapable of arriving at a theoretical view of the apparent autonomy of law, or of considering abstractly the relationships between plural legal forms, including those of the state, in different countries.[176]

Franz and Keebet von Benda-Beckmann similarly observe that although the literature on legal pluralism is extensive, 'it mainly consists of case studies, on the one hand, or of very general summary statements simply reproducing the official, state-law version of legal pluralism on the other'.[177] They in fact even go so far as to deny that it is an explanatory theory at all, merely referring to legal pluralism as a 'sensitising concept'.[178] Therefore, due at least in part to these three factors, currently there is a very limited theoretical foundation for addressing the sorts of questions this study asks about improving the relationship between the *kastom* and state legal systems in Vanuatu. The next section discusses the material that makes up this limited foundation, then Chapters 7 and 8 build from this basis a new framework and methodology for analysing and reforming relationships between plural legal orders.

Using legal pluralism as a normative tool

The principal contributors to the development of a legal pluralist approach to law reform to date have been Morse and Woodman.[179] In the late 1980s, they developed a number of broad categories for the main formal legal measures the State could take regarding customary law.[180]

The first category is negative measures, including prohibition of conduct either required or permitted by customary law and denial of validity of the legal consequences that would otherwise be conferred by a customary norm.[181] The second category is positive measures, and this contains three subsets. The first is admittance as fact, which can be viewed as not amounting to an acceptance of the legal nature of customary law. The second is incorporation of law, by which the state law admits into its own body of norms a customary law norm or portion of that norm. They point out, however, that this is problematic particularly when it comes to procedural norms, as particular procedures are often inseparable in practice from the social institutions within which they operate and so their incorporation is likely to be narrowly limited unless there is a profound reform of state institutions. It should be noted that all the approaches suggested so far fit within the weak pluralist approach. The third subset of approaches, however, moves beyond a state-centralist approach. Morse and Woodman refer to them as 'measures of acknowledgment' and define them as 'measures by which state law expressly or impliedly provides that state institutions do not have an exclusive capacity to perform certain functions to do with law, which customary law is competent to perform'.[182] For example, through a measure of acknowledgment, state law accepts the capacity of customary law to constitute an institution with legal powers, such as a traditional assembly with power to enact law or to adjudicate in disputes.

Morse and Woodman set out three ways of classifying the measures of acknowledgment. The first is the type of power, which can be either a legislative acknowledgment or a measure of norm-applying acknowledgment, such as adjudication. The second way of classifying the measures of acknowledgment is according to the State's characterisation of each. The State may assert either that it has conferred the power itself on the customary institution or that it is recognising existing, legitimate powers. The latter approach implies abandonment of any dogma of a state monopoly of legitimate authority and will not allow the State to circumscribe the powers or to abrogate them as could be done in the former instance. Morse and Woodman note that the latter approach is unlikely to be accepted by a state due to its challenge to the State's monopolistic powers. The third way of classifying the measure of acknowledgment is whether the state law confers on a state institution powers concurrent with those granted or recognised as held by the customary institution or whether it provides that the customary institution is the sole holder of the powers of the type designed. In the former case, a difficulty will arise as to how to resolve conflicts between the two institutions given that the State necessarily concedes its lack of competence to determine the scope of the powers of the customary institution. Morse and Woodman suggest that this can be solved only by some overriding law, based, for example, on the notion of the binding force of agreement between the populations of the two constituencies.

Morse and Woodman's analysis of different measures of acknowledgment is an important start to the development of an analytical framework. They demonstrate that when discussing deep legal pluralism, the foremost issues are processual rather than normative and that the questions that arise are what can be termed structural in nature. The second point to emerge from their discussion is that a measure of acknowledgment must be between the State and a mechanism that exists independently of the State—in other words, that has not been constituted by state laws. The analysis, however, is also very limited, particularly in regard to the lack of concrete examples that Morse and Woodman can point to of such measures of acknowledgment in reality.[183] It is therefore not possible to tell from their analysis under what circumstances the various measures of acknowledgment could be effective. Morse and Woodman themselves acknowledge that they are merely trying to initiate the development of such a theory, rather than to present a finished framework, and consequently they do not move in any detail beyond the broad description just outlined.

More recently, Woodman has drawn a distinction between institutional recognition, 'where a law accepts the existence of institutions of another law, and provides that the activities of these institutions or some of them to produce legally valid effects',[184] and normative recognition that 'consists of the recognising law providing that in certain cases the norms of the other law will be applied by the institutions of the recognising law instead of its own norms'.[185] The former type of recognition is associated with deep legal pluralism and the latter with state legal pluralism. This distinction is useful as it clearly illustrates the different responses legal systems are required to make depending on the type of legal pluralism involved. This point is developed further in Chapter 7, which seeks to explore all the different potential types of institutional recognition possible in a given jurisdiction.

A further contribution in this area is von Benda-Beckman's suggestion that one way to analyse the differential use of indigenous, neo-traditional and state institutions in former colonial countries is to look at the variations in the politico-legal structure of the overall system.[186] He suggests that rather than asking, as is usually done, whether or not folk institutions have been recognised by being incorporated into the official/colonial/national system, it is more fruitful to ask whether or not state/neo-traditional institutions have been placed within or outside the indigenous political system and the socio-spatial jurisdictions of its institutions.[187] Although he acknowledges that limited data make such analysis difficult, he conducts a comparison of the differential use of such institutions in a number of former British African colonies and West Sumatra. His findings are that state courts are used more frequently if they are located below or at the top level of the non-state justice system and less frequently if placed outside indigenous political structures.[188] He concludes that the structural location of 'folk institutions' is more important in terms of their containment rates and use than other factors such as their degree of Westernisation.[189]

von Benda-Beckman's hypothesis seems to be backed up by Westermark's study of village courts in Agarabi, Papua New Guinea. Westermark notes that

> the presence of the administration fostered the creation of unofficial courts by village officials, providing forums that were perceived both

to be linked to the official system and to operate in a way generally acceptable to the community. Such a combination of an ostensibly official status and acceptable style led to an active use of the courts by community members.[190]

Another useful suggestion arising from Westermark's work comes from his disagreement with Abel's assertion, made in relation to Africa, that pre-capitalist informal legal institutions cannot be used as a model for institutionalising informal forums under capitalism.[191] He argues that the village courts in Papua New Guinea have generally been successful as they have emerged from the cultural and historical variability of the country and, importantly, 'because the links between the national and local level were not drawn taut in the development of the courts, each court area was free to express this variability'.[192] This idea of not drawing the links 'taut', while anathema to a traditionally legalistic approach, is also an extremely valuable insight, even if the view of village courts, while not totally false, might have been somewhat prematurely rosy.[193]

In recent years, there also has been increasing interest in normative questions concerning state and non-state justice systems from a different interest group—namely, law reform and development agencies, many of whom have realised the importance of traditional and informal systems as complements to the formal system, especially in post-conflict situations, and also that these systems might need reform in order to become fairer and more effective.[194] The UK Department for International Development has been particularly active in this respect and has generated a number of studies of non-state justice systems, mostly in Africa and South America.[195] Law reform commissions in various countries, including Australia,[196] New Zealand,[197] Malawi, Fiji[198] and, perhaps to the greatest extent, South Africa,[199] have also produced a number of reports and studies. Finally, there has been some interest in the area by NGOs, such as Penal Reform International,[200] the US Institute of Peace[201] and the United Nations.[202] Blagg comments that the emerging practices in relation to issues surrounding non-state justice systems by these organisations involve a '"synthesis and synergy" approach to law reform, involving a gradual convergence of Indigenous and non-Indigenous values, beliefs and practices'.[203] There is a broad acceptance that to have any chance of success the approach must be far more sophisticated than, for example, merely integrating customary law into the state system. For example, Fitzgerald argues:

> There needs to be institutional space or spaces created for the accommodation of Aboriginal law within the broader Australian legal system. There must be institutional design for the administration of a local order by Aboriginal communities. There must be 'pods of justice' distinct in form and function, autonomous but contributing to a federal whole.[204]

Conclusion

The preceding discussion has demonstrated that, although no comprehensive framework has yet been proposed by legal pluralist scholars or law reform or donor agencies,[205] the makings of such a tool are present. These include: the growing number of empirical studies, generated by legal anthropologists and donor organisations, [206] into how non-state justice systems are really operating in many countries; the recognition of the centrality of structural relationships between plural legal orders; the importance of avoiding a state-centralist approach to issues of law reform; the conceptual distinctions between normative and institutional pluralism; and the need to consider the nature of the links between plural legal orders. These ideas are developed further in Chapter 7, which proposes a typology of models of relationship between state and non-state justice systems based on a comparative study of the treatment of non-state justice systems across various jurisdictions. This in turn allows an investigation into the possibilities of relationships in which state and non-state justice systems continue to work within their own normative and processual frameworks, in ways that are mutually supportive and, in the best case, constitutive of justice.

ENDNOTES

[1] Franz von Benda-Beckman observes that such normative orders generally owe their existence and normative validity to the pre-colonial political and legal system, irrespective of what the official legal system says about them. It is important to distinguish them from hybrid institutions that are officially recognised or fully constituted by colonial/national law but based on pre-existing indigenous institutions. von Benda-Beckmann, Franz 1985, 'Some comparative generalizations about the differential use of state and folk institutions of dispute settlement', in Anthony Allott and Gordon R. Woodman (eds), *People's Law and State Law: The Bellagio papers*, p. 188. Moore observes in the African context that, on gaining independence, each African country had to ask itself the same questions: to what extent should there be a unitary system and to what extent should a multiplicity of local legal systems continue to operate? Can national centralisation of control and some degree of local autonomy in these matters be reconciled? Moore, Sally Falk 1992, 'Treating law and knowledge: telling colonial officers what to say to Africans about running "their own" native courts', *Law and Society Review*, vol. 26, p. 26.

[2] In fact, it is increasingly being recognised that legal pluralism exists even in Western societies and this state of affairs is contributed to by the growth of transnational laws and the presence of large groups of migrants who bring their own systems and observances of law with them to their adopted countries. See, for example, Shah (*Legal Pluralism in Conflict*), who discusses legal pluralism in the United Kingdom. Tamanaha says simply, 'Legal Pluralism is everywhere.' Tamanaha, Brian 2007, *Understanding legal pluralism: past to present, local to global*, St John's University School of Law Legal Studies Research Paper Series, no. 07-0080, p. 1.

[3] Morse and Woodman note that 'little work has been done to date to build a comparative theory for state policies towards customary laws'. Morse, Bradford and Woodman, Gordon (eds) 1988, *Indigenous Law and the State*, p. 5.

[4] Woodman argues that indirect rule is 'an institutional device, involving a form of legal pluralism'. Woodman, Gordon 1996, 'Legal pluralism and the search for justice', *Journal of African Law*, vol. 40, p. 152. He later expands on this in Woodman, Gordon 2007, 'The possibilities of co-existence of religious laws with other laws', in Erik Sand et al. (eds), *Religion and Law in Multicultural Societies*, p. 9. See also Tamanaha, *Understanding legal pluralism*, p. 13.

[5] Hart, H. L. A. 1961, *The Concept of Law*, 2nd edn, p. 170.

[6] Hughes supports this, arguing that '[t]he body of Pacific jurisprudence concerned with the relationship between introduced customary law fits largely within the tradition of classical legal positivism'. Hughes,

Robert 2003, 'Legal pluralism and the problem of identity', in Anita Jowitt and Tess Newton Cain (eds), *Passage of Change*, p. 332.

[7] MacLachlan, Campbell 1988, 'The recognition of Aboriginal customary law: pluralism beyond the colonial paradigm—a review article', *International and Comparative Law Quarterly*, vol. 37, no. 2, p. 382.

[8] See Chapter 5 under 'The relationship between the courts and the *kastom* system' for a description of the place of customary law in Vanuatu's state legal framework.

[9] Vaai, The rule of law and the Faamatai, p. 31.

[10] Westermark, George 1981, Legal pluralism and village courts in Agarabi, PhD thesis, The University of Washington, p. 4.

[11] Narokobi, Bernard 1986, 'In search of a Melanesian jurisprudence', in Peter Sack and E. Minchin (eds), *Legal Pluralism: Proceedings of the Canberra Law Workshop VII*, p. 215.

[12] See, for example, Scaglion, R. 1983, *Customary Law in Papua New Guinea: A Melanesian view*, Law Reform Commission of Papua New Guinea; Powles, Guy 1997, 'The common law at bay? The scope and status of customary law regimes in the Pacific', *Journal of Pacific Studies*, vol. 21, p. 61; Ottley, Brian and Zorn, Jean 1983, 'Criminal law in Papua New Guinea: code, custom and courts in conflict', *American Journal of Comparative Law*, p. 251; Findlay, Mark 1997, 'Crime, community penalty and integration with legal formalism in the South Pacific', *The Journal of Pacific Studies*, vol. 21, p. 145; Ntumy, M. 1995, 'The dream of a Melanesian jurisprudence: the purpose and limits of law reform', in Jonathan Aleck and Jackson Rannells (eds), *Custom at the Crossroads*, p. 7; Corrin Care, Jennifer 2001, 'Customary law in conflict: the status of customary law and introduced law in post-colonial Solomon Islands', *University of Queensland Law Journal*, vol. 21, no. 2, p. 167; Brown, Ken 1986, 'Criminal law and custom in Solomon Islands', *Queensland Institute of Technology Law Journal*, vol. 2, p. 135; Corrin Care, Jennifer and Zorn, Jean 2001, 'Legislating pluralism: statutory "developments" in Melanesian customary law', *Journal of Legal Pluralism*, vol. 46, p. 49.

[13] Stewart, A. 2000, 'The contribution of feminist legal scholarship', in A. Stewart (ed.), *Gender Law and Social Justice*, p. 11, cited in Griffiths, Anne 2004, Customary law in a transnational world: legal pluralism revisited, Paper presented at the Customary Law in Polynesia Conference, Auckland, 12 October 2004, p. 18.

[14] Zorn, Jean and Corrin Care, Jennifer 2002, '"Barava tru": judicial approaches to the pleading and proof of custom in the South Pacific', *The International and Comparative Law Quarterly*, vol. 51, no. 3, p. 635.

[15] The approach taken by legal scholars in regard to Vanuatu is discussed in further detail in Chapter 5 under 'The relationship between the courts and the *kastom* system'.

[16] Aleck, Jonathan 1997, 'Beyond recognition: contemporary jurisprudence in the Pacific islands and the common law tradition', *Queensland University of Technology Law Journal*, vol. 7, p. 139.

[17] Ibid., p. 143.

[18] Sack, Peter and Minchin, Elizabeth (eds) 1986, *Legal Pluralism: Proceedings of the Canberra Law Workshop VII*, p. 6.

[19] See, for example, the *Underlying Law Act 2000* of Papua New Guinea and the *Customs Recognition Act 2000* (no. 7) of Solomon Islands. For an extensive commentary and comparison of these two pieces of legislation, see Corrin Care, Jennifer and Zorn, Jean 2001, 'Legislating pluralism: statutory "developments" in Melanesian customary law', *Journal of Legal Pluralism*, vol. 46, p. 49.

[20] Roberts, *Order and Dispute*, p. 13; Moore, Sally Falk 1978, *Law as Process: An anthropological approach*, pp. 85–8.

[21] For a summary of the jurists' traditional view of law in non-Western societies in the eighteenth century and early nineteenth century, see Vaai, Saleimoa 1995, The rule of law and the Faamatai: legal pluralism in Western Samoa, PhD thesis, The Australian National University, pp. 10–19.

[22] For a discussion of this in the African context, see Moore, 'Treating law and knowledge'.

[23] Snyder identified these periods. Snyder, Francis 1981, 'Anthropology, dispute processes and law: a critical introduction', *British Journal of Law & Society*, vol. 8, no. 2, p. 144.

[24] For an overview of the other major monographs, see ibid. (pp. 142–3).

[25] Roberts recounts the story of Sir James Frazer being asked whether he had ever met any of the people he wrote about, replying 'God forbid!'. Roberts, Simon 1979, *Order and Dispute: An introduction to legal anthropology*, p. 189.

[26] Malinowski, Bronislaw 1967, *Crime and Custom in Savage Society*, pp. 15–16.

[27] Ibid., pp. 15–16.

[28] Humphreys, Sally 1985, 'Law as discourse', in Sally Humphreys (ed), *The Discourse of Law: History and anthropology*, p. 242.

[29] Moore, 'Treating law and knowledge', p. 22.

[30] Sack, Peter 1985, 'Bobotoi and Pulu Melanesian law: normative order or way of life?', *Journal de la Societe des Oceanistes*, vol. 41, p. 16.

[31] Narokobi, Bernard 1989, 'Law and custom in Melanesia', *Pacific Perspectives*, vol. 14, no. 1, p. 17.

[32] Ibid.

[33] Moore, 'Treating law and knowledge', pp. 22–3.

[34] Hoebel, Adamson and Llewellyn, K. 1941, *The Cheyenne Way: Conflict and case law in primitive jurisprudence.*

[35] Snyder, 'Anthropology, dispute processes and law', p. 67.

[36] Gluckman, Max 1955, *The Judicial Process Amongst the Barotse of Northern Rhodesia (Zambia).*

[37] Gulliver, Paul 1963, *Social Control in an African Society.*

[38] Bohannan, Paul 1957, *Justice and Judgment among the Tiv.*

[39] Humphreys, 'Law as discourse', p. 243.

[40] Rouland, Norbert 1994, *Legal Anthropology*, p. 37.

[41] Humphreys, 'Law as discourse', p. 244.

[42] Ibid., p. 244.

[43] Snyder, 'Anthropology, dispute processes and law', p. 67.

[44] Mundy, Martha and Kelly, Tobias 2002, 'Introduction', in Martha Mundy (ed.), *Law and Anthropology*, p. xvi.

[45] Ibid., pp. xvi–xvii.

[46] Conley, M. and O'Barr, W. 1993, 'Legal anthropology comes home: a brief history of the ethnographic study of law', *Loyola of Los Angeles Law Review*, vol. 27, p. 49.

[47] Mundy and Kelly, 'Introduction', p. xvii.

[48] Snyder, 'Anthropology, dispute processes and law', p. 160.

[49] Zorn, Jean 1990, 'Lawyers, anthropologists and the study of law: encounters in the New Guinea Highlands', *Law and Social Inquiry*, p. 274.

[50] Ibid., p. 275.

[51] Mundy and Kelly, 'Introduction', p. xviii.

[52] von Benda-Beckmann, 'Some comparative generalizations about the differential use of state and folk institutions of dispute settlement', p. 187.

[53] Riles argues that 'anthropologists interested in law and lawyers working on questions of culture lately have experienced their enterprise as professionally marginalized, devoid of theoretical innovation, and even uninteresting'. Riles, Annelise 1994, 'Representing in-between: law, anthropology, and the rhetoric of interdisciplinarity', *University of Illinois Law Review*, no. 3, pp. 597–8.

[54] Ibid., p. 605.

[55] Ibid., p. 643.

[56] See, for example, Shah, *Legal Pluralism in Conflict.*

[57] Mundy asserts that today work in this field is geographically 'very much a North American specialty'. Mundy and Kelly, 'Introduction'.

[58] Rouland, *Legal Anthropology*, p. 51.

[59] Griffiths, 'What is legal pluralism?', p. 39.

[60] Tamanaha, *Understanding legal pluralism*, p. 1.

[61] Sack, Peter and Minchin, Elizabeth (eds) 1986, *Legal Pluralism: Proceedings of the Canberra Law Workshop VII*, p. 1. Compare this with Woodman, who comments that this is 'strictly speaking, without sense'. Woodman, Gordon 1998, 'Ideological combat and social observation: recent debate about legal pluralism', *Journal of Legal Pluralism*, vol. 42, p. 48.

[62] Santos, *Toward a New Legal Common Sense*, pp. 89, 91.

[63] Griffiths, 'What is legal pluralism?', p. 3.

[64] Griffiths, Customary law in a transnational world, pp. 8–13.

[65] The other conceptions that have been advanced have been Pospisil's notion of legal levels, Smith's structural conception of pluralism based on corporate groups and Ehrlich's theory of the 'living law'. These are all summarised in Griffiths, John 1986, 'What is legal pluralism?', *Journal of Legal Pluralism*, vol. 24, pp. 15–29. More recently, Chiba proposed the three-level structure of law, which consisted of official law, unofficial law and legal postulates. Chiba, Masaji (ed.) 1986, *Asian Indigenous Law: In interaction with received law*. He refined this theory to the three dichotomies of law in pluralism—namely, official versus unofficial law, legal rules versus legal postulates and indigenous law versus transplanted law. Chiba, Masaji 1989, *Legal Pluralism: Towards a general theory through Japanese legal culture*, ch. 12.

[66] Moore, Sally Falk 1978, 'Law and social change: the semi-autonomous social field as an appropriate subject of study', *Law as Process: An anthropological approach*, p. 56.

[67] Ibid., p. 57.

[68] Ibid., p. 58.

[69] Merry, Sally 1988, 'Legal pluralism', *Law & Society*, vol. 22, no. 5, p. 881.

[70] Westermark, George 1986, 'Court is an arrow: legal pluralism in Papua New Guinea', *Ethnology*, vol. 25, no. 2, p. 131.

[71] Ibid.

[72] Ibid.

[73] Woodman, 'Why there can be no map of law', p. 384.

[74] Ibid., p. 385.

[75] Ibid., p. 390.

[76] Ibid.

[77] Riles, 'Representing in-between', p. 641.

[78] Griffiths, John 1995, 'Legal pluralism and the theory of legislation—with special reference to the regulation of euthanasia', in Hanne Petersen and Henrik Zahle (eds), *Legal Polycentricity: Consequences of pluralism in law*, p. 210, cited in Woodman, 'Why there can be no map of law', p. 383.

[79] Woodman, 'Why there can be no map of law', p. 383, and Woodman, 'Ideological combat and social observation, p. 22.

[80] Harris, Olivia (ed.) 1996, *Inside and Outside the Law: Anthropological studies of authority and ambiguity*, p. 7.

[81] Hughes, 'Legal pluralism and the problem of identity', p. 336.

[82] von Benda-Beckmann, Franz 2002, 'Who's afraid of legal pluralism?', in *Legal Pluralism and Unofficial Law in Social, Economic and Political Development: Papers of the XIIIth International Congress of the Commission on Folk Law and Legal Pluralism, 7–10 April, 2002, Chiangmai, Thailand*, p. 293.

[83] Roberts, 'After government?', p. 12.

[84] von Benda-Beckmann, Franz 1988, 'Comment on Merry', *Law and Society Review*, vol. 22, no. 5, p. 897; Snyder, 'Anthropology, dispute processes and law', p. 156.

[85] von Benda-Beckmann, 'Who's afraid of legal pluralism?', p. 292.

[86] Tamanaha poses this question and says that for legal pluralism the answer is very much 'the coherence and development of an important conceptual insight'. Tamanaha, Brian 1993, 'The folly of the "social scientific" concept of legal pluralism', *Journal of Law and Society*, vol. 20, p. 212.

[87] This issue arose at the first conference of Folk Law and Legal Pluralism and has continued as a controversy. For a report of the conference, see Allott, Anthony and Woodman, Gordon (eds) 1985, *People's Law and State Law: The Bellagio papers*.

[88] von Benda-Beckmann, Franz 1986, 'Anthropology and comparative law', in Keebet von Benda-Beckmann and Fons Strijbosch (eds), *Anthropology of Law in the Netherlands: Essays on legal pluralism*, p. 92.

[89] Roberts (*Order and Dispute*, p. 23) commented that, for example, Hobbes depicted law as rules 'commanded' on the subject by the sovereign.

[90] Roberts, 'After government?', p. 24.

[91] Tamanaha, 'The folly of the "social scientific" concept of legal pluralism', p. 205.

[92] von Benda-Beckmann, 'Anthropology and comparative law', p. 92.

[93] Hoebel, Adamson 1954, *The Law of Primitive Man*, p. 28.

[94] Moore, 'Law and social change', p. 56.

[95] Benton, Richard 2004, Lexicography, law and the transformation of New Zealand jurisprudence, Paper presented at the Symposium on Concepts in Polynesian Customary Law, Auckland, 2004, pp. 1–2.

[96] Griffiths, 'What is legal pluralism?', p. 38.

[97] Ibid.

[98] A very elaborate one was recently suggested by Franz and Keebet von Benda-Beckman (2006, 'The dynamics of change and continuity in plural legal orders', *Journal of Legal Pluralism*, vols 53–4, pp. 12–14).

[99] Merry, 'Legal pluralism', p. 871. See also Franz and Keebet von Benda-Beckman's response to this. Ibid., pp. 15–17.

[100] Merry, 'Legal pluralism', p. 879.

[101] Tamanaha, 'The folly of the "social scientific" concept of legal pluralism', p. 192.

[102] Ibid. It should be noted that Tamanaha has recently taken a different view of legal pluralism to that expressed earlier. Tamanaha, Brian 2001, *A General Jurisprudence of Law and Society*.

[103] See Franz von Benda-Beckman ('Who's afraid of legal pluralism?') for a comprehensive rebuttal of these arguments.

[104] Tamanaha, *Understanding legal pluralism*, p. 29.

[105] Woodman, 'Ideological combat and social observation', p. 43.

[106] Roberts suggests that '[i]t is perhaps tempting to conclude that this story [about the difficulties of defining law] vindicates the view adopted by Karl Llewellyn that it is best to avoid becoming embroiled in general efforts at definition at all'. Roberts, Simon 2005, 'After government? On representing law without the State', *The Modern Law Review*, vol. 68, no. 1, p. 22.

[107] Woodman, 'Ideological combat and social observation', p. 45.

[108] Merry, 'Legal pluralism', p. 889.

[109] Humphreys, 'Law as discourse', p. 251.

[110] Santos, *Toward a New Legal Common Sense*, p. 93.

[111] Sack and Minchin, *Legal Pluralism*, p. 10.

[112] von Benda-Beckmann, 'Comment on Merry', p. 898.

[113] von Benda-Beckmann, 'Anthropology and comparative law', pp. 92–3. See also von Benda-Beckmann and von Benda-Beckmann, 'The dynamics of change and continuity in plural legal orders', pp. 13–14.

[114] He expands on these ideas in later work. von Benda-Beckmann, 'Who's afraid of legal pluralism?', p. 278.

[115] Twining, William 2003, 'A post-Westphalian conception of law', *Law and Society Review*, vol. 37, p. 250.

[116] Tamanaha, *Understanding legal pluralism*, p. 35.

[117] See also Berman, 'Global legal pluralism', p. 1178.

[118] Fitzpatrick, Peter 1984, 'Law and societies', *Osgoode Hall Law Journal*, vol. 22, no. 1, p. 116.

[119] Sack and Minchin, *Legal Pluralism*, p. 3.

[120] Ibid., p. 4.

[121] Ibid., p. 3.

[122] Griffiths, 'What is legal pluralism?', p. 3.

[123] Zorn, 'Lawyers, anthropologists and the study of law', p. 293.

[124] Merry, 'Legal pluralism', p. 879.

[125] Ibid.

[126] Roberts, 'After government?', p. 18.

[127] Griffiths, 'What is legal pluralism?', p. 3.

[128] von Benda-Beckmann, 'Comment on Merry', p. 900.

[129] Fitzpatrick, 'Law and societies', p. 117.

[130] Ibid.

[131] Ibid.

[132] Ibid., p. 116.

[133] Rouland, *Legal Anthropology*, p. 58.

134 See further in Chapters 7 and 8.

135 Woodman, 'The possibilities of co-existence of religious laws with other laws', pp. 3–4.

136 Griffiths, 'What is legal pluralism?', p. 8.

137 Ibid.

138 Woodman, 'Legal pluralism and the search for justice', p. 158.

139 Although it is classified positivist below in the section 'Positivism in Melanesia'.

140 Griffiths, Customary law in a transnational world, p. 5.

141 Woodman has also commented that 'since it will not present distinct, coherent or easily recognizable legal orders, the distinction between pluralism within an order (legal pluralism in the weak sense) and that between different orders (legal pluralism in the strong sense) will disappear'. Woodman, Gordon 2002, 'Why there can be no map of law', *Legal Pluralism and Unofficial Law in Social, Economic and Political Development: Papers of the XIIIth International Congress of the Commission on Folk Law and Legal Pluralism, 7–10 April, 2002, Chiangmai, Thailand*, p. 391.

142 von Benda-Beckman, 'Who's afraid of legal pluralism?', p. 275.

143 Fitzpatrick, Peter 1985, 'Underdevelopment and the plurality of law', in Anthony Allott and Gordon R. Woodman (eds), *People's Law and State Law: The Bellagio papers*, p. 249.

144 It is easy to see how as soon as one begins discussing structure, a state-centralist approach can start to creep in as a consequence of the (lawyerish) desire to regulate clearly the relationships between the different legal orders. This is taken up in Chapters 7 and 8.

145 Greenhouse, Carol 1985, 'Mediation: a comparative approach', *Man (N.S.)*, vol. 20, p. 93.

146 Ibid., p. 108.

147 Ibid., pp. 96–7.

148 Franz von Benda-Beckman also argues that the structure of indigenous and state institutions is particularly important, as discussed below in the section 'The possibilities and limitations of legal pluralism for Melanesia'.

149 For example, volumes 53 and 54 of the *Journal of Legal Pluralism* are dedicated to the dynamics of change and continuity in plural legal orders.

150 von Benda-Beckman and von Benda-Beckman, 'The dynamics of change and continuity in plural legal orders', p. 19.

151 Svesson, Tom 2005, 'Interlegality, a process for strengthening indigenous peoples' autonomy: the case of the Sami in Norway', *Journal of Legal Pluralism*, vol. 51, p. 74. It should be noted that Santos (*Toward a New Legal Common Sense*, p. 437) proposes a slightly different definition of inter-legality that, while stressing its dynamic nature, does not contain a normative component.

152 Santos, Boaventura de Sousa 2006, 'The heterogeneous state and legal pluralism in Mozambique', *Law and Society Review*, vol. 40, p. 46.

153 Webber, Jeremy 1995, 'Relations of force and relations of justice: the emergence of normative community between colonists and aboriginal peoples', *Osgoode Hall Law Journal*, vol. 33, p. 627.

154 Ibid., p. 629.

155 von Benda-Beckmann and von Benda-Beckmann, 'The dynamics of change and continuity in plural legal orders', p. 7.

156 Berman also argues that '[p]luralism is...principally a descriptive, not a normative, framework. It observes that various actors pursue norms and it studies the interplay, but it does not propose a hierarchy of substantive norms and values.' Berman, Paul 2007, 'Global legal pluralism', *Southern California Law Review*, vol. 80, p. 1166.

157 Woodman, Gordon 1999, 'Legal theory, anthropology and planned legal pluralism', in Keebet von Benda-Beckmann and Harald Finkler (eds), *Papers of the XIth International Congress Folk Law and Legal Pluralism: Societies in transformation*, p. 30.

158 See, for example, Government of the United Kingdom 2003, *Safety, Security and Access to Justice*, GRC Exchange, Department for International Development, viewed 2 February 2005, <http://www.grc-exchange.org./g_themes/ssaj_workshop0303.html>

159 Twining, 'A post-Westphalian conception of law', pp. 248–9. See also von Benda-Beckmann and von Benda-Beckmann, 'The dynamics of change and continuity in plural legal orders', p. 17.

160 Merry, 'Legal pluralism', p. 885.

161 Griffiths', 'What is legal pluralism?', p. 4.

[162] Rouland, *Legal Anthropology*, p. 58.

[163] Sack and Minchin, *Legal Pluralism*, p. 3.

[164] Ibid., p. 14.

[165] Hughes, 'Legal pluralism and the problem of identity', p. 330.

[166] Santos (*Toward a New Legal Common Sense*, p. 90) argues that to date, however, the political claims of legal pluralism have not been clearly articulated and separated from its analytical claims, but that '[t]he paradigmatic debate of modern law requires that such an acknowledgment be fully made and indeed conceived as one of the premises of the debate'.

[167] Ibid., p. 30.

[168] Hughes, 'Legal pluralism and the problem of identity', p. 334.

[169] Ibid., p. 336.

[170] Rouland, *Legal Anthropology*, p. 52.

[171] Ottley and Zorn, 'Criminal law in Papua New Guinea', p. 254.

[172] Ibid., p. 299.

[173] For example, Griffiths ('What is legal pluralism?', p. 1) explicitly stated that his aim was to 'establish a descriptive conception of legal pluralism'.

[174] Both of these factors are due to the fact that anthropologists rather than lawyers have generated much of the material. In addition, anthropologists are traditionally wary of 'venturing outside the bounds of academic investigation'. Westermark, Legal pluralism and village courts in Agarabi, p. 296. Franz von Benda-Beckman ('Some comparative generalizations about the differential use of state and folk institutions of dispute settlement', p. 191) notes that anthropological discussions of dispute management that take account of pluralistic situations at all have usually been concerned with the analysis of the factors determining the choice of (one type of) an institution and with the style of dispute management within institutions.

[175] Snyder, 'Anthropology, dispute processes and law', p. 163.

[176] Ibid., p. 163.

[177] von Benda-Beckmann and von Benda-Beckmann, 'The dynamics of change and continuity in plural legal orders', p. 1.

[178] Ibid., p. 14.

[179] Berman (in 'Global legal pluralism') has also recently developed a series of nine 'procedural mechanisms, institutional designs and discursive practices for managing hybridity'. His focus, however, is primarily on relations between different state systems in the international context, rather than non-state systems.

[180] Morse and Woodman, *Indigenous Law and the State*.

[181] Ibid., p. 7.

[182] Ibid., p. 17.

[183] Ibid.

[184] Woodman, 'The possibilities of co-existence of religious laws with other laws', p. 8.

[185] Ibid., p. 9.

[186] von Benda-Beckman, 'Some comparative generalizations about the differential use of state and folk institutions of dispute settlement', p. 190.

[187] Ibid., pp. 190–1.

[188] Ibid., p. 197.

[189] von Benda-Beckman, 'Anthropology and comparative law', p. 197.

[190] Westermark, Legal pluralism and village courts in Agarabi, p. 22. In an earlier report, he observes that while village courts are officially structured as the lowest level in the national judicial system, the village court officials perceive another forum beneath them, which Westermark calls the 'outside court'. The officials who participate in the outside court do not dissociate themselves from the village court, but rather make explicit appeals to its coercive powers in their handling of disputes. Thus, from the perspective of those who manage them, the two forums do not stand in opposition as official and unofficial courts, but rather serve to support each other. Westermark, George 1978, 'Village courts in question: the nature of court procedure', *Melanesian Law Journal*, vol. 6, nos 1–2, pp. 87–8.

[191] Westermark, 'Court is an arrow', p. 147.

[192] Ibid., p. 147.

[193] See Chapter 7 (under 'Sharing of procedures') for a more detailed description of the PNG village courts.

[194] Government of the United Kingdom, *Non-State Justice and Security Systems*, p. 1.

[195] See <http://www.gsdrc.org/>

[196] Australian Law Reform Commission 1986, *The recognition of Aboriginal customary laws*, Report no. 31.

[197] New Zealand Law Commission 2006, *Converging currents: Custom and human rights in the Pacific*, Study Paper 17.

[198] Filimone, Ratu Ralogaivau 2005, *Problem Solving—Community Based Courts Across the Fiji Islands*, Fiji Law Reform Commission.

[199] South African Law Commission (SALC) 2003, *Report on traditional courts and the judicial function of traditional leaders*, Project No. 90.

[200] Penal Reform International 2000, *Access to Justice in Sub-Saharan Africa: The role of traditional and informal justice systems*.

[201] See, for example, Hohe, Tanja and Nixon, Rod 2003, *Reconciling Justice: "Traditional" law and state judiciary in East Timor*, United States Institute of Peace.

[202] For example, the UN Commission on Human Rights held an Expert Seminar on Indigenous Peoples and Administration of Justice in Madrid in 2003. See also Stavenhagen, Rodolfo 2004, *Report of the Special Rapporteur on the Situation of Human Rights and Fundamental Freedoms of Indigenous Peoples*, United Nations Commission on Human Rights.

[203] Blagg, Harry 2005, *A New Way of Doing Business? Community Justice Mechanisms and Sustainable Governance in Western Australia*, Law Reform Commission of Western Australia, Project no. 94, p. 319. See also International Centre for Criminal Law Reform and Criminal Justice Policy, School of Criminology and Simon Fraser University 1995, *Putting Aboriginal Justice Devolution into Practice: The Canadian and international experience*, Workshop report, viewed 16 November 2006, <http://www.icclr.law.ubc.ca/Publications/Reports/Aboriginal.PDF>

[204] Fitzgerald, T. 2001, *The Cape York Justice Study Report*, Government of Queensland, p. 113.

[205] Schärf, the New Zealand Law Reform Commission and the UK Department for International Development have set out various different models in their publications, but have not attempted to propose any sort of general analytical framework for them. Schärf, Wilfried 2001, 'Policy options on community justice', in Wilfried Schärf and Daniel Nina (eds), *The Other Law: Non-state ordering in South Africa*; New Zealand Law Reform Commission 2006, *Report of Proceedings*, New Zealand Law Commission Workshop on Custom and Human Rights in the Pacific, Nadi, Fiji, 2006; Government of the United Kingdom 2004, *Non-State Justice and Security Systems*, Department for International Development, United Kingdom.

[206] Although it should be noted that the literature covers only a limited number of countries and often only small parts of those countries. It also often is frustratingly general in the real mechanics of the operation of both systems and their relationships, such as, for example, not distinguishing clearly between concepts of appeal and re-hearings.

3. Tradition and transformation in leadership structures and conflict-management mechanisms

This chapter surveys the ethnography of Vanuatu from first contact with Europeans to the present day, drawing out the main themes in relation to conflict management and indigenous leadership structures. The motifs elicited will serve as an introductory framework within which the current debates about the *kastom* system and the role of chiefs can be more readily understood and appreciated. In addition, the extreme versatility of ni-Vanuatu in adapting to the enormous changes brought about by increasing influence and control by the outside world becomes apparent.

The discussion differentiates three periods: the period between when the first ethnographers arrived in Vanuatu and the Condominium (roughly the last part of the nineteenth century and the early twentieth century); the period of colonisation by the French and British (1906–80); and post-independence (1980 onwards). Each section includes an analysis of how the leadership structures and conflict-management systems changed over the period under consideration.[1]

Leadership structures and conflict management in the nineteenth century and early twentieth century

The furthest back it is possible to find ethnographic materials on Vanuatu is the late nineteenth century.[2] By this time, however, in some parts of the country there had already been more than 100 years of contact with Europeans. One terrible result of this contact, which significantly changed 'traditional' society forever, was the massive depopulation resulting from the introduction of diseases for which the indigenous population had no immunity. Deacon records how this depopulation resulted in the loss of enormous amounts of traditional knowledge, stating that out of the dead 'so many, so terribly many, are the old men, the last men who "know"…At every turn it is "the men who knew [who] are dead"'.[3] Another development profoundly affecting the society during this early period was the establishment of missions throughout the archipelago. This resulted in a demographic move, encouraged by the Church, bringing together people living in smaller hamlets or settlements to establish nucleated villages. Often the move was from the interior villages to the coast.[4] This had a significant effect on the extant leadership structures, as community groups were ripped apart, separated from their land and new communities created.[5] A final development that significantly impacted on patterns of life in this period was the movement of men between Vanuatu and the sugar plantations of Queensland.[6] As a consequence of these various events, it is likely that the leadership structures and conflict-management mechanisms discussed below are not entirely traditional, but we have no way of knowing in *which* ways they have been changed.

Leadership structures

Traditionally, there were two broad groups of leadership structures or political power systems in Vanuatu: the graded system in the north, and a partly hereditary, partly elective system based on titles in the centre and south. Within these two broad groups, however, there were many different permutations and combinations.[7] As Bonnemaison states, 'It is as if it were a part of the Melanesian genius to take the model it receives, as it spreads from place to place, and complicate it as much as humanly possible to put a local stamp on it.'[8]

The graded system

In the north of Vanuatu (from Epi to the Torres Islands), men—and occasionally women, particularly in the northern matrilineal groups[9]—traditionally achieved status through the publicly graded society (there was often also a series of 'secret' societies existing alongside the public societies). This institution was called variously '*sukwe*', '*maki*', '*huggwe*' and '*nimangki*' (*nimangki* will be used in this study) and was said to be a 'path of peace';[10] in other words, it was an alternative to using war to achieve status. Characteristically, it consisted of a series of grades, arranged in ranked order, that could be gained by performing certain rituals—typically, the killing of pigs—and paying various amounts of other traditional 'money' such as mats, weavings, shell money and whale teeth. The higher the grade, the more pigs that needed to be amassed—often more pigs than any one man had, so he was required to muster supporters to act as sponsors.[11] Thus, Jolly and Bonnemaison point out that to achieve a high grade, a person needed to have the ability to develop networks of supporters and also to have the support of those dignitaries who held the keys to power.[12] This system had the effect of vesting considerable power in richer and older men who, however, were obliged to use their wealth for the promotion of new works or the sponsoring of further cycles of the *nimangki*, either by themselves or others. The *nimangki* system thus involved a continual series of ritual exchanges of gifts. Patterson draws attention to the fact that even in this system, men benefited from demonstrating connections to powerful descendants—from their current place and beyond.[13]

The question of whether men of high rank were automatically leaders was not seriously examined until William Rodman's doctoral research in Ambae in the 1970s, where the publicly graded society still existed.[14] Rodman queried earlier assumptions that the graded society was the basis of power and authority and argued that it created a social, but not a political, elite. To become a leader, further qualities were required, such as ambition and personal traits such as generosity that were not required to progress through the *nimangki*.[15] Jolly also argued that rank and leadership were 'disjunct' in South Pentecost and pointed to examples of men of low rank wielding considerable power in village meetings and men of high rank being politically inconsequential.[16] Bonnemaison concurs, stating:

> Men of high grade do not, however, embody pure political power in the sense in which we generally understand the word 'chieftainship'. They undoubtedly have every means of becoming 'leaders' if their natural authority and charisma lend themselves to it, but it is not necessarily something that goes without saying.[17]

As all these scholars were writing on the basis of observations made more than a century after contact, it was, however, possible that the lack of automatic equation of high rank to leadership position was due to changes consequent on outside contact.

Early accounts lack details about what sorts of power or authority leaders and/or men of high rank are likely to have had. This gave rise to debate about whether or not indigenous decision making in the graded system was traditionally autocratic or consultative. Premdas argued that traditional decision making was 'consultative, involving discussion over issues until consensus was attained'.[18] Rodman, however, argues that this is contrary to the historical and ethnographic record and that 'before intensive contact, chiefs tended to consult local opinion, but often they were more autocratic than democratic in their behaviour. Especially in the northern islands, high ranking chiefs...possessed the ultimate sanction, the legitimate right to order an offender's execution.'[19]

Other scholars support Rodman's comments.[20] For example, Speiser, quoting Coombe's account of the 'ultimate penalty' in North Pentecost, also graphically illustrates the power of leaders during early times: 'to be eaten was the extreme penalty of chiefly law—if say a great man's pig be stolen or one of his wives kidnapped...to carry the sentence out strictly, the body must be cooked in the *gamal* and portions distributed among every man, woman and child in the village'.[21]

Hereditary/mixed systems

There are fewer studies during this period of leadership structures in the central and southern regions, where the leadership structure was more similar to Polynesian concepts of hereditary chieftainship.[22] These systems are traditionally associated with pyramidal power structures, hereditary leadership and absolute authority, although the extent to which all these features are present in the chiefly systems of Vanuatu is debatable, as discussed below. The existence of chiefly systems in the south during this period could be explained partly by the fact that from Tongoa southwards there was considerable Polynesian influence, resulting in various political, linguistic and ritual changes and borrowings.[23]

As a result, from south-east Ambrym southwards, power at this time was often 'conjoined with several hereditary posts'.[24] It seems clear, however, that there was not a purely hereditary system in many areas, if any at all. MacClancy has therefore said that inheritance of leadership was not by strict primogeniture,[25] and Guiart has commented that 'it was not inherited at all':[26] a young man would not be given responsibilities that went with a chiefly title unless and until he was considered capable of handling the responsibilities. These comments accord with Spriggs' findings that in Aneityum during this period there was a 'patrilineal hereditary chieftainship, tempered to some extent by the necessary approval of the "principal men" of the group'.[27] Facey's reconstruction of traditional Nguna describes the political structure as 'hierarchical', in which different orders of chiefs exist, from the 'high' or 'dominion' chief through to 'small' chiefs. She also found that although chiefly titles were hereditary, 'there was room for a man with great personal ambition and strength to thrust himself into power'.[28]

The powers of these chiefs, however, do accord with the Polynesian concept of chief. It appears therefore that in central Vanuatu the highest order of chiefs in particular had 'formidable powers'. A chief could order death and also other penalties, such as the destruction of a man's possessions or the pronouncement that a man was fit only for slavery, whereupon another chief could claim him for his servant.[29]

The island that has proved to have the most difficult leadership structure to analyse, and which has been the focus of most anthropological attention in the south, is undoubtedly Tanna. Gray, in analysing the ethnography of leadership in Tanna, observes that 'the picture of traditional leadership on Tanna is not at all clear'.[30] Although Humphreys in his 1926 study on Tanna found that each village had a single chief and that 'in the old days' this chief had 'practically absolute' power over the people of his village,[31] Speiser stated that '[w]hether such chiefs had real factual authority depended entirely on their character; it is unlikely they ever occupied an almost divine position as in some Polynesian islands. Nor were they entirely independent of the men's assembly.'[32] A third perspective is provided by Guiart, who, writing some 30 years later, observed, 'Tanna is a society of carefully preserved rank, organised in such a way that few people outrank all the others.'[33] He found that 'at least one-fourth of the men in the island…[hold one or another privilege] and proudly assume its possession as a sign of rank'.[34]

Maintenance of law and order and conflict-management mechanisms

The available literature suggests that the mechanisms used for managing conflicts during the period depended on the relationship between the conflicting parties: the closer the relationship, the more peaceful the mechanism employed and, conversely, the more remote the relationship between the disputants, the more war-like the resolution.

Intra-community disputes—whether a community was constituted by a clan or a village or a different grouping varying from place to place—appear to have been approached at least initially in a peaceful manner. In some areas, it appears that meetings were used to resolve such disputes. Speiser therefore observed that in the north 'there were actual court sessions in which the men of the *suque* groups gathered together and deliberated on the case'.[35] In other areas, however, such formal mechanisms did not exist. Deacon states that 'there is in this island [Malekula] the minimum of organised legal machinery' and even where there are men 'to whom the word "chief" is not inapplicable', they do not have any judicial or administrative functions.[36] Rather, the influence they might have had over their fellow tribesmen was due to their wealth. In the absence of formal mechanisms such as council meetings, it would appear that the onus was on individual disputants to resolve the disputes between themselves, perhaps with the aid of community leaders. Speiser supports this supposition and observes that 'the public did not interfere in private feuds and even the chiefs had no direct jurisdiction here'.[37]

Disputes that had effects outside the village, however, would be dealt with differently. If an act perpetrated by a member of the village caused the village as a whole to be in danger from reprisals, penalties would be imposed on that person, depending on the severity of the harm that had befallen the village.[38] The types of redress that are referred to in these early accounts include payback killing, swapping of live people, 'blood money' in terms of pigs to be paid and, in one instance, burning.[39]

Disputes between communities were dealt with through wars followed by ceremonies, creating either permanent or temporary peace. It has been traditional in the ethnography of Vanuatu to present a picture of widespread and fairly continuous warfare between rival groups throughout the archipelago before the arrival of the missionaries.[40] Archaeologist Andrew Hoffman, however, queries such a portrayal, emphasising that most ethnographers arrived in Vanuatu at least 100 years after first contact with Europeans. On the basis of his research, he attributes the warfare described by early anthropologists largely to the depopulation of the country resulting from diseases introduced by the Europeans, which led to people blaming 'sorcerers' for causing the deaths and consequently setting a series of revenge killings in train.[41]

In the late nineteenth century, however, warfare was certainly pervasive and common. Speiser noted that typical causes of wars were 'the abduction of women and revenge for what is conceived to be sorcery or death due to sorcery. Blood revenge caused feuds to go on without remission and war to be waged between two regions for generations without the cause always being known.'[42] Layard comments that another cause is 'insults of various kinds, which in turn bring forth counter-insults and in any case drag in their train recriminations based on disputes that may have smouldered for generations'.[43] Tonkinson, in his reconstructed account of the late nineteenth century in Ambrym, referred to 'intervillage disputes and blood feuds' in which killings were usually of the 'payback' type and 'involved the ambush of an individual on a path or in his garden, by a small band of men, patrilineally related to one another, who used bows and arrows for the attack'.[44] Facey records that in Nguna an act such as a murder or theft of a woman would result in long-lasting animosity and intermittent violent flare-ups. Facey states that 'retributive night raids were made to even a score, and in the light of day the village might find several of its members dead or missing—the latter having been taken captive, destined to be cooked and ritually consumed'.[45]

Pre-contact, any wars that did occur seldom resulted in the loss of many lives since the weapons used were rudimentary. Once sandalwood traders introduced guns in the early nineteenth century, however, the wars became increasingly violent, leading Speiser to refer to 'the war of extermination between the natives which was waged almost systematically and is one of the major factors in the extinction of the native people'.[46]

In a society accustomed to war, ways of making peace were of central significance. Deacon found that in Malekula peace could be established by different ceremonies depending on whether a permanent peace or a temporary peace was desired. To make a temporary peace, 'one or more pigs are paid by each side to the elder brother of the man or men in the enemy's camp whom they had killed'.[47] To make a permanent peace, though, necessitated the making of an elaborate peace dance and 'a small pig [was] presented to their opponents by those who have suffered most damage in the conflict'.[48] Speiser commented generally that the principle on which a peace was concluded was invariably that the losses on each side should be balanced out.[49] Layard also states that 'no war, once started and once one death has occurred, can cease until the number of dead on both sides is equal'.[50] He explains that this could lead to the situation in which the victors in a war are left in such a state of 'taut nerves' that it is they, rather than the vanquished, who must sue for peace:

> The only solution, therefore, is that they should themselves offer one of their number as victim to restore the balance demanded by the honour of both parties. So they seek out the least desirable member of their own

clan, approach him from behind, seize him, truss him up like a pig, decorate him for sacrifice, and send him to the enemy, those who deliver him bearing a cycad leaf, emblem of peace. As a rule the victim is sent, if possible, alive, and it is said that the enemy thus appeased force him to dig a pit for the fire in which he is to be roasted, and then sacrifice him with all the ritual due to an enemy captured in battle, and then eat him.[51]

In addition to private agreements, meetings of leaders and war, there were other sociological factors that operated to keep checks on the frequent commission of anti-social acts. These, according to Deacon, included 'fear of the anger of the ancestral spirits', 'the desire for prestige and the fear of public contempt or ostracism' and the dependence of the members of the community on each other.[52] In relation to this last point, Deacon emphasises the fact that every man needs the cooperation of his kinsfolk and clansfolk: failure in his obligations towards them will be repaid in kind.[53] Deacon also draws attention to the fact that the life of a man in Malekula is a public one, with 'daily activities for the most part carried out…in full view of other people'. He suggests that this is also a fact of 'considerable sociological importance' in the maintenance of law and order.[54] Speiser similarly notes that '[d]isputes in the village itself become catastrophes only under exceptionally unfavourable conditions because the fact of living together in such proximity soon makes a reconciliation imperative'.[55]

Another form of social control used extensively was black magic. Leaders were considered to have either extensive supernatural powers themselves or magic men working for them who were able to manipulate these powers on their behalf. In relation to Tanna, Bonnemaison refers to magic as being the 'prison of the chiefs' in traditional ideology, 'representing the means of enforcing obedience and of punishing those who disregarded the code of social relations'.[56] Spriggs also found on Aneityum that the chiefly power was based 'on ritual rather than physically coercive powers—power of sorcery against enemies, power over the elements to control success in agriculture and fishing'.[57] In relation to south-east Ambrym, Tonkinson characterises the chiefs' 'alleged possession of a variety of sorcery techniques and their exclusive right to resort to sorcery' as 'a vitally important element in maintaining control over their followers'.[58] Deacon notes that on Malekula the 'belief in the effectiveness of magic is very strong' and every man who has sufficient wealth can 'purchase the services of highly skilled magicians by whose arts they can inflict damage and suffering on those who oppose or threaten them, and in this way they are able to wield power beyond the reach of men of lesser means'.[59] A final indigenous system used to control conflict was the *naflak* system, which was popularly supposed to have been introduced in Efate in the 1600s by the powerful chief Roy Mata.[60]

With regard to the substantive content of the laws at the time, or what Deacon calls 'the standards traditionally approved by the community of which they are members', these are described only in a general way in the existing literature, such as 'not to fight'.[61] Speiser goes somewhat further in describing what he refers to as the 'natives' idea on law', when he comments:

> They are based on the natural law that any wrong must be requited by a like. Every stolen pig must be replaced by one of equal value, murder must be requited by murder on the other side or by a suitable sum of blood money, and wars can be ended when both sides have lost the same number of dead. A settlement can also be reached by the side with the most fatal casualties being supplied with a corresponding number of living men. These can then be killed or they can be admitted to the clan corporation as substitutes for the dead.[62]

These early accounts emphasise a number of points about leadership and conflict management in Vanuatu in the early twentieth century and before. The first is the enormous variety of leadership structures that existed throughout Vanuatu and the range of authority that leaders had over their communities. The second is the pervasive use of war and violence to resolve disputes between groups with a degree of separation (inter-village, inter-island) and the use of peaceful means to resolve disputes between closely related groups (inter-clan or intra-village). The third is the importance of exchanges of pigs and gifts in achieving peace and the notion of achieving a 'balance' between opposing parties.

Leadership structures and conflict-management mechanisms during the Condominium

During the Condominium period, there were three legal systems: the English, the French and the Condominium.[63] The Condominium purported to directly regulate indigenous affairs; in accordance with Article 8 of the Protocol,[64] Native Courts were established in 1928 to apply native law to natives. The Protocol directed condominium officials to 'cause a collection of native laws and customs to be made' and provided that customary law 'should be utilised for the preparation of a code of native law, both civil and penal'.[65] It seems, however, that no such project was undertaken and the native criminal codes that were produced were based almost entirely on French and British jurisprudence, with a few 'indigenous' elements such as the prohibition on witchcraft.[66]

The extent to which there was a real engagement with the regulation of ni-Vanuatu during this period, as opposed to the mere passage of legislation, has not been closely studied. The Condominium was centred in the capital, Port Vila, and provided very little administrative structure outside it.[67] Although the British and the French appointed district agents, who periodically toured the islands, collecting taxes, holding court hearings and taking people away to jail, it was primarily the missionaries who had a significant impact on the day-to-day lives of rural ni-Vanuatu.[68] It thus appears that few resources and limited manpower were directed by the government towards conflict management, especially outside the areas populated by Westerners. Scarr observed that even by 1911 the Condominium police force was 'reckoned to be practically useless outside Vila'.[69] As a result, the indigenous leadership structures and conflict-management mechanisms continued to be vital to the local communities. These structures and mechanisms were, however, themselves affected by the actions of the colonial government and the increasing Christianisation of society.[70]

Leadership systems

The leadership structures changed significantly during this period in three major ways: the 'creation' of the institutions of chiefs by the missionaries and later the Condominium Government; the emergence of new paths to power through the Church and the government; and the consequent lessening and, in places, elimination of the influence of the *nimangki*.

The Presbyterian missionaries were the first to actively create 'chiefs' throughout Vanuatu, based on the model of leadership they had 'found' in central Vanuatu. This development was later formalised by the Condominium.[71] Rawlings noted that, in Efate before 1909, chiefs were installed by the missionaries, one of whom wrote in that year, 'I suppose that during all these years I have installed over a dozen [chiefs] at different villages.'[72] Jolly states that the role of 'chief' was introduced into South Pentecost by the colonial powers in the late 1940s, whereas it had been introduced in Ambrym in the 1930s and earlier in Ambae and Tanna.[73] Jolly adds the comment that, '[u]nlike other parts of the archipelago, the first generation of chiefs appointed were on the whole powerful and respected men...Similarly in most of the Christian villages, the chiefs appointed were already leaders'.[74] By the early 1950s, however, the role had 'fallen into disrepute amongst the traditional people' in South Pentecost.[75]

The role of these government and missionary-appointed chiefs was to be the broker between the village and outsiders such as the government and traders. MacClancy comments that 'since these "chiefs" were not just appointed in the southerly isles, the Bislama term *"jif"* came to mean "village leader", a post not necessarily legitimated by heredity'.[76] Even in central Vanuatu, where traditional leaders most approximated the idea of chiefs, the missionaries identified converts instead of local hereditary leaders to fulfil the role of chiefs, thus undercutting the local system.[77]

In addition to the creation of chiefs, the Condominium opened up other new roads to power. One was the institution of government assessors, established by the Protocol to act as consultants in cases presented to the Native Court, which was presided over by the district agents. The role of assessors was, however, gradually expanded and in some districts they unofficially settled minor disputes themselves.[78] In discussing the role of assessors in Ambae, Rodman characterised them as 'middlemen' who maintained control of the flow of cases between the discrete levels of law (government and local).[79] Rodman also noted that most disputants understood that the consequence of non-compliance with the assessor's decision was that the case would go to the Native Court.[80] Facey noted that in Nguna the people who were appointed as assessors were, like government chiefs, often men who already had positions of authority and were respected in their own community.[81] In Ambae, however, William Rodman argued that the people who were appointed assessors, while initially satisfying none of the traditional prerequisites for leadership, had their credentials validated by established leaders so they could in turn gain indirect access to the coercive sanctions of the national government and a voice in decisions made in the Native Court.[82]

The churches were another source of authority and prestige. Men aspiring to power could establish themselves as a member of the clergy or other position in the church hierarchy. Education, employment by the government and skill at business also all became new roads to power.[83]

While these new roads were opening, traditional paths to power and authority were being closed. MacClancy therefore states that 'secret societies became less active and, with the banning of warfare, fighting lost its prestige and village leaders their ability to apply coercive sanctions'.[84] The publicly graded system also went into significant decline in most parts of the country. Gray reports that, due to the fact that the Church disapproved of the *nimangki* ceremony,[85] 'the leaders of Vao society today do not depend upon the traditional ritual performance of *nimangki* for confirmation of their status'.[86] Scarr, describing the Presbyterian mission as 'the most active and successful' in Vanuatu, points out that it 'had no respect for their proselytes' traditional culture, which to them was a manifestation of the forces of evil'.[87] They therefore 'set out to destroy the traditional culture' and the 'attainment of rank by the ceremonial slaughter of pigs was a particular object of their disapprobation'.[88] Bonnemaison poignantly recounts the abandonment of the grade-taking system in the Torres Group:

> [I]n 1894 the highest graded man in the Torres Islands, Tequalqual, asked to be baptized. The missionary requested that he first relinquish his grade. Along with his kin, Tequalqual erased the path he had followed in the course of his life: over the next few days, he killed fewer pigs of decreasing value and ate at more common hearths. On reaching the lowest level of the hierarchy, the chief stated that he was 'free' and was then bapitized. The grade system was abandoned in the Torres Islands.[89]

During this period, there are numerous references to the diminution of the authority of traditional leaders. Gray points out the consequences that the removal of the power of physical coercion had on leaders' ability to enforce decisions, observing that 'whereas in the past the only sure escape from the chief's authority was death, today a young man may escape merely by seeking employment on a plantation and thus in fact shrug off the chief's control of his life'.[90] Charpentier stated that towards the end of the Condominium, young people best described as 'half-baked' went back to their villages 'with or without an educational certificate, but all full of more or less well-assimilated knowledge'.[91] This led them to resent customary authority traditionally wielded by the elders as they had 'nothing but contempt for the elders barely able to read and write'.[92] 'It is no exaggeration,' he remarks further, 'to state that at village level there was a power vacuum.'[93] Jacomb commented that the Condominium had 'weaken[ed] the already shadowy power of the Chief by practically telling his tribe not to obey him'.[94] Other factors undermining the traditional authority of the leaders were the spread of Christianity, whose teaching and doctrine de-legitimised the use of sorcery,[95] which had been one of the bulwarks of their authority, and also the weakening of the obligations of kinship by the economic pressures of a cash and wage economy.[96]

During this period, therefore, the roads to power changed significantly. The essential characteristics of leadership, however, largely continued: the ability to form networks, to have influence, to gain knowledge and to be a focal point for exchange. At this time as well, we see the beginnings of confusion about rights to leadership that is so common today. Thus, Tonkinson records:

> In south-east Ambrym, as in many other parts of the country, the graded society collapsed rapidly following early contact with Europeans…a few of the grade names or titles have been handed down as personal names, leading some men to assume that their forebears who had achieved a high rank were therefore chiefs. On the basis of this belief some men have pressed claims to be chiefs, thus confusing the achieved and non-inheritable ranked status with that of ascribed, inherited chiefly status. Such confusion is widespread.[97]

Maintenance of law and order and conflict-management mechanisms

There were also significant changes to the maintenance of law and order and the management of conflicts during this period. Due to the cessation of warfare and the embargo on the use of coercive physical force by the community leaders, conflicts were resolved at the non-state level, either through a form of public meeting and the imposition of fines or through private agreements.[98] Although some mention is made of public meetings in earlier writings,[99] during this period such meetings came to assume a primary role in the management of conflicts—a role they continue to have today.

Public meetings as a mechanism for managing conflict are today inextricably linked to chiefs and chiefly councils. Although there is no clear record of their development, there are some suggestions that chiefly councils were a missionary-led initiative, at least in some islands. In relation to Aneityum, Proctor states that Reverend John Inglis 'urged the chiefs to act jointly when faced with conflict among their subjects'. At his suggestion, they developed the practice of sitting together to conduct trials and impose punishments.[100] Scarr notes that the Presbyterians established a local government system 'based on meetings of the senior men of the community, who formed a "court" for the trial of breaches of the moral code and petty offences'.[101] Scarr observes: 'Wherever Christianity had a foothold, a local government of this sort was set up, with courts of whose decisions the missionaries or native mission teachers were the inspiration, chiefs were generally mission-nominees and "policemen" who acted as the executive arm.'[102]

Another influence was the establishment by the Condominium Government of local government councils, whose main responsibilities were to maintain law and to keep villages sanitary.[103]

The main features of public meetings were public talking and the payment of compensation to balance the account between the disputing parties. It can be surmised that these meetings varied in form throughout the archipelago and probably resembled Western 'courts' to a greater or lesser degree, depending on the extent to which the area was visited by the government representatives, the influence of the Church and also, no doubt, on the views of the observer. Thus, Tonkinson refers to the chiefs holding 'court sessions',[104] while Jolly describes 'very informal' meetings to which people 'drifted in casually' and '[c]hildren wander in and out'.[105]

In Ambae, Rodman explains that there are a number of stages in the meeting. The first is concerned with a full expression of issues and evidence by the defendant or contending parties. Witnesses are then asked to comment on these accounts and to contribute their own versions of the events. The second phase of the meeting is when 'young and low ranking men at the hearing interrogate the defendants, and each other. Discrepancies are perforated, evidence is contested, ramifications are explored...The old leaders wait, listening, reflecting.'[106] During the third stage, 'different solutions are tested against community sentiment'.[107] The *ratahigi* (a high-ranking leader) then articulates a decision relating to the case that encapsulates the views of the community. The meeting concludes with 'the irenic reinstatement of parties to the dispute or the wrongdoer into Lonanan society'.[108] Elsewhere, Rodman points out that 'Aoban legal traditions place a premium on the reintegration of offenders into everyday life and on the conciliation of former enemies'.[109] He later elaborates on this important point:

> [D]aily face-to-face contact with one's neighbours is unavoidable. Men rely on each other for everything from garden produce to marriage partners. A legacy of resentment and recrimination at the end of the hearing might as well be as injurious to the accusers as to the accused.[110]

Muller describes different procedures and reports observing two 'courts', during which 'the natives passed judgment on some cases of poisoning' in Malekula. He described one in particular, where an older man was accused of poisoning a young girl by throwing some poisoned leaves, which struck her on the chest. She died about a week later. Some 25 adult men were present at the 'court' and eight women sat within earshot. Very few people spoke except for the defendant and the victim's father, but after a couple of hours the defendant realised that everyone was convinced that he was guilty. The negotiations over a penalty then began, with the eventual outcome that he paid a similar amount to the bride price the father would have realised had his daughter married. The defendant was persuaded to shake hands with the father before leaving the hearing.[111]

From these two descriptions and other observations made by anthropologists during this period, it is possible to draw out a number of features of these meetings. The first is that the people who led these meetings varied considerably from place to place. Rubenstein remarks that in theory the 'leaders in settling such disputes are "chiefs"—government-appointed executives—and "assessors"—government-appointed adjudicators', who 'listen and decide on the merits of each case'. In practice, however, there were also other intermediaries between the parties present, such as members of the local political party *nagriamel*.[112] In Ambae, Rodman states that 'despite the withdrawal of their power to seek revenge and settle differences with other leaders through physical coercion', law and peace remain 'inextricably linked to the authority of the Lonanan *ratahigis* [high-ranking men]'.[113] It therefore appears that in some places the traditional leaders continued to be responsible for law and order, while in others those who followed newer roads to authority found themselves in charge.

The second feature is the procedures followed in the meetings, which appear to have been more consultative than authoritative. Rodman states that in Ambae 'the link between a leader and his followers [rests] in great measure on rule by consent rather than coercion'.[114] Thus, at meetings to resolve disputes a leader is expected to act as spokesman solely for the consensus reached by the participants.[115] As a successful resolution to any public meeting depends on the formation of a consensus, the *ratahigi* must 'be a persuader, a compromiser, a sifter of facts and a non-partisan spokesman for any settlement that might lead to harmony'.[116] In relation to South Pentecost, Jolly notes that at the end of the meeting the leaders suggest a resolution that they believe will achieve unanimity and end the talk. Jolly observes that 'although there is a strong emphasis on consensus, influential leaders can dominate by oratory and can manipulate consensus to their advantage'.[117] Tonkinson comments along the same lines that in south-east Ambrym 'decisions are taken only after protracted discussion in which everyone has the opportunity to comment and offer suggestions, [but that] chiefs often act to steer the meeting towards consensus and a decision'.[118] In Tanna as well, public speaking is central to the process. Lindstrom notes that the settlement of disputes involves first a debate and discussion in which 'good speaking (agreement) re-establishes good speech'.[119] He notes that '[i]slanders conceive of local debate processes and products more in terms of the finding—rather than negotiating—of consensus'. [120]

A third feature is the way in which decisions reached at meetings are enforced. As the sanctions for a resolution were consensual rather than coercive, one of the strongest ways to exact compliance by the offender was the use of shame. Rodman draws attention to the 'intrinsic fragility' of the leader's role in resolving disputes,[121] noting that the leader's decision 'is contingent upon a belief by an offender in the legality and fairness of the imposition rather than upon a notion that retribution will be forthcoming if pigs are not paid'.[122] Elsewhere he also notes the restraining power of negative public opinion:

> Public scorn and ridicule are two of the most powerful weapons possessed by a leader seeking to preserve his *tamata*. A meeting is a vehicle for shaming a lawbreaker. To be scrutinized by the curious and the indignant, to be questioned and condemned by any man who wanders in from the road—the possibility of such a situation installs dread in every Longanan.[123]

As a replacement for the use of force, the ultimate threat that community leaders could use was to send the case to the State for adjudication. In regard to Malo therefore, Rubenstein reports:

> In many such cases, participants may turn to the government in an attempt to solve them. This is, in a sense, an ultimate threat. Regardless of how capricious the government may seem at times, there is a recognition by the Maloese that the government does hold an ultimate power.[124]

A final feature of these meetings is the relationship this mechanism has with the State. It appears that the village leaders (either traditional or government appointed) dealt with most cases themselves, but they used the government courts as a backup for persistent recidivists or murder or serious assault. [125] In his ethnography of Ambrym in the 1960s, Tonkinson observed that a chief would seek outside support only in cases of serious disputes or of an individual rebelling against court judgments, when he would refer the matter to the area chiefs' meeting.[126] Larcom's description of the situation in Malekula accords with that described by Tonkinson. She found that before independence, 'the division between local and colonial justice had settled into a stable system, with expectations and results relatively clear to both the Mewun and the BDA [British district agent]'.[127] Rodman states in relation to Ambae that 'the evidence is clear that local leaders, for their own purposes, engaged in a kind of dialogue with the state: they helped the state maintain an illusion of control in return for occasional access to the state's coercive sanctions'.[128]

From the perspective of the State, there were mixed opinions about these meetings (or courts, as they were referred to). The British High Commissioner, for instance, reported in 1906 that their existence posed 'a likely challenge to the new administration', while his deputy 'regarded it with more favour', given the 'inability of the Condominium to establish any administration at all in native affairs outside Efate'.[129] In an illuminating footnote, Tonkinson notes:

> Chiefs' courts, though illegal, are essential to the maintenance of law and order in most areas of the New Hebrides, so, pending official recognition, District Agents in most areas have unofficially agreed to set up guidelines for the activities of these courts…Punishments are unofficially limited…and the courts are encouraged to record their judgments if possible. In practice the chiefs' courts hear almost all offences and only the more serious ones are reported to the District Agent.[130]

Unfortunately, there is no record of whether any guidelines were ever drawn up to regulate the village courts, as foreshadowed in the note.

Leadership structures and conflict management post-independence

There are a number of ethnographic studies relating to Vanuatu since independence.[131] Anthropological studies during this period were hampered by a moratorium on all research in Vanuatu from 1985 until 1995.[132] After the moratorium was lifted there was a fairly constant stream of researchers in Vanuatu, but, with the exception of Rousseau, none focused on issues of conflict management.[133] Before dealing with leadership structures and conflict-management mechanisms, I will discuss the debates concerning the meaning of *kastom*, which have been the focus of many anthropologists during this period.

Kastom and the 'invention of tradition'

One of the major themes in the ethnographic literature in this period is the meaning of '*kastom*' and its importance in Vanuatu in the development dialogues taking place today. The intention of this survey is not to present a comprehensive overview of the considerable body of literature on this topic but, rather, to highlight some of the main themes relevant to the present study. These are: the meaning of *kastom*; the question of whether, when ni-Vanuatu speak about *kastom* today, it accurately represents 'true' custom or tradition, or whether it is rather an 'invention'; and third, if *kastom is* a recreation of the past and what significance this has for reform and development proposals in Vanuatu today.

What is *kastom*?

Kastom is a concept that appears repeatedly in the ethnographic, historical and popular discourse of independent Vanuatu. While acknowledging that *kastom* is a contested concept[134] and that the meaning of *kastom* has changed over time,[135] it is possible to discern in the literature two general categories of views about the meaning of *kastom*. One view sees *kastom* as referring to certain distinctive features of a way of life—for example, styles of singing and dancing or weaving mats.[136] The other sees *kastom* as a notion that has expanded over time to include a whole way of life.[137] To an extent, these two views are playing themselves out today in the forms of the Vanuatu Cultural Centre (VCC) and the National Council of Chiefs (NCC). The VCC has focused on areas such as art, ritual knowledge and artefacts, traditional stories and other sorts of traditional knowledge—namely, the material and ceremonial side to *kastom*.[138] The NCC on the other hand is increasingly advocating a view of *kastom* as a cultural whole and pushing for the State to recognise this expanded view of *kastom*—for example, by legislating for chiefly powers.

A fundamental point made by all commentators is that the use of *kastom* today draws a self-conscious distinction between '*fasin blong ol man ples*' (the way of indigenous inhabitants) and foreign ways. Bolton convincingly argues that, despite the suggestions of authors such as Keesing, Jolly and Thomas that the self-conscious reification of 'culture as *kastom*' is a product of the colonial encounter, in fact, ni-Vanuatu already had a self-conscious formulation of difference before European contact. What the Europeans, or particularly the missionaries, did, however, in their efforts to impose Christianity and to stamp out the former ways of living, was to create *kastom* as a category that could be opposed to European practices.[139] Thus, originally *kastom* was dialectically contrasted with '*skul*', which represented the new way of life brought by Christian missionaries and was symbolised by the education system they established. In these earlier times, Christianity was associated with 'light' and progress and *kastom* with 'darkness' and backwardness.[140]

In the time leading up to independence, however, there was a gradual shift in the way in which ni-Vanuatu started to view *kastom*. Rather than being seen as something to be ashamed of, it was seized on by the Vanua'aku Party and the francophone opposition parties as a symbol that could be used to unite the whole country (which until the creation of the colonial state had never had a national identity) and also to highlight the importance of the difference between *man ples* and their colonial masters.[141]

The decision to use *kastom* as a guiding ideology for the new state has, however, given rise to a question central to the present study: what relationship should *kastom* have with introduced foreign concepts? This question was first raised in relation to Christianity as—certainly by the mid-1970s, and in many places much earlier—Vanuatu became a deeply Christian country. The solution adopted was to stop talking about *kastom* as being in opposition with *skul* and to start to argue that *kastom* and the Church must come to an accord 'and achieve a mutually dependent balance like that of a canoe and outrigger'.[142] This did not prove particularly problematic, partly because, as Hume explained in relation to Maewo, this was what was happening in practice to a large extent anyway.[143]

The revival of material aspects of *kastom*, those associated with a more museological view of *kastom*—such as pig killing, kava drinking, traditional dances and costumes—has proved relatively uncontentious. The difficult question has been how to deal with the relationship between the wider sense of *kastom* as a cultural whole and the new state system. Jolly argues that this question has arisen in three contexts: the incorporation of *kastom* leaders as an advisory council within the State, the decentralisation of justice and the return of all rural land to the customary owners.[144] To these I would add a fourth context: the role of so-called 'universal human rights' and other democratic institutions in Vanuatu today. Speaking at a conference on *kastom* and the constitution, the Secretary of the Malvatumauri observed that the principles of *kastom* could not easily be accommodated within the democratic system. He succinctly stated that the question was '*Hao nao bae tufala imaret?*' (how can these two things be married?). The logical corollary from this question he sees as '*sapose tufala imaret, who nao ihusband mo who nao iwife?*' (if the two are married, then who will be the husband and who will be the wife?).[145] At the time leading up to independence, *kastom* was deliberately left vague and undefined. Tonkinson comments that 'its utility as a rallying point depends heavily on its confinement to an ideological level, indivisible and unexamined'.[146] Now, however, 20 years after independence, as is apparent from the remarks in the conference quoted above, serious questions are being asked about the place of *kastom* that require a closer analysis of the utility and relevance of various aspects of *kastom* today, as is done in this study.

Kastom as 'invention'?

The second issue is the extent to which the *kastom* that is referred to today is a historically accurate representation of the past.[147] Keesing refers to 'invention' of *kastom* and the 'refashioning' of the pre-colonial past, arguing that there is a wide gap between the authentic past and the representations of the past in contemporary ideologies of cultural identity. He states:

> The portrayals that idealise the precolonial past not only incorporate conceptual structures and premises of colonial discourse and elevate symbols as reactions against colonial domination. In many respects, they also incorporate Western conceptions of Otherness, visions of primitivity, and critiques of modernity. The imagined ancestors with whom the Pacific is being repopulated—Wise Ecologists, Mystical Sages, living in harmony with one another, cosmic forces and the environment—are in many ways creations of Western imagination.[148]

This theme is picked up by a number of other scholars, who illustrate how *kastom* is being reinvented or recreated today, stressing that whereas *kastom* was previously fluid, accommodating of change and deliberately borrowing from and incorporating notions from outside influences, today it is being recreated as something far more fixed, changeless and unresponsive to foreign influence. For example, Tonkinson argues that 'ni-Vanuatu concerns about the ownership and truth of *kastom* reflect a more rigid view of the past and an "uncustomary" attitude towards cultural differentiation'.[149]

Larcom also documented the different views the Mewun of Malekula had of *kastom* before and after independence. She found that, before independence, *kastom* was 'an incomplete, creative product of continual invention'. After independence, however, this notion had changed, and today *kastom* was seen more as a 'codified tradition'.[150] Like Tonkinson, Larcom argues that '[c]ontemporary needs are apparently more effectively satisfied by reference to fixed truths rather than to fluid and dynamic representations of culture'.[151]

The issue of the authenticity of *kastom* is tied up to a degree with the question of to what extent indigenous culture can change on its own accord. It has frequently been pointed out that classic ethnography about Melanesian society portrays it as largely changeless and static, changing only with the arrival of the Europeans.[152] Early commentators such as Speiser and Deacon were indeed convinced that the culture would soon disappear under the influence of the West, and felt a duty to record it to preserve it for posterity.[153] According to this view, culture or *kastom* is an almost rarefied object that cannot be exposed to the winds of change for fear that it will crumble and turn to dust. Jolly challenges such a view in her critique of Babadzan: 'If they (the "natives") are no longer doing "it" they are no longer themselves, whereas if colonisers are no longer doing what they were doing decades ago, this is a comforting instance of Western progress.'[154]

Even as recently as 1985, Rodman pointed out that his description of legal innovation in Ambae was a radical departure from the existing literature. He attributes this to the 'legal centralist' view of the law that sees innovation as being something that the State introduces into a local community, and refuses to recognise the possibility of innovation existing outside the State.[155] These two viewpoints about the capacity or need for *kastom* to change are also clear in modern ni-Vanuatu debates about *kastom*. There are some who argue, as Chief Philip Tepahae does, that 'custom has never changed from the time of our ancestors until today'.[156] On the other hand, there are those such as Maxime Korman, the former Prime Minister of Vanuatu, who argue that *'everi samting igat evolution blong hem. Mi believem se kastom tu igat evolution'* (everything evolves. I believe that *kastom* evolves as well).[157]

The significance of *kastom* as invention

Closely tied up with the issue of the authenticity of *kastom* is the third issue raised by the literature: whether or not the fact that aspects of *kastom* are to some extent an invention really matters. Jolly has argued in response to claims about the 'invention of tradition' that these 'spectres of inauthenticity' are finally not a significant issue and that it is for people to present themselves as they see fit.[158] According to this view, what is important is how people perceive themselves and their culture today. Keesing also reflects that perhaps it does not matter whether the multiple pasts being recreated and invoked are mythical or real, pointing out that political symbols work by radically condensing and simplifying 'reality'.[159] White similarly argues that 'the focus on cultural invention draws attention away from the substantial cultural and historical continuities that give so-called invented forms much of their emotional and political power'.[160] There are others, however, such as Bolton, who argues that, for ni-Vanuatu today, the expression of *kastom* has effects on the present.[161] Curtis makes the important point that 'configured continuity' associated with *kastom* 'is intimately connected not only to representations of past and present, but also in imaginings of the future'.[162] Although neither author takes this next step, the logical corollary of their arguments is that it is significant to argue about what should be credited with the label of '*kastom*' if future directions are based on it. Keesing also finally concludes that the reality behind imagined pasts really does matter, as it is all too easy to edit out of the pre-tribal past aspects such as violence, the domination of women and youth and exploitation and to create a romantic version of an idealised primitive past. He urges a more radical, more deeply reflexive Pacific discourse with regard to pasts and power and 'a critical deconstruction of conceptualisations of "a culture" that hide and neutralize subaltern voices and perspectives'.[163]

From the basis of the fieldwork done for this study, there can be no doubt about the power of *kastom* to validate all kinds of behaviour and attitudes. This was demonstrated by the debate about whether or not the subordinate role of women was justified in *kastom*, discussed in Chapter 1.[164] Consequently, the question of what can legitimately be called *kastom*, and who has the right to speak 'for *kastom*' today, is very much a live issue in Vanuatu that must be confronted, if possible, with the reflexivity advocated by Keesing.[165]

Leadership structures in Vanuatu today

Today, it is widely accepted that chiefs are traditional leaders with a right to speak for *kastom*.[166] Bolton comments that the 'conflation between chiefs and *kastom*…is so taken for granted in Vanuatu today that it is hard to unpick'.[167] The discussion above, however, demonstrates that traditionally there have been very few places in Vanuatu where the leaders could be considered 'chiefs' in the sense that chiefs are understood today (as leaders—often hereditary—with a stable power base and authority over an entire community). Thus, Lindstrom comments that '[t]oday's *kastom jifs*, although undoubtedly *kastom*, are not simply customary. The emergence and construction of the popular identity *jif*, from a plethora of local leadership positions, were shaped by the events and interests of postcontact, colonial society'.[168]

Bolton, in her article based on an interview with the first President of the National Council of Chiefs, sheds light on the development of chiefs as an institution in Vanuatu since independence.[169] The first time that chiefs were formalised as a group was in 1974, when the decision was made to include four chiefs to be elected to the Representative Assembly to 'represent custom'.[170] This initial step, however, proved intensely controversial and the problem of electing these four chiefs became such a major issue that it prevented the assembly from meeting at all.[171] One of the significant difficulties in the election process was the determination of to what extent a chief should embody traditional modes of authority and how traditional modes of authority should be applied in making that decision.[172] A solution to the impasse was finally negotiated in the form of the creation of a Council of Chiefs to advise the Representative Assembly on all matters concerning *kastom*. Bolton noted that this decision depoliticised chiefs.[173] At their second meeting, the council changed their name to Malvatumauri, linking the institution to indigenous sources of power and status and reinforcing the perception that the position of chiefs was derived from pre-colonial practice.[174]

Lindstrom explains that, since its creation, the Malvatumauri has 'engaged in a strategic process of elaborating and defining chiefly identity and prerogatives'.[175] One of the ways it has done this is by codifying *kastom* law, producing in 1983 a book of *kastom polisi* dealing with village-level disputes and designed 'particularly to keep women and youth under closer control and to make chiefly supervision of village activities more muscular'.[176] Another way is the creation of an official chiefly hierarchy that extends down to six regional councils, into various area councils and terminates in many village councils of chiefs.

There are a number of ethnographies that describe contemporary chiefs in Vanuatu.[177] One of their main themes is the continuous dispute over the right to chiefly title. For example, Sherkin comments that on one island there are two different, local versions of rightful chieftainship, which consequently divide island opinion in half. One of the difficulties is that references to the pre-mission past are the main impetuses used in claiming chiefly titles, but 'consistent problems arise, as the multiple and diverse versions of life prior to missionary arrival can never be substantiated; much knowledge of *kastom*, including oral histories has gradually been forgotten. Thus, the power struggle among chiefs continues'.[178]

Another theme is the continuous tension between chiefs and the State. Lindstrom points out that, although in some respects chiefs and the State share interests in shoring up chiefly political power, chiefs also present potential dangers to the State. Consequently, state politicians have been nervous about how much power and independence to give to chiefs.[179] These two themes are discussed further in Chapters 4, 5 and 6.

Conflict management

There are three ethnographic accounts of changes that took place in various communities around the time of independence that illustrate the dynamism of *kastom* conflict-management mechanisms.

Rodman, Larcom and Facey all discuss initiatives by local leaders to create new legal orders in the wake of the vacuum left by the withdrawal of the Condominium Government. In Ambae, the leaders devised a code of laws—a combination of customary and non-customary laws—and used the written codes in dispute processing.[180] Rodman noted that the main forces for ensuring compliance with the system were: people's ingrained values, which predisposed them to conform to the court's judgments; the multiplex ties between people, which meant that it was in the disputant's own best interests to accept a compromise and settle conflict; and the final option of vigilante justice.[181] In relation to this last option, Rodman observed that it was remarkable how rarely the chiefs resorted to the threat or use of physical coercion.[182] Within the system, the chiefs reached their decisions in open hearings after full consultation with the concerned parties. Further, Rodman notes that '[l]eaders rarely reach unpopular decisions that go against the community grain. They are sensitive to popular opinion, well aware that too many bad calls will leave them with a blemished reputation and reduced authority.'[183]

The laws emphasised compensation and reconciliation and always required disputing parties to exchange valuables in public after the case had been heard in court to 'wipe out the offense'.[184]

Facey notes that about the time of independence, as in Ambae, in Nguna, high chiefs gathered to draft some laws for the community. These laws were 'explicitly modelled on the ten commandments'[185] and dealt with minor offences such as stealing and swearing; the regulation of sexual behaviour, specifically adultery and fornication; abortion; lack of respect for chiefs; non-payment of fines (for which it was recommended the chief's police should take the person's possessions) and extended residence of jobless Ngunese in Port Vila (all relevant concerns today). Facey notes that 'what all of these proposed "laws" have in common is the desire on the part of the chiefs to shore up, and then extend, their authority'.[186] During this period, public and private meetings held by a council comprising mostly titled members dealt with offences. The assessors, who continued to execute their functions after independence, ensured that murder, violent assault and rape were all reported to the central police. At the end of council meetings, 'when a crime affects a particular person the guilty party must make reparation to both the injured party and the village chiefs and shake hands with all of them. This is said to restore "good heart" by erasing ill will on all sides.'[187]

In contrast with Rodman and Facey, Larcom found that, after independence, 'the Mewun [in Malekula] lost the power of force that had supported social order; in exchange they gained little additional autonomy for their dispute-settling process, which they had effectively controlled for quite some time'.[188] Consequently, they looked to the government to replace the district agent. The government, however, did not leap into that role and left them largely to their own devices, leaving the Mewun to complain that they needed clear laws defined from above, as the trouble would not 'die' as it had in the past.

In addition to these studies, all done shortly after independence, there are three anthropologists who have investigated issues surrounding conflict management more recently. Rousseau's doctoral research, based in Port Vila, involves an examination of the way in which *kastom* is brought into court proceedings and the incomplete or unsuccessful integration of customary law and state law. She finds that although a common attitude exists that such integration is necessary, there are considerable difficulties in doing this, concluding:

> Despite co-operation between the two spheres, and the ability of people to choose to invoke one or the other, a fundamental incompatibility exists due to the need in kastom for the achievement of simultaneity in time and space, matched by a convergence of understanding achieved through objectification that enables relations to be re-established and continue into the future.[189]

The achievement of simultaneity in *kastom* refers to the sense of completion that a settlement in *kastom* has, and the way in which a dispute is 'explained by and incorporated into a history of interaction between the two parties, resulting in a comprehensible chain of events'.[190] These issues are discussed further in Chapter 5 in the context of an examination of reasons for a previous failure of integration between the *kastom* and state systems.

Mitchell's fieldwork in the Blacksands settlement around Port Vila also offers some insights into issues of conflict management in Vanuatu today. She finds that young people are frequently afraid of police and she attributes this largely to police brutality.[191] Mitchell explains that the *kastom* system is 'qualitatively different' from police violence, which involves physical beatings and strategies of humiliation.[192] In *kastom*, although violence exists, talking and respect are central.[193] Mitchell also draws attention to the 'contested nature of *kastom* and "white man's" system of justice', noting that they 'are often identified as competing ways in which to articulate, contain and resolve violence'.[194] In a case study of a murder in Blacksands, Mitchell highlights a number of problematic features of the state legal system, noting that local people find many of the evidentiary laws that restrict admissibility of evidence incomprehensible. She also explained that, in the case, the two men charged with murder were found not guilty and hence did not make a *kastom* exchange. As a result, they cannot gain respect and when they go back to their village peace will not have been restored. The issues raised by Mitchell are also expanded on in Chapters 4, 5 and 6.[195]

Finally, Hess includes an analysis of a *kastom* meeting to resolve a land dispute as part of her doctoral study on Vanua Lava. She analyses the oratorical strategies used by the speakers and the way in which the chairman of the meeting mediates. Hess finds that the parties explicitly distinguish between their processes and those of a 'white-man's court', noting that *kastom* is 'portrayed as the only way to create peace by finding consensus (*agrimen*) rather than making a court-like decision, where one party wins and the other loses'.[196] Hess's observations are also drawn on in Chapter 4.

Conclusion

This chapter has described three different layers of leadership structures that have developed in Vanuatu. The first layer is the immense variety of leadership structures that existed pre-contact, only a few of which fitted into the anthropological ideals of 'chief' and 'big-man', with the rest incorporating various combinations of elements of both. During this period, leadership functions were often shared among different members of the community, so that there would be several powerful men responsible for the operation of different aspects of the community. The missionaries and the Condominium Government created the second layer. They created the institution of 'village chiefs' and 'assessors', giving to the holders of these positions responsibilities that leaders in the first layer had previously exercised, such as the management of conflicts and dealings with outsiders on behalf of the community. The third layer was created shortly before independence when the colonial powers established a National Council of Chiefs. This structure, providing yet another road to chiefdom—through public election—was later enshrined in the constitution and given an advisory role to the government. This background of multitudinous and competing leadership structures explains why, as discussed in Chapter 4, rights to chiefly titles in Vanuatu are so hotly contested today and disputes concerning them are so difficult to resolve.

The survey of the literature also offers important insights into how conflict management is likely to have been conducted in pre-contact Vanuatu and how these mechanisms changed during the time of colonisation and independence. We saw that earlier, more autocratic methods, relying on coercive force and supernatural powers, gradually gave way to more consultative approaches. The most prominent of these is the institution of the public meeting, where talking is central and earlier notions of restoration of loss (in the form of compensation rather than dead bodies) and the powerful forces of public shame, kinship ties and obligations are also incorporated. The development of this mechanism, and other innovations in conflict management, especially around the time of independence, demonstrate the dynamism and adaptability of the *kastom* system—a theme returned to in later chapters.

Finally, we have seen that the main catalyst for the adaptations just discussed was the introduction of competing legal orders—first the Condominium and later the Vanuatu State. This theme is pursued in later chapters, which argue that the state and the *kastom* systems each have a profound effect on each other and so need to be studied together to form a complete picture of conflict-management mechanisms in the country today. The relationship between indigenous conflict-management mechanisms and the government has been shown to have always been ambiguous. In the colonial period, the government relied on these mechanisms to maintain law and order, given its limited reach, but its unease in doing so was demonstrated by the lack of formalisation of any linkages or formal recognition of the right to exercise jurisdiction. The local leaders during this period were likewise wary of the government, keeping the management of conflicts largely under their control, but using the Native Court as an ultimate threat to ensure compliance or to deal with persistent troublemakers. As we will see, this unofficial relationship has changed very little today, with the state government now relying on the chiefs in rural and urban areas to manage conflicts in the absence of sufficient government resources. What has changed, however, is the preparedness of the chiefs to accept these responsibilities in the absence of any support or recognition by the government of their work. This provides the context for the bedevilled question of the relationship between the State and the *kastom* system that is discussed in the rest of this study.

ENDNOTES

[1] With the exception of William Rodman, anthropologists in the first two periods have not focused particularly on conflict management. Consequently, in order to form a picture of how conflict management occurred in these periods, it has been necessary to piece together fragments from many places of information, often included as throw-away comments or in footnotes. Care has been taken to compare as many different sources as possible to achieve a picture that is consistent with the observations of many commentators.

[2] The earliest anthropologists in Vanuatu were Codrington (1891), Speiser (1913) and Rivers (1914), who made some general surveys of Vanuatu; Deacon (1926) and Layard (1914), who carried out in-depth field studies, both in Malekula; and Humphreys (1923), who did an ethnographic survey of the southern islands. In addition to these very early ethnographies, there are some later ethnographers such as Tonkinson (1968, 1981, 1982), Gray (1971) and Facey (1983), who attempt to piece together an understanding of how areas in Vanuatu would have functioned before colonisation or the arrival of the missionaries.

[3] Quoted in MacClancy, *To Kill a Bird with Two Stones*, p. 86.

[4] Rawlings, 'Foundations of urbanisation', p. 80.

[5] Rodman, *Masters of Tradition*, pp. 16–17; Patterson, Mary 2002, 'Moving histories: an analysis of the dynamics of place in North Ambrym, Vanuatu', *The Australian Journal of Anthropology*, vol. 13, no. 2, p. 211.

[6] See also Wawn, *The South Sea Islanders and the Queensland Labour Trade*; Shineberg, 'The sandalwood trade in Melanesian economics, 1841–65'.

[7] Patterson states that 'leadership is a "fuzzy categrory" in an ill-defined field' and that 'even in the most apparently hierarchical political systems, leadership is resistant to typology and to delineations that emphasise either structure, or process, rather than the complex interaction between them'. Patterson, Mary 2002, 'Leading lights in the "Mother of Darkness": perspectives on leadership and value in North Ambrym, Vanuatu', *Oceania*, vol. 73, p. 127.

[8] Bonnemaison, 'Graded societies and societies based on title', p. 200.

[9] Jolly, Men, women and rank in South Pentecost, p. 291; Rodman, Margaret 1981, 'A boundary and a bridge: women's pig killing as a border-crossing between spheres of exchange in East Aoba', in Michael Allen (ed.), *Vanuatu: Politics, economics and ritual in island Melanesia*, p. 85.

[10] Bonnemaison, 'Graded societies and societies based on title', p. 210.

[11] MacClancy, *To Kill a Bird with Two Stones*, p. 7.

[12] Jolly, Men, women and rank in South Pentecost, p. 284; Bonnemaison, 'Graded societies and societies based on title', pp. 202–3.

[13] Patterson ('Leading lights in the "Mother of Darkness"', p. 129) argues that '[i]n the emergence of leaders, the interplay between precedence in an apparently fixed hierarchy related to place and origin, and achievement in an inherently competitive system that required great organizational skill and political acumen and a forceful personality was a delicate matter'.

[14] The furthest that Deacon goes in this regard is to note that 'such high rank [in the *nimangki*] carries with it considerable influence but probably nothing which could be truly regarded as authoritative powers'. Deacon, Bernard 1934, *Malekula: A vanishing people in the New Hebrides*, p. 47.

[15] Rodman, Men of influence men of rank, p. 14.

[16] Jolly, Men, women and rank in South Pentecost, pp. 297–8.

[17] Bonnemaison, 'Graded societies and societies based on title', pp. 202–3.

[18] Premdas and Steeves, *Decentralisation and political change in Melanesia* , p. 53.

[19] Rodman, 'The law of the State and the state of the law in Vanuatu', pp. 60–1.

[20] For example, Blackwood describes the authority a powerful high-ranked man in Ambae (a *ratahigi*) would have had as follows: 'In the pre-contact period of endemic hostility between groups, *ratahigi* enjoyed an extreme position of dominance and some real sanctions in exercising control in the community. Underpinning such a leader's position and authority were the *matagelos* [a following of youths] who provided a police force and an element of coercive sanction to a leader's power.' Blackwood, Peter 1981, 'Rank, exchange and leadership in four Vanuatu societies', in Michael Allen (ed.), *Vanuatu: Politics, economics and ritual in island Melanesia*, pp. 51–2.

[21] Speiser, Felix 1923, *Ethnology of Vanuatu: An early twentieth century study*, p. 218.

[22] Though 'Polynesia' itself was never completely chiefly in this respect—for example, Tuvalu, Tokelau and Niue all had very weak chieftaincies, if any at all.

[23] Rawlings, Gregory 1995, *Urbanisation, Kastom, Economic Practice and the Dynamics of Social Change in a Vanuatu Peri-Urban Community: The case of Pango Village, South Efate—a field report*, p. 78.

[24] MacClancy, *To Kill a Bird with Two Stones*, p. 14; Guiart, Jean 1996, 'Land tenure and hierarchies in Eastern Melanesia', *Pacific Studies*, vol. 19, no. 1, p. 17.

[25] MacClancy, *To Kill a Bird with Two Stones*, p. 14.

[26] Guiart, 'Land tenure and hierarchies in Eastern Melanesia', p. 18.

[27] Spriggs, Matthew 1981, *Vegetable Kingdoms: Taro irrigation and Pacific prehistory*, p. 58.

[28] Facey, Ideology and identity, p. 52.

[29] Ibid., p. 47.

[30] Gray, The emergence of leaders in the New Hebrides, p. 96.

[31] Humphreys notes that '[i]n the case of any delinquency amongst his people the chief dealt with the offender, pronounced judgement and ordered punishment. Even if death was the penalty commanded, his prerogative seems to have been absolute.' Humphreys, C. B. 1926, *The Southern New Hebrides: An ethnological record*, p. 35.

[32] Speiser, *Ethnology of Vanuatu*, p. 304. It should be noted that as Spesier was on a 'bus-stop' tour of the islands when he made his survey, his observations can be only superficial in most cases.

[33] Guiart, 'Land tenure and hierarchies in Eastern Melanesia', p. 19.

[34] Ibid., p. 21. A more sophisticated and nuanced explanation of the leadership structure can be found in Bonnemaison's ethnography of Tanna. Although the period in which he lived in Tanna (at various times from 1968 to 1981) was significantly after contact, his discussion of the three traditional 'images of power' that existed in Tanna helped to explain the confusion of other earlier commentators on the nature of authority in Tanna. According to Bonnemaison, the first of these images of power is the *yremera*, the 'honour' of the community, who is linked with great ceremonial exchanges and controls the traditional roads of alliance. The second is the *yani niko*, who represents the political will, takes control in times of war and highlights the *yremera*'s glory and speaks on his behalf. The third is the *naotupunus*, who works with agrarian magic and is the sanctioned mediator of supernatural forces. Further, the titles for these different forms of leadership are transferred in different ways. The clan leaders choose the *yani niko* on the basis of his human and intellectual properties, while the *yremera* receives his title as a child. Bonnemaison (*The Tree and the Canoe*, pp. 150–1) concludes: 'Thus, Tannese society seems to be a syncretic combination of "Melanesian" and "Polynesian" elements.'

[35] Speiser, *Ethnology of Vanuatu*, p. 306.

[36] Deacon, *Malekula*, p. 47.

[37] Speiser, *Ethnology of Vanuatu*, p. 306.

[38] Ibid.

[39] Ibid.

[40] Some even go so far as to describe warfare as 'endemic' in parts of Vanuatu—for example, Tattevin, in regard to South Pentecost, noted in Jolly, Margaret 1979, Men, women and rank in South Pentecost, PhD thesis, The University of Sydney, p. 298.

[41] Interview with Andrew Hoffman, Vanuatu Kaljoral Senta (Port Vila, 12 November 2004).

[42] Speiser, *Ethnology of Vanuatu*, p. 211.

[43] Layard, John 1942, *Stone Men of Malekula: Vao*, p. 594.

[44] Tonkinson, *Maat Village Efate*, pp. 16, 18.

[45] Facey, Ideology and identity, pp. 41–2.

[46] Speiser, *Ethnology of Vanuatu*, p. 213.

[47] Deacon, *Malekula*, p. 224.

[48] Ibid.

[49] Speiser, *Ethnology of Vanuatu*, p. 215.

[50] Layard, *Stone Men of Malekula*, pp. 598–9.

[51] Layard in Vao documents this escalation of violence—depending, in part at least, on the degree of separation between the disputing parties. He states that attempts will be made to settle peacefully disputes between members of the same clan and, if not, then only clubs will be used. With regard to disputes between villages on the same side of the island, the conflict is fought with clubs or spears at

pre-arranged times in special fighting grounds. With regard to disputes with other small islands or villages on the mainland, however, the methods are ambush and surprise and poisonous bows and arrows. Layard (*Stone Men of Malekula*, p. 598) observes that 'man-traps and poisonous spined shells laid in the path are used only against a foreign foe'.

52 Deacon, *Malekula*, p. 47.

53 Ibid.

54 Ibid., pp. 47–8.

55 Speiser, *Ethnology of Vanuatu*, p. 303.

56 Bonnemaison, *The Tree and the Canoe*, p. 179.

57 Spriggs, *Vegetable Kingdoms*, p. 59.

58 Tonkinson, 'Church and kastom in Southeast Ambrym', p. 241.

59 Deacon, *Malekula*, pp. 49–50.

60 The story that is told widely today is that in order to restrict tribal fighting, Roy Mata requested that representatives gather in the centre of Efate, bringing with them an item of importance such as yam, breadfruit or octopus. These then became the symbols of the new matrilineal clans that were established throughout Efate, whose members were thus prevented from engaging in warfare with each other. Rawlings, Gregory 1999, 'Foundations of urbanisation: Port Vila Town and Pango Village, Vanuatu', *Oceania*, vol. 70, no. 1, p. 79. Although the legend of Roy Mata as the origin of this system is contested, the *naflak* system continues today and is becoming increasingly important in land-dispute cases and even disputes over chiefly title, largely because it is a matrilineal system and all the other systems on Efate are patrilineal (Interview with a chief from Efate, Port Vila, 20 March 2007).

61 He does point to one specific offence, which is a certain type of curse such as 'you are as good as dead'. He observes that such curses are held to be serious insults and the compensation of a pig may be demanded (Deacon, *Malekula*, p. 50). This appears to continue to be the case today: in a discussion with an anthropologist living on Maewo, I was told about a recent case in which a man had made such a curse to someone else and this was treated very seriously and he was required to pay a pig as compensation.

62 Speiser, *Ethnology of Vanuatu*, p. 306.

63 Each of the two powers retained sovereignty over its nationals, and people who were present in the Condominium who were not French, British or indigenous were required to 'opt' for either system within one month of their arrival.

64 The *Protocol Relating to the New Hebrides* between Britain and France signed in 1914 and ratified in 1922.

65 Article VIII(4) in Weisbrot, David 1989, 'Custom, pluralism and realism in Vanuatu: legal development and the role of customary law', *Pacific Studies*, vol. 13, no. 1, p. 68.

66 See New Hebrides Condominium, *Joint Regulation 12 of 1962*.

67 Jacomb, *France and England in the New Hebrides*, pp. 30–3, 68–70.

68 Jacomb (ibid., p. 68) records in that when the 'natives' have troubles 'it is not to the Government they instinctively turn, it is to the Missionary'.

69 Scarr, *Fragments of Empire*, p. 241. See also ibid. (p. 65), where Jacomb says that the 'police force inspires the beholder with mingled feelings of admiration and despair'.

70 The anthropologists who worked in Vanuatu during this period were as follows: Jolly (1979, Men, women and rank in South Pentecost) conducted fieldwork in south Pentecost, focusing on questions of rank in the graded system and what these meant for men and women; Tonkinson (1968, *Maat Village Efate: A relocated community in the New Hebrides*) did a study that investigated the social and cultural changes and continuities of community for south-east Ambrym people who resettled near Vila; Gray (1971, The emergence of leaders in the New Hebrides, MA thesis, University of Auckland) studied the factors affecting the development of leaders among the 'New Hebrideans'; Margaret and William Rodman conducted extensive fieldwork in Longana, Ambae, first during the Condominium (1968–71) and follow-up fieldwork at later intervals after independence. Rodman, Margaret 1976, Spheres of exchange in a northern New Hebridean society, Masters of Arts thesis, McMaster University; Rodman, William 1977, 'Big men and middlemen: the politics of law in Longana', *American Ethnologist*, vol. 4, p. 525. Although their interests were originally in land use and the graded society, both developed an interest in issues surrounding law and order. William Rodman in particular went on to write a series of articles in which he discussed the legal innovations that took place in Longana due to the withdrawal of the Condominium Government, which will be discussed in the next section. Lindstrom conducted fieldwork

in Tanna, focusing on the way in which knowledge conferred power in that community. Lindstrom, Lamont 1981, Achieving wisdom: knowledge and politics on Tanna (Vanuatu), PhD thesis, University of California, Berkeley. Finally, Rubenstein did an ethnography of Malo Island, examining the connections that men and women had to land. Rubenstein, Robert 1978, Placing the self on Malo: an account of the culture on Malo Island, New Hebrides, PhD thesis, Bryn Mawr College.

[71] Jolly, Men, women and rank in South Pentecost, p. 36; Bolton, Lissant 1998, 'Chief Willie Bongmatur Maldo and the role of chiefs in Vanuatu', *Journal of Pacific History*, vol. 33, no. 2, p. 183.

[72] Rawlings, 'Foundations of urbanisation', p. 82.

[73] Jolly, Men, women and rank in South Pentecost, p. 36.

[74] Ibid., p. 36.

[75] Ibid.

[76] MacClancy, *To Kill a Bird with Two Stones*, p. 20.

[77] Bolton, 'Chief Willie Bongmatur Maldo and the role of chiefs in Vanuatu', p. 182.

[78] Rodman, 'Big men and middlemen', pp. 527–8.

[79] Rodman, 'Gaps, bridges and levels of law', p. 75.

[80] Ibid., p. 80.

[81] Facey, Ideology and identity, p. 152.

[82] Rodman, 'Big men and middlemen', p. 532.

[83] Allen, Michael 1981, 'Innovation, inversion and revolution', in Michael Allen (ed.), *Vanuatu: Politics, economics and ritual in island Melanesia*, p. 131.

[84] MacClancy, *To Kill a Bird with Two Stones*, p. 24.

[85] Gray, The emergence of leaders in the New Hebrides, p. 31.

[86] Ibid., p. 32.

[87] Scarr, *Fragments of Empire*, p. 237.

[88] Ibid., p. 237.

[89] Bonnemaison, *The Tree and the Canoe*, p. 65.

[90] Gray, The emergence of leaders in the New Hebrides, p. 205.

[91] Charpentier, 2002, p. 169.

[92] Ibid.

[93] Ibid.

[94] Jacomb, *France and England in the New Hebrides*, p. 71.

[95] See Tonkinson, who describes the changes in belief in sorcery in Ambrym resulting from the widespread conversion to Christianity. Tonkinson, Robert 1981, 'Church and kastom in Southeast Ambrym', in Michael Allen (ed.), *Vanuatu: Politics, economics and ritual in island Melanesia*, pp. 256–61.

[96] Gray, The emergence of leaders in the New Hebrides, p. 206.

[97] Tonkinson, 'National identity and the problem of kastom in Vanuatu', p. 311.

[98] Making peace in Longana is the same as restoring law—both are accomplished by the payment of a pig to a *ratahigi*. Rodman explains, 'The legal system is flexible, not in its categorisation of offenses, but in the options available to a leader after a wrongdoing has been discovered.' Rodman, William 1973, Men of influence men of rank: leadership and the graded society on Aoba, New Hebrides, PhD thesis, University of Chicago, pp. 256–7. He points out that the leader can ignore it and refer it to either another leader or the Condominium Government; or he can call a public meeting; or he can summon the misdemeanants, determine relative guilt and decree *haradai* (the payment of a pig to 'wipe away blood'). Rodman suggests that public meetings are called to resolve a dispute or shame a wrongdoer in preference to a private hearing based on a number of different factors, including whether or not witnesses must be summoned.

[99] See, for example, Tonkinson's ('Church and kastom in Southeast Ambrym', pp. 240–1) discussion of village councils during the pre-contact period.

[100] Proctor, 'Scottish missionaries and the governance of the New Hebrides', p. 353. There are also suggestions that 'Native Courts' were promoted by the Presbyterians on other islands as well, particularly Futuna.

[101] Scarr, *Fragments of Empire*, p. 236.

[102] Ibid., pp. 236–7.

[103] Premdas and Steeves, *Decentralisation and political change in Melanesia*, p. 53.

[104] Tonkinson, 'Church and kastom in Southeast Ambrym', p. 255.

[105] Jolly, Men, women and rank in South Pentecost, p. 294.

[106] Rodman, Men of influence men of rank, p. 270.

[107] Ibid., p. 271.

[108] Ibid., p. 273.

[109] Ibid., p. 271.

[110] Ibid., p. 274. Jolly (Men, women and rank in South Pentecost, p. 292) undertakes a similar analysis of conflict-management meetings in South Pentecost, noting that such meetings are called primarily for disputes over women and land, but also for sorcery accusations, disputes with Christian natives and debts. She states (p. 294) that the meetings follow the contours outlined by Rodman for Ambae.

[111] Muller comments that there had been substantial prejudice against the defendant before the court hearing and that he had been convicted of poisoning some time before. There had been a good deal of discussion about whether or not to give him over to the government, but people were dissuaded by the fact that they were afraid that he would die in jail, and also that if he did go to jail the father would not have received the money and the pig. Muller, Kal 1972, 'Field notes on the small Nambas', *Journal de la Société Des Océanistes*, vol. 28, no. 35, pp. 248–9. While these accounts present functioning conflict-management mechanisms, this does not appear to have been the case everywhere throughout the archipelago. For example, in regard to Malo, Rubenstein observes that although traditionally the Maloese saw their traditional land-tenure system as almost a codified body of laws that was completely respected and final, the knowledge and respect for these laws had diminished. This was a result of the 'perceived failure of powerful individuals within society to create, constitute, or enforce rules for land tenure' and also 'confusion as to what land principles may now be and how some of these principles rank in respect of relative strength and efficacy' (Rubenstein, Placing the self on Malo, p. 33).

[112] Nagriamel was a political movement based in Santo and led by the charismatic Jimmy Stevens. The movement called for a return to customary ways of life and the return of land to ni-Vanuatu.

[113] Rodman, Men of influence men of rank, p. 247.

[114] Ibid., p. 15.

[115] Ibid., p. 17.

[116] Ibid., p. 268.

[117] Jolly, Men, women and rank in South Pentecost, p. 297.

[118] Tonkinson, 'Church and kastom in Southeast Ambrym', p. 255.

[119] Lindstrom, Lamont 1981, 'Speech and kava on Tanna', in Michael Allen (ed.), *Vanuatu: Politics, economics and ritual in island Melanesia*, p. 385.

[120] Lindstrom, 'Traditional cultural policy in Melanesia', p. 375. Lindstrom discusses the procedures followed in meetings in some detail and makes two important observations. The first is that the consensus that is reached might not indicate much about the future of the behaviour of those consenting. As no meeting member has executive powers to enforce the decisions 'discovered' in the debate, there is no obligation, other than a moral one, to support a meeting's decision. Although disputes are therefore rarely permanently resolved through such meetings, they do have value because the dispute is at least temporarily resolved and can thus end the social avoidance that is the automatic result of a continuing dispute between participants. The second point is that in meetings the participants build up a public and communal version of the 'truth' of the dispute. In doing so, the meetings reproduce relations of inequality and power. Consequently, the parties depend on the mediation of powerful third parties, and parties who do not have the right to speak, such as women and young men, might have their voices unheard and unrepresented in the final story that emerges.

[121] Rodman, Men of influence men of rank, p. 291.

[122] Ibid., p. 292.

[123] Ibid., p. 266.

[124] Rubenstein, Placing the self on Malo, p. 35.

[125] With regard to Ambae, Rodman (Men of influence men of rank, p. 285) similarly notes: 'Murder and major assault are the only two instances of lawbreaking in which Native Court is inevitable; for any other transgression, outside intervention is an unpleasant option to be exercised after all other attempts at mediation fail.' In regard to Malo, Rubenstein (Placing the self on Malo, p. 35) commented on the fact that of the 16 cases he observed, only five were considered to be 'finally settled', as follows:

'The Maloese themselves recognise their inability to solve many of these cases, as the record indicates. Judges are themselves in conflict of interest, principles and facts are muddled, and political factionalism is rife. In many such cases, participants may turn to the government in an attempt to solve them. This is, in a sense, an ultimate threat. Regardless of how capricious the government may seem at times, there is a recognition by the Maloese that the government does hold an ultimate power.'

[126] Tonkinson, *Maat Village Efate*, p. 73.

[127] Colonial law was enforced by a Native Court, a meeting of colonial and local Mewun leaders held every month. The BDA essentially dealt with any cases that included assault, statutory rape and adultery. The assessor was responsible for dealing with the rest. Appeals went to the BDA and he had the power to imprison people. Larcom notes that '[e]ven when the BDA presided, most legal cases were in effect settled according to Mewun rather than European standards of justice'. Larcom, Joan 1990, 'Custom by decree: legitimation crisis in Vanuatu', in J. Linnekin and L. Poyer (eds), *Cultural Identity and Ethnicity in the Pacific*, pp. 179–80. An extremely useful insight into the operation of the Native Courts and the work of the district agents is provided in Bresnihan, Brian and Woodward, Keith 2002, *Tufala Gavman: Reminiscences from the Anglo-French condominium of the New Hebrides*, edited by two former district agents. It appears from most accounts that, as suggested by Larcom, the district agents adapted Native Court procedures very much to fit in with the local circumstances. Bresnihan (p. 99) remarks, 'Criminal cases…were also very time consuming. All parties involved had to be allowed to speak and it sometimes took many hours to unravel the facts and establish why the crime had been committed in the first place.' A number of district agents also commented on the fact that their work was made much easier because the defendants almost never pleaded not guilty and they 'provided the police with necessary evidence, as a point of honour', 'happily' accepting their sentence (pp. 247, 273, 216). It appears that at times even the substantive law was changed to fit local conditions and needs. Charpentier (in Bresnihan and Woodward, above) comments that in south Malekula traditionally adultery was punishable by death, however, '[w]ith the arrival of the missions, such a settlement was no longer possible'. He (pp. 161–2) explains that 'a kind of legal hiatus had come into being with which the District Agents were often asked to deal. Thus, a substantial proportion of the prisoners in the gaols of the Condominium had been convicted for reasons that in the West, would certainly not have brought them there.'

[128] Rodman, William 1993, 'The law of the State and the state of the law in Vanuatu', in Virginia Lockwood et al. (eds), *Contemporary Pacific Societies: Studies in development and change*, p. 61.

[129] Scarr, *Fragments of Empire*, p. 237.

[130] Tonkinson, *Maat Village Efate*, pp. 72–3.

[131] There are six anthropologists whose work is particularly relevant to the central issues in this study. Rodman on Ambae: Rodman, William 1983, 'Gaps, bridges and levels of law: middlemen as mediators in a Vanuatu society', in William Rodman and Dorothy Ayers Counts (eds), *Middlemen and Brokers in Oceania*, p. 69; Rodman, William 1985, 'A law unto themselves: legal innovation in Ambae, Vanuatu', *American Ethnologist*, vol. 12, p. 603; Rodman, 'The law of the State and the state of the law in Vanuatu', p. 55. Lindstrom on Tanna: Lindstrom, Lamont 1984, 'Doctor, lawyer, wise man, priest: big-men and knowledge in Melanesia', *Man*, vol. 19, no. 2, p. 291; Lindstrom, Lamont 1990, 'Straight talk on Tanna', in K. A. Watson-Gegeo and G. M. White (eds), *Disentangling Conflict Discourse*, p. 373; Lindstrom, Lamont 1997, 'Chiefs in Vanuatu today', in Geoffrey White and Lamont Lindstrom (eds), *Chiefs Today: Traditional Pacific leadership and the postcolonial state*, p. 211. Larcom on Malekula: 'Custom by decree'. Facey on Nguna: Facey, Ellen 1983, Ideology and identity: social construction of reality on Nguna, Vanuatu, PhD thesis, University of Sydney. Rousseau on Port Vila: Rousseau, Benedicta 2004, The achievement of simultaneity: *kastom* in contemporary Vanuatu, PhD thesis, University of Cambridge. Hess on Vanua Lava: Hess, Sabine 2005, Person and place on Vanua Lava, Vanuatu, PhD thesis, The Australian National University.

[132] Curtis explains that one of the main ideas behind the moratorium is the idea that *kastom* belongs to the future ni-Vanuatu and should be 'kept' for them to write up. Curtis, Tim 2002, Talking about place, PhD thesis, The Australian National University, p. 78. See also Bolton, Lissant 1999, 'Introduction', *Oceania*, vol. 70, no. 1, p. 1; Regenvanu, Ralph 1999, 'Afterword: Vanuatu perspectives on research', *Oceania*, vol. 70, no. 1, p. 98.

[133] Rousseau, The achievement of simultaneity.

[134] See, for example, Keesing, Roger 1982, 'Kastom in Melanesia: an overview', *Mankind*, vol. 13, no. 4, p. 297.

[135] Bolton, Lissant 1993, Dancing in mats: extending kastom to women in Vanuatu, PhD thesis, University of Manchester, p. 69.

[136] Ibid., p. 85; Jolly, Margaret 1992, 'Custom and the way of the land: past and present in Vanuatu and Fiji', *Oceania*, vol. 62, pp. 340–1.

[137] Jolly, 'Custom and the way of the land', p. 341.

[138] Philibert, Jean-Marc 1986, 'The politics of tradition: toward a generic culture in Vanuatu', *Mankind*, vol. 16, no. 1, p. 3.

[139] Bolton, Dancing in mats, p. 84.

[140] Jolly, 'Custom and the way of the land', p. 341.

[141] Ibid., p. 343.

[142] Bolton, Dancing in mats, p. 94.

[143] Hume, 'Church and custom on Maewo, Vanuatu'. Although, see Tonkinson, Robert 1982, 'National identity and the problem of kastom in Vanuatu', *Mankind*, vol. 13, no. 4, pp. 308–9.

[144] Jolly, 'Custom and the way of the land', p. 343.

[145] Selywn Garu (Author's notes from the Conference on *Kastom* and the Constitution, University of the South Pacific, Emalus Campus, Port Vila, Vanuatu, 4 October 2004).

[146] Tonkinson, 'National identity and the problem of kastom in Vanuatu', p. 310.

[147] This debate was initiated by the pioneering special edition of the journal *Mankind*. See Keesing, Roger and Tonkinson, Robert (eds) 1982, 'Reinventing traditional culture: the politics of *kastom* in island Melanesia', *Mankind* Special Issue, vol. 13, no. 4.

[148] Keesing, Roger 1989, 'Creating the past: custom and identity in the contemporary Pacific', *The Contemporary Pacific*, vol. 1, nos 1–2, p. 29.

[149] Tonkinson, 'National identity and the problem of kastom in Vanuatu', pp. 311, 312. He discusses how in Ambrym in the years around independence there was a self-conscious revival of old practices, even to the extent of one chief importing people from other areas who still had memories of how to make *kastom* objects, even though there were private criticisms that imported *kastom* might not be the '*tru*' (real) *kastom* of the *ples* (p. 311).

[150] Larcom, Joan 1982, 'The invention of convention', *Mankind*, vol. 13, no. 4, p. 336. She observed that several copies of Deacon's ethnography of the Mewun were circulating in the community, and discussed the propensity to draw on Deacon's book to search for precedents to be used in settling disputes in preference to the consensual ways of settling land disputes at public meetings that had hitherto occurred.

[151] Ibid., p. 330.

[152] See, for example, Rodman, 'Gaps, bridges and levels of law', pp. 603–4.

[153] This was due to their view of indigenous society as essentially static and also to the enormous rate at which the population was dying out as a result of diseases introduced by the Europeans. In a letter home in 1926, Deacon wrote, 'Probably during the next 50 years civilization will have penetrated to every area of the world & we shall see then what races have gone under & which are going to survive as competitors in the evolution of mankind. We have a long start in the race; & should eliminate a good many: e.g. the New Hebrides are almost bound to go.' Gardiner, Margaret 1987, *Footprints on Malekula: A memoir of Bernard Deacon*, p. 33.

[154] Jolly, Margaret 1992, 'Spectres of inauthenticity', *The Contemporary Pacific*, vol. 4, no. 1, p. 57.

[155] Rodman, 'Gaps, bridges and levels of law', p. 621.

[156] Tepahae, Chief Philip 1997, *Chiefly power in Southern Vanuatu*, reference" > Discussion Paper 1997/9, State, Society and Governance in Melanesia Research Paper Series, The Australian National University, <http://rspas.anu.edu.au/melanesia/research.php>, p. 1.

[157] Author's notes from the Conference on *Kastom* and the Constitution, University of the South Pacific, Emalus Campus, Port Vila, Vanuatu, 4 October 2004.

[158] Jolly, 'Spectres of inauthenticity'.

[159] Keesing, 'Creating the past', p. 19.

[160] White, Geoffrey M. 1997, 'The discourse of chiefs', in Lamont Lindstrom and Geoffrey White (eds), *Chiefs Today: Traditional Pacific leadership and the postcolonial state*, p. 232.

[161] Bolton, Dancing in mats, p. 79.

[162] Curtis, Talking about place, p. 76.

[163] Keesing, 'Creating the past', p. 37.

164 See also Facey's doctoral study on Nguna in which she is concerned to illustrate 'how a particular construction of the past is being propagated…by present day holders of positions of power and authority in order to lend authority to the politico-religious structures in which their positions lie' (Ideology and identity, p. 188).

165 See also Chanock, Martin 1978, 'Neo-traditionalism and the customary law in Malawi', *Journal of African Legal Studies*, vol. 16, p. 80, in which he argues that 'historical research into the "legal environment" in which pre-colonial law turned into the "customary law" of the colonial period could help to correct the process by which Africa is being given an authoritarian law invalidly claiming to embody its indigenous legal genius'.

166 Bolton, 'Chief Willie Bongmatur Maldo and the role of chiefs in Vanuatu', p. 180.

167 Ibid., p. 185.

168 Lindstrom, 'Chiefs in Vanuatu today', p. 212.

169 Bolton, 'Chief Willie Bongmatur Maldo and the role of chiefs in Vanuatu'.

170 Ibid., p. 185. Bolton notes that this illustrates a change of role for the chiefs from representing their community in non-traditional contexts, as they did during the Condominium, to representing the community's traditional face to outsiders, and suggests that this 'significantly, and subtly, underlines the identification of chiefs as traditional leaders'.

171 Ibid.

172 Facey (Ideology and identity, p. 248) noted that the difficulty stemmed from the fact that the structure of Melanesian society differed from district to district and from island to island, with the result that there was no uniform system of chiefly authority.

173 Bolton, 'Chief Willie Bongmatur Maldo and the role of chiefs in Vanuatu', p.185.

174 '*Mal*' meaning chief and '*vatu*' meaning stone, island or place. In the past, when they ordained chiefs, they took their authority from stones. '*Mauri*' means something that is alive, that grows in the light. Bolton 'Chief Willie Bongmatur Maldo and the role of chiefs in Vanuatu', pp. 190–1.

175 Lindstrom, 'Chiefs in Vanuatu today', p. 218.

176 Ibid., p. 219.

177 See, for example, ibid.; Bolton 'Chief Willie Bongmatur Maldo and the role of chiefs in Vanuatu'; Jolly, *Women of the Place*, p. 249.

178 Sherkin, Samantha 1999, Forever united: identity construction across the rural–urban divide, PhD thesis, University of Adelaide, p. 66.

179 Lindstrom, 'Chiefs in Vanuatu today', p. 227.

180 Rodman, 'A law unto themselves'.

181 Rodman, 'The law of the State and the state of the law in Vanuatu', p. 64.

182 Ibid.

183 Ibid., pp. 63–4.

184 Rodman, 'A law unto themselves', p. 615.

185 Facey, Ideology and identity, p. 162.

186 Ibid., p. 166.

187 Ibid., p. 170. She noted that at the time of her study there was a widespread perception of a number of contemporary problems facing Ngunese society. Moreover, while there was agreement that the problems existed, there were two different points of view as to what was causing them. The general population lay the blame on the behaviour of individual chiefs, who were accused of no longer serving as examples for people to follow, thus leading to people losing respect for them and making them in turn unable to control their people (p. 224). The chiefs, on the other hand, argued that Nguna's troubles stemmed from a general lack of respect for customary and Christian rules and for those authority figures whose job it was to see those rules were upheld. This difficulty is said to derive from things beyond their control, including loss of chiefly sacred spirits, inadequate support from their aides and widespread deviation from traditional behavioural patterns (p. 230). As is discussed in Chapter 5, these two opposing views also came across clearly during my fieldwork.

188 Larcom, 'Custom by decree', p. 180.

189 Rousseau, The achievement of simultaneity, p. 45.

190 Ibid., p. 139.

191 Mitchell, 'Violence as continuity', pp. 196–7.

192 Ibid., p. 198.
193 Ibid.
194 Ibid., p. 204.
195 Ibid., pp. 201–3.
196 Hess, Person and place on Vanua Lava, Vanuatu, p. 201.

4. *Mat, kava, faol, pig, buluk, woman*: the operation of the *kastom* system in Vanuatu today

This chapter explores the current operation of the *kastom* system through the analysis of a number of initial hypotheses in light of later research.[1] Due to space constraints, it is not possible to provide a full ethnographic account of the whole *kastom* system throughout Vanuatu. Consequently, this chapter focuses on its most salient aspects, especially those that affect its relationship with the state system. It also draws out some of its main principles and fundamental concepts (what Chiba would call the *legal postulates* of the system),[2] including those of respect, reciprocity, shame, balance and the importance of the community. The discussion is based primarily on fieldwork conducted between 2003 and 2006, and also some of the ethnographic works discussed in Chapter 3 as well as a report commissioned by the Ministry of Internal Affairs[3] as a preliminary step in drafting Chiefs Legislation (a project discussed in Chapter 5).

As a preliminary matter, however, I would like to discuss my use of the terms '*kastom* system' and 'conflict management'. The choice of terminology for the non-state system of conflict management in Vanuatu is problematic because there is no one term that ni-Vanuatu use to refer to it. Some refer to 'sitting down in the *nakamal* or *nasara*' (the place where dispute management is often carried out),[4] some to 'straightening' a conflict 'at the level of *kastom*' or 'in *kastom*', some to 'giving' the conflict 'to the chiefs' and others use a handful of other descriptive phrases. The essential features of the system as shown by these phrases are that the system is indigenous and administered by non-state leaders (chiefs) in their own places of authority. In this study, the term '*kastom* system' is used, the word '*kastom*' meaning generally 'our way of doing things',[5] thus capturing the most significant feature of the system. Support for this terminology also comes from Hess, who observes that '[t]oday the notion of *kastom* is actively used to stress the participatory "found" public consensus that distinguishes it from adversarial Western legal systems, which entail decisions for someone and therefore also against someone'.[6]

It is recognised that there are some who would argue that the *kastom* system should not be called a 'system' at all. First, it could be said that Vanuatu is so diverse that there are *many* different indigenous legal systems—as many as there are functioning subgroups, to use Pospisil's argument—rather than just one.[7] While this is certainly true, and the substantive laws and procedures used vary significantly throughout the country, there are common threads that unify them: the emphasis on peace and harmony in the community, on restoring relationships, on the use of chiefs to facilitate agreement, on community involvement in the processes and on the achievement of settlement by the payment of compensation. So just as the study of the 'civil law system' and the 'common law system'[8] is legitimate despite the fact that they include within them many different legal systems and subsystems, so too is the study of the *kastom* system despite the variation in its operation throughout Vanuatu.[9]

It might also be argued that the use of the term 'system' is misleading because it implies a coherence and structure that the *kastom* system does not have, being more a collection of subsystems than one with a clear national or even provincial structure, although this is gradually changing as new reforms are effected.[10] To attempt to overcome such problems, some scholars have used other terms—for example, Griffiths[11] prefers to speak of 'orders' rather than systems to avoid assumptions of systematic bodies of law, while Woodman instead speaks of 'legal fields'.[12] There are, however, two reasons why the term 'system' is used in this study. First, all legal systems suffer from these criticisms to an extent, as Keebet von Benda-Beckmann argues:

> Law is not an amorphous set of norms and principles but neither is it a tightly structured system. This is not even the case for western legal systems, despite the efforts of centuries of legal scholarship. Law typically consists of clustered sets of norms, principles, concepts and procedures.[13]

Therefore, as the use of the term system is retained for the State, and the differences in coherence are ones only of degree, it is legitimate to use it for the *kastom* system as well for epistemological coequivalence. Second, and more importantly, the term system carries with it the concept of interconnectedness, which is important in identifying the fact that although these subsystems operate within a particular social setting, they increasingly have relations with each other, and that these relationships are significant.[14] Thus, in this study, the term system is used to refer to the state and the *kastom* processes, while disclaiming any pretensions to coherence that the term suggests. Seymour-Smith supports this approach, arguing that the key to the productive use of the term system in anthropology is 'the recognition that such systems do not exist in reality but are analytical devices which we may impose in order to investigate our data more fruitfully'.[15]

A final justification is that the *kastom* system is conceived of as such by many involved in its administration. For example, the Secretary of the Malvatumauri, in the context of a protest about prison conditions,[16] recently stated:

> We made a ceremony and then the Chiefs handed the prisoners over to the other system of governance, that's the police again. So, it was really *from one system to the other and making sure that both systems, protocols, procedures, are observed in the whole process.* Yesterday, we believe that

we observed the two procedures for the two systems and we feel that we are quite satisfied with what we've done yesterday[17] [my emphasis].

The term 'conflict management' is used in preference to others such as 'dispute resolution'. It is broad enough to include processes that go beyond dealing merely with particular disputes, thus allowing a study 'of the relationship of rule orders to behaviour'.[18] It also encompasses processes that manage conflicts, rather than necessarily reaching fixed and permanent settlements. These broader parameters are necessary when discussing the *kastom* system, as often what occurs is a continuing exercise in managing the various consequences of a particular conflict or conflicts. For example, if a violent dispute breaks out between two villages there might need to be a move by the chief from one village to send a payment, such as a pig, first of all to the other chief in order to ease the tension. Then, some days later, a meeting might be held at which temporary agreement is reached and a *kastom* settlement is made, but the conflict might still be one that exists until some new circumstances give it reason to fire up again, thus it cannot be considered to have been resolved.

The pervasiveness of the *kastom* system

The *kastom* system, in one form or another, exists in every village and town in Vanuatu. It is indisputably the way in which the majority of conflicts in every rural and urban community in the country are managed, and even cases managed by the state system often have some level of involvement with the *kastom* system.[19]

The central idea of the *kastom* system is that the chief or chiefs of a community are responsible for managing conflicts. They do so through holding a public meeting with the parties involved where the conflict is extensively discussed, responsibility allocated and amends made through the making of a *kastom* payment by one or both of the parties. Around this '*stampa*' (base) there is great variation in the form the *kastom* system can take.

The *kastom* system in almost every island is divided into different levels, although the number of these levels and the formality of the divisions between them de facto and de jure vary from island to island. Generally, the first level (after attempts to resolve a conflict at a family level have been unsuccessful) is the village chief or chiefs. Next, some communities have a 'ward' council made up of chiefs from several villages, then there is often an area council comprising representatives of the various ward councils in a particular area, and then sometimes an island-level (often including offshore islands)[20] or a provincial-level chiefly council as the penultimate level. The Malvatumauri is at the top of this structure, representing chiefs at a national level. Although there have been chiefly councils in Vanuatu for decades now, some provincial governments[21] and the Malvatumauri have recently been instrumental in formalising and mobilising the different levels of chiefly councils as part of their efforts to promote greater engagement of the chiefs in governance and conflict management.[22]

In the two towns of Port Vila and Luganville, the organisation of the *kastom* system is slightly different due to the many different island communities who live there. Each community has its own chief or chiefly representative[23] in town and many have chiefly town councils, depending on the size of the particular community.[24] As the organisation of these representatives is often ad hoc, some people are criticised for being 'self-styled' chiefs and their right to exercise authority is questioned. Generally, when a conflict involves people from different communities the different chiefly councils will sit to hear the conflicts together.[25] The chief of the South West Bay Malekula community in Vila gave the following example:

> A young man from our area had decided to leave his wife who was from Ambae. We had to call the chiefs from Ambae and Malekula to sit together to sort that out. Both chiefs chaired the meeting. After the meeting to finalise the judgment, we have what we call a native court, where chiefs go to finalise the penalties, chiefs sit together to discuss the penalty. They then call the meeting back and say this is our decision—it is always a two or three man decision when judging something serious.

In the two towns there are also town councils of chiefs with chiefly representatives from the different communities living in the towns that are not from Efate or Santo. Similar bodies have also been established in some of the bigger villages in the islands where there are diverse communities living together.[26] In some urban areas, there are also 'suburban' councils of chiefs, such as the Freswota Council of Chiefs, comprising chiefs from that community.

All these different levels of councils and, at the village level, individual chiefs are responsible for managing conflicts that members of their community are involved in. The sorts of matters that they deal with vary depending on a number of factors, including the chiefs' own assessment of their jurisdictional capabilities and power, community support for the *kastom* system, the wishes of the conflicting parties and the accessibility of the state system. In some places therefore the *kastom* system is used just to resolve minor cases, whereas in other places it deals with cases as serious as murder. The issue of which system should hear which case is currently a major problem, as is discussed in Chapter 6.[27]

Diversity in conflict management

The validity of the hypothesis that there is a significant diversity in conflict-management practices across Vanuatu can best be tested by separately examining the various stages involved in the management of a conflict.

The people in charge of the management of the conflict

When the research began, I thought that only chiefs were responsible for managing conflicts but, as with so much else, the truth was much more complex. In fact, a wide variety of people are responsible for the management of conflicts in different communities (although chiefs are the primary decision makers), including:

- a chief alone or with one or two assistants[28]
- a non-chiefly or chiefly chairman who directs proceedings together with a council of chiefs who decide the matter[29]
- a chief together with a council comprising elders and 'small' (or lesser) chiefs[30]
- a chief who appoints representatives from the supporters of the two parties to act as judges[31]
- several chiefs[32]
- a chiefly chairman together with a council of four counsellors and a woman's representative[33]
- several 'small chiefs' who direct the proceedings and the 'big chief' who says nothing until making a decision at the end.[34]

There is such a wide range of practices that it is difficult to make any reliable predictions about which form will be found at which level and in which place, but where the concept of levels of chiefly councils is firmly established, the councils are more likely to comprise chiefly representatives from the different areas involved. In some areas, there are also other office-holders, such as secretaries who take minutes of the meeting and village police officers who are used by the chiefs to enforce their orders.[35]

Before the meeting

A *kastom* meeting is almost always initiated by one of the parties or one of their family members approaching the chief or his representative. In some areas, the person must also give the chief some money in order to initiate the proceedings.[36] In most areas, the chief or his assistants will then call a meeting to resolve the case, but in other areas the chief or his assistants will go to talk with the people involved in the conflict first of all—to see if it can be resolved without a meeting and also to collect evidence that can be used at the meeting. The formality with which this is done varies: in some areas it is just a matter of the chiefs or assistants talking with the conflicting parties,[37] while other areas have a highly formalised system. For example, in Mele, the village police go to take statements and then bring their reports to the council members a day before the scheduled meeting and they then discuss the cases, sometimes sending the police back to get more information to 'balance' the story.

The other variation in what occurs before a meeting is whether or not there is physical aggression by one of the parties or their families towards the other. The only island where this appears to be a regular part of the *kastom* process is Tanna, where sometimes the victim's family will attack the defendant either before the meeting or at the start of the meeting.[38] While this is not officially sanctioned, there is often an unspoken agreement not to interfere with this physical retaliation and any harm suffered is then taken into account when 'weighing' the compensation due to one or both sides. A senior police officer in Santo observed that Tannese chiefs in Luganville often allowed the victim's family to assault the defendant before the chiefs 'sat down' to resolve the conflict, remarking 'now everyone knows what to expect if they are invited to a meeting by Tanna chiefs!'.[39]

At the meeting

There are a number of different procedural variations in the meetings, which are generally held in the community *nakamal* or *nasara*.[40]

Who attends?

The one uniform practice of *kastom* meetings is that they are public events. At a minimum, the two parties and their families are present, and often the community in general as well. The community attendance might be limited to one community or might include neighbouring villages. For example, in Tanna, when the chief of one of the parties calls a meeting, he will generally invite members of neighbouring villages to attend. The reason for this is said to be, alternatively, to keep the peace or to give 'balance' to the discussion. Although community members are present, they might not all physically sit down in the same area—some (especially women and young people) might stay outside the *nakamal*, often listening and staring in through the openings. In the towns in particular, it is also common to invite other people involved with the parties in some way, such as employers or fellow employees. The chief blowing on a conch shell, which makes a loud and distinctive sound, or the sounding of the slit-gong drum, traditionally notifies the community that the meeting is in session.[41] The atmosphere at one meeting has been evocatively described as follows: 'the meeting is called—there are different rumours flying around—whilst people are waiting for the meeting to start they form little groups and discuss the matter informally.'[42]

Who speaks?

In general, the essence of all *kastom* meetings is to give a chance to the two parties and other interested members of the community to fully express themselves; in Bislama, this is called '*serem toktok*' (sharing talking). In the majority of islands, both parties are invited to speak for themselves—first the complainant and then the defendant—and the leaders of the meeting question them. The system is thus far more inquisitorial than adversarial, although the parties may also question each other. Where the matters are disputed,[43] the two parties often bring witnesses, who are also questioned. In general, the community is also free to participate in the discussion: often the chairman, who gives permission to people to speak once they have raised their hand, controls their participation. Many respondents stressed that the chairman had the right to stop people from talking if they digressed too much from the subject at hand, but in general there was a great deal of tolerance for wide-ranging and repetitive talking. An anthropologist commented on the purpose of the speaking in meetings as follows:

> I believe these legal processes are more intended to give space for each party to present their view so they don't feel aggrieved. Public speech is so important in Vanuatu, even if the content is absurd or repetitive. It is important the people feel they have had their say. If there is a notion of justice in this it is in the opportunity to externalise your grievance.[44]

A chief similarly commented that his mediating strategy was 'to let everyone have their say and vent their emotions of frustration and anger and then…[w]hen everyone was exhausted' to lead them 'to find peace among themselves'.[45]

There are, however, some variations to this general pattern. In some islands, women are not allowed to talk in the *nakamal*. This *kastom* is changing fast throughout most of Vanuatu and today appears to be maintained primarily in Tafea Province.[46] In the *kastom kot* observation[47] study, women spoke in 58 per cent of cases; they were too scared to speak in 8 per cent of cases; they were not allowed to speak in 29 per cent;[48] and in one case the chief was allowed to speak to the woman involved alone. If a woman is one of the parties to the conflict and is not allowed to talk then she will have someone representing her. The practice of having someone speaking on behalf of one of the parties is not limited just to women, it happens for youth and occasionally for adult men.[49] It is more common in the southern islands and is said to be a way of avoiding direct confrontation in meetings. Another way of doing this is to address questions to a person or group not involved in the conflict.[50] Many people from all over Vanuatu also commented that in *kastom* meetings people often talked in parables, and that it was not direct like the state system.[51]

How is a decision reached?

Unlike in the state system, where the decision about culpability is separate from the decision about penalty, in the *kastom* system, there is often no clear distinction drawn between these two types of decisions. The procedures used throughout Vanuatu to determine the outcomes of *kastom* meetings present a complete spectrum of decision-making styles, ranging from those chiefs who make a decision themselves and announce it to the parties who have to either accept it or take it to another body, to those chiefs who act as facilitators, encouraging the parties to come to their own decisions, to chiefs delegating the decision making to others and acting just as a chairperson of the proceedings. Thus in some islands it would even be wrong to characterise what occurs as decision making, as the parties themselves refer to what occurs as more of a 'disentangling' of a conflict through talking.[52] As such, the line between arbitration and mediation is blurred in theory and practice.[53] For example, one respondent describes the process in Ambae:

> Once the parties have put their cases and [their points of] view the meeting breaks off after having elected some judges. These judges are not formally nominated; it is just known which people have the most knowledge and wisdom and have been fair in the past. These people then go away and discuss between themselves what to do and then return and announce how the reconciliation is to be reached. The parties are then called to comment on the decision and if there is disagreement then the meeting will not end until agreement is reached. The contribution of both parties is significant in coming to a reconciliation.[54]

A similar procedure occurs in Erromango, where, when all the talking has finished, the counsellors go away and come to a decision about what to do. They come back and announce the decision and ask if everyone is happy. If people are not then they have to go away and come back with another decision.[55]

In North Pentecost, in contrast, as the following example shows, there is far less participation by the parties in the final decision:

> When there is a meeting everyone gathers in the *nakamal* and the chairperson of the village council tells the chiefs that they will be responsible for making a decision. The chairperson directs the meeting. He is chosen by the village but is not necessarily a chief. Everybody talks, to give evidence and so on. At the end of the talking everyone goes outside and leaves the chiefs to discuss the issue and come to a decision. Then they come back inside and the chiefs say what their decision is. Then everyone goes back to their houses to look for pigs and red mats…There is never any negotiation about the *faen* [fine].[56]

Similarly, in Mele, once the decision has been pronounced by the paramount chief there is no disputing it, but this decision has generally been arrived at as a result of the talking and negotiating between the 'small chiefs' and the parties.

The most party-inclusive model is found in some parts of Tanna, where the complainant and all of his or her family and friends sit down in one area, the defendant and all of his or her family and friends sit in another and groups representing the other villages sit in other areas.[57] The talk then 'goes around and around' until a decision is reached that everyone accepts.[58] In Vanua Lava as well, there are times when the chiefs will send the parties away to make a decision between themselves.[59] The decision that is made generally involves an order that one or both parties must make a payment of some sort. The words that are used to describe this payment vary: in some places, it is referred to as a *kastom faen* (fine), in others a *kastom* settlement or *kastom* compensation.[60] In this study, the term '*kastom* payment' is generally used. Today many payments are in cash, although *kastom* payments of pigs,[61] pig tusks, mats, kava and root crops are also used, especially in rural areas.[62] Sometimes there are other orders that can be made, such as that a party should not go to a particular area or should not engage in the same conduct again.[63]

The issue of how chiefs or the parties or counsellors come to a decision is far more complex and is linked to the purposes or aims of the *kastom* meetings, and that, as discussed below, is a fluid issue at the moment. Traditionally, there was not so much importance attributed to the question of what had really occurred: what was important was finding out how relationships had been damaged and what needed to be done to restore them. There was an assumption that the mere fact that there had been a social disturbance meant that the parties had done something wrong—as one respondent said, '[L]ong kastom loa yu rong finis i stap—yu mas talem i no yu' (in *kastom* there is the presumption that you are guilty and you must prove that you are not).[64] Another relevant factor is that in the past people were prepared to follow a chief's orders even when they were in fact innocent, because of a belief that the truth would eventually come out and then they would gain respect for their behaviour in accepting the chief's decision. One respondent observed:

> People knew that if a judgment was not right, if they went along with it then they would be better off in the end because it would become clear eventually that they were right. There are some sayings that support people in this belief. One is that 'the truth is sharp', in other words, you can't hide it as it will cut through everything. Another refers to the hard inside part of a tree, and says that even if the tree trunk is rotten and covered with mud, eventually this hard central bit will come out. So even if a judgment was biased against you, you went along with it to maintain the reconciliation, confident that you would eventually be vindicated.[65]

Today, however, there is increasing emphasis on making sure that people are made to pay only for misbehaviour they have really done, and hence chiefs are being pressured to justify their decisions or the way they 'skelem toktok' (weigh the speech), especially by members of their communities who have been educated about the state system. There is therefore a developing interest in issues of proof and evidence.

There are a number of different mechanisms used today by chiefs to help them decide whether or not a complaint against someone is justified. Some chiefs maintain that they can tell when someone is lying because they live with the people and know their character. There is also a lot of reliance on the wisdom of certain people who are believed to be able to tell whether someone is telling the truth or not. Another factor is that villages are small places and there is a general belief that if someone has done something wrong then it will not be possible to hide that fact, making it relatively easy to compel a confession. It is also believed that if everyone involved is present then gradually through talking and questioning of witnesses the truth will come out and what has happened will be revealed. In this respect, there is reliance on the fact that people will feel shame for having done something bad to someone else and so eventually they will want to confess to be able to restore the relationship. Sometimes as well the case is 'put on hold' to see if more evidence comes to light. For example, if a boy swears that he did not get a girl pregnant then they just wait for the baby to be born and they see who it looks like.[66] A final method, used primarily in the north, is for the chiefs to call the priests or the Melanesian Brotherhood[67] to make people tell the truth. A respondent explains that people in rural areas believe that if you lie to one of these people something terrible will happen to you. The belief in priests and the brotherhood is strongest in those areas that are predominantly Anglican—for example, Pentecost, Maewo, Ambae, Torba Province and Luganville and Vila to an extent.[68] In the Banks Islands, a chief reports that if people do not confess then he gets a priest to come, who usually manages to find out if the person has done something wrong or not. He said this was the only way he had to find out if something was true or not.[69]

In regard to their investigative role, the chiefs have quite wide-ranging powers to 'faen' everyone who they consider to have transgressed kastom, even if the complainant did not complain about that person's misconduct. For example, in Ambae, the following case occurred:

> The case was a case about 'jealousy': a man suspected that his wife, a nurse, was having an affair with Z, one of her co-workers. Initially a village court heard the case and it was settled, but then Y started to talk to the jealous husband, stirring him up and suggesting that his wife and Z had been lying. The case then was taken up again at the area level where the chiefs 'found' that although the wife had not had an affair with Z she had provoked the jealousy because she had once telephoned him when she was away and had told him she was calling from a different place than the place she actually was. The end result was that the wife was ordered to pay a faen, but the heaviest penalty was imposed on Y who had to pay a faen to the chief, to Z and to the husband for the trouble he had caused.[70]

After the meeting

In many cases a reconciliation or *kastom* ceremony of some sort is held, either immediately after the meeting or a few days later. This might be the time when the *kastom* payments are made or they might have been made before or after if the parties do not have sufficient means to pay immediately. Whether or not such a ceremony is held seems to depend on whether the matter is serious and relations need to be mended. In the *kastom kot* observation study, 33 per cent of cases involved a ceremony in which the parties drank kava or ate together, there was an apology, a *kastom* payment was made or the parties shook hands. In 45 per cent of cases, however, there was no ceremony.[71] A provincial officer comments that the reconciliation ceremony is important because it is where you publicly say what you have done is wrong and that you will do better in the future. This ceremony symbolises that agreement has been reached.[72]

In the Banks Islands, the reconciliation ceremony is held several days after the meeting. By this time, people's tempers have cooled and they come together to share food and kava and to shake hands and make peace. One chief said if this ceremony was held directly after the meeting the 'feelings are too strong'.[73] In the Torres Islands, the reconciliation ceremony involves a kava ritual. One person makes the kava and gives two shells of kava to each party who then have to drink the shells all at once. This is said to symbolise washing the sin of the conflict from your eyes because the truth and facts of the world enter your body through your eyes. From that moment on the grievances should be buried.[74] In some places, parties make *laplap*[75] for each other and eat together[76] and in other places they exchange *kastom* payments, give and accept leaves of plants of special meaning—such as *namele* (cycad) and *nanggaria* (croton) leaves—and shake hands. Chiefs very rarely miss an opportunity to give a speech about how the parties should now be friends and not commit this sort of behaviour in the future.

The restorative nature of the *kastom* system

There has been much written about the restorative nature of traditional practices in the South Pacific[77] and this aspect of the *kastom* system is constantly promoted by all respondents. I lost count of the number of times respondents stated that in *kastom* both parties won, but in the state system one party won and one lost.[78] Certainly, the basic principles of the *kastom* system as enunciated by the chiefs, and as practised in the majority of instances recorded in this research, are restorative, particularly in that they focus on restoring relationships that have been damaged by the conflict. The *kastom* systems also emphasise compensation, repair of harm, prevention of future harm, reintegration of offenders and communication of the shamefulness of law-breaking, often followed by a '*kastom sori*'[79] (sorry, apology) and forgiveness. Hess explains that being '*sori*' 'is a key concept in ni-Vanuatu ideas about being human' and the word 'could be approximately glossed in English as grief, regret, compassion, sympathy and empathy'.[80] In addition, there is also empowerment of multiple stakeholders (not necessarily all women and all youth) to tell their own stories in their own way. Many chiefs explained that the restorative nature of *kastom* decisions was necessitated by the small-scale nature of their communities. Because people live in a communal society where everyone helps each other, if there is a conflict this '*mekem i had sipos yu no mekem fren bakegen from bae oli no helpem yu*' (makes it hard if people do not restore friendship because they will not help each other).[81]

Two of the main stated aims of any *kastom* meeting are restorative—namely, '*blong mekem [tufala pati] sekhan mo kam gudfala fren bakegen*' (to make the two parties shake hands and become good friends again)[82] —and to allow the defendant to '*klinim fes*' (literally, 'clean his face', meaning remove the sense of shame and restore respect to the wrongdoer in the face of the community). The first aim thus focuses on restoring relationships between the disputing parties, while the second is concerned with reintegrating the wrongdoer into the community, allowing any avoidance that might have been practised before the meeting (as a result of the feelings of shame or of anger) to cease.[83] The concept of shame is thus intrinsically linked to reconciliation, and Hess explains that in Vanuatu the ability to feel shame 'is seen as a positive attribute of a person'.[84]

The restorative nature of *kastom* decisions is manifested in a number of ways. First, everyone—the parties, their families and their community—is involved in the process. This means that everyone is able to fully understand the issues and background to what has happened. As one respondent comments, in *kastom*, the defendant is asked to explain his or her behaviour, allowing everyone to come to a level of understanding.[85] A related point is that the investigation into what happened is free and wide ranging. A chief gave an example of the holistic approach taken in *kastom*:

> In *kastom* if John comes and looks at Brown and Brown swears at him, John fights him. In court if a man says that he fought the man then he is punished but the one who swore does not get any punishment. So John goes and fights him again. The way that the ni-Vanuatu look at it is to ask who started the conflict and to punish that person as well.[86]

Because of this approach, payments in *kastom* are often two way, with each party paying each other an amount of the same or different weight. An important aspect of *kastom* is a concern to make sure that the person who has lost or been found to have been in the wrong is not left feeling bitter. Therefore even in cases where only one party is in the wrong, the other side will also often pay something to make sure there is peace between them. One chief explains this by saying that in *kastom* when one party wins he then feels *sori* for the other party and so gives him something so as not to deprive him completely. He gave an example of a conflict over land and said that the winning side might tell the losing side that he could live on a piece of the land that was in conflict. He contrasted this with the state system, where the losing side would have to leave the land.[87] Even when the payment is just in one direction, however, there are other ways of making the outcome reciprocal. For example, in Pentecost, at the end of a *kastom* meeting the parties eat and drink kava together and it is primarily the responsibility of the complainant to light the fire in the *nakamal* and to provide the kava and food. Lindstrom's observations about the importance of balance in exchanges of goods in Vanuatu are relevant here, and he states that '[a]s imbalance in exchange adversely affects other spheres of life (the body physic and social) a judicious and balanced exchange of goods repairs imbalance in those areas'.[88] He gives the following example: 'Young brothers, sadly brought to violence by excess of drink, exchange not only the monetary contents of their pockets but also the shirts off their backs as they re-establish balance and good feeling in their relations with each other.'[89]

Another restorative element is the focus on compensation. In some respects, the payment that must be paid is a very literal attempt at compensation—for example, in some islands, a man who has killed someone must 'replace a life with a life' by giving one of his daughters to the family of the victim.[90] Where the damage is less easy to quantify, however, an amount is set having regard to the surrounding circumstances. Often more than just straight compensation is involved and sometimes this element of the compensation is referred to as a '*kastom sori*' or apology rather than a payment, because it arises from a desire on the part of the wrongdoer to say sorry for what has occurred, and it will be paid to many people involved in the conflict.[91]

For example, in Tanna, there was a case where a woman had 'adulterous affairs' with three 'boys' from three different villages.[92] Everyone confessed what had happened and the chiefs decided that each boy had to pay a big pig and a big head of kava. One pig went to the village chief 'to make his heart happy again', another went to the husband and the third went to the wives of the three boys. It is very common for chiefs to receive part of this payment because committing an offence in a chief's jurisdiction is seen as being in itself an act of disrespect to the chief, and this is often perceived to be just as serious as the offence itself.[93] For example, in 2004, a young girl from Ambae, living in one of the peri-urban communities around Vila, killed her newborn baby, which provoked a great deal of community shock and outrage. A *kastom* meeting was held at which the chiefs from Ambae paid a *kastom* payment of pigs, mats and roosters to the Efate Island Council of Chiefs (the Vaturisu). The chief of the Vaturisu stated, 'I declare that [in *kastom*] nothing further is to be said of the incident. Our *nasara* is clean as we turn to a clean page and there is no more bad feeling anymore.'[94]

While these principles of compensation and restoration are present in most cases decided in Vanuatu, there are also a number of cases where the chiefs use *kastom* to impose punitive sanctions on the wrongdoers.[95] The aims of such decisions seem much less about reconciliation than about punishment, and sometimes revenge.[96] For example, a young respondent reported:

> I will tell you about a case of a relative of mine. She had *flatem* [had sexual relations with] all the men around her and made lots of women very angry with her. The chiefs tried everything they could to stop her—they cut off her hair, and they all whipped her. Then finally they sent her back to the island. She stayed there for ten years and she saw how hard life was there, not like getting paid money for sex, and now she has come back to Vila ten years later a changed woman. Now she stands next to the chiefs to assault the women who have children with no fathers!

Chiefs also beat people (especially youth), make them cut grass or perform other manual labour, grind kava and even run around naked in public as punishments. Occasionally, chiefs also order exile or banishment. For example, the chief of Emae said that if a member of the community caused trouble he had the right to send him out of the area. He explained that 'if a wild dog is inside the yard with your pigs and is slowly eating them, will you save it? No.'[97] This remedy was resorted to in 2006 in Luganville when chiefs from Sanma Province resolved that a family, originally from Paama, had to leave the island after allegations that the family was behind the assault of a chief from east Santo.[98]

There are also some areas where some 'payback' types of *kastom* still exist. For example, on the island of Malo, there is a *kastom* that if someone is killed then their family has the right to attack the defendant's family by chasing them out of the village and destroying their property and killing a member of the family. A respondent reported that the chiefs of Malo recently authorised a family of a deceased person to do this, but the family was stopped before they caught and killed anyone.[99] Like the state system, the *kastom* system is therefore also not intrinsically restorative rather than punitive.

Privileging the community over individuals

Three major findings emerge in relation to the hypothesis that the focus of the *kastom* system is on peace and harmony in the community rather than individual justice. First, there is no doubt that restoring peace and harmony to the community is the guiding rationale behind most chiefly decisions.[100] A chief from Pentecost stated: 'under the *kastom* system peace is collectively owned by a group or community and the community has got a collective accountability to peace.'[101] There appears to be an almost unspoken fear in the minds of many chiefs that their communities could at any moment erupt into chaos, and hence they must deal with conflicts quickly, and in a way that discourages other conflicts from flaring up. The metaphor of a fire was often used to convey the sense that small sparks must be contained to avoid a massive blaze.[102] Related to this is the fact that a person involved in an incident is not seen as an individual, but part of a family unit[103] or, as is increasingly the case in mixed communities, a member of a particular island.[104] Therefore the whole community quite literally is involved in the conflict, as they are likely to be either the victim's or the defendant's family or a close contact.[105] Families and not individuals also often make payments, in turn building up the network of obligations and counter-obligations ni-Vanuatu society is based on. For example, in Pentecost, the chief will make a payment on behalf of someone from his village. They do not have an obligation to pay back the chief with material objects, but there is an obligation to respect the chief. In Ambae, the chief will make the payment, but then the troublemaker must pay him back.

The second major finding is that the focus on ensuring peace and harmony in the community at times conflicts with the restorative notions of the *kastom* system. In other words, victims who might not really be happy with the decision are forced to accept it and 'shake hands' for the good of the community. This is particularly a problem for women, who are often made to stay in abusive relationships for the sake of community stability. One respondent explains that in *kastom* if there is a problem in the home then the decision is taken on the basis of the interests of the family unit; there is always an emphasis on putting the family unit back together. Traditionally, there is the concept that one suffers for the good of the community; the general approach is that couples have to stay together even if one has been wronged.[106]

The third finding is that the focus on ensuring peace and harmony in the community is being increasingly called into question as people engage more with modernity and start learning about individual rights and justice. This makes them more reluctant to accept that the needs of the community should prevail over their needs. Many women are also becoming increasingly aware that reference to the good of the community can conceal power dynamics that favour men over women. Thus a counsellor at the Vanuatu Women's Centre observed that even if the *kastom* meeting created peace in the community, the woman still did not have peace, explaining further that the *kastom* system did not look at a woman as a whole being.

The tension between the needs of the community and individual rights is fully appreciated by many chiefs, but they see prioritising the community over the individual as a choice they must make. For example, the Secretary of the Malvatumauri stated, '[O]n Pentecost justice at times is not the priority, but peace is.' This view was also expressed by another chief, who stated that in *kastom* the good of the community was paramount: individuals 'will be given their day' but if 'at the end of the day' the community would suffer then the community must be given priority.[107]

Kastom procedures and *kastom* law

The initial question to be investigated was whether in *kastom* procedures were more important than substantive laws. On further reflection, however, I realised that the real question was whether or not the procedural aspects of the *kastom* system were just as, or more, difficult to reconcile with the state system as the substantive laws. Analysing this question requires a three-stage approach: are there substantive laws in the *kastom* system? Are the differences between substantive laws in the two different systems problematic? Are the differences between procedural approaches in the two systems more or less problematic?

The first question therefore is whether there are substantive laws in the *kastom* system. Many authors warn against using concepts of Western jurisprudence, such as 'rules' or prohibitions to describe Melanesian ways of resolving conflicts, as the use of such terms is said to 'sit uneasily with the ethnographic evidence'.[108] In the *kastom* system today, however, the concept of substantive laws, by which is meant a relatively precise norm with a sanction for disobeying, is widespread. The laws that are spoken about, and increasingly written down,[109] appear to have three sources: *kastom*, the state system and Christianity.

Kastom laws generally relate to regulating kinship relationships[110] or prohibitions of various kinds (for example, a chief may put a *namele* leaf[111] on the beach, which signifies that people must not gather resources from that reef), protection of the environment and respect.[112] Some crimes from the state system are also slowly being introduced into the *kastom* system, such as the crime of rape, which did not exist in the same way in *kastom*.[113] The third category of laws is derived from Christianity; thus people will talk about the prohibition on 'coveting' something or on 'fornication'. There are also of course general laws prohibiting people from stealing, assaulting each other, damaging property and so on, which probably come from all three sources.

It is clear that *kastom* laws vary throughout Vanuatu, but it is difficult to determine to what extent.[114] Most respondents agreed that the fundamental principles of *kastom* remained constant throughout the country, but there were variations in details such as appropriate amounts of *kastom* payments and laws relating to respect and kinship.[115] One chief stated, '[W]e do everything similar, but how we present it in a ceremonial way is different.'[116] There are a number of indications that the differences between various *kastom* laws do not pose huge difficulties in resolving conflicts in practice. The Chief Justice and the Chief of the Malvatumauri—men who would be expected to be aware of the differences between *kastom* in different parts of the country—stated that the differences in substantive *kastom* were not of much importance. Also the town councils of chiefs in Luganville and Port Vila manage to deal with the different laws among the various communities without too much difficulty.

Given that there are therefore substantive laws in the *kastom* system today, the second question is whether or not differences between them and the laws of the state system are likely to be problematic. One of the clear findings of the research was that, with the exception of some human rights provisions in the constitution[117] that were widely criticised as being inconsistent with *kastom*, no respondent complained about the particular substantive content of the state system.[118] It could be that this is due to a lack of true understanding by the majority of the population of the substantive content of state laws. An alternative reason could be that ni-Vanuatu are used to accepting different *kastom* laws and to finding ways of minimising the difficulties these pose. This suggests that differences between state law and *kastom* law might similarly be able to be negotiated, because people are used to doing so and because the content of substantive *kastom* laws has changed over time anyway, incorporating state laws and Christian laws.[119]

The final question therefore is whether differences between the procedures in the state and *kastom* systems are more or less problematic than the differences in substantive laws. Except for the complaints about the laws relating to human rights in the constitution, every criticism of the state system and example of the difficulties with it made during this study related to procedures rather than substance. This suggests that differences in procedures are more problematic than differences between substantive laws. As the Chief Justice stated, the focus of reform needed to be on the legal structures and systems—'the basket'—rather than the substantive law or what was inside the basket. He observed that that could come afterwards: 'the people can fill the basket with their laws.'[120]

The dynamism of the *kastom* system

There are two main findings from the fieldwork that support the hypothesis that the *kastom* system is dynamic: the conscious adaptations made to the *kastom* system by the chiefs, and the widespread open-mindedness of the chiefs and their willingness to embrace new ideas. This attitude was summed up by a statement made by a former President of Vanuatu when he said, '[E]*vri samting i gat evolution blong hem. Mi belivim se kastom i gat evolution*' (everything evolves. I believe that *kastom* evolves too).[121]

The development of the *kastom* system in the past few decades is apparent from a comparison of the anthropological material discussed in Chapter 3 with the system described above. Some changes are due to conscious attempts by the chiefs and chiefly organisations to deal with the challenges that continue to confront them, and others are unconscious changes as a result of influence from the state system. One of the most obvious conscious changes is the introduction or formalisation of the levels of chiefly councils[122] and the process of appeal. Although the word '*apil*' is used often,[123] what occurs is more like a rehearing or a renegotiation at a higher level than a strict review of the decision of the chief at the lower level. For this reason, some chiefs prefer the word 'referral',[124] as this more accurately describes what happens. For example, in Nguna, a small island in the north of Efate, a conflict will first be dealt with at village level. If the paramount chief of his village cannot solve it, he will ask the paramount chiefs of some neighbouring villages to come to help. If there is still no resolution, it will go to the body for the whole of Nguna, the Turuduaki Council of Chiefs, then it can be appealed to the Council for Nguna and Pele (the adjoining island) and, if still a problem, it will go to the Efate Island Council of Chiefs.[125] Although traditionally there was almost certainly the possibility of bringing a third body into the management of a conflict community leaders were having difficulties resolving, this formal referral structure is a relatively recent innovation of the *kastom* system. There is some criticism of the process of appeals[126] as they are seen to prolong a conflict and to make final reconciliation difficult: as one respondent put it, with appeals, chiefs '*no save flatem kwik taem*' (cannot quickly finish the conflict).

Another conscious change is the writing down of *kastom* laws. The movement to start to draft what are universally referred to as 'by-laws' appears to have been started by the Malvatumauri, who drafted their by-laws shortly after independence.[127] Almost every place visited in the course of this research had either written their by-laws, was doing so or was considering doing so. The reasons given for doing so were mixed and included the following:

- it will make it easier to judge conflicts
- if they are not written down they will be forgotten as the young people do not know them
- it will harmonise the different rates of penalty among the different villages/throughout the province
- if a chief goes to court then he has to be able to justify the decision he has made
- if the laws are written down the people cannot question the chiefs' authority—it is 'in black and white'[128]
- to counter the criticisms of young people who say that because the laws are not written down they have no legal effect
- if everyone in the community participates in the writing of the laws then they cannot argue with them
- in order to try to reclaim some territory for the chiefs that has been taken by the State.[129]

The same reasons for drafting by-laws probably prompted the development of the keeping of records of *kastom* meetings and the creation of positions of secretaries that is increasingly occurring in chiefly councils. In the *kastom kot* observation study, I was astonished that in 58 per cent of cases there was someone who took minutes of the meeting. It is, however, important to consider the extent to which these innovations really work in practice. Thus when I asked whether or not the by-laws were really *used* in judging cases, the answers were very vague and chiefs often generally indicated that there was a copy 'somewhere'. A similar response was given when I asked to see the records of the minutes taken in the meetings, with many chiefs admitting with a laugh that they were *'olbaot nomo'* (all over the place). There are many other examples of conscious adaptation from the state system, including: the creation of village police,[130] the introduction of the concept of payment of fees to get chiefs to hear cases[131] and even the development by some chiefly councils of summons forms and letterheads.[132]

The other aspect of the dynamism of the *kastom* system is the open-mindedness and flexibility of approach displayed by the majority of chiefs interviewed for this study. Many others, including the leaders of the two major women's organisations in Vanuatu, also remarked on this feature. It is illustrated by one of the by-laws from a ward council in Penama Province, which, roughly translated, states:

> The Council does not agree that women should wear shorts but we understand that they have the right to so she can wear shorts so long as they come down to her knees and she does not wear them in front of her brother or some other relatives or else she will be fined.

During the fieldwork, chiefs continually told me that they wanted to have training and assistance to enable them to *'leftemap'* (lift up) their system.

Challenges for the *kastom* system today

An early hypothesis is that the *kastom* system is currently facing considerable challenges to its survival. Much of the evidence suggests that indeed it is facing significant difficulties and there are some who question its ability to continue to play such a major role in conflict management if it continues to be unsupported by the State and outside agencies. As one respondent said, '[S]*istem blong jif i wik mo mifala i fraet se bae i brokbrok*' (The system of chiefs is weak and we are afraid it will break). A High Chief from Pentecost similarly stated that 'the *kastom* system is being eroded every day'.[133] In some places, such as South Santo and some of the Banks Islands, these difficulties are such that the *kastom* system is almost no longer functioning, with the result that the inhabitants of these areas are becoming more and more dependent on the scarce police resources available. The limitations of the chiefly system at present to control law and order in urban environments were also brought home by two incidents of breakdowns of law and order that occurred in Santo and Vila in late 2006 and March 2007, respectively. In relation to the Santo incident, a newspaper reported that '[w]hat was particularly disturbing was that Chiefs from all Provinces were not able to reach a common ground in the "traditional" way to try and solve the issue'.[134] Similarly, in the days leading up to what became the March 2007 riots, the chiefs attempted to calm the situation by holding meetings, but these erupted into violence that the chiefs were unable to contain, and three people were killed.[135] The challenges facing the *kastom* system today can be divided into roughly four groups: the problems with determining chiefly title; problems of loss of respect leading to difficulties with enforcement and lack of power; problems of misbehaving chiefs and the lack of mechanisms to deal with them; and the erosion of the authority of chiefs by societal changes.

Too many chiefs

Chapter 3 discusses the fact that, although chiefly title is not a traditional part of ni-Vanuatu culture, except to a limited extent in the central islands, today the institution of chiefs is entrenched throughout the country. As a result of the lack of a firm indigenous basis for this institution, attempts by the missionaries and the colonial and national governments to artificially create various types of chiefs and chiefly bodies, and the considerable movement of people that has occurred in the country in the past 100 years, today there is considerable confusion and disagreement about who has the right to be the chief in many communities throughout Vanuatu.

The lack of a clear road to chiefly title has a number of consequences. First, there are many people laying claim to being a chief and also many different types of chiefs in the various communities around Vanuatu (I was told about small chiefs, big chiefs, assistant chiefs, paramount chiefs, *kastom* chiefs, community chiefs and church chiefs). One respondent told me that when she went back to her island community after a number of years of absence she was shocked to find that 'every household has got a chief!'.[136] This proliferation of chiefs leads to the devaluation of the position of chief, as these people are increasingly no longer perceived as being special or authoritative.[137]

Even more importantly, disputes over chiefly title often involve disagreement about who has the right (or obligation) to manage conflicts. For example, a number of respondents said that a person who had become a big-man through the graded system should not necessarily be the chief who looked after the community; 'He can just judge the pigs!' said one cheeky respondent. Such disputes have the potential to completely stymie the *kastom* system. In two places visited during this study, conflicts over who should be on the chiefly council had caused the council to stop functioning,[138] and in many other places conflicts over chiefly title were causing great instability and even violence,[139] as well as undermining people's respect for the decisions made through the *kastom* system. A recent report into community governance highlighted the problems caused by conflicts over chiefly title, stating that in one village a dispute over chiefly title had caused 'village life [to fall] apart. Violence became the norm and many people left the village fearing for their safety'.[140]

There is also a related problem of the appropriate institution to adjudicate on rights to chiefly title—an issue that has been tossed backwards and forwards between the state courts of all levels and various *kastom* bodies for the past number of years.[141] There are three major ways that are used in Vanuatu today to determine right to chiefly title: community election/appointment,[142] the graded system (which generally involves killing pigs) and the hereditary or bloodline system. I found these systems to be used all over and fairly indiscriminately, with people claiming they were chiefs on the basis of one, two or three of these criteria. As one respondent puts it, at the moment, the system of chiefs is *'olbaot'* (all over the place). My favourite example of this is a chief from Santo who said, 'I am a *kastom* bloodline chief. My grandfather killed 1,000 pigs which made him a paramount chief and gave the right for all the generations that come after to call themselves chiefs.'[143] This man had managed to link the graded system, the hereditary system and the new concept of 'paramount' chiefs all together in his ancestry.[144]

In an attempt to resolve the problems of conflicts over chiefly title, the Malvatumauri has at various times attempted to create a register of all the chiefs in Vanuatu; however, they have had enormous difficulty in finding what the criteria should be to register them.[145] A recent report suggests that this process has in fact exacerbated the problem of conflicts over chiefly title because '[m]any chiefs now appear to believe that being recognised as the rightful chief will convey significant future benefits, and the position is therefore more attractive'.[146]

'Respek hemi lus' (Respect has been lost)

Many of the chiefs' previous sources of power are no longer workable: the State has a monopoly on the use of force, chiefs are no longer revered for their supernatural powers[147] and they often no longer have control over community land.[148] Consequently, chiefs today rely entirely on one fragile source of power: respect. The concept of respect is extremely important in Vanuatu. It involves living harmoniously and peacefully with others; looking after community and family members and the environment; observing social norms; participating in and supporting cultural practices; acting with appropriate behaviour; and honouring and obeying community leaders and also various kinship relations.[149] Respect has also been referred to as the cornerstone of the *kastom* system and the glue that holds society together. It is, however, currently under threat and this is manifested in two major ways: people not obeying chiefly decisions and people refusing to come to meetings.

While everyone agrees that respect for chiefs has significantly diminished, and in some places has even been lost, there are a variety of opinions about the reasons for this. In general, the chiefs blame social changes such as increasing reliance on the cash economy, education and the younger generation lacking respect for their wisdom. A typical response from the chiefs was that *'yangfala ting se oli save moa bitim ol olfala'* (young people think they know more than old people). A variation on this was one chief, who said with a chuckle, '[W]e say, "More school, more stupid"!'[150] Another major reason is that the chiefs say they are faced with people challenging them by saying that what they have ordered goes against the constitution or that their laws are not written down in 'black and white' and therefore do not have to be obeyed. Non-chiefly respondents, however, suggested a different range of reasons, citing many of the types of chiefly misbehaviour, discussed below.[151]

Problems of enforcement of *kastom* payments

One of the major ways in which the diminishing respect for chiefs is manifested throughout Vanuatu is the growing difficulties chiefs are having in getting people to follow their orders or the decisions made during meetings. This was mentioned to be a problem by almost every chief interviewed, although the extent of the problem varied significantly. In some areas, it was reported that the non-following of chiefly orders was a compounding problem: the more people did not make *kastom* payments, the less other people felt compelled to do so.

The chiefs try to overcome this problem in a number of ways. Some tell people they can pay in food or mats instead of cash and others set time limits in which the payment must be made. Another approach is for the chief to tell other chiefs that the person has not made the payment and ask them to refuse to help that person if he or she later encounters trouble.[152] Others call on various representatives of the State to try to support them (usually this is the police, but in some instances other authorities are involved)[153] or threaten to send the case to the courts. An alternative approach tried in Mele village is to have some younger educated men sitting with the chief on his council and this has apparently helped considerably in getting young people to respect the council decisions.

Orders to carry out community work would appear at first glance to be a way around the problem of non-payment of fines, but in practice it does not appear to work anywhere. Chiefs often mentioned that community work was a good idea, and that it had worked well during the time of the Condominium, but then gave various reasons as to why they did not use it. These reasons—such as the need to supply tools and food for the people doing it—seem to be a bit spurious.

Perhaps the real reason for it is closer to the insightful comment made by an old man to the effect that in the days of the Condominium people accepted community work but today the reaction of the younger generation is different: they do not feel comfortable exposing people to public shame. This means that if the chief gives an order to do community work, the people might challenge the chief.[154] It is for this reason that there is a push for councils of chiefs to be the ones who have the responsibility for overseeing community work, rather than individual chiefs.

Problems of people attending meetings

Another way the lack of respect manifests itself is that people do not attend *kastom* meetings. If the main parties do not turn up then the meeting has to be adjourned, with the inevitable result that the matter is not dealt with.[155] This problem is pervasive across Vanuatu. Chiefs deal with it in a variety of ways: fining people for not obeying them, sending the case to the police (which causes frustration when the police send it back), asking the police to bring people to the meeting, getting a higher chiefly council to look at the case and developing their own police force. They also use the threat of the State to help them, as is demonstrated by the following example:

> There was a disagreement between the Council and some boys from one village. The Council had put down a rule that alcoholic drinks could not be sold near the vicinity of the Council house. But some boys set up a fundraiser in the vicinity and sold alcoholic drinks. I wrote to them and asked them to attend a meeting and they refused. So I sent another letter that threatened to involve the police from Ambae and so they came and I presided over the meeting.[156]

Chiefly misbehaviour

The most common complaint respondents made about the *kastom* system was the problem of bias or favouritism by chiefs. In small-scale communities everyone is related in some way to each other, and indeed one of the strengths of the system is that it allows decisions to be made on the basis of a full understanding of all the people and surrounding circumstances involved in an incident. Today, however, there is considerable concern about chiefs favouring one side over the other due to political or religious alliances or a close family connection. This concern is most likely exacerbated by increasing knowledge about how the state system functions[157] and the importance placed on independence of the judiciary. As a consequence, disgruntled parties complain increasingly about chiefly favouritism (and use it as a justification for why they do not have to follow the chiefs' orders).[158] In the *kastom kot* observation study, six out of 20 respondents who answered the question stated that they considered the decision reached by the chiefs in the meeting they had observed was not fair, and six out of 18 stated that they thought that the chiefs had been biased.[159]

The other types of misbehaviour complained about are involvement in politics, not setting good examples with their own behaviour and breaking their own laws. For example, in one incident, a chief put a *tabu* on collecting trochus shell on the reef and then broke his own *tabu*, leading to a very tense situation. Traditionally, community leaders did not mix with other members of the community, even cooking on their own '*tabu* fire', and this preserved their mystique and authority. Today, however, they live with the community and are subject to the same temptations as community members, and are easily discovered if they transgress their own laws. Some further reasons for the decrease in the ability of chiefs to command respect include a perception that they are lazy in doing their work and some are considered to be greedy, as they will not hold meetings unless they are paid a sitting allowance.

An extreme example of chiefs failing to act as good leaders, and instead actually spearheading criminal activity, is the riots in Vila on 3 March 2007 that led to the deaths of three people. According to various reports, chiefs from Tanna ordered a man from Ambrym to be 'beaten into submission' to reveal the names of the people alleged to have committed black magic,[160] and at least one chief was behind the decision to go on a killing rampage, apparently 'urging the mob to this course of action saying the only way to deal with sorcery was to kill the sorcerers'.[161] Other chiefs who tried to stop the riots were powerless to do so. According to the newspaper, 'The young people were adamant they would no longer listen to their chiefs because they had taken too long to solve the matter.'[162] This in turn illustrates the limitations of the *kastom* system in urban communities in dealing with mob violence, as is also shown in the Santo incident in 2006 discussed above.

Lack of disciplinary mechanisms

The preceding section has shown that many of the weaknesses with the *kastom* system at present are related to individual chiefs losing respect through their own behaviour, as well as through circumstances beyond their control. This indicates that one of the main challenges facing the system is the ability to regulate the behaviour of individual chiefs and make them accountable for their actions.

Although there are a number of factors with the potential to keep a check on the chief's exercise of power—loss of community approval leading to expectation that the chief will resign; appeals to other levels of the *kastom* system; overruling of decisions made by chiefs by state courts; and the decision by other chiefs to remove a chief from his position—in practice, it is often extremely difficult to regulate the use of chiefly power. It is very easy for chiefs to hide behind demands for respect to get away with acting badly or inappropriately. Further, other chiefs are often reluctant to interfere in the community of another chief out of respect. The Secretary-General of Torba Province states that when a chief is involved in a conflict then the conflict can easily get out of hand because other chiefs cannot deal with the problem and so they have to rely on the state system stepping in. Appeals to state courts, however, are not always possible due to access issues, and appeals to higher levels of the *kastom* system might also be problematic. For instance, one young respondent complained that the system of appeal was no help because often the same person would be sitting on the council at each level so you could never get an independent review of the first decision.[163] The Secretary of the Malvatumauri explained that often villages contacted the Malvatumauri in desperation because they were fed up with their chief who was causing problems in the village, but due to the lack of a developed structure of chiefly councils in many parts of the country, the Malvatumauri was often not in a position to be able to do anything to assist either.[164] Thus, although there is increasing need for ways to control the exercise of chiefly authority, there is currently no effective way to do so.

Chiefs and modern society

Further challenges to the *kastom* system today come from the multitude of changes posed by increasing modernisation. In addition to the effects of the state system discussed in the next few chapters, the increasing participation of the community in the cash economy rather than the *kastom* economy, over which the chief has considerable control,[165] and the development of a more individualistic mentality among community members, there is the increasing mobility of society and the issue of education and training. Traditionally, one of the factors encouraging people to follow a chief's orders was the limited opportunity to escape from the very small community of which he was the leader and the social ostracism that would follow from failing to obey. Today, however, wrongdoers can escape from the chiefs by taking a boat to one of the two towns, leaving the chiefs feeling powerless and frustrated.

The second challenge is that as society becomes increasingly educated by a Western-based education system, chiefs are having greater difficulties being respected and winning arguments against those more educated than themselves. Many are tired of being publicly humiliated or defeated by such people, commenting that they are able to '*trekem yu long wan foreign wei yu no save*' (trick you in a foreign way that you do not understand).[166] As a consequence, many chiefly respondents expressed a great desire for training in conflict management and to learn about how the state system worked.

The major problems within the *kastom* system identified above can be summarised as in Table 4.1.

Table 4.1 Problems within the *kastom* system

- Disputes over chiefly title are causing the system to break down in some parts of the country.
- Respect for chiefs is decreasing.
- Many chiefs in Vanuatu today experience difficulties requiring people to follow their orders and to attend meetings.
- Some chiefs engage in favouritism or bias in their work, are lazy and/or greedy and break their own taboos.
- Often there is no effective means to redress unfairness caused by chiefs or to regulate chiefly behaviour.
- Women and youth are denied a voice in some parts of the country and are discriminated against by the substance of the decisions made in many areas.
- Many chiefs have low morale and question their capacity to continue with their responsibilities in the face of increasing challenges from youth about their right to assert their authority.

Widespread support for the continuation of the *kastom* system

During the course of the fieldwork, although there were many criticisms of the *kastom* system, there was not a single person who advocated its abolition. The following reasons were given for liking the *kastom* system and for wanting it to continue to manage conflicts in Vanuatu. First, it is an indigenous system and thus has legitimacy in the eyes of the people. As one respondent said, '[W]e need our own system to straighten us. We cannot be adopting a foreign system because that will always bring friction.'[167] Second, the *kastom* system is accessible to everyone and can deal with matters quickly. This is particularly important in small communities where the tensions from an unresolved conflict can fester and cause further problems. Third, the *kastom* system is familiar for people and its procedures are understandable. An element of this is that in *kastom* everything happens in the same place and is dealt with by the same people, as opposed to the state system, where there are many institutions involved: police, prosecution, courts and prisons. Fourth, people feel that they are supported in the *kastom* system by their families and not isolated or publicly humiliated[168] as they are in the state system. Fifth, there is no stigma attached to being found a criminal as there is in the state criminal system.[169] Sixth, the *kastom* system is perceived to be cheaper than the state system, where people have to pay for lawyers and the courts.[170] Seventh, in *kastom* people receive compensation, but in the state criminal justice system they do not receive anything.[171] Finally, the factor that was stressed by everyone was that in *kastom* at the end of the meeting the parties were friends again, whereas in the state system people were still bitter towards each other because in *kastom* both parties 'won' whereas in the state system one 'won' and one 'lost'.

Women and the *kastom* system

The issue of how the *kastom* system treats women is controversial and viewpoints vary considerably. Generally, men were more inclined than women to state that the *kastom* system supported women; educated women were more inclined to be critical of the *kastom* system (although not uniformly) than uneducated women; and women from the south claimed they were treated more unfairly than the women from the north. There were a significant number of respondents, male and female, who stated that they believed that the *kastom* system did help women, that chiefs listened well to women and assisted them and that women felt comfortable using the *kastom* system. There were, however, also many who complained about the way the *kastom* system treated women. This section will discuss first of all some of the major ways in which the *kastom* system is said to disadvantage women and then examine the ways in which it is said to support women or has the potential to do so.

In many areas, women participate actively and vocally in *kastom* meetings,[172] but in a considerable number of communities, women's participation is either limited or non-existent. As discussed above, in some areas, women are not permitted to speak in *kastom* meetings. In relation to Tanna, Lindstrom states that '[w]omen and young men generally remain in the audience. They lack personal qualifications to make statements; these belong to socially powerful men.'[173] Lindstrom further observes that 'meetings are a procedure that reproduces relations of inequality and power'.[174] In other areas, although women are *permitted* to speak, they are often inhibited from doing so due to shyness or because they are afraid of being laughed at or spoken to roughly or questioned in public about private matters. There is also the problem that, as one respondent said, 'women talk but they are not heard'.[175] One respondent told me that women often felt there was no point speaking because they knew they would always be blamed anyway, especially in cases of sexual assault and adultery.[176] The problem of not being heard is demonstrated in a case study from Lindstrom's work in Tanna:

> Tonga had gone over the head of her in-laws to ask Rapi, the big-man of a neighbouring village to convene and witness a meeting. Her agenda (complaints against in-laws for not helping her with childcare; against her husband for not building her a decent house and for adultery) were only fleetingly raised by discussants. Rapi, and other witnesses who closed the debate, enunciated and redirected the problem to be an uppity daughter-in-law.[177]

There is also a perception that women are often fined more heavily than a man or punished for conduct for which a man would not be punished. For example, one young man reported that if a girl and a boy had sex then the chief would tend to punish the girl and say that it was her fault for causing the problem, when it was just as much the boy's fault.[178] The Director of the Vanuatu Women's Centre stated that there were many cases where the chiefs in Vila sent women back to the islands because they had extramarital affairs, but they rarely sent men back who did the same thing. She gave the following example:

> We had a case where there was a woman who had left her husband about 3 years before and [had] come to Vila. She would go back and visit the man and the children sometimes. Then she met a new man in Vila and wanted to be with him. The chiefs held a meeting and said that she had to go back to the island. But the chiefs didn't know that the woman's husband was diabetic and thus impotent which made him very frustrated and aggressive.[179]

There were mixed views about the extent to which chiefs were prepared to deal with domestic violence and sexual abuse.[180] A number of women said that the chiefs did listen to them and lectured their husbands and fined them, but that the men did not listen to the chiefs and continued with their abuse. The majority of women, however, were of the view that chiefs did not act enough in cases of domestic violence. The Director of the Vanuatu Women's Centre stated, '[W]e have not yet seen active support by the chiefs to deal with sexual abuse and violence against women.'[181] In many places, it is accepted that it is only if the woman is seriously injured, or if the beating occurs in public, that the chiefs will do something. This is illustrated by one of the 'by-laws' in a village in Maewo: *'yu no save kilim waef blong yu long yad blong narafala man'* (you cannot hit your wife in the yard of another man).[182] Some respondents said that some chiefs blamed women for domestic violence.[183] For example, one respondent said that if a man beat his wife because she was complaining to him all the time, or did not have dinner ready on time, some chiefs would authorise the man to beat her and would make the woman pay a *faen*. One woman reported that a chief had said to her in such a situation: *'yu yu woman, ples blong yu hem i blong mekem evri wok long haos'* (you are a woman and it is your job to do all the housework). Chiefs are said to be sympathetic to the men because they are their friends or because they are also a man. One respondent commented, '[O]*li yusem kastom blong stan bihaen'* (they hide behind *kastom*).[184] Another woman observed that chiefs favoured men because they did not want to be seen to be putting the man down, as this would harm the chief's reputation in the community. Women are also often blamed, rather than supported, for having a *'pikinini blong rod'* ('child of the road'—an illegitimate child).

A less widespread, but extreme problem is that in some areas women are treated as chattels by the *kastom* system. For example, sometimes women or girls are given away as part of *kastom* payments—hence the title of this chapter.[185] A young actor recounted the following incident:

> Last year there was a case involving two men in a boat and one killed the other. No-one knew what had happened, but then one night the man was drunk and told his wife that he had blood on his hands but not to tell anyone. She went straight to her family and they went to the chiefs who put out the word that they would '*katem nek blong hem*' [cut his neck]. The man heard this and became very frightened and so instead of having a meeting, he just made a '*sori*' instead and gave a girl from his family to the other side.[186]

A police officer in Tanna confirmed that a way of making peace was to give a woman to replace the life that had been taken.[187] The practice also exists in Malekula[188] and in Erromango—not just for murder but for adultery. One man explained that if he took someone's wife then he must give that person his daughter to '*talem mi sori*' (say sorry). He explained, '*Mining blong hem big wan: mi spoelem property blong yu, mi mas givim wanem we mi bin stilim*' (The significance of it is important: I am saying that I have spoiled some property of yours and so I am giving back what I have stolen).[189] In some areas, if a woman runs away from her husband and a bride price has been paid, the chief will force her to go back, as the belief is that a man owns a woman if he has 'paid' for her.[190]

Finally, there are very few places where women are involved in decision making in the *kastom* system. This is problematic because, as one respondent explains, men do not understand the life of a woman. There are a few exceptions to this. In Vanua Lava, there is a female chief who was elected a few years ago[191] and also one in Mere Lava. Some villages or areas also have certain women who act as spokeswomen for other women inside the councils, and sometimes the chief's wife acts informally in this capacity. In Dillons Bay, the main town in Erromango, there is a women's representative on the chiefly council. Her role is to act as a link between the chiefs and the women of the community, bringing up issues at the council meetings that women want discussed and passing on decisions and so on to the women.[192] She said that her role was good because many women found it hard to explain their thoughts to men but they felt comfortable going through her. She is, however, only one woman against many men, so if the men do not want to hear what she has to say, they do not listen and they become angry with her.[193]

Despite these many ways in which women are discriminated against by the *kastom* system, there is a vast amount of support by women and women's groups in general for the *kastom* system. The general view is that there are problems, but these can be fixed and are worthwhile fixing because the alternative—reliance on the state system—also has its problems and does not have many of the advantages of the *kastom* system. I spoke with a number of representatives of women's groups at a national and a regional level and they all affirmed the fact that the chiefs at an individual level were very receptive to their awareness-raising work and supportive of many of their projects and ideas.[194] The head of the Vanuatu National Council of Women stated that the *kastom* system would be preferable to deal with a woman's complaints than the state system, provided the right person was the chief.[195] The Director of the Vanuatu Women's Centre stated that since they had started working with communities they had never been thrown out of a village, and often they found that after they had held their awareness-raising sessions the chiefs were very grateful and said that they had been wrong in their preconceptions about the work they did.[196] She was, however, at pains to contrast the receptive and open-minded response of chiefs at a village and provincial level with that of chiefs at a national level, who had not made any public declarations in support of women.

Youth and the *kastom* system

The initial hypothesis was that the *kastom* system was unfair to youth, particularly because some oft-repeated rhetoric was that the chiefs did not understand young people and that young people did not respect chiefs and were '*strongheds*' (troublemakers). This study found that in fact the situation was more complicated than either of these two stereotypes suggested and that although there were significant problems with its treatment of youth, there was also a great deal of support for the continuation of the *kastom* system by young people in Vanuatu today.

One of the major problems for youth in the *kastom* system is in having their voices heard. For example, in Tanna and Aniwa, young people cannot speak on their own behalf in meetings, but have people speaking for them.[197] Even when they have the right to speak, however, there are still often difficulties with communication. Thus, the Director of Youth and Sports stated that young people had trouble being heard by their elders and were often not trusted by them. There are no special procedures for dealing with youth in the *kastom* system, but in many places the chiefs say they just give the youths a warning or a lecture rather than a *faen*. Young people also complain that the chiefs do not do anything for young people to deter them from committing criminal activities, such as providing sporting and employment opportunities. This is a point also made by Bolton, an anthropologist, who argues that 'if older people want younger people to stay in the islands they have to have things for them to do which are interesting. In the past, ritual and ceremony kept life buzzing. Young people had a lot of objectives and goals, because they had to achieve certain status.'[198]

The common response that young people gave when asked to respond to the accusation that they did not respect chiefs was that the chiefs should act in a way that deserved respect and they would give it to them. They complain that many chiefs are biased and double faced: telling the youth to behave and then behaving in inappropriate ways themselves. They also felt that many chiefs were concerned only with getting money from the parties and not with making justice.

The attitude of youth towards the future of the *kastom* system was generated by a quantitative survey.[199] The major finding was that youth wanted chiefs and courts involved in dealing with criminal conflicts. Ninety-three per cent of respondents stated that if they were involved in some kind of trouble they would prefer the chiefs to deal with it rather than the courts.[200] When asked whether they would want the courts or the chiefs to deal with a person who made trouble for them, however, the results were far more even—with 57 per cent preferring chiefs and 43 per cent the courts.[201] They were also asked whether they thought the courts or the chiefs should deal with a range of different types of offences and the answers showed that generally they felt that chiefs should deal with the less serious offences, such as small-scale theft and assault, and also domestic violence. They were roughly evenly divided about who should deal with cases of drunkenness, but overwhelmingly wanted the courts to deal with cases of large-scale theft, rape, murder and underage sexual intercourse.[202] The results can be seen in Table 4.2.

Table 4.2 Survey of attitudes of youth in Vanuatu (n = 150) [203]

Type of offence	Prefer chiefs to deal with it (%)	Prefer state system to deal with it (%)
Small-scale theft	86	12
Assault	70	30
Domestic violence	67	33
Drunkenness	52	46
Large-scale theft	15	86
Rape	18	82
Murder	4	95
Underage sexual intercourse	13	85

The research therefore shows that there are some respects in which the *kastom* system is unfair to youth, particularly in relation to giving them a fair hearing. It also shows, however, that young people support the *kastom* system in principle and want it to continue, with the state system, to play a role in managing conflicts in the future. In this respect, it confirms the findings of the Juvenile Justice Project.[204]

Conclusion

This study has demonstrated that the *kastom* system plays a fundamental role in conflict management in Vanuatu today. On a practical level, it is the first, and often the only, level at which the majority of conflicts are dealt with in rural and urban areas. Given the weakness of the state system, the *kastom* system is thus critical to the maintenance of law and order in Vanuatu today. Second, on an ideological level, the whole population views the *kastom* system as being *their* system, one that they understand, find accessible and consider legitimate, even while recognising that it requires reform. It was notable that even the majority of women and youth, two groups that were often discriminated against or marginalised by the system, strongly supported its continuation.

There is an extraordinary variety in the procedural and substantive features of the *kastom* system throughout the archipelago. The range of procedures used—from basic mediation through to almost autocratic decision making—is another reflection of the Melanesian genius for diversity, which is discussed in Chapter 1. Despite this variety, however, it is possible to clearly identify several core principles that form the base of the *kastom* system throughout Vanuatu: the emphasis on respect and on restoring relationships; the holistic approach to the conflict; the prioritising of community harmony; the importance of public talking and community participation; and the notions of reciprocity, shame, feeling *sori* and balance. These are the features that allow ni-Vanuatu to distinguish 'their' system from the state system, even while simultaneously separating 'their' *kastom* from that of a person from a different *ples*.

This study has also shown that the *kastom* system today is weak and in need of reform. In much of the rest of this study, the argument will be made that the *kastom* system needs to be given more capacity and recognition. It is, however, currently facing many serious challenges and if it is not given more support in the near future, it might no longer be able to take on a greater role or even continue doing the work it currently performs. The Secretary of the Malvatumauri recently stated:

> If you ignore, if donors ignore the chiefs, then the possibility of something happening like in the Solomons is increased, yeah, that is what we see. That is why we try very hard to make the donors

understand that they must support us, that you must support the traditional systems as well.[205]

In this regard, Nelson's comments in the context of Papua New Guinea are also pertinent. He argues that the broad terms of 'fragile' and 'weak' are concerned most with institutions of central government and so are the strategies for strengthening them. There has been less consciousness of the radical changes that have been taking place in the traditional systems, but it should be recognised that '[w]eakness, fragility and failure occur in the traditional systems of village government'. [206]

The most obvious weakness of the *kastom* system today is the erosion of respect for chiefs and the decisions made by them, leading to problems of enforcement, but this could be seen as symptomatic of many other problems with the system. The erosion of respect is due in part to systemic issues beyond the control of any one individual, such as the forces of modernisation and the operation of the state system—as discussed in the next two chapters—but also to the behaviour of individual chiefs. There is a widespread perception that many chiefs are biased, and there are also frequent problems with chiefs who break their own *tabus* or who are lazy or incompetent in some way. This leads to an erosion of respect for the chiefs, in turn discouraging chiefs from doing their best, thus perpetuating a downwards spiral. A major factor in this cycle is the current absence of an effective way for a community to free itself of such chiefs. The introduction of such a mechanism, as well as improved processes to determine legitimate claims of chiefly title, are important challenges that must be taken up, in addition to any reform of the relationship the *kastom* system has with the state system.

In light of the above, it is fortunate that one aspect of the *kastom* system that has come out very strongly through the research is the enormous capacity for, and willingness to, change on behalf of the chiefs. This flexibility and dynamism, together with the firm platform of community support for the *kastom* system, augur well for its ability to overcome the many challenges it faces.

ENDNOTES

[1] The chapter subtitle is the order of *kastom* payments that is used by some chiefs and chiefly councils.

[2] Chiba (*Asian Indigenous Law*, p. 7) describes these as 'a value principle or value system specifically connected with a particular official or unofficial law, which acts to found, justify and orient the latter'. See also Shah, *Legal Pluralism in Conflict*, pp. 2–7.

[3] Garu, Selwyn and Yaken, Jack 2001, *Chiefs' Legislation Project Report*, Ministry of Internal Affairs.

[4] The word *'nakamal'* in Vanuatu is used to refer either to a cleared area near the chief's house or near the central banyan tree in a village, which is used as a meeting place, or else to the meeting house itself. In Efate and the Shepherds, the term *'nasara'* is often used rather than *nakamal*, but it has the same meaning.

[5] For example, *kastom medicine* refers to traditional approaches to healing and *kastom dress* refers to the types of clothing that were worn before the arrival of the Europeans. I have not referred to *kastom law*, as might seem consistent with these other two examples, first because it would be unnecessary as

this is provided by the context of the study (for the same reason I refer to the state system rather than the state system of criminal justice), and second because for ni-Vanuatu the legal system is not something apart and separate from other aspects of life. As Narokobi says, '[L]aw is not quantifiable as an autonomous institution, but is an aspect of the total way of life of the people.' Narokobi, Bernard 1989, *Lo Blong Yumi Yet*, p. 3.

[6] Hess, Person and place on Vanua Lava, Vanuatu, p. 196.

[7] Pospisil, Leopold 1974, *Anthropology of Law: A comparative theory*, p. 98.

[8] Indeed, in my position as a lecturer at the University of the South Pacific, I teach 'the common law criminal justice system' to students from 12 different jurisdictions.

[9] Franz and Keebet von Benda-Beckmann ('The dynamics of change and continuity in plural legal orders', p. 18) also comment that 'there may be system-internal pluralism in the sense that the same legal system may contain duplicatory regulations of the same set of activities or domains'.

[10] For example, the *National Council of Chiefs Act (2006)* establishes a uniform system of island councils of chiefs and urban councils of chiefs throughout Vanuatu. This act is discussed in greater detail in Chapter 5.

[11] Griffiths, 'What is legal pluralism?', p. 36.

[12] Woodman, 'Ideological combat and social observation', p. 54.

[13] von Benda-Beckmann, Keebet 2002, 'The contexts of law', *Legal Pluralism and Unofficial Law in Social, Economic and Political Development: Papers of the XIIIth International Congress of the Commission on Folk Law and Legal Pluralism, 7–10 April, 2002, Chiangmai, Thailand*, p. 299. See also von Benda-Beckmann and von Benda-Beckmann, 'The dynamics of change and continuity in plural legal orders', p. 18. Woodman (in Allott and Woodman, *People's Law and State Law*, p. 18) also argues that state laws are 'neither internally self-consistent logical systems nor clearly bounded from other normative orders'.

[14] Keebet von Benda-Beckmann, 'The contexts of law'.

[15] Seymour-Smith, Charlotte 1986, *The Macmillan Dictionary of Anthropology*, p. 275.

[16] Discussed in further detail in Chapter 5 under 'The relationship between the prisons and the *kastom* system'.

[17] 'Vanuatu: chiefs step in to end jail-break impasse', *Pacific Beat*, 10 May 2006, <http://abc.gov.au/ra/pacbeat/stories/s1635039.htm>

[18] Chanock, Martin 2000, 'Introduction', in Sally Moore (ed.), *Law as Process*, p. xviii.

[19] It is not possible to quantify the exact percentage of cases dealt with by each system due to the lack of accurate record keeping in the *kastom* system. Anecdotal accounts suggest that the percentage dealt with by both systems varies throughout the country depending on the accessibility of the state system, but 80–90 per cent of cases dealt with by the *kastom* system was the most common estimate by key actors from both systems.

[20] For example, the Efate Island Council of Chiefs, the Vaturisu, includes chiefs from the offshore islands of Nguna, Pele, Lelepa, Moso and Emau.

[21] For example, in Penama, the different levels of councils have been called the 'Penama system' by the province. When chiefs were asked about whether this was a new system or just a new name, however, they were vague in their responses, just suggesting that the general idea had been there before. Although such initiatives are often welcomed by the chiefs and communities involved, they can also cause problems as, for example, occurred in Ambae when the Penama system effectively cut across the authority of the locally developed Lakalakabulu Council of North Ambae.

[22] For example, the *National Council of Chiefs Act 2006*, which establishes a structure of chiefly councils headed by the Malvatumauri. This act is discussed in greater detail in Chapter 5.

[23] Who may or may not be a chief in his or her own right, but is often a more minor chief than the 'real' authority on the island.

[24] For example, there is a town council of chiefs from East Ambae in Vila and also one for South-West Bay, Malekula, as well as many others.

[25] The only council that I came across that did not do this was the Lakalakabulu Council of North Ambae, which insisted that only its members act as decision makers.

[26] For example, in Dillons Bay, Erromango, the Dillons Bay Council of Chiefs comprises chiefs from different communities.

[27] See Chapter 6 under 'Dispute and confusion over jurisdiction'.

28 This is very common at the village level for minor offences.

29 This is very common at the area level and above.

30 This is another variation found at area and ward levels.

31 This pattern is found in Tanna.

32 This is often the pattern found at the ward level, where a village chief cannot deal with the matter and so calls some chiefs from neighbouring villages to help him.

33 This occurs in Dillons Bay, Erromango.

34 This occurs in Mele, Efate.

35 For example, in Mele and Nguna.

36 For example, in Erromango in Dillons Bay, if a person has a problem they give vt200 to the chief and register their name.

37 In Nguna, the chiefs will collect information before a meeting is held and hold a meeting only if there is enough evidence.

38 A chief in a town council of chiefs told me about a case involving a man who had an affair with his sister-in-law. The village chief first dealt with the matter but the man did not agree with the decision so it went to the area council. At this meeting, the council allowed the family of the cuckolded man to beat up the defendant. The council also ordered the man to pay vt20 000 and a cow and a head of kava. The man appealed to the town council, which upheld the decision to make the man pay vt20 000 but rescinded the obligation to pay for the cow and the kava because he had been beaten. The chairman explained that normally it was not permitted to fight in the *nakamal*, but the family involved was from Tanna and that was their *kastom*.

39 Interview with a senior police officer (Santo, 18 November 2004).

40 A traditional meeting house or place (see the introduction section).

41 This no longer happens in many communities, particularly not those living in urban areas.

42 Interview with a man from Ambae (Port Vila, 15 March 2004).

43 As in the state system, it is often not necessary to determine guilt as the defendants accept they have misbehaved, but increasingly people are challenging the complaints against them. In the *kastom kot* observation study, roughly one-third of the defendants denied they had done something wrong.

44 Interview with Carlos Mondragon, an anthropologist who lived in the Torres for three years (Port Vila, 21 July 2004). The importance of 'rhetoric' in conflict management is also highlighted by Santos (*Toward a New Legal Common Sense*, p. 86), who argues that it is a structural component of the law and defines it as 'not only a type of knowledge, but also a communication form and a decision-making strategy based on persuasion or conviction through the mobilization of the argumentative potential of accepted verbal and non-verbal sequences and artifacts'.

45 Hess, Person and place on Vanua Lava, Vanuatu, p. 203.

46 Tafea Province comprises the southern islands of Tanna, Aniwa, Futuna, Erromango and Aneitym.

47 One planned research methodology for this study was to attend and observe *kastom kot* meetings. Unfortunately, I was not able to attend *kastom* meetings personally except on one occasion. This was due to the fact that as *kastom* meetings did not occur at regular and predetermined times and places, the only way to attend such meetings was for someone involved in them to contact me and tell me that they were on. As I spent only short periods outside of Vila, I was not in a village at any time such a meeting occurred. In Vila, despite continued requests to participants and organisers of such meetings, I was not invited to any *kastom* meetings. To overcome this, law students and VCC fieldworkers were engaged to observe *kastom* meetings in their villages and then to record their observations on a form I devised. A number of anthropologists were consulted about the wisdom of this and they all agreed that as long as account was taken of the fact that it would be a perception of what was happening, it would be an interesting methodology to try. Twenty ni-Vanuatu law students were engaged before their long summer break. I had a meeting with them to discuss my research and what I wanted them to do. Unfortunately, only two of them gave me back completed forms. I also gave the forms to about 60 fieldworkers from the Vanuatu Cultural Centre (fieldworkers were ni-Vanuatu who were engaged by the VCC to collect cultural material from the community they reside in. They come from all around Vanuatu and gather together at a workshop once a year to present their findings as a group). In the end, I received reports of 24 different *kastom* meetings. These reports are referred to throughout as the *kastom kot* observation study.

48 All the cases where the women were not allowed to speak occurred in Tafea Province.

[49] In the *kastom kot* observation study, the parties talked for themselves in 66 per cent of cases. In 16 per cent, both parties were represented and in 12 per cent of cases the male party spoke but the youth or woman who was the other party was represented.

[50] So they will, for example, ask a question to a group that represents another village, but the other party will know the question is intended for them and answer either directly or indirectly. This indirect questioning is also a way of showing respect. In Erromango, this technique is often used where youth are involved: the chief will speak harshly to the father but the youth will know that the criticisms are intended for him or her.

[51] Hess also states that '[w]hen talking about taboo topics, such as sex, shame, conflict...or mistakes, people often use euphemisms'. Hess, Person and place on Vanua Lava, Vanuatu, p. 212.

[52] See, for example, Hess's comments in relation to Vanua Lava. Hess, Person and place on Vanua Lava, Vanuatu, p. 203. See also Lindstrom, 'Straight talk on Tanna'.

[53] Greenhouse, 'Mediation'.

[54] Interview with a man from Ambae (Port Vila, 15 March 2004).

[55] Interview with a man from Erromango (Erromango, 18 May 2004).

[56] Interview with a man from North Pentecost (Port Vila, 30 August 2004).

[57] Some people said that the judges in the *nakamal* were the four men who represented the four '*kastom* roads' that were the ways out of the village to places beyond. Others said there was no judge, while yet others said that the chief of the village was the judge.

[58] Originally, the side that managed to get the most support would 'win' regardless of the merits of the case, but now the system is moving more towards having decisions made based on what is said in the meeting.

[59] Hess, Person and place on Vanua Lava, Vanuatu, p. 201. She remarked, however, that at the end of the meeting she observed, although the chairman kept insisting that he was not making a decision, 'he still made everybody follow his vision of the outcome of the meeting' (pp. 216–17).

[60] The nature of this payment is discussed more in the section under 'The restorative nature of the *kastom* system' (this chapter).

[61] There are many different types of pigs, all with different values. The most valuable are those pigs with rounded tusks, which have been developed by knocking out the pig's two upper incisors. As the bottom incisors grow they curve around and gradually pierce the cheek to grow back inside and form a full circle. Of course, pigs that have tusks like this cannot eat normally and must have someone (normally a woman) prepare a mash for them to eat. To produce a pig with fully rounded tusks takes about seven years.

[62] In 2007, the Year of the *Kastom* Economy, there were initiatives to discourage the use of cash in *kastom* payments.

[63] In the *kastom kot* observation study, the decision in almost all the cases was that payments had to be made and there were also orders made such as: a boy should not go near a particular girl; a person should not go near a piece of land belonging to another person; a man should stop assaulting his wife; another man should leave his mistress and return to his wife; and in a witchcraft case a man had to touch the Bible.

[64] Many respondents stressed that the fact that in *kastom* there was no presumption of innocence.

[65] Interview with a man from North Pentecost (Port Vila, 30 August 2004).

[66] Interview with a man from Erromango (Erromango, 18 May 2004).

[67] Discussed in Chapter 1 under 'Religion and denomination'.

[68] Interview with a man from North Pentecost (Port Vila, 11 May 2004).

[69] Interview with a chief from Vanua Lava (Vanua Lava, 23 October 2003).

[70] Interview with a chief from Ambae (Ambae, 29 September 2003).

[71] This question was not answered in 20 per cent of cases.

[72] Interview with the Assistant Secretary in Torba Province (Vanua Lava, 23 September 2003).

[73] Interview with a chief from Vanua Lava (Vanua Lava, 21 October 2003).

[74] Interview with Carlos Mondragon, an anthropologist who had lived in the Torres Islands, north Vanuatu, for three years (Port Vila, 21 July 2004).

[75] Traditional food cooked in a ground oven.

[76] For example, in Santo, the disputing parties are often told to make a *laplap* (a traditional meal cooked in a ground oven) for each other.

[77] For example, Dinnen, Sinclair and Jowitt, Anita (eds) 2003, *A Kind of Mending: Restorative justice in the Pacific islands*.

[78] See also Hess, Person and place on Vanua Lava, Vanuatu, pp. 201–2.

[79] This word can also be spelled '*sore*'.

[80] Hess, Person and place on Vanua Lava, Vanuatu, pp. 85–7.

[81] Interview with a man from Erromango (Erromango, 18 May 2004).

[82] Interview with a chief from Erromango (Erromango, 20 May 2004).

[83] In some cases where this does not occur the avoidance becomes semi-permanent, lasting decades, and is often how new villages and new churches are formed. For example, in 2004–05, there was a dispute over chiefly title and religion in the village of Siviri on the island of Efate. As a consequence, one group moved inland and established a new village, Malafau.

[84] Hess, Person and place on Vanua Lava, Vanuatu, pp. 87–8.

[85] Interview with a man from Ambae (Port Vila, 15 March 2004).

[86] Interview with Port Vila Town Council of Chiefs (Port Vila, 26 May 2004).

[87] Ibid.

[88] Lindstrom, Achieving wisdom, p. 109.

[89] Ibid.

[90] Another example is when someone has stolen a particular item of property, such as a chicken, they will be told to return the chicken.

[91] Interview with an Efate chief (Port Vila, 21 March 2007). This is also discussed in the case study in Chapter 6.

[92] This case also illustrated the practice of the victim's family assaulting the defendants before a meeting because in this case the husband got a group of his boys together and they went and fought the three boys. The police were notified but they went and asked a high chief if he could resolve the situation, so he called a meeting. It seems that the fighting was not even discussed; rather, the subject of the meeting was the cause of the fighting: the woman's affairs.

[93] It is also possible that the *sori* is made by people other than the offender, such as the offender's family or chiefs. For example, in 2007, the father of a boy who was killed in the 3 March riots accepted a *kastom* apology from members of the Tanna community in Santo. See Waiwo, Elenor 2007, 'Father accepts sorry for son's death', *Vanuatu Daily Post* (Port Vila), 10 March 2007, p. 6.

[94] Garae, Len 2004, 'Vaturisu says Ambae chiefs set example', *Vanuatu Daily Post* (Port Vila), 7 October 2004, p. 3.

[95] A similar point is made by Sally Falk Moore ('Treating law and knowledge', pp. 32–3), who writes, 'I would argue that the "social equilibrium" presentation of African disputational logic is a mixture of African self-idealization and colonial/anthropological political theory. It is also not without some foundation in fact, but it is a well-edited version of the facts. According to this interpretation of "traditional life", the disputants are obliged to work out mutually agreeable settlements because they are fated to go on living together in the same community. Collective pressures encourage them to achieve a harmonious settlement. That is surely sometimes a part of the story, but it is emphatically the view from the outside. As I have written elsewhere on the question of collective liability, the view from the inside is of a much more competitive, much less harmonious entity. Within these groups there are factions and sub-segments and individual interests. There are superiors and inferiors. There are more and less powerful persons in these communities, and they can mobilize more or fewer individuals in the local political arena. Individuals can not only be discredited, they can be expelled. What appears to be an equilibrium from the outside is often a temporary moment of agreement in which a dominant segment of the group has prevailed and everyone recognizes that predominance and acquiesces in all public behaviour. This is what often gives the appearance of unanimity to collective decision making.'

[96] For example, the man Tanna/man Ambrym riots discussed below under 'Chiefly misbehaviour'.

[97] Interview with a chief from Emae (Port Vila, 22 September 2004).

[98] Binihi, Ricky 2006, 'Family Ulas prepared to leave Luganville', *Vanuatu Daily Post* (Port Vila), 3 August 2006, p. 6. This incident is discussed in more detail in Chapter 6 under 'Dispute and confusion over jurisdiction'.

[99] The chiefs were charged with damage to property but they argued in their defence that they had the right in *kastom* to retaliate in this way. The magistrate dismissed this argument. I asked the Public Prosecutor who recounted this incident to me whether there was a copy of this judgment but she told me that the magistrates did not write down their judgments.

[100] I was told it was essential to ensure peace and harmony inside the community almost as much as the fact that in *kastom* both parties 'won'.

[101] Lini, Hilda Motarilavoa 2006, Indigenous laws and *kastom* system, Paper presented at the Vanuatu Judiciary Law Conference, Port Vila, 2006, p. 2.

[102] This belief often appeared incongruous given the extremely peaceful and sleepy appearance of most villages in Vanuatu.

[103] See the comment about 'dividuality' in Endnote 10 in Chapter 6.

[104] See Chapter 1 under 'Place' for a discussion of islandism.

[105] Interview with a man from Ambae (Port Vila, 15 March 2004). He went on to note that to some extent this had changed now.

[106] Interview with a judge (also a chief) (Port Vila, 20 August 2004).

[107] Ibid.

[108] Sillitoe, *An Introduction to the Anthropology of Melanesia*, p. 149. See also the discussion in Chapter 2 under 'The legal anthropological approach' on the place of norms in customary legal systems. Gordon and Meggitt commented that the influence of Malinowski, who derided any study or analysis of 'codes, courts, and constables', also contributed to the scholarly focus on the broader field of processes of social control rather than the analysis of customary law in Melanesia. Gordon, Robert and Meggitt, Mervyn 1985, *Law and Order in the New Guinea Highlands*, p. 192.

[109] This development is discussed in further detail under 'The dynamism of the *kastom* system'.

[110] These range from the people with whom one can have sexual relations to the different types of behaviour one should adopt with different members of the family—for example, the prohibition in some areas on brothers and sisters talking to each other once they have reached puberty.

[111] The *namele* is a type of cycad and its leaves are used to mark *tabu* places. Its importance is shown by the fact that it appears on the Vanuatu national flag.

[112] This is a wide-ranging notion that includes the prohibition on women drinking kava in some places, a woman not being allowed to be in a tree that men pass underneath and people speaking out of turn at meetings. Respect is discussed further under '"*Respek hemi lus*" (Respect has been lost)'.

[113] In *kastom*, the idea of consent—central to the state crime of rape—was not considered an issue. What was problematic was sexual intercourse outside societal boundaries, such as adultery and cross-kinship sexual relations. Today, many chiefs use the word 'rape' when in fact they are not referring to forced intercourse but forbidden intercourse (because the parties are not married, for example), but some use it to mean '*fosem woman*' (force the woman).

[114] The by-laws that have been written suggest there is a lot of differentiation in relation to the *kastom* laws relating to kinship and respect but this could result from the differing judgments of the people who wrote them down as to what should be included.

[115] Respondents often talked about 'our *kastom*' and 'their *kastom*', but when pressed as to the differences they would mostly respond that the quantum of the fine was different in different communities.

[116] Interview with a chief from Efate (Port Vila, 21 March 2007).

[117] Freedom of movement and freedom of religion are the principal problems.

[118] There were of course many general comments to the effect that it did not sufficiently reflect the cultural context of Vanuatu.

[119] This is discussed further in Chapter 5.

[120] Interview with Chief Justice Lunabek (Port Vila, 7 February 2002).

[121] Maxime Korman, former Prime Minister of the Republic of Vanuatu (Author's notes from the Conference on *Kastom* and the Constitution, University of the South Pacific, Emalus Campus, Port Vila, Vanuatu, 4 October 2004).

[122] The latest move in this direction is the *National Council of Chiefs Act 2006*, discussed in Chapter 5.

[123] People also often say that the conflict '*mas ko long nekis level*' (must go to the next level) or else '*tekem nekis step*' (take the next step).

124 A group of chiefs (Author's notes from the Vanuatu Judiciary Conference, University of the South Pacific, Emalus Campus, Port Vila, Vanuatu, 26 August 2006).

125 Interview with a chief from Nguna (Nguna, 31 October 2003).

126 See in particular the comments about the appeal structure for the Customary Land Tribunals in Simo, Joel 2005, *Report of the National Review of the Customary Land Tribunal Program in Vanuatu*, Vanuatu Cultural Centre, p. v.

127 See Malvatumauri, 'Kastom polisi blong Malvatumauri'. The impetus behind making by-laws also comes from the provincial governments, as they are given power under the *Decentralisation Act* (Cap 127) to make regional laws, which also includes criminal offences. Provincial administrators in Penama and Torba Provinces mentioned that they were involved in collecting chiefly by-laws.

128 Interview with a chief from Nguna (Nguna, 31 October 2003). See also Larcom ('Custom by decree'), who discusses the power of the written word in local communities in Malekula.

129 For example, in Mota Lava, they have included penalties for killing someone. They said this was because the last time someone was killed the police came and took the suspect and he was tried and all he was given was a suspended sentence. The family of the victim waited and waited for the man to pay *'sak'* (compensation for the 'head' of the person who was killed) but it never came. They therefore want to be prepared to deal with these cases in future. They said they had the right to deal with these cases because Father Walter Lini had told them chiefs should deal with cases of murder rather than sending them to the police (Interview with a chief from Mota Lava, Mota Lava, 21 October 2003).

130 In Mele, for example, there are village police who even wear a special uniform and who work on behalf of the chief to provide security and to take statements from people making complaints. I asked why they wore a uniform and they told me that the effect of this was to *'mekem spirit blong wok blong mifala strong, igat pawa'* (make our work spirit strong and give power) (Interview with a village police officer, Mele, 31 May 2004).

131 For example, the Lakalakabulu Council of Chiefs charges vt6000 'sitting fees'. Many other chiefly councils also charge sitting fees, although the amounts vary. The highest I encountered was vt15 000 per case, charged by the Sanma Council of Chiefs. Such measures have created problems because people complain that chiefs have the attitude of *'pem mi sipos yu wantem mi mekem'* (pay me if you want me to do something).

132 For example, the Lakalakabulu Council of Chiefs has a summons and letterhead with its logo on it, which comprises the *kastom* symbols of a mat and a bird as well as the blue and white check of the police.

133 Lini, Indigenous laws and *kastom* system.

134 Lini, Lora 2006, 'Law and order situation in Luganville questioned', *Vanuatu Daily Post* (Port Vila), 22 August 2006, p. 6.

135 The newspaper reported, 'A meeting was supposed to have taken place on Saturday to solve the issue followed by reconciliation but apparently the situation got out of hand after a fight broke out that resulted in the stabbing and subsequent death of Keinoho'. See 'Two confirmed dead in Ambrym and Tanna clash', *Vanuatu Daily Post* (Port Vila), 5 March 2007, p. 1; see also Garae 2007c; 'Malvatumauri to meet over riots', *Vanuatu Daily Post* (Port Vila), 9 March 2007, p. 3.

136 Interview with the head of the Vanuatu Rural Development Training Centres Association (Port Vila, 16 June 2004).

137 This devaluation is being assisted by the increasingly common practice of communities 'awarding' chiefly titles to government ministers and even to prominent businessmen. This is often done for reasons of 'respect' but also clearly sometimes purely for pecuniary motives. For example, the *Vanuatu Daily Post* reported that a community in South Santo had awarded the President of the Vanuatu National Party a chiefly title. It then reported that the community 'petitioned [the president] to build a new road from the main road to their village'. See Waiwo, Elenor 2005, 'Than receives new chiefly title', *Vanuatu Daily Post* (Port Vila), 25 October 2005, p. 6.

138 The Dillons Bay Council of Chiefs and the Nikoletan Island Council of Chiefs in Tanna.

139 For example, the conflict concerning the chiefs of central Pentecost, which resulted in the police being sent in (who then added to the violence themselves). See Ombudsman of Vanuatu 2003b, *Public report on police brutality during operation on Central Pentecost*, VUOM 16, <http://www.paclii.org.vu>

140 Kalontano, Alice, Vatu, Charles and Whyte, Jenny 2003, *Assessing Community Perspectives on Governance in Vanuatu*, Foundation of the Peoples of the South Pacific International, p. 117. The report goes on to say that a village council was set up with an equal representation of chiefs from the competing

factions, and that this had returned some peace to the village, but that '[r]esolving who is the village's paramount Chiefs [sic] remains a critical issue for the community, and there is high likelihood that tensions will surface again'.

[141] In the past few years, there have been a few isolated attempts by individual judges to engage with the *kastom* system in an informal and ad hoc way when dealing with such cases. For example, in *Tenene vs Nmak* (2003, VUSC 2, <http://www.paclii.org>), the Supreme Court sent a case to the Malvatumauri for its determination on the issue of chiefly title and then used the recommendations from the meeting as the basis of its decision. On another occasion, the Chief Justice appointed three people knowledgeable in *kastom* to sit with him and hear a case about the right to chiefly title. See Forsyth, Miranda 2003, 'Determining chiefly title: from courts to custom and back again', *Alternative Law Journal*, vol. 28, no. 4, p. 193.

[142] This ranges from a formal type of election with all members of the village voting to an informal system, where the elders identify a suitable person to be the chief on the basis of their perceived leadership qualities. For example, in the Torres Islands group, many chiefs are elected on a yearly basis but I met one who was appointed 22 years ago and who continues to hold the position today.

[143] Interview with a chief from Santo (Santo, 16 November 2004).

[144] Further, the criteria used do not necessarily correspond to the areas where there were traditionally ranked and hereditary systems (as discussed in Chapter 3). For example, one old chief in the Banks (which had a graded system before the arrival of missionaries and had since become an elected system) told me that he was a bloodline paramount chief 'like Queen Elizabeth'.

[145] They make up three different forms: one for communities where chiefly title is hereditary, one where chiefs are elected and one where the graded system is used. Each community was told to use the form that best suited it, but some communities took all three forms while others refused to use any, saying it did not fit them.

[146] Mavromatis et al., *Implementation of the* Customary Land Tribunal Act No 7, 2001, p. 12.

[147] Although there is still a very strong belief in black magic, during the colonial period, the practice became available to all people through inter-island exchange, rather than being practised just by traditional leaders. See Rio, Knut 2002, 'The sorcerer as an absented third person: formation of fear and anger in Vanuatu', *Social Analysis*, vol. 46, no. 3, p. 137.

[148] See Note below.

[149] One respondent stated that 'the term "respect" in my mother tongue [North Pentecost, Raga dialect] is "BINIHI MARAHI"; in transliteration it may be broken down to mean—BINIHI: thought and MARAHI: heavy, big, weighty. So *rispek* can mean just "being thoughtful"'.

[150] A chief at the Vanuatu Judiciary Conference (Port Vila, 28 August 2006).

[151] A final reason proffered by some respondents is that chiefs are interested only in cases that involve sexual matters because they can pry into all the private sordid details, and are not interested in helping to deal with other sorts of cases. As one respondent stated, '[J]*if ia hem i gud nomo blong tokabaot problem blong ol woman*' (this chief is only good for dealing with sexual issues).

[152] Interview with a police officer stationed in Ambrym (Port Vila, 8 November 2004).

[153] For example, one case in Santo involved some boys who stole from an aid post. The council said they must pay a fine of vt2000, but they refused to do so. The chief asked the Health Department to write a strong letter to the two boys, which they then did, and one of the boys paid but the other did not. The chief stated that there was nothing more he could do.

[154] Interview with an elder from Santo (Santo, 16 November 2004).

[155] For example, this occurred in the case study discussed in Chapter 6.

[156] Interview with a man from North Pentecost (Port Vila, 30 August 2004).

[157] For example, some respondents stated that because the chiefs had no way of finding proof, and no written guidelines to follow, they tended to make decisions on the basis of 'favour only'.

[158] For example, Hess describes one case she observed where one of the chiefs who decided on the fines was the father of one of the accused, and his son paid the lowest fines. She comments, 'The whole ceremony was heavily criticised both for the outcome as well as the process.' Hess, Person and place on Vanua Lava, Vanuatu, p. 47.

[159] Some communities have ways of limiting the potential of bias in the *kastom* system. For example, in Ambae, a traditional notion of the idea that judges should not be too closely related to the parties involved exists (Interview with a man from Ambae, Port Vila, 15 March 2004). The Lakalakabulu Council has developed this into a rule that the parties are asked if they agree with the selection of judges and

if a party does not want one judge then he or she must stand down. Apart from this council, however, I did not come across any other areas where there is more than a general principle that people should not judge cases where they might have a conflict of interest.

160 'The roots of the man Tanna/man Ambrym row', *The Independent* (Port Vila), 11 March 2007, p. 3.

161 Ralph Regenvanu, former Director of the Vanuatu Cultural Centre. See Regenvanu, Ralph 2007, State of emergency, Posting to the Vanuatu Research Interest Group, 5 March 2007. The President of the Port Vila Town Council of Chiefs stated, 'I would have thought their primary role was to maintain peace and unity in their jurisdiction, island, province and country. In other words, it was not their duty to instigate the use of black magic or violence'. See Garae, Len 2007, 'Chief Tarilama says chiefs, police to be blamed', *Vanuatu Daily Post* (Port Vila), 13 March 2007, p. 3.

162 'The roots of the man Tanna/man Ambrym row', *The Independent* (Port Vila), 11 March 2007, p. 3.

163 Interview with members of Wan Smol Bag Theatre Group (Port Vila, 15 April 2004).

164 Interview with Secretary of the Malvatumauri (Port Vila, 27 July 2006).

165 A man from North Pentecost stated that traditionally the chiefs were seen as being the ones who controlled the use of the land and as a consequence if someone did not obey them then the chief could reduce the part of land that person was entitled to use. Today, however, with the increasing emphasis on individual ownership of land that power is starting to be reduced (Interview with a man from North Pentecost, Port Vila, 26 July 2007).

166 Interview with a man from Erromango (Erromango, 18 May 2004).

167 Interview with the Head of the Vanuatu Rural Development Training Centres Association (Port Vila, 16 June 2004).

168 Only one respondent stated that in *kastom* she felt that all her 'dirty washing was hung out' in public.

169 Although in *kastom* there is certainly an element of public shaming, the offender is then reintegrated back into the community through the payment of fines and making a '*kastom sori*'.

170 Although, as mentioned above, in many places in Vanuatu, chiefs demand sitting fees to manage cases.

171 The law has just changed (partly as a result of recommendations by the author) and now it is possible for complainants to receive compensation in a criminal case. See the *Penal Code (Amendment) Act 2006* (s 40).

172 For example, in Erromango, women generally feel confident about speaking to men as a group and so, if at the end of a meeting the women are not happy with the way the judges have judged a case and feel that a burden has been unfairly placed on a woman, they will say so and the judges will have to go back and come up with a decision the women will accept.

173 Lindstrom, 'Straight talk on Tanna', p. 388.

174 Ibid., p. 387.

175 Interview with Merilyn Tahi, Director of the Vanuatu Women's Group (Port Vila, 7 May 2004).

176 This respondent said that even if a woman was raped she would be blamed and made to pay a fine or sent away from the village.

177 Lindstrom, 'Straight talk on Tanna', p. 395.

178 In many communities, a woman walking alone is seen as inviting sexual attention, so there will be little sympathy for her if she finds herself in trouble as a result of this.

179 Interview with Merilyn Tahi, Director of the Vanuatu Women's Group (Port Vila, 7 May 2004).

180 There is a specific problem with the treatment of rape in the *kastom* system because traditionally in *kastom* there is no concept of rape as such; rather, the problem is if the girl has sex with a boy to whom she is not married or to whom she is related or to whom she falls pregnant. For this reason, one of the solutions to a case of rape is for the chief to order the man to marry the girl. I was confronted with this once when I went to prosecute a rape case on the island of Epi and the defendant was not present in court because he was with the victim, now his wife, in hospital awaiting the birth of their first child.

181 Interview with Merilyn Tahi, Director of the Vanuatu Women's Group (Port Vila, 7 May 2004). She was speaking mostly about chiefly organisations rather than individual chiefs.

182 Interview with Gaia Fisher, anthropologist (Port Vila, 11 November 2004).

183 Interview with members of Wan Smol Bag Theatre Group (Port Vila, 15 April 2004).

184 Interview with Merilyn Tahi, Director of the Vanuatu Women's Group (Port Vila, 7 May 2004).

[185] For example, the *Tanna Law* (Article 5) states that the punishment for killing someone through sorcery is to give a girl to the chief, presumably for him to keep as a wife or daughter.

[186] Interview with members of Wan Smol Bag Theatre Group (Port Vila, 15 April 2004).

[187] Interview with a senior police officer (Tanna, 24 February 2004).

[188] A respondent told me of one case in Malekula a few years ago where a man had committed murder and went to prison but when he came back there was still hurt in the community so he gave his 10-year-old daughter as a fine to the other family. She noted wryly that the girl cried and cried but it did resolve the problem between the families and create a linkage between the two groups.

[189] Interview with a man from Erromango (Erromango, 18 May 2004).

[190] Interview with the Chief Executive Officer of the Vanuatu National Council of Women (Port Vila, 16 April 2004).

[191] Apparently what happened was that the elected chief made people work on the provincial holiday and two women publicly criticised him. The chief therefore called another election and one of the women was nominated and elected.

[192] She also said that her other role was to clean the meeting room and to organise the food for the meeting.

[193] Interview with women's representative on Dillons Bay Chiefly Council (Erromango, 19 May 2004).

[194] This was also confirmed on an individual level by some of the respondents. Some women commented that they had really seen changes since awareness about domestic violence and sexual offences was raised. One woman told me that after attending a workshop on domestic violence she felt able to 'preach' to her husband about his abusive behaviour and 'today there is peace in the home at last'. A man who had attended a workshop on gender issues told me that it had really opened his eyes and now he helped his wife with the washing of clothes and looking after the children.

[195] Interview with the Chief Executive Officer of the Vanuatu National Council of Women (Port Vila, 16 April 2004).

[196] A counsellor at the Women's Counselling Service in Santo said that chiefs often viewed the centre as being just for women and tried to stop victims going there as they said the chiefs were there for everyone. Generally, however, after they have explained their purpose to chiefs, chiefs cooperate with them. Many chiefs allow them to go to meetings with women and sit with them and tell them whether what the chiefs have decided is correct according to the law. The chair of the Committee Against Violence Against Women in the Banks Islands also stated that 'we hold hands with the chiefs and the area council secretary to block domestic violence' (Interview with chair of Committee Against Violence Against Women, Banks Islands, Vanua Lava, 21 October 2003).

[197] Interview with the Director of Youth and Sports (Port Vila, 11 June 2004).

[198] Makin, Bob 2005, 'Lissant Bolton on women and trade in Vanuatu', *The Independent* (Port Vila), 27 November 2005, p. 18.

[199] The questionnaire was used in this study to counterbalance the fact that the majority of informants in the in-depth interviews were older than twenty-six years and thus the views of youth were not adequately represented. It also aimed to clarify the finding from an earlier survey conducted by the Juvenile Justice Project in 2001 that ni-Vanuatu youths preferred chiefs rather than police to deal with them if they were involved in a dispute. See Rousseau, *The Report of the Juvenile Justice Project*. The questionnaire was carried out by members of the Young People's Project (which worked through the Vanuatu Cultural Centre) in 2003, with 158 informants from 17 different islands, as part of a broader empirical survey they were conducting. Potential problems of misrepresentations of the questionnaire were addressed in the questionnaire design by working with ni-Vanuatu colleagues to ensure the questions were clear and also by asking the same question in several ways. The potential for misunderstanding by the informants was also limited by the way the questionnaire was administered. Each youth was interviewed by a YPP fieldworker, who wrote his or her reply onto the questionnaire. The fieldworker was therefore able to clarify any misunderstandings the respondent might have had.

[200] The most common reasons for this choice were that: preferring chiefs meant that they had respect and trust for their culture, that courts could not solve trouble amicably like chiefs and that chiefs could not send people to prison and the fine was lower than in the court system.

[201] The major reasons for preferring chiefs are that chiefs will bring about peace and settle the conflict amicably and if the case goes to the courts there will still be division among people. The major reasons for preferring the courts are that courts will give appropriate punishment and will prevent the crime being committed again.

[202] I also asked whether they thought that if someone had stolen many times or raped someone or had killed someone they should be ordered to pay a fine or should be sent to prison and 95 per cent responded that the person should be sent to prison, mostly because the person was seen to have caused trouble, had broken the law and would learn a lesson in prison and so would not do the same thing again. The final question was whether they thought that if someone was a troublemaker in Vila or Luganville they should be sent back to the island. Eighty-two per cent felt that they should be, and the most common reasons given for this were that if they remained in town they might lead others astray; the parents, chiefs and elders on the island could give advice and reform the person; and that the person would create a bad image of their island in town. The major reason given for not wanting them to be sent back was that they might cause trouble on the island. Only seven respondents stated that it would be against the person's constitutional rights to be sent back against their will, which supports the observation of many respondents that many young people are not aware of their rights under the constitution.

[203] Some tables do not add up to 100 as not all respondents answered all the questions.

[204] Discussed in Chapter 1 under 'Age'.

[205] 'Vanuatu chief calls for support for traditional law agencies', *Radio New Zealand International*, viewed 9 June 2006, <http://www.rnzi.com/pages/news.php?op=read&id=24582>

[206] Nelson, Hank 2006, *Governments, states and labels*, Discussion Paper 2006/1, State, Society and Governance in Melanesia Research Paper Series, The Australian National University, viewed 10 March 2007, <http://rspas.anu.edu.au/melanesia/research.php>, p. 6.

5. The relationship between the state and *kastom* systems

This chapter examines the current relationship between the *kastom* system and various state institutions—namely, the courts, police, prisons, Public Prosecutor's Office, Office of the Public Solicitor and the Malvatumauri. The last is included although it is not part of the criminal justice system because it is the state body that, at least nominally, represents the *kastom* system at a state level. We shall see that adopting this broad ambit generates a far more nuanced account of the relationship between the two systems than has previously been produced by legal scholars who have focused solely on how substantive customary law has been used by the courts. This is because it permits an investigation of the formal and informal institutional relationships between the two systems in all areas of the criminal justice system. In addition, as Keebet and Franz von Benda-Beckman argue, examining 'the connections between the various co-existing substantive and procedural legal norms, the actors using them, and in particular the political and administrative authorities and decision-making institutions of the respective systems' is a major aid in understanding change in plural legal constellations.[1]

The chapter also considers the current condition of each state institution and the views of stakeholders concerning it. The capacities of these various institutions are related to their empirical and their normative relationships with the *kastom* system: a strong, well-functioning and accessible state institution is likely to have, and to require, a very different relationship with the *kastom* system than one that is under-resourced and strained to breaking point. In addition, the condition of each institution is relevant to issues of legitimacy. As Dinnen argues in relation to Papua New Guinea, 'the weak performance of PNG's formal law and justice system, particularly its criminal justice system, is as much an outcome of its lack of legitimacy, as it is a consequence of shortage of resources, "technical" or otherwise'.[2]

A final theme of this chapter is the discrepancy between the operation of the state legal system in theory and in practice, compared with the *kastom* system, where there is far greater synergy between the two.

The courts

There are four levels of courts in Vanuatu. The highest is the Court of Appeal, comprising judges from neighbouring countries in the South Pacific in addition to Vanuatu Supreme Court justices. The next level is the Supreme Court, comprising four judges, one of whom is based in Santo and the others in Port Vila. Under the Supreme Court come the Magistrates' Courts. The magistrates are all ni-Vanuatu and most have a law degree.[3] The Island Courts, authorised by the *Island Courts Act* (Cap 167) to be established by the Chief Justice wherever he thinks appropriate, are at the bottom of the court hierarchy and to date seven Island Courts have been established.[4] In addition to these courts there are Customary Land Tribunals whose establishment and jurisdiction are governed by the *Customary Land Tribunal Act 2001*. Their sole purpose is to resolve disputes based on customary land.

The current condition of the court system

The courts in Vanuatu are widely perceived as being independent and impartial and the judiciary is greatly respected. Due to Vanuatu's particular geography, however, the relative newness of the state system and resource issues, there are a number of fundamental problems with their current operation. The first is that the court system is *physically* inaccessible to many ni-Vanuatu. The Supreme Court has only two registries—one in Vila and one in Santo—and tours the islands on a periodic basis depending on funding arrangements and case loads, often meaning cases must wait for a year or more before they are heard. Even at the Magistrate's Court level, not every province has a registry and, consequently, everyone involved in a case must either travel a long way to the court or wait for many months, if not years, for the court to come to them on tour. Further, in criminal cases where the defendant is transferred from his or her home island to Santo or Vila, the people who have been affected by the crime—the victim and the community—are often completely excluded from the process (for example, when there is a plea of guilty).[5] As a result, people do not feel part of the process, do not understand what has happened and feel they have not had a chance to give their side of the story. The courts are also generally perceived as *financially* inaccessible, as the court fees, especially in the Supreme Court and Court of Appeal, are out of reach for most ni-Vanuatu.[6]

The second problem is that many ni-Vanuatu see the court system as being a foreign system. The general distrust and lack of ownership of the system are illustrated by the fact that many people refer to the courts as *'kot blong waetman'* (white man's court). The procedures used by the state courts are also foreign for the majority of defendants and witnesses. A legal officer commented that people often did not understand why they had won or lost a case.[7] A particular problem many ni-Vanuatu face is understanding why the state system deals only with the particular complaint and not the background factors or even crimes preceding it (all highly relevant in a *kastom* meeting, as discussed in Chapter 4), and this can cause a great deal of confusion and anger as people feel that 'their' side of the story has not been told. Further, in the higher courts and even some Magistrate's Courts, the language used is English, which is not understood by the majority of the population, or at least not at the level it is used in the legal context. It was also clear from this study that many ni-Vanuatu, particularly women and youth, did not know their legal rights and saw the courthouse as frightening and confusing. This results in false pleas of guilty, as discussed in the next chapter, and also raises real doubts as to the capacity of the system to achieve justice.

A third problem is the delays in the system.[8] Normally, there are delays in hearing cases of between six and 18 months in Vila and Santo. In other places, where the courts visit only when there are sufficient cases, the delays are much greater.[9] On some occasions, when the court finally does arrive, the cases are dismissed 'for want of prosecution' because a state prosecutor has not come on tour. Further, the number of cases before the courts keeps increasing. One judge stated that the magistrates and judges were 'bogged down with work' but more files kept piling up. Perhaps because of this, the courts are not seen by the wider community to be able to move quickly enough to 'put out the fire' before a dispute gets out of hand. In contrast, the speed with which chiefs can resolve matters is regularly commented on. In a small community, this is often essential, as an unresolved dispute can lead to property damage, arson and even physical retaliation. Additionally, a normalisation in relations is needed to allow the interdependent relationships to mend and for the social capital (especially trust) necessary for development to be restored.

There are also problems with enforcement of court orders, especially in rural areas and with Island Court cases. The previous magistrate on Tanna stated that warrants of execution were very rarely served, even for Magistrate's and Supreme Court cases. In Santo as well, there is very little enforcement of orders so fines are not paid. Some respondents commented that they did not care if cases went to the courts or not because they just did not pay the fines and there was no follow up. Many people involved in the administration of the Island and higher-level courts confirmed this perception.

There are particular problems facing the Island Courts. Perhaps the most significant is that they are not operating in many places due to lack of payment of sitting fees for the judges. For example, the police prosecutor responsible for Island Courts in Santo reported in 2004 that they had to cancel all the sittings for the rest of the year because the justices' sitting fees had not been paid for the past four months. A further problem is that the justices who serve in the courts are often uneducated and left to manage the courts with little or no training. Adding to their difficulties is the fact that the laws they are meant to be administering are written only in English (and complicated 'legal' English at that) and there is not a functioning system of supervision by the Magistrates' Courts. As a result, many of the criticisms made of the Island Courts were the same as those levelled at chiefs: they were accused of favouritism and of involving politics in disputes, leading to an undermining of their authority. The comment was frequently made that if the justices were faced with a defendant who was a bit educated he could easily 'turnturnem olgeta' (confuse them) and they became lost.[10] It is to be hoped that recent training programs and strengthening initiatives begun in 2006 improve this current situation.[11]

The relationship between the courts and the *kastom* system

The relationship between the courts and the *kastom* system will be analysed by distinguishing between the institutional pluralism and the normative pluralism that exist between the two systems.[12] The reason for this approach is to try to tease out the exact nature of the relationship of the two systems, in turn allowing a more satisfactory consideration of what sort of relationship they should and could have.[13]

The relationship between customary law and state law

This section is concerned with the potential for, and the reality of, the use by the state system of substantive norms from the *kastom* system.[14] As this area has been the main focus of previous scholars investigating the relationship between customary law and state law, this discussion is relatively short.[15] The basic position can be summed up very simply: despite the ability at a jurisdictional level to integrate substantive customary law into case law, the courts to date have not done so. This is one illustration of the considerable disjuncture between written law and the practical reality of the state legal system in Vanuatu.[16]

At a formal statutory level there is considerable scope for the role of customary law in the state criminal justice system. After independence, introduced laws were retained 'until otherwise provided by parliament',[17] with a clear intent evident in the constitution that these would be gradually supplanted by an indigenous legal system. The constitution provides that introduced laws should be applied 'wherever possible taking due account of custom'.[18] Further, it provides that 'customary law shall continue to have effect as part of the law of the Republic of Vanuatu'.[19] The judiciary is charged by Section 47(1) to 'resolve proceedings according to law' and, if there is no rule directly applicable, to make a decision 'according to substantial justice and wherever possible in conformity with custom'.[20] Other relevant legislative provisions are Section 65(2) of the *Judicial Services and Courts Act 2000*, which allows all courts to construe any act or law 'with such alterations and adaptations as may be necessary' for 'the purposes of facilitating the application of custom', and Section 65(3), which gives the courts inherent and incidental powers to apply custom. Finally, the *Law Commission Act* (Cap 115) provides that one function of the commission is to recommend reforms that reflect the 'distinctive concepts of custom' (Section 7[a]).[21]

Although these provisions seem to accord customary law a significant place in the legal system, it is also possible to read into the constitution hints of wariness about customary law. Section 47(1), for example, suggests that the drafters of the constitution were torn between a desire to embrace customary law and to reject those parts of it not in conformance with the standards of a modern nation-state. The constitution also contains a Bill of Rights outlining the fundamental rights and freedoms enjoyed by all citizens,[22] some of which are perceived as limiting the application of customary law.

Further, the constitution does not provide any procedures as to how courts are to inform themselves about the relevant customary law in particular cases, leaving this to Parliament in Article 51. To date, Parliament has failed to address this issue and this omission has contributed to the difficulties the courts have faced in utilising customary law. The constitution did, however, provide two possible mechanisms for the integration of customary law into the state system: Article 51, which allows Parliament to appoint as assessors people 'knowledgeable in custom' to sit on the higher state courts, and Article 52, providing that Parliament is to legislate for the establishment of village courts, in which chiefs should play a role, with jurisdiction over customary and other matters.[23]

Pursuant to Article 51, Part VIII of the *Criminal Procedure Code* (Cap 136) provided for assessors to sit in the Supreme and Magistrates' Courts alongside the judiciary to assist in their determination of the guilt of the accused. There was, however, limited opportunity to integrate a customary perspective as the assessors were not required to have any particular knowledge of customary law[24] and it was not required for their decision to be followed, although if the judge or magistrate did not wish to follow their decisions they were required to give reasons for this.[25] It is unclear to what extent assessors were really used in practice, but they were formally abolished by the *Criminal Procedure (Amendment) Act 1989*. It appears that the reason for their abolition was that the then expatriate Chief Justice considered that they did not serve a useful function and, moreover, the necessity to provide them with proper instructions was too onerous a duty on the judiciary.[26]

The second potential mechanism in the constitution to integrate the use of customary law is the institution of Island Courts. These courts can be viewed as an example of an attempt at weak legal pluralism, dressed up to look like deep legal pluralism, but in fact not legal pluralism at all. The *Island Courts Act 1983* (Section 1) provides that the Chief Justice may establish Island Courts throughout Vanuatu 'as he sees fit'. The attempts at weak legal pluralism in this act are demonstrated in two ways. First, the courts are required to comprise three justices knowledgeable in the custom of the island, at least one of whom must be a chief (Section 3[1]). This suggests an intention for the Island Court justices to use customary law in making decisions. Second, Section 10 provides that 'an island court shall administer the customary law prevailing within the territorial jurisdiction of the court' to the extent that it is not inconsistent with any written law or contrary to justice, morality and good order.

The specific jurisdiction of each court is, however, defined in the warrant that establishes it[27] and no warrant to date has given any general or specific customary law jurisdiction. Rather, the warrants indicate that the focus of the courts' jurisdiction is minor introduced law matters.[28] Thus, as Weisbrot noted in 1989, the Island Courts operated as less formal Magistrates' Courts rather than as officially sanctioned custom courts.[29] Rousseau, working more than a decade later, reached the same conclusion, stating that '[i]n the case of the island courts, supposedly designed to bring *kastom* into state law as procedure, the result appears as the imperfect enforcement of existing state legislation'.[30] These observations were also confirmed by my fieldwork, with Island Court justices drawing distinctions between the types of law they administered in the courts and the law they administered in the *nakamal*.

The reason for arguing that the Island Courts have been 'dressed up' to look like deep legal pluralism comes from some commentary made pertaining to Island Courts, seemingly in response to government announcements concerning them. Larcom, an anthropologist writing shortly after the passage of the *Island Courts Act*, wrote that the act

> was a crucial step in the government's attempt to construct and solidify a national cultural identity. The Act was intended to grant decision-making authority over most local jural matters to local institutions. Apparently recognizing the inability of national legal codes to regulate social order in the villages, the government now sought to hand issues of law and justice back to village courts.[31]

This statement suggests that at the time of the passage of the act, the government was intending to convey the message that the act in fact was giving power to manage disputes back to the chiefs, or to at least engage in a relationship with the *kastom* system. A statement made by the Malvatumauri in 1992 confirms this impression:

> Although the *Island Courts Act* was passed in 1983, the Island Courts have never achieved this unifying function [that the pre-existing systems of customary justice would become part of the judicial system of the country]. The Island Courts have always been seen as part of the court system and the chiefs have continued to exercise customary justice in the *nakamal* or *nasara*.[32]

As can be seen from the current legislative framework for the courts, however, there is no provision made for chiefs to use substantive customary law or procedures inside the Island Courts. The Island Courts have therefore by and large not achieved either deep or weak legal pluralism on even a theoretical level.[33] As a result, as one respondent observed, the Island Courts presently '*float nomo*' (just float), being neither satisfactory state courts nor *kastom* courts.

A further mechanism that has the potential to facilitate the introduction of customary law into the state system is Section 38 of the *Penal Code (Amendment) Act 2006*.[34] This provides that the court may 'promote reconciliation and encourage and facilitate the settlement in an amicable way, according to custom or otherwise'.[35] This provision is potentially quite radical as it allows the courts to use customary norms and procedures to determine the substantive outcome of cases. Further, it envisages the courts applying these principles outside the state system, rather than bringing them into the state system and incorporating them into state normative processes. As such, it comes close to allowing a process of deep legal pluralism, although it is still the state system that determines how the customary law is used. Unfortunately, however, this section and its precedent have rarely, if ever, been used in practice, although judges and lawyers agree that theoretically it is a good idea. The reasons given for the lack of use of the provisions are vague, but it can be surmised that no-one is exactly sure how it should be used. The Chief Justice in fact explicitly commented that there was a need for a clearer mechanism to be included, with more detail and assistance given about exactly how to use the section, and yet this was not done in the recent rewriting of the section into its current form.

Thus, as the former Director of the Vanuatu Cultural Centre has stated, although the constitution leaves the road open for judges and lawyers to use customary law in their decisions and arguments, and for politicians to make laws about how custom can be used, all of these institutions have so far failed to do so.[36] There is a great deal of debate as to whose responsibility it is to change this. Politicians argue it is up to the judges, the judges say it is up to the legislature to legislate ways for customary law to be used[37] and to the lawyers to make submissions based on customary law,[38] and the lawyers say it is up to the judges to encourage the use of customary law.[39]

Apart from a refusal by any one group to take ownership of the issue of the lack of development of what Narokobi refers to as a 'Melanesian jurisprudence', many other reasons are cited for the failure of customary law to play a role in the substantive law of the State.[40] The first is the place in the legal hierarchy that the constitution has given to customary law. Paterson has observed that the extent to which courts, including Island Courts, in Vanuatu can apply customary law and the relationship between customary law and the common law are 'shrouded in some obscurity'.[41] As customary law comes after the constitution and legislation, and arguably also after the common law as a source of law, the door is left open for courts to argue that customary law has only a 'fill-in' role—in other words, it is only if there is no other law available that the court must look to custom. As Vanuatu still applies the laws of England and the laws of France as applied to, or made for, the New Hebrides before 1980, to the extent that they are not expressly revoked or incompatible with the independent status of Vanuatu, there are not very many areas in which an ancient British law cannot be dredged up.[42]

A second reason that has been advanced as an explanation is that customary law varies so much from community to community and island to island that it is not possible to apply it as a homogenous body of law at a national level.[43] This was the view put forward by Justice Cooke in *Boe & Taga vs Thomas* (1980–94, Van LR 293), in which he noted:

> Mr Rissen further submitted that I should consider the custom of the parties in assessing damages. I regret that I cannot accede to this submission of Mr Rissen as custom varies so much in each village throughout Vanuatu that it would be quite impossible to lay down guidelines for those dealing with the matter.

According to this view, if a norm of customary law does not exist throughout Vanuatu, it cannot be recognised as a rule of law, as due to the principles of *stare decisis*, this would result in it becoming a precedent for the whole country.

A third reason is that the legal profession in Vanuatu has been, and still significantly remains, expatriate and trained in the common law tradition. The former Chief Justice, Justice d'Imecourt, observed in *Banga vs Waiwo*:[44]

> What Parliament has not done so far, and I venture to say, is unlikely to do, is to do away with the element of British 'Common Law and Equity' that apply [sic] in Vanuatu. After 16 years of Independence, it would be difficult to do so. Further more, it is likely to cause enormous upheaval in the legal system if it sought to do so now. One need only to consider the fact that virtually all the country's lawyers, including the Ni-Vanuatu lawyers are common law trained.

This factor has had a significant impact on the inhibition of the development of a Melanesian jurisprudence. As Bourdieu notes, 'The individual is always, whether he likes it or not, trapped…within the limits of the system of categories he owes to his upbringing and training.'[45] Consequently, this has meant that lawyers and the judiciary have felt more comfortable in applying the common law than customary law and have, in general, shied away from pushing the boundaries established by the constitution.[46]

Fourth, although Parliament is charged by Article 51 of the constitution to 'provide for the manner of the ascertainment of relevant rules of custom', it has not done so. Consequently, there is confusion about how customary law is to be used as a source of law by the courts, contributing to the judiciary's reluctance to use it in preference to easily accessible introduced laws. Weisbrot states:

There is nothing to provide some guidance as to the integration of custom in the western-style courts on such matters as: (1) the definition of custom; (2) the subject areas in which custom is or is not applicable; (3) the modes of ascertainment and rules of evidence and procedure with respect to adducing custom in the courts; (4) the standards (if any) against which the recognition of custom must first be tested; (5) the regime to be followed in the event of a conflict of customary laws; (6) the method by which a person must establish (or refute) membership in a customary group, and so on. The experience elsewhere in the Pacific suggests that in the absence of strong guidelines and incentives to utilise custom it is very difficult for customary law to develop in a coherent and comprehensive manner.[47]

The question of how customary law is to be proved has been considered by the courts, and although views vary, the general approach seems to be that set down by Chief Justice d'Imecourt in *Banga vs Waiwo*, in which he states, 'Although it is conceivable that there might not be a need for strict rules regarding the obtaining of evidence of a particular custom if and when the need arises to establish a particular custom, evidence must, nevertheless, be obtained and a clear custom must be established'.[48] Norms of customary law must therefore be proven to the courts in the same way as facts, creating a substantial burden on the party wishing to use the norm.

Finally, there is the view that the natures of common law and customary law are fundamentally different. Customary law is seen to be 'flexible, fluid, capable of being used in different ways at different times'.[49] As a consequence, it is argued that bringing customary law into the state system would essentially change its nature, crystallising it and making it into an inflexible precedent—thus losing its value and purpose. Ntumy argues that when a legal norm of customary law is sanctioned by the State, either through legislation or the norm-creating activity of the courts, it is instantly converted by state power from customary form to state law. It then ceases to be customary law. Ntumy observes, 'Efforts to legislate customary law by an external political power are, therefore, the antithesis of custom.'[50]

These various reasons go some way to showing the difficulties, theoretical and practical, of using customary law in the state system, and in explaining why judges, lawyers and legislators continue to put the question of the use of customary law into the 'too-hard basket'. In the final two chapters, this thesis argues that these difficulties can be overcome largely by asking broader questions about the institutional and procedural relationships of the two systems and instituting reforms that allow each to feed through into the other system.

The relationship between the kastom system and the court system

This section is concerned with the relationship between the two systems on an institutional level. In other words, to what extent does the state system accept, formally or informally, the *kastom* system's power and right to manage conflicts? On a theoretical level, the inquiry is really the extent to which deep legal pluralism exists in Vanuatu today.

On a formal level, there is only one mechanism for the state system to recognise the operation of the *kastom* system in the area of criminal law: Section 39 of the *Penal Code (Amendment) Act 2006*,[51] which provides that the court must take into account any compensation made or due by the offender under custom. The section thus allows the court to recognise that a defendant might have already been punished by the *kastom* system and to modify the sentence in light of that punishment. A classic example of how this occurs in practice is described in the case of *Waiwo vs Waiwo and Banga*:[52]

> [V]ery often, the Magistrate will not be surprised to see appearing before the Court…next to the Accused, his custom chief. The chief pays respect to the bench and informs the Court that they have already dealt with the matter in custom and the Defendant or Accused is already punished for his wrongdoing…The Court explain[s] to the chief concerned the position within the criminal law, the Accused [i]s dealt with accordingly and the Court then invites the chiefs to explain the custom.

There are, however, still problems with the way courts take *kastom* payments into account as mitigating features.[53] First, the court is not permitted to stay or terminate the proceedings in light of the fact that the *kastom* system has already dealt with the matter. Second, there is very little inquiry into whether the parties are satisfied with the settlement or whether or not the payment has been appropriate according to the *kastom* of the relevant area. Further, the Court of Appeal has ruled that a customary payment may affect the quantum of the sentence but may not change the nature of the sentence.[54] As a result, a customary payment may reduce a fine or prison term, but may not change a prison term into a fine or a suspended sentence. Apart from this restriction, the courts have hitherto been inconsistent in their approach to the value that a customary payment should be given. Some Supreme Court decisions indicated the development of a rule that a customary payment would reduce a sentence by one-third (in the same way that a plea of guilty would), in order to 'formally recognise the role that custom can play in the criminal justice system'.[55] This half-formulated rule was, however, dismissed by the Court of Appeal in *Public Prosecutor vs Niala* (2004, VUCA 25), in which their honours commented that a 'precise mathematical deduction' was not appropriate.[56]

An important aspect of the relationship between the two systems is the effect that each has on the workload of the other. Thus, it is clear that today the work of the *kastom* system in managing conflicts significantly reduces the burden placed on the state court system. This is recognised by some involved in the state system. For example, a judge commented that he was afraid that respect for chiefs was disappearing and that 'once that disappears the courts will be swamped with so much the number of judges and magistrates will have to be increased significantly'.[57] The work of chiefs in resolving matters at a community level also often prevents disputes from getting out of hand and ending up with the involvement of the state system. This was acknowledged by a Supreme Court judge who commented during sentencing that '[i]f community leaders deal with the issue at first sight, problems such as this, leading to death could have been avoided'.[58]

Views of stakeholders about the relationship

All the key players involved in the court system interviewed for this study, including lawyers, judicial officers and prosecutors, stated that they considered there was not enough of a relationship between the two systems at present and that there should be more recognition of the *kastom* system by the state system. For example, one judge commented, 'The [justice] structure has to take into account the local structure and it is currently not taking it into account in a way that allows the community to have access to justice.'[59] Another judge remarked that for the ordinary person the highest court of the land did not give any weight to *kastom*, but that this was wrong and *kastom* should be given some weight in the system. He further observed, 'There is good wisdom in terms of mechanisms and methods of both systems. These can be combined.'[60] Another judicial officer stated that although there should be a natural progression between the decisions of the chiefs and the state courts, in fact there was a 'void' between the two systems, meaning that when matters reached the state courts they were dealt with as fresh matters and all that had been done by the chiefs was disregarded.[61] Finally, a senior government lawyer stated that very little recognition was given by the state system to the steps taken by the chiefs to ensure that peace and harmony prevailed.[62]

Although there is a considerable majority of opinion that the relationship should be more clearly defined than it is at present, there is a great deal of uncertainty about how this can be achieved.[63] There was hesitation by many actors in the state system about the idea of legislating for chiefly powers. For example, the Chief Justice stated that defining the chiefs' role would immediately limit their scope, condemning them to 'live in a bucket' and become dependent for their powers. Rather than legislating for chiefly powers, most non-chiefly respondents proposed a wide variety of creative suggestions about how exactly it would be best to 'marry' the two systems, some of which are discussed in the final chapters.

In summary, therefore, the two systems operate very much independently of each other, despite the belief of the overwhelming majority of the stakeholders that they should work together in some way. This, combined with the fact that the court system is currently over-stretched, inaccessible to a sizeable percentage of the population and still largely viewed as foreign, suggests that there is plenty of scope to strengthen the relationship so as to ease the workload of the state system and to help it to attain a degree of legitimacy in the eyes of the population.

The Vanuatu Police Force

The police force has two wings: the Vanuatu Police Force (VPF) and the paramilitary wing, the Vanuatu Mobile Force (VMF).[64] There are 547 police officers organised into two main police commands: one in Port Vila and one in Luganville. Within these there are four main police stations[65] and eight police posts.[66] This means that there are many islands with no police presence and many parts of islands where getting to a police post can take several days.

The condition of the police today

The VPF today suffers from a negative public image and a negative self-image. In regard to the latter, a report into the state of the VPF in 2003 finds that the police 'do not generally feel positive about the job that the force is doing' and are concerned that they 'do not receive sufficient training, that resources were not managed appropriately and that they were being underpaid and their general welfare neglected'.[67] An analysis by Penama Province paints a typical picture of the situation of police outside the two urban centres:

> Penama Police service is severely affected by budgetary constraints and low moral[e]. This constraint seems to be exacerbated by an ineffective system of administration, which affects proper distribution of resources allocated to the Provincial Police Services. Resources budgeted for the Penama police services do not seem to be appropriated to the Provincial police station at Saratamata but rather used up elsewhere by other provinces or municipalities.[68]

During this study, police regularly complained that they were unsupported by the government and hampered in carrying out their duties. In rural areas in particular, the lack of resources such as vehicles or boats means that the police are significantly hindered in carrying out investigations and arresting and summonsing people to attend court.[69] For example, the sole police officer on the island of Ambrym discussed a murder investigation he was conducting, complaining that not only did he not have a vehicle to travel to the murder scene and to interview witnesses, he did not even have a notebook, and was required to pay for phone cards out of his own salary to call headquarters in Port Vila to try to obtain more funding. A statement made by the Acting Commander of the

Central Investigation Unit in the local newspaper illustrates the feeling of frustration with the system: 'We are helpless. We can't even detect and apprehend the suspects which is our mandate. We are helpless in managing the crime trend because we lack vital resources in terms of transport facilities, proper telecommunication systems and manpower and human resources.'[70]

It must also be noted, however, that a lot of people are cynical about police claims that they do not have sufficient manpower or resources, especially in urban areas, commenting that police officers are often seen just hanging around and that police trucks are often seen in front of kava bars.[71] The negative self-image of the VMF leads to problems of discipline, to low morale and to a generally lax attitude towards the work of policing. Lawyers and other actors in the state system therefore complain about the lack of proper investigation of cases and care in drafting charges.[72]

The police force's low self-image is also reflected in its public image. Newton Cain found that '[t]here are generally very low levels of [public] confidence in the capacity of the police to address issues that are important to groups within the community' and that '[t]here is a growing belief within the community that there is very little point in seeking recourse to the police, as their response is either non-existent or inadequate'.[73] The two biggest complaints made about the police are that they will not assist when requested and that they have a culture of employing unnecessary violence. Complaints about the police not going to assist victims of crime are legendary throughout Vanuatu. When I asked a group of young people what happened if you went to make a complaint with the police, the reaction was instantaneous: half of them made a gesture of tearing up paper and throwing it away, explaining that the police threw the complaint away as soon as the complainant left the room. In rural areas, people complain that the police are so remote they cannot contact them, and when they do, the police ask them to pay for them to come, as they cannot afford the cost of fuel. In 2007, the *Vanuatu Daily Post* reported, 'There is a general perception of the Luganville Police that they will rarely do anything'.[74] Despite these negative views, people are generally of the view that the police are needed in all areas of Vanuatu and that their presence does help to control crime.

Police brutality has been widely documented.[75] Rousseau comments that '[t]he level of violence employed by the police seems to be an "open secret" in Vanuatu—known, but infrequently acted upon'.[76] One senior bureaucrat stated that in urban areas police brutality was common, with the police regularly forcing people to confess by punching and slapping them.[77] In many cases, the victims of this violence accept it,[78] but increasingly there have been complaints and demands for compensation. The most public of these arose from *Operesen Klinim-Not* (Operation Clean-Up the North) in Santo, which resulted in a number of court cases relating to police brutality. In one, the parties complained that they had been 'subjected to verbal abuses, physical assaults extending from undressing in an open field, dancing naked in pairs, pinching of private parts with pliers, kicking with boots, hitting with rifle butts and truncheons, licking boots and toilet brush'.[79]

There are mixed views regarding the way the police deal with women. Some women perceived the police to be more powerful than the chiefs in dealing with problems such as domestic violence, incest, teenage pregnancies and underage sex. There is, however, a culture of domestic violence in the VPF itself, which undermines the confidence of victims in the police.[80] For example, one woman who was married to a police officer told me that he regularly beat her so the women in her area knew that there was no point complaining to him about domestic violence. A study conducted by the legal officer at the Vanuatu Women's Centre between 1995 and 1996 found that '[g]enerally speaking domestic assault is treated [by the state criminal justice system] as a matter less likely to require outside intervention, and when intervention is undertaken, the punishment tends to be less severe than if it had not been domestic violence'.

It further found that 'when women seek the intervention of the legal system the statistics show a significant failure on the part of the police to impose bail conditions to protect them from further assault and pressure to withdraw their complaint'.[81] The study concluded that, although the formal legal system in Vanuatu offered some significant protection to women and had a constitutional guarantee of their equal status with men, it often failed to enforce women's rights.[82] The amendments to the law since this study, primarily the development of Domestic Violence Protection Orders[83] by the Supreme Court, have alleviated this situation to an extent, allowing women to apply directly to the court for an order of protection. Women are, however, still dependent on the police for the enforcement of these orders and sometimes police tell them that it is not their work, that it is the woman's fault or that the woman must serve the order herself. Many police take the view that violence against women is a private matter and they will not interfere. This attitude was illustrated by a senior police officer, who commented that cases that were 'merely domestic issues'—for example, where a husband hit his wife because she had been with another man—were sent back to the chiefs.[84] Police also often send women complainants to the Vanuatu Women's Centre instead of taking their statement and prosecuting the offender. The physical inaccessibility of police posts, especially in rural areas, also means that police are not an option for many women in dealing with criminal activities.[85]

The relationship between the police and the *kastom* system

The relationship between the police and the *kastom* system is complex and varies considerably throughout the country. The official VPF policy since 2000 has been that chiefs should be encouraged to work with the police and to manage 'minor' offences themselves, leaving the police to the work of resolving the 'serious' crimes. This policy has not been reduced to written form in any detail and is very much a pragmatic one; the police rely on the chiefs to keep law and order to a great extent in practice, and officially recognising this fact might be seen as an attempt to control the nature of that reliance. A senior police officer summed up the situation by stating that the police and the chiefs worked together, but there was no continuous link between them—no 'hotline'—so at times they worked together and at other times they did their own thing.[86]

There is enormous variation in the implementation of this policy throughout the country. To an extent, these differences are created by the different individuals involved in each system, but also by variations such as the size of the community compared with the number of police officers servicing the area, the resources of the particular police post[87] and the strength or weakness of the *kastom* system in the area. An example of an area where the police and the *kastom* system have a very close relationship is Tanna. The officer in charge of the police station on Tanna spoke in glowing terms about the fact that in *kastom* '*dei afta tomorrow tufala save fren*' (the next day the two are friends), whereas in the state system '*wan mas lose and wan mas win*' (one has to lose and one has to win). He said that because his officers were fed up with people lodging complaints and then withdrawing them after the matter had been resolved in *kastom*, he made it a rule that people had to discuss the matter with their chief first. If they still want to lodge a complaint they have to come with their chief or with an elder certifying it has passed through the chief's hands first. If they do not, they are sent to read a notice, which provides that if they lodge a complaint and then wish to withdraw it, they have to pay a fee of vt1000 (about half a term's school fees). Apparently, since this new rule came into effect no-one has lodged a complaint with the police.[88] In contrast, in Erromango, there is no police post and the police come only a few times a year, if that. The chiefs are very dismissive of the work of the police, saying they come and take statements but then do nothing and the cases just 'go to sleep'. A third level of relationship occurs in Ambrym, where there is only one police officer. That police officer said that sometimes when he had completed his investigations into minor cases it was too hard to send the files back to Vila or Santo so he called the chiefs together and presented them with the findings of his investigations and told them to 'judge the case in *kastom*'.[89] A final situation is Santo, where there is quite an antagonistic relationship between the chiefs and the police. The chiefs complain that the police do not help them, but the police say they do not assist the chiefs because there is no law to allow them to do so.

Ways the police assist the *kastom* system

The police assist with the *kastom* system in a variety of ways. On occasions, chiefs ask the police to come to *kastom* meetings to 'keep the peace'. Generally, police will be requested to do this only when the meetings involve people from different communities, as this is when tensions are highest, or else very serious cases, such as those concerning allegations of black magic. An example of this was a meeting held in Vila in 2005 to deal with disputes between people from different parts of Tanna. The *Vanuatu Daily Post* reported:

> Police and VMF quickly calmed a raging fire by cooling down the dreaded fury of approximately 400 Tannese from attacking Chief Koro's men as soon as the opening prayer ended with an 'amen'. Scores of young men fuelled by instinct for revenge surged forward only to be stopped by the Police and VMF.[90]

Occasionally, police are also asked to bring people to meetings. At times, this merely involves bringing people who would be willing to come anyway but do not have transport or else are not aware of the meeting. It may, however, also involve bringing people who do not wish to attend the meeting. Generally, the police do not use force, relying on their position as authority figures to convince people to go with them. On occasions, however, police do forcibly pick up people, as occurred in *Public Prosecutor vs Kota and Others* (1989–94, 2 VLR 661):

> The police were consulted at the Police Station, and 2 police in a police truck, together with Mathias Teku, went to the house where Marie Kota was living, and forced Marie to go to the meeting. I find it most astonishing and abhorrent that Vanuatu Police had anything to do with this matter. And had it not been for the fact that they were firstly requested, and secondly agreed to go, this matter would not be where it is today. The Vanuatu Police had no authority in the legislation of this country to act as they did in this case, to bully and force a person to attend a meeting, and I propose to take this matter up to the Chief Commissioner of Police.

The police are sometimes also involved in the enforcement of orders made by the *kastom* system. In most instances, this simply involves the police going to people who have refused to make their *kastom* payments and telling them that they should pay. At other times, the police write letters directing people to pay. It appears that for the most part force is not used to compel people to pay fines, although I was told reasonably often by the chiefs that sometimes they requested the police to take an offender to the police holding cell and to beat him or detain him for the night as punishment.[91] It is difficult to assess how much this really occurs in practice, and how much it is merely the unfulfilled desire of the chiefs, as only a few police officers admit to doing it. The cases in which the police are most often said to use force involve the enforcement of decisions by the chiefs to send people living in the urban areas back to their home islands. Despite the case of *Kota*,[92] it appears that some police continue to assist chiefs, generally those from their community, in forcibly putting people onto boats to send them back to their home islands.

Ways the *kastom* system assists the police

There are also a number of ways in which the *kastom* system assists the state system. First, the chiefs help the police with locating defendants and witnesses. For example, a senior police officer stated that when the police went to look for a suspect in a village they must first see the chief of the village and he would then tell them where to find the suspect.[93] As the concept of an address is relatively foreign in Vanuatu, such assistance is invaluable. For example, in a recent murder case in Ambrym, a chief was sent to the village of the suspects to ask them to voluntarily surrender.[94] The chiefs also assist by maintaining peace in their communities and dealing with conflicts 'on the level of *kastom*' before the police arrive, thereby often stopping situations from getting out of hand. This is particularly important in communities that can take the police several days to reach. The *kastom* system also relieves the burden on the police to an enormous extent by dealing with a large percentage of criminal cases—minor and serious. It is clear that if the *kastom* system stopped operating, the VPF, stretched as it already is, could not possibly meet the law and order needs of the community.

On a number of occasions since independence there have been riots of one kind or another and the police have relied heavily on the chiefs to restore law and order. For example, during the 1998 riots, sparked by political instability and concerns over the management of the Vanuatu National Provident Fund, order was restored only with the assistance of the chiefs. The Commissioner of Police at the time stated that '[d]evelopments in recent days have proved that the traditional ways of maintaining our society and people is [sic] still very much alive'.[95] Similarly, in 2002, the chiefs also assisted the police to restore calm in the tensions arising from the appointment of a new police commissioner. In contrast with those earlier occasions, two recent breakdowns in law and order—one in Santo at the end of 2006 and the other in Vila in March 2007—involved failure on behalf of the police and the chiefs to manage group violence.[96] These two situations illustrate the weak state of both systems of law and order and also point to failures in the relationship between them, as will be discussed in the next chapter.

View of stakeholders about the relationship

The views of the chiefs concerning the police vary considerably. The general view is that the police perform a valuable function, but that they should be more responsive to the needs of the chiefs. This point was made prominently during the March riots in 2007, when the police had allegedly been informed by chiefs before the violence that trouble was brewing and their help was needed, but the police refused to provide any assistance, even after the riots started and people were killed and houses burnt down.[97]

The police and others involved in the enforcement of law and order in a government capacity are for the most part extremely complimentary about the *kastom* system, pointing out its many benefits and explaining how it does a lot of the work of maintaining peace in the communities. For example, a state official commented that in reality it was not the police that solved problems, it was the chiefs.[98] The police legal advisor similarly stated, '[W]hen we have a problem then we look at police work but also look at traditional way, because once a fire is lit then it is necessary to use *kastom* to *kilim daon fia* [put out the fire].'[99] The former Commissioner of Police, Robert Deniro, stated that their partnership with the chiefs up to now had been informal, but very effective and fruitful. Another important finding concerning the relationship between the police and the *kastom* system was that all the actors were concerned that the relationship between the two systems should be clearer to avoid disputes over which cases each should deal with and to clarify what demands the chiefs could legitimately make of the police.[100] For example, the police legal advisor suggested that there should be some legal framework to give recognition to the role played by chiefs and police, and if the chiefs and police could work together as part of a restorative justice system this would reduce disputes.[101]

The police are also often outspoken about their belief that the chiefs have a *responsibility* to maintain law and order in their communities, and often blame the chiefs for 'not doing their work properly' when situations of conflict arise. For example, in 2004, the Police Chief of Staff called on the Port Vila Town Council of Chiefs to send their unemployed young people back to their islands. He is reported to have said: 'There is no need [for] the chiefs to wait for a law to order the unemployed to go home because…common sense dictates that people without jobs in Port Vila immediately become a burden on their friends and relatives and the state.'[102]

The problems generated by such disagreements between the police and the chiefs over the responsibility to deal with certain situations are discussed further in the next chapter.

A final point emerging from the research is the difference between the views of the chiefs and the police about which party should control the relationship. The police are clearly of the view that *they* should be the ones telling the chiefs what matters to resolve and when they will give them assistance, whereas the chiefs generally view the police as being primarily there to assist them, and hence become frustrated when they fail to do so.

The prisons

At present, there are two prisons for male prisoners and one for female prisoners in Port Vila, a prison at Luganville in Santo[103] and also one at Lakatoro in Malekula.[104] In addition, on islands where there are police posts there is often a room that is used as the police holding cell. In 2006, the management of the prisons was transferred from the police to the civilian Department of Correctional Services (*Correctional Services Act 2006*).

The condition of the prisons today

The poor conditions of Vanuatu's prisons have been highlighted by Amnesty International, which referred to the cruel and inhumane conditions in the 'decaying, overcrowded former colonial prison[s]',[105] and also by the Vanuatu Ombudsman.[106] The local newspapers and various reports by aid donors also regularly comment on them.[107] The research for this study found structural problems with prison buildings rendering them dangerous during earthquakes and cyclones; prisoners' lack of protection from the elements as a result of large holes in the roofs, resulting in prisoners sleeping in sodden clothes and bedding; blocked showers and toilets; overcrowding;[108] lack of any sort of rehabilitation activities apart from sporadic visits by local church groups; lack of separation of violent criminals and defendants on remand; lack of facilities for juvenile[109] and female prisoners (except in Vila);[110] lack of cooking facilities and a lack of security.[111] In 2005, the Chief Inspector of Prisons stated that the police could do nothing much about the security of the prisoners because of the poor condition of the prisons, commenting that '[w]e only counsel them about not running away from jail'.[112] All the people involved in the administration of the prisons are very critical of them. The former Assistant Superintendent of Prisons stated, '[I]f we continue the way we are it is a losing battle. We are not winning anything.'[113]

In 2006, the prisoners staged a break-out in protest over the conditions they faced, complaining about 'poor diet, disgusting toilets, dilapidated building, no exercise, no visitation from family and no access to telephone calls or medical treatment'.[114] High-risk prisoners also complained of being shackled in chains with other prisoners at all times, even for bathing and going to the toilet, for up to eight months at a time.[115] The response by the police to the prisoners' claims was ambiguous: in the same breath that they said the claims were exaggerated and unfounded, they justified their treatment for a number of reasons, including the prisoners' ability to 'escape in a blink of an eye'.[116]

It is to be hoped that the transfer of authority from the police to the Department of Correctional Services (which occurred in 2006) improves the condition of prisoners in Vanuatu. Transparency International has, however, cast some doubt on whether the proposed reforms will in fact solve the deep-seated problems in the prisons, commenting that 'the new bills [do] not adequately ensure that prisoners are kept in safe conditions and that minimum international standards for prisoners' and prison conditions are met'. Since the change in authority, there have been regular letters of complaint in the newspapers, alleging that prisoners are allowed to get drunk in prison, are allowed to freely wander around town and that they have used the prison house as a repository for stolen goods.[117]

On a more theoretical level, there are debates in Vanuatu about the concept of imprisonment per se. A substantial percentage of the population, especially chiefs, is critical of imprisonment for a variety of reasons. One is that imprisonment alienates people from their communities. For example, the head of the Vanuatu Council of Churches stated that in the traditional systems when people were punished they were still a member of the community, they still participated. In prison, however, there is isolation from the community and this remains even after they have come out of prison. Also, because the prisoners have been removed from their community, they tend to remain in town and do not go back to their island community after they have served their sentence.[118]

Another criticism is that merely imprisoning an offender does not allow for the relationships between him/her and the victim and the community to be mended. A respondent stated:

> In law when you put a man in jail then he will come out still cross and it will not finish. If he sees you on the road somewhere he will think about the fight you had. But if all the chiefs sit down with the two parties and fix it in *kastom* then at the same time we can drink kava and forget…it is finished.[119]

A prisoner made a comment along the same lines, despairing that when a person went to prison even for a long time, the problem was still there when they came out and it never finished. A chief identified a further problem, commenting that the problem with prisons was that when the prisoner was released he assaulted the person who put him there.

Many respondents also noted that sending people to prison harmed their dependants. This is often the justification used by chiefs attempting to remove cases from the state system. For example, in *Public Prosecutor vs Munrel*,[120] the court referred to the fact that there had been letters from the local chiefs setting out the difficulties that imprisonment would cause and even a letter from the victim asking the court to return the defendant to look after her children. The former President of the Malvatumauri stated:

> [I]f you put someone in jail for an example who is married, has got…[a] wife and children back at home, once you put that person into jail we say in custom that it looks like you've put more burden on the whole family now because he should be at home to look after the kids, the

woman cannot look after the children by herself. So we say in custom, putting people in jail you put more burdens on the whole family.[121]

Finally, some officials in the state system are of the view that imprisonment does not really work as an effective deterrent. A legal officer in the Public Prosecutor's Office stated that although some people learned from being prosecuted and did not repeat their mistake, there were a lot of people who were prosecuted who went to jail and then when released continued with the same behaviour.[122] A judicial officer similarly commented that people came out of jail and repeated what they had previously done.

Despite these criticisms, it appears that the majority of the population accepts that prisons are necessary as a last option for dealing with persistent 'strongheds'. A significant percentage of the population also believes that prison sentences are currently too lenient and not imposed in enough cases, particularly in relation to sexual offences.

The relationship between the prisons and the *kastom* system

Until 2006, it would have been accurate to state that there was no relationship at all between the *kastom* system and the prisons. In 2006, however, two developments initiated a relationship of sorts between the two systems. The first was the Correctional Services Project, which was funded by NZAID and started in 2005. The project was initiated by the Amnesty International report discussed above, and an initial feasibility study concluded that 'the demand for correctional services was likely to increase in coming years, and that urgent action was required to update the management and operations of these services in Vanuatu'.[123]

The project devised a number of reform proposals that 'create opportunities for linkages between *Kastomary* processes and the Courts'.[124] A central proposal was the establishment of a Community Probation Service, which adopted a 'Community Justice Process'. This process is said to build on and strengthen the Vanuatu tradition of community participation in the justice process and to preserve and enhance the existing practice of chiefs resolving disputes in a traditional context. The process is based on the idea that at a number of points there are opportunities for matters to be referred back to community leaders for resolution and reconciliation. This proposal is quite general and does not address many of the difficult questions arising from the interaction of the two systems.[125]

Perhaps because of these unresolved issues, although the general policy documents generated by the task force engage in a direct way with the relationship between *kastom* and the state system, the real legislative provisions that have emerged from the process[126] focus almost entirely on the state system.[127] The changes relating to *kastom* are relatively minor: a broadening of the court's ability to take a customary payment into account in sentencing;[128] the ability of the court to order compensation to be paid to a victim as part of criminal proceedings;[129] the creation of community work options; and the establishment of a probation service.[130] Of these, the last development has the most potential, as probation officers will liaise between the two systems, thereby creating better linkages between them and bringing issues in their relationship to the fore.

The second relationship between the prisons and the *kastom* system was an incident in 2006 in which 20 prisoners escaped from a prison in Vila and sent a letter to the Malvatumauri, asking that it publicise their concerns about the conditions they faced in prison.[131] The Malvatumauri took the case on board, stating, 'It is the role of chiefs to maintain peace in the community and when someone is in trouble and enters our *nakamal*, we take him back peacefully.'[132] The chiefs organised a peaceful walk through town with the prisoners and officers from the Prime Minister's Office, performed a custom ceremony, obtained an assurance from the government that the prisoners' concerns would be taken up and handed the prisoners back to the authorities. It remains to be seen whether or not this incident precipitates a closer relationship between the prisoners and the chiefs, as it has given rise to much public debate. For example, a letter in the *Vanuatu Daily Post* stated: 'maybe let's put the chiefs in front of the Rehabilitation program of the correctional service institute because the so-called prisoners have expressed that in reality, they have confidence in the chiefs—maybe from there we can move on.'[133]

The Public Prosecutor and the Public Solicitor

The Public Prosecutor has an office in Vila and one in Santo.[134] The Public Solicitor's Office was established under Article 56 of the constitution and its role is to provide legal assistance to needy people or to any person on being directed to do so by the Supreme Court.[135]

The condition of the prosecution and Public Solicitor

The prosecution and the Public Solicitor have been besieged with problems in recent years. There is an extremely high staff turnover in both offices, with a pattern of new lawyers being employed but leaving as soon as they can find work in the more profitable private sector, resulting in there being very few lawyers with much experience working in the office at any one time.[136] The lack of lawyers and lack of experience mean that cases are regularly mishandled, overlooked and, in the case of the prosecution, dismissed by the court 'for want of prosecution'.[137]

A further problem is the centralisation of the two offices in Vila. Due to budgetary constraints, it is difficult for the lawyers to tour the islands to prosecute and defend, meaning that cases must wait for long periods before they can be heard. This has clear ramifications for the ability of prosecutors to secure convictions as during this time evidence is often lost, witnesses disappear and memories fade. For example, the local newspaper reported that in August 2005 seven criminal cases were adjourned in Santo following the absence of representatives from the prosecution and Public Solicitor.[138] The situation is even worse in the islands. In 2004, the court visited Gaua and dealt with cases concerning intentional assault and destruction of property going back to 2001 due to lack of police prosecutors.[139] As the Public Solicitor has no office even in Luganville, there is growing dissatisfaction with the situation and criticism that the government is not meeting its constitutional obligations to afford a lawyer to everyone charged with a serious offence.[140]

A final major problem for the prosecution is the service of summonses to defendants and witnesses. There is a continuing dispute between the police and the prosecution over responsibility for the service of summonses—a time-consuming job that requires the use of a vehicle, and these are in short supply. As a result, summonses are frequently not served and, again, the courts regularly dismiss huge numbers of cases 'for want of prosecution'.[141]

The relationship between the prosecution and the Public Solicitor with the *kastom* system

The relationship between the prosecution and the *kastom* system is informal and centres mostly on negotiation with chiefs about the appropriate forum for particular cases to be settled in. Chiefs will therefore often approach the prosecution and ask for cases to be dropped as they have either been, or will be, dealt with in *kastom*. There is no official policy for legal officers in the prosecution on how to deal with these kinds of situations, and as a result there is a great deal of variation in the approaches of the individual prosecutors. A recent Court of Appeal decision, *Public Prosecutor vs Gideon*,[142] clearly sets out what the correct 'legal' response to a request to drop a case after a *kastom* payment should be:

> Customary settlement in this case was initiated by a letter from the village Chief to the respondent demanding the payment of a fine of VT30,000, a pig and mats by a specified date, failing which criminal charges would be laid against him. The demands of the letter were duly met but that did not prevent the criminal charge being laid against the respondent who might well entertain some sense of grievance…We are concerned…at the suggestion in the letter that performance of customary settlement could somehow influence the laying of criminal charges in this case. We desire to dispel any notion that customary settlement can have such an

effect in an offence as serious as occurred in this case where the public interest dictates that criminal charges must be laid.

These statements, however, reflect an idealised view of the prosecution process rather than the reality, as a significant number of cases *are* dropped after representations from complainants and chiefs.[143] The problems that these sorts of negotiations over forum raise are discussed further in the next chapter. Conversely, a legal officer said that a lot of people came after a chief had already dealt with a case and said they were not happy with the way the chief had decided the case.

The Public Solicitor relates with the *kastom* system largely by getting information about customary payments that have been performed in order to use this as a mitigating factor in sentencing submissions.

The Malvatumauri

The closest thing to state recognition of the *kastom* system is the establishment of the Malvatumauri.[144] The Malvatumauri comprises chiefs who are elected every four years from every region in Vanuatu and it meets only twice a year.[145] The role given to the Malvatumauri by the constitution is limited. It has 'a general competence to discuss all matters relating to custom and tradition' and also it 'may make recommendations for the preservation and promotion of ni-Vanuatu culture and languages'.[146] It is not, however, mandatory for any legislation to be given to it for discussion or approval. As a result, very few pieces of legislation are ever submitted to it and to date it has not played a very significant role.

In recent years, however, the Malvatumauri has become more active in establishing structures for chiefly councils and attempting to establish procedures for registering chiefly title. It has also become more vocal in expressing dissatisfaction with the powers of chiefs in general, arguing that the State should legislate for chiefly powers in relation to conflict management. As early as 1983, the Malvatumauri produced its 'Custom Policy', which set out a codified set of customary laws purportedly applicable to the entire country and covering many of the same issues as the *Penal Code Act*, such as murder and damage to property.[147] In 1990, the chiefs told the Constitutional Review Committee that 'although they currently have a role to play in villages and island courts, they still face problems since the *Constitution* does not give them enough power to straighten out all problems'.[148] Then in 1992, the Malvatumauri proposed to the government that it should establish 'customary courts'. It is clear from this proposal that the chiefs envisage that the 'chiefly system of justice' should become part of the state court system rather than operating outside and parallel to it.[149] The memorandum that accompanied the custom courts proposal notes that:

- the chiefly system of justice remains important in most areas of Vanuatu, particularly those in which there is little police presence or control
- as it is a working system, which is acknowledged by all, it is wrong to treat it as some type of alternative system of justice; it should be brought fully into the judicial system
- at the same time, it is open to abuse; conflicts of interest may not be acknowledged, unwritten rules may be altered and decisions may be unfair with no realistic right of appeal.[150]

It appears that little was done in response to this proposal until the establishment of the Chiefs' Legislation Project in 2000. The government established this project, presumably as the result of pressure from the Malvatumauri. The aim of the project was to 'examine the chiefly institution in its traditional and cultural context with the view to translate it to accommodate any potential threats to internal peace and stability' and thus to 'legalise the roles and functions of chiefs throughout the country, in a way that would be adaptable to contemporary Vanuatu so as to assist, facilitate and generally be conducive to nation building'.[151] The project approached the issue of the lack of customary law in the state system from an almost polar opposite direction to that adopted by the legal academics discussed above. Right from the start, the focus was on how the *kastom* system was operating and the problems it was facing, rather than any examination of the written laws and the state courts.

The first step in the project was the commissioning of a study into the chiefly systems and various roles of chiefs in Vanuatu today and into the views of relevant key stakeholders in order to 'assess and advise upon the scope for the legislation of the chiefly systems and their roles and examining compatible avenues of adapting these systems with the government and judicial systems'.[152] The study was undertaken in 2001 and a report was produced, which set out a number of findings about the operation of the *kastom* system and its relationship with the State. The findings of this report are broadly consistent with those of the present study, although in a much simplified form.[153]

The report recommended that two pieces of legislation be drafted: a Chiefs' Bill, which 'must acknowledge and empower the chief in his roles and functions both as an individual chief and collectively with other chiefs in courts and other areas where the chief has a role';[154] and a Village Courts Bill, which 'will give recognition and official status to the custom courts and shall provide for their developments and improved administrations'.[155] As the report was mostly a sociological survey rather than draft legislation, it was given to an experienced law professor to turn into legislative form. Due to a number of difficulties, the work on the legislation did not begin until 2005. The draft was given to the Malvatumauri, who then edited it considerably, removing many of the safeguards concerned with the appointment and dismissal of chiefs.[156]

The Bill for the National Council of Chiefs Act (2006) that emerged from this process moves away from the balanced approach advocated in the 1992 proposal. Although most of the bill is concerned with the organisation of the Malvatumauri and the establishment of councils of customary chiefs on the islands and in urban areas, there was an attempt to give chiefs the unlimited power to 'resolve disputes according to local customs' (Sections 13[1][a] and 14[1]) and to make 'by-laws' (Sections 14[2] and [3], 15 and 16). The bill also provided that chiefly councils could require the assistance of the police to enforce their penalties and that police officers 'must provide such assistance'—again, with no limitations on this power (Section 16[3]).[157] These provisions, however, were removed even before the bill went before Parliament[158] and the act that was passed was concerned solely with the organisation of various chiefly councils (*National Council of Chiefs Act 2006*). The Secretary of the Malvatumauri commented at the Judiciary Conference in 2006 that the act that had finally been passed through Parliament was like a dog that had had all its teeth removed and yet the dog was still expected to hunt pigs.[159]

Conclusion

The previous three chapters have used a legal-pluralist perspective to provide a window into the complex operation of conflict management in Vanuatu. We have seen how focusing on institutions, processes and principles rather than purely on substantive norms has allowed a more holistic picture to emerge than has previously been possible. Further, exploring the points of interaction of the two systems has generated rich data concerning the dynamics of legal pluralism and the characteristics of the linkages between the two systems. These data lead to a number of tentative conclusions about the nature of legal pluralism in Vanuatu today.

Since colonisation, ni-Vanuatu have been faced with at least two systems of law that they can and do draw on, depending on particular circumstances (such as the accessibility and strength of the systems and the nature of the conflict) as well as personal preferences (such as support for or mistrust of *kastom* chiefs/the State or colonial powers, and belief about which system will lead to a more advantageous outcome). The legitimate scope of the two systems has never been formalised; instead, the unofficial division of jurisdiction has been left to individual institutions and administrators to negotiate, and the results of this process have and do vary considerably over time and place.

Overall, the current linkages between the systems are largely informal, dynamic and subject to continuous negotiation. We have also seen that, ironically, there is less real engagement between the two systems in practice in those few areas where legal pluralism is legislatively provided for[160] than other places where unofficial relationships and allocations of responsibility between the two systems have been created by the individuals involved.

Svesson draws a distinction between a situation of *legal pluralism*, where legal systems operate in parallel, and *inter-legality*, where there is 'continuous interaction in the main between different legal perceptions, thereby influencing and shaping new normative orders adapted to considering cultural diversity'.[161] Generally in Vanuatu, we have seen little evidence of inter-legality in this sense, as the development of the state system has not been influenced perceptibly by the *kastom* system. More importantly, and perhaps symptomatically, there has also been little active dialogue between the two systems or interchange of different legal views. This is due in part to the lack of centralisation of the *kastom* system, endemic political instability and the difficulties of communication in Vanuatu generally, but also to the lack of institutional spaces for such dialogue to occur.[162] During the Condominium, district agents and assessors were formally charged with liaising between the two systems and found themselves confronted with particular situations requiring them to reconcile procedural and substantive differences between the two systems. Since independence, such roles have disappeared and there is very limited opportunity for conflicts between the systems on the level of legal principle to arise and be articulated in this way.

At present, however, the lack of real engagement between the two systems means that the main 'hotspots'[163] between them, rather than operating at the level of contested legal principles, involve disputes over jurisdiction, particularly in relation to cases involving women and youth. This issue is complicated by the fact that *kastom* is often used as a vehicle for chiefs and others to express concern about, and try to regain control over, the societal changes being precipitated by the growing engagement with globalisation. The problems caused by such disputes are discussed at length in the next chapter.

A cause of increasing tension between the two systems is also the State's heavy reliance on the *kastom* system, especially in rural areas, coupled with its reluctance to contribute any resources or recognition in return. It was perhaps inevitable that the chiefs have become tired of being treated as the unpaid and unacknowledged assistants of the state system and are increasingly vocalising demands for legislative recognition of chiefly powers. In the past, the state system has been able to brush off such demands by trotting out platitudes about the authority and power of the chiefs resting in community respect, but it is unlikely that this response will be tenable for much longer, especially given evidence of the partial unravelling of respect shown in the previous chapter.

A further important finding to emerge from the discussion is that today the state system is failing to meet many of the challenges it is confronted with in terms of capacity and human rights standards. The major problems within the state system identified in this chapter can be summarised (Table 5.1).

Table 5.1 Problems with the state system

- The state courts lack legitimacy and are viewed by many as an alien system in which people feel unable to properly tell their story (*'kot blong waetman'*).
- Women and children in particular find the state system confusing and frightening and their justice needs are often not satisfied by it.
- The state system is inaccessible to a large proportion of the rural population due to its limited geographical reach.
- The state system is very slow, especially in remote areas where the courts tour only sporadically.
- The state courts often exclude community participation due to the practice of court sittings taking place in the urban centres rather than the communities in which the crime occurred.
- The state courts are pushed to breaking point with their workload.
- State court orders are often not enforced, especially in the lower levels of the courts.
- The police are under-resourced, under-trained and affected by low morale.
- There is a culture of police brutality, which causes juveniles particularly to regard police officers with fear rather than as a source of assistance.
- The prison buildings are decrepit and prisoners are held in circumstances that breach their human rights.
- Many in the community see imprisonment as a punishment serving no real benefit and causing significant hardship to the family and community of the offender.
- The prosecution and the Public Solicitor are under-resourced and understaffed and have little reach outside Port Vila.

Thus, any discussion of the relationship between the *kastom* system and constitutional rights and freedoms should take place in a context that acknowledges that the state system itself currently breaches a number of fundamental rights, in particular freedom from inhumane treatment (the treatment of prisoners), equal treatment under the law (the treatment of women by the police) and the right to a fair hearing within a reasonable time (the failure by the courts to deal with cases in a timely manner). In addition, we have seen that generally the *kastom* system is far more consistent than the state system in meeting the expectations and demands of its users. These findings suggest a continued need for the *kastom* system in Vanuatu, as the state system cannot meet the current needs of the population by itself and is unlikely to be able to do so in the near or even distant future given the additional factors of population explosion and urban drift.

Finally, there was a strongly held belief by the majority of respondents that the current gap between the two systems should be bridged in some way, but there was a lack of consensus about how best to achieve this. The lack of progress on this issue since independence, despite considerable will and legislative scope to do so, suggests that more than a new legal framework is needed. How much more is discussed in Chapter 8.

ENDNOTES

[1] von Benda-Beckman and von Benda-Beckman, 'The dynamics of change and continuity in plural legal orders', p. 32.

[2] Dinnen, Sinclair 2002, *Building bridges: law and justice reform in Papua New Guinea*, Discussion Paper 2002/2, State Society and Governance in Melanesia Research Paper Series, The Australian National University, viewed 31 May 2007, <http://rspas.anu.edu.au/melanesia/discussion.php>, p. 14.

[3] There are currently resident magistrates in Port Vila, Luganville and Malekula, who go on tour to neighbouring islands subject to funding and case loads, and there is also a registry of the Magistrate's Court in Vanua Lava.

[4] In Vanua Lava, Santo, Malekula, Efate, Ambae, Tanna and Pentecost.

[5] Many times, the difficulties of communication are such that even the complainant is not notified of the result of the proceedings.

[6] Except in the case of applications for Domestic Violence Protection Orders in the Supreme Court, for which the court fee is quite low and no lawyer is necessary. Although there is a Public Solicitor, the office is overworked and has only one office, in Vila (see below under 'The Public Prosecutor and the Public Solicitor'). As a result, people often feel compelled to pay for a lawyer or to be unrepresented, and lawyers' fees are notoriously high.

[7] Interview with a government legal officer (Santo, 15 November 2004).

[8] At the opening of the court in 2007, the Chief Justice announced that there were 1171 cases lodged with the Supreme Court the previous year and only 205 completed, 2325 cases lodged with the Magistrate's Court and only 1749 completed and the Island Courts received 764 and completed 388. See Garae, Len 2007, 'Chief Justice opens courts', *Vanuatu Daily Post* (Port Vila), 10 February 2007, p. 1.

[9] Paterson, Don 2004, *Report on Customary Law Research Project*, AusAID, p. 37.

[10] Interview with a state police prosecutor (Santo, 18 November 2004).

[11] The Chief Justice announced at the opening of the court in 2007 that the Pacific Judicial Development Program had trained 225 Island Court justices and that a senior administrator for the Island Courts had been appointed. See Garae, Len 2007, 'Chief Justice makes new appointments', *Vanuatu Daily Post* (Port Vila), 14 February 2007, p. 2.

[12] These terms were coined by Woodman: see Chapter 2 (under 'The possibilities and limitations of legal pluralism for Melanesia') for a discussion concerning them.

[13] Previous analysis of the role of customary law in Vanuatu, and indeed elsewhere throughout the region, either has not taken account of the institutional side at all or has conflated it with the consideration of substantive customary law. There are, however, enormous differences between the state courts using customary law in their decisions on the one hand, and the state courts recognising decisions made by other institutions administering those norms on the other.

[14] The previous chapter discussed how the *kastom* system used substantive norms from the state system.

[15] See, for example, Weisbrot, David 1988, 'Law and native custom in Vanuatu', *Law and Anthropology*, vol. 3, p. 103; Weisbrot, David 1989, 'Custom, pluralism and realism in Vanuatu: legal development and the role of customary law', *Pacific Studies*, vol. 13, no. 1, p. 65; de Deckker, Paul and Faberon, Jean-Yves 2001, *Custom and the Law*; Powles, Guy 1997, 'The common law at bay? The scope and status of customary law regimes in the Pacific', *Journal of Pacific Studies*, vol. 21, p. 61; Powles, Guy 2004, Some thoughts on the future of customary law in Pacific island states, Paper presented at the Australasian Law Teachers Association Conference, Darwin, July 2004; Ottley, B. 1992, 'Custom and introduced

criminal justice', in R. James and I. Fraser (eds), *Legal Issues in Developing Society*, p. 128; Ottley, Brian 2002, 'Reconciling modernity and tradition: PNG's underlying law act', *Reform*, vol. 80, p. 22; Ottley and Zorn, 'Criminal law in Papua New Guinea'; Corrin Care, Jennifer 1999, 'Customary law and human rights in Solomon Islands: a commentary on *Remisio Pusi v James Leni and Others* (cc 218/1995, unreported [High Ct., Solom. Is.])', *Journal of Legal Pluralism and Unofficial Law*, vol. 43, p. 135; Corrin Care, Jennifer 2001, 'Customary law in conflict: the status of customary law and introduced law in post-colonial Solomon Islands', *University of Queensland Law Journal*, vol. 21, no. 2, p. 167; Corrin Care, Jennifer 2002, 'Wisdom and worthy customs: customary law in the South Pacific', *Reform*, vol. 80, p. 31; Corrin Care and Zorn, 'Legislating pluralism'; Zorn, 'Lawyers, anthropologists and the study of law'; Zorn and Corrin Care, '"Barava tru"'; Scaglion, *Customary Law in Papua New Guinea* ; Fraser, Ian 1999, 'Legal theory in Melanesia: pluralism? Dualism? Pluralism long dualism?', *Journal of South Pacific Law*, vol. 3, <http://paclii.org.vu/journals/fJSPL/index.shtml>; Dinnen, Sinclair 1995, 'Custom, community and criminal justice in Papua New Guinea', in Jonathan Aleck and Jackson Rannells (eds), *Custom at the Crossroads*, p. 148; Narokobi, 'Law and custom in Melanesia', and *Lo Blong Yumi Yet*; Paterson, Don 1995, 'South Pacific customary law and common law: their interrelationship', *Commonwealth Law Bulletin*, vol. 21, no. 2, p. 660; Paterson, *Report on Customary Law Research Project*; Ntumy, 'The dream of a Melanesian jurisprudence'; Newton Cain, Tess 2001, 'Convergence or clash? The recognition of customary law and practice in sentencing decisions of the courts of the Pacific island region', *Melbourne Journal of International Law*, vol. 2, no. 1; Vaai, Saleimoa 1997, 'The idea of law: a Pacific perspective', *The Journal of Pacific Studies*, vol. 21, p. 225; Jowitt, 'Indigenous land grievances, customary land disputes and restorative justice'; Hughes, 'Legal pluralism and the problem of identity'; James, R. 1992, 'A comparative view of the underlying law', in R. James and I. Fraser (eds), *Legal Issues in Developing Society*, p. 146; Aleck, 'Beyond recognition'; Aleck, Jonathan and Rannells, Jackson 1995, *Custom at the Crossroads*.

[16] This is not to deny that this is not the case in other jurisdictions as well.

[17] Government of Vanuatu n.d., *Constitution of the Republic of Vanuatu*, Article 95(2).

[18] Ibid.

[19] Ibid.

[20] Ibid., Article 47(1).

[21] In fact, the Law Commission has never been established.

[22] Government of Vanuatu n.d., *Constitution of the Republic of Vanuatu*, Article 5.

[23] Ibid., Article 52.

[24] *Criminal Procedure Code* (Cap 136, Section 153), repealed by the *Criminal Procedure Code (Amendment) Act 1989*.

[25] *Criminal Procedure Code* (Cap 136, Section 185) (this section does not appear to have been repealed but it makes no sense without the sections that have been repealed).

[26] Interview with Professor Paterson (Port Vila, 12 October 2005).

[27] Section 1 provides that the Chief Justice may define the jurisdiction of each court 'as he shall see fit'.

[28] Jowitt, Anita 1999, 'Island courts in Vanuatu', *Journal of South Pacific Law*, vol. 3, <http://paclii.org.vu/journals/fJSPL/index.shtml> The warrants of appointment for the Island Courts that exist authorise them to determine certain minor criminal offences specified in the *Penal Code* (Cap 135) and other legislation, civil claims relating to contracts and torts not exceeding vt100 000 and claims for maintenance of legitimate family and also illegitimate children.

[29] Weisbrot, 'Custom, pluralism and realism in Vanuatu', p. 115.

[30] Rousseau, The achievement of simultaneity, p. 171.

[31] Larcom, 'Custom by decree', p. 176.

[32] Malvatumauri, 'Kastom polisi blong Malvatumauri'.

[33] For a thorough critique of the Island Courts, see Jowitt, 'Island courts in Vanuatu'.

[34] This replaces, and somewhat expands, the repealed Section 118 of the *Criminal Procedure Code* (Cap 136).

[35] The previous section provided that after doing this the court may 'thereupon order the proceedings to be stayed or terminated', but this phrase is not present in the new section, although the court has a general power to discharge a matter.

36 Ralph Reganvanu, Director of the Vanuatu Cultural Centre (Author's notes from the Conference on *Kastom* and the Constitution, University of the South Pacific, Emalus Campus, Port Vila, Vanuatu, 4 October 2004).

37 When I asked one judge why he did not encourage lawyers to make submissions on the basis of customary law he said that the problem lay with the legislature, who had a duty to further develop the principles about custom being part of the law 'set down boldly in the constitution' (Interview with a judge, Port Vila, 20 August 2004).

38 Interview with a judge (Port Vila, 5 September 2003).

39 For example, one lawyer said that he did not feel there would ever be any point raising issues of *kastom* in his arguments, except for mitigation because '*kastom* is not written and so in that respect it is not recognised' (Interview with a lawyer, Port Vila, 10 September 2003).

40 Narokobi, 'In search of a Melanesian jurisprudence'.

41 Paterson, 'South Pacific customary law and common law'.

42 This is demonstrated by the case of *Boe & Taga vs Thomas* (1980–94, Van LR 293), in which the court was considering the question of compensation for the death of a child. Justice Cooke justified ignoring *kastom* by finding that two old English acts—namely, the *Fatal Accidents Act 1846* and the *Law Reform (Miscellaneous Provisions) Act 1934*—applied and that he was therefore not compelled to turn to *kastom*. Further, in all the courts, customary law can be applied only if it is 'not in conflict with any written law and is not contrary to justice, morality and good order' (*Island Courts Act*, Cap 167, Section 10). If a higher court trained in the common law tradition determines the ideas of justice, morality and good order, this also has the potential to severely limit its use.

43 See, for example, Corrin Care, 'Customary law in conflict', p. 174.

44 *Banga vs Waiwo*, 1996, VUSC 5, <http://www.paclii.org.vu>

45 Bourdieu, Pierre and Wacquant, Loic 1992, *An Invitation to Reflexive Sociology*, p. 126.

46 See, for example, Forsyth, Miranda 2006b, 'Sorcery and the criminal law in Vanuatu', *LawAsia*, p. 1, in which I discuss the difficulties state law has had in dealing with sorcery in Vanuatu.

47 Weisbrot, 'Law and native custom in Vanuatu', p. 115.

48 *Banga vs Waiwo*, 1996, VUSC 5, http://www.paclii.org.vu

49 Zorn, Jean 1991, 'Making law in Papua New Guinea: the influence of customary law on common law', *Journal of Pacific Studies*, vol. 14, no. 4, p. 24.

50 Ntumy, 'The dream of a Melanesian jurisprudence', p. 10.

51 This provision replaces the repealed Section 119 of the *Criminal Procedure Code* (Cap 136), which provided much the same, although it used the word 'may' instead of 'must'.

52 *Waiwo vs Waiwo and Banga*, 1996, VUMC 1, <http://www.paclii.org.vu>

53 For an interesting discussion of how other courts in the region have dealt with the issue of taking into account customary remedies. See New Zealand Law Commission, *Converging currents*, pp. 180–4.

54 *Public Prosecutor vs Gideon*, 2002, VUCA 7, <http://www.paclii.org.vu>

55 Interview with a judge.

56 For a further discussion, see Paterson, Don 2006, 'Customary reconciliation in sentencing for sexual offences: a review of *Public Prosecutor v Ben and Others* and *Public Prosecutor v Tarilingi and Gamma*', *Journal of South Pacific Law*, vol. 10, no. 1, <http://paclii.org.vu/journals/fJSPL/index.shtml>

57 Interview with a judge (Port Vila, 20 August 2004).

58 Tinning, Esther 2004, 'Court sentences brothers and sister for assault', *Vanuatu Daily Post* (Port Vila), 11 September 2004, p. 8.

59 Interview with a judge (Port Vila, 20 August 2004).

60 Interview with a judge (Port Vila, 5 September 2003).

61 Interview with a judicial officer (Port Vila, 5 April 2004).

62 Interview with a senior government lawyer (Port Vila, 10 September 2003).

63 See a report of detailed discussion about this at the Vanuatu Judiciary Conference in 2006. Forsyth, Miranda 2006a, *Report on the Vanuatu Judiciary Conference 2006: The relationship between the* kastom *and state justice systems*, University of the South Pacific, <http://paclii.org.vu/vu/2006_jud_conf_report.html>

[64] There have been considerable tensions between the two wings that have been played out in the saga involving the appointment of a new Commissioner of Police in 2002, resulting in the arrest of the Police Services Commission, including the Attorney-General, the Secretary to the President and the Ombudsman.

[65] In Port Vila, Luganville, Malekula and Tanna.

[66] One in Sola, two in Ambae, one in Pentecost (which is not currently operational), one in Aneitym, one in south Malekula, one in Epi and one in Tongoa.

[67] Newton Cain, Tess 2003, *Final Report Base Line Survey Organisational Climate Survey*, AusAID.

[68] Penama Province 1994, *Penama Social Development Plan*.

[69] The Secretary-General of Torba Province further explained that this lack of resources placed significant limits on the ability of the police to deal effectively with crime because if an officer wanted to go to another island he must apply for an impress from headquarters and this could take a month. Consequently, if there is an emergency the police cannot react quickly.

[70] Joy, Shirley 2003, 'Police plead for government support to fight crime', *Vanuatu Daily Post* (Port Vila), 22 October 2003.

[71] In fact, most recently, when I hailed a police truck for assistance, the two people driving told me that they were not, in fact, police officers, but that they could drive me to the police station if I wanted them to!

[72] Interview with a lawyer (Santo, 18 November 2004). I experienced this also during my year as a prosecutor.

[73] Newton Cain, *Final Report Base Line Survey Organisational Climate Survey*.

[74] Lini, 'Law and order situation in Luganville questioned'.

[75] See Super, *A Needs Assessment of Juvenile Justice Issues in Fiji and Vanuatu*; Mitchell, *Young People Speak*; Morgan, *Conference Report of the Governance for the Future*; Rousseau, *The Report of the Juvenile Justice Project*; Ombudsman of Vanuatu 2002, *Public report on the unlawful arrest and detention of Mrs Aspin Jack*, VUOM 11, http://www.paclii.org.vu; Ombudsman of Vanuatu 2003b, *Public report on police brutality during operation on Central Pentecost*, VUOM 16, <http://www.paclii.org.vu>

[76] Rousseau, The achievement of simultaneity, p. 202.

[77] Interview with the Director of Youth and Sports (Port Vila, 11 June 2004).

[78] A youth representative in a rural community reported that the police often gave very severe beatings, sometimes requiring hospitalisation, but the youth believed it was the policeman's right to do this if the person did not surrender.

[79] *Working Group for Justice vs Government of the Republic of Vanuatu*, 2002, VUSC 55, http://www.paclii.org.vu

[80] Mason, Merrin 2000, 'Domestic violence in Vanuatu', in Sinclair Dinnen and Ley Allison (eds), *Reflections on Violence in Melanesia*, p. 119.

[81] Ibid., p. 128.

[82] Ibid.

[83] *Civil Procedure Rules* (2002, Part 16, Division 4).

[84] Interview with a senior police officer (Port Vila, 29 July 2003).

[85] Interview with the Director of the Vanuatu Women's Centre (Port Vila, 7 May 2004).

[86] Interview with a senior police officer (Port Vila, 6 April 2004).

[87] For example, a police post without a vehicle or Magistrate's Court will rely more heavily on the chiefs than one with these resources.

[88] I was there only three weeks after the new policy.

[89] Interview with a police officer (Port Vila, 8 November 2004).

[90] Garae, Len 2005, 'Chiefs diffuse Tanna fight', *Vanuatu Daily Post* (Port Vila), 8 August 2005, p. 1.

[91] See also Rousseau, The achievement of simultaneity, pp. 207–8.

[92] *Public Prosecutor vs Kota and Others* (1989–94, 2 VLR 661).

[93] Interview with a senior police officer (Port Vila, 29 July 2003). Examples of the benefits of the chiefs and police working together are regularly reported in the local newspapers. For example, in 2004, the police launched an operation in Malekula to deal with outstanding criminal cases dating back to 1999 that had not been dealt with due to a shortage of manpower at the police post. The police worked closely with the chiefs, who delivered the suspects to the police station and the police then decided which

cases to put before the court and which to refer back to the chiefs to solve. See Walter, Matthew 2004b, 'Forty suspects netted in Malekula operation', *Vanuatu Daily Post* (Port Vila), 26 November 2004, p. 2.

[94] Garae, Len 2005, 'Tension high after Ambrym killing', *Vanuatu Daily Post* (Port Vila), 11 October 2005, p. 3. After the 3 March riots in 2007, the *Vanuatu Daily Post* also reported the Minister of Internal Affairs saying, '[T]he chiefs of the two communities of Tanna and Ambrym have already been informed to get those that are involved in the problem to surrender by sunset yesterday afternoon' ('Two confirmed dead in Ambrym and Tanna clash', *Vanuatu Daily Post* [Port Vila], 5 March 2007, p. 1).

[95] Wittersheim, Eric 2005, *Melanesian elites and modern politics in New Caledonia and Vanuatu*, Discussion Paper 1998/3, State Society and Governance in Melanesia Discussion Paper Series, The Australian National University, <http://rspas.anu.edu.au/melanesia/discussion.php> See also Amnesty International 1998, *No Safe Place for Prisoners*.

[96] These two incidents are discussed in further detail in Chapter 4 under 'Chiefly misbehaviour' and Chapter 6 under 'Dispute and confusion over jurisdiction'.

[97] 'Two confirmed dead in Ambrym and Tanna clash', *Vanuatu Daily Post* (Port Vila), 5 March 2007, p. 1; 'West Ambrym chiefs willing to supply local food to victims', *Vanuatu Daily Post* (Port Vila), 10 March 2007, p. 3; 'The roots of the man Tanna/man Ambrym row', *The Independent* (Port Vila), 11 March 2007, p. 3; Regenvanu, State of emergency.

[98] Interview with a secretary-general (Ambae, 3 October 2003).

[99] Interview with a police officer (Port Vila, 14 April 2004).

[100] See also the discussion on this issue at the Vanuatu Judiciary Conference in 2006. Forsyth, *Report on the Vanuatu Judiciary Conference 2006*.

[101] Interview with police legal advisor (Port Vila, 14 April 2004).

[102] Garae, Len 2004, 'Police want unemployed sent home', *Vanuatu Daily Post* (Port Vila), 25 November 2004, p. 3.

[103] It was recently reported that there were 162 inmates in Port Vila and Luganville and that prison authorities spent more than vt500 000 each month on inmates' food. See Willie, Royson 2005, 'Inmates remind president of deteriorating prisons', *Vanuatu Daily Post* (Port Vila), 29 October 2005, p. 2.

[104] There was a prison at Isangel, Tanna, which was destroyed by a cyclone in 2003.

[105] Amnesty International, *No Safe Place for Prisoners*. Amnesty reported the major problems as being 'prison buildings made unsafe by earthquakes and water seepage, insufficient food for prisoners and a lack of safe accommodation for female prisoners. In August 1998, a female prisoner was held for a month in a prison evacuated by all male prisoners because the building was considered "too dangerous"'.

[106] Ombudsman of Vanuatu 1999, *Public report on prison conditions and mismanagement of the prison budget*, VUOM 15, http://www.paclii.org.vu The Ombudsman's report found that 'food rations, the type of bedding, the level of hygiene, the need for segregation of prisoners, the lack of exercise, rehabilitation and library all resulted in conditions far below the desired standards'. Further, it revealed that there were problems with the funding of the prisons as only a fraction of the funds earmarked for the prisons really went to them, the rest being spent on police requirements.

[107] There have been proposals to build new prisons since as early as 1987 (see Amnesty International, *No Safe Place for Prisoners*), but to date little has been done. Recently, however, NZAID has committed itself to the Correctional Services Project, which involves the building of new prisons in the near future.

[108] Overcrowding is such a major problem that some judicial officers are reluctant to sentence people to imprisonment because the jails are too full. The only way the issue of the overcrowding of prisons has been 'addressed' has been for the President and the minister responsible for prisons to regularly release prisoners well before they have served their full sentence—traditionally in bulk on Independence Day or periodically throughout the year (Article 38 of the constitution provides that '[t]he President of the Republic may pardon, commute or reduce a sentence imposed on a person convicted of an offence. Parliament may provide for a committee to advise the President in the exercise of this function.' The minister is given the power under Section 30 of the *Prisons [Administration] Act* [Cap 30]). This issue was discussed by the Vanuatu Court of Appeal in the decision of *Public Prosecutor vs Atis Willie* (2004, VUCA 4, http://www.paclii.org.vu), which found that powers of presidential pardon 'are being used very extensively' and that 'the need for a consistent and transparent approach in any mechanism which would have the effect of reducing the actual times spent in prison is overwhelming'. The court concluded: 'On the data which is [sic] currently available it is difficult to be confident that there are not major variations in the treatment of prisoners because of the way in which these two powers are presently being exercised. This has the potential to totally undermine the Court in its duty of delivering justice equally to all citizens as they are duty bound to provide, when there are subsequent mechanisms where

the exercise is not grounded in those same fundamental policies.' Possibly as a result of this judgment and also as a consequence of the appointment of a new president, who was formerly a lawyer and a judge, it appears that this practice has been substantially halted. See Willie, 'Inmates remind president of deteriorating prisons'.

[109] As a consequence, juvenile prisoners are sentenced to imprisonment in the same facilities as mature criminals. For example, in the case of *Public Prosecutor vs Ben and others* (2005, VUSC 108, http://www.paclii.org.vu), three fifteen-year-olds were sentenced to five years' imprisonment. See also Super, *A Needs Assessment of Juvenile Justice Issues in Fiji and Vanuatu.*

[110] As a consequence, in some cases, women prisoners are not sentenced to imprisonment, despite the fact that this might be the most appropriate sentence. For example, in a recent case, the Court of Appeal gave a female defendant a suspended sentence, stating, 'Nor can we ignore the absence of a female prison in Santo so that if she were now imprisoned, she would be physically removed from her children and her island in being transported to Port Vila for incarceration' (*Public Prosecutor vs Niala*, 2004, VUCA 25, http://www.paclii.org.vu).

[111] Each prison I visited often left the front gate wide open and, not surprisingly, the newspaper often reported incidents of escaping prisoners. Recently at my work, we received an email from the head of the Police Intelligence Analysis Unit notifying us that '49 prisoners at the Ex French Center escaped from lawful custody last night' and that '[s]ome of this escapees are very high risk and are known for Unlawful entry and likely to commit other offences [sic]' (Frazer Tambe, <ftambe@vanuatu.gov.vu>, 30 May 2007). The next day the newspaper reported that in fact the 49 prisoners (of 62 detainees) had just *walked out* of prison in protest over the food. See Garae, Len and Jerety, Johnety 2007, 'Walkout offenders to be prosecuted', *Vanuatu Daily Post* (Port Vila), 31 May 2007, p. 1.

[112] Binihi, Ricky 2005, 'All runaway prisoners behind bars', *Vanuatu Daily Post* (Port Vila), 4 August 2005, p. 5.

[113] Interview with a police officer (Port Vila, 6 April 2004).

[114] 'Twenty escape from inhuman treatment', *The Independent* (Port Vila), 14 May 2006, p. 3.

[115] Ibid.

[116] 'Protest over human rights of prisoners', *Vanuatu Daily Post* (Port Vila), 16 May 2006, p. 4.

[117] See, for example, Police Concern Officer 2007, 'Complaint against Correctional Services Management', *Your Letters, Vanuatu Daily Post* (Port Vila), 20 April 2007, p. 5; Repeated Theft Victim 2007, 'Have you been offered a "great deal" for electronics?', *Your Letters, Vanuatu Daily Post* (Port Vila), 3 March 2007, p. 7; Kaloran, Morris 2007, 'Correctional services ensure rehabilitation and reintegration', *Vanuatu Daily Post* (Port Vila), 14 March 2007, p. 4.

[118] Interview with a pastor (Port Vila, 7 June 2004).

[119] Interview with a fieldworker from Tanna (Port Vila, 22 September 2004).

[120] *Public Prosecutor vs Munrel*, 2005, VUSC 75, http://www.paclii.org.vu

[121] Australian Broadcasting Corporation (ABC) 2007, 'Time to talk', *ABC Radio Australia*, viewed 27 April 2007, <http://www.abc.net.au/timetotalk/english/radio/stories/TimeToTalkTranscript_418691.htm>

[122] Interview with a legal officer in the Public Prosecutor's Office (Santo, 17 November 2004).

[123] NZAID 2005, *Proposed Vanuatu Community Probation Service: Summary report*, p. 1.

[124] The project established a task force of senior ni-Vanuatu employed in the state justice system and the Malvatumauri and held 'extensive consultations…with a number of stakeholders and interest groups in five of the six provinces'. See NZAID, *Proposed Vanuatu Community Probation Service*, p. 34.

[125] Such as: what offences, if any, should never go to *kastom* first? What happens if one party goes to *kastom* and the other to the police? What happens if the chiefs make a decision and it isn't followed by the parties? What happens if the chief's decision involves a breach of the constitution or is unfair? Can there be an appeal from a chief's decision to the court?

[126] The *Penal Code (Amendment) Act 2006*, the *Criminal Procedure Code (Amendment) Act 2006*, the *Island Courts (Amendment) Act 2006* and the *Correctional Services Act 2006.*

[127] The major changes are the establishment of a new Department of Correctional Services, removing the responsibility for prisons from the police, the establishment of a probation service, the abolition of the early release provisions, the establishment of a community parole board and the building of new prisons, which will house prisoners according to their classification of risk and provide rehabilitation programs. The proposals for a diversion program have not been accepted by Parliament but will reportedly be resubmitted at a later date.

[128] The new Section 39 of the *Penal Code (Amendment) Act 2006*, replacing Section 119 of the *Criminal Procedure Code* (Cap 136), as discussed above under 'The relationship between the courts and the *kastom* system'.

[129] *Penal Code (Amendment) Act 2006* (Section 40).

[130] *Correctional Services Act 2006* (Part 5).

[131] Lini, Lora 2006, 'Escapees seek chiefs' help', *Vanuatu Daily Post* (Port Vila), 8 May 2006, p. 1.

[132] 'Police breakout: chiefs maintain peace', *The Independent* (Port Vila), 14 May 2006, p. 2.

[133] 'Re: protest over human rights of prisoners', *Vanuatu Daily Post* (Port Vila), 22 May 2006, p. 7.

[134] Currently, there are four ni-Vanuatu lawyers working in the Vila office and none at the Santo office. There are also a number of police who have been trained as state prosecutors who prosecute in the lower courts.

[135] Section 5(1) of the *Public Solicitor's Act* (Cap 177). The Public Solicitor's Office currently has four ni-Vanuatu lawyers and an Australian adviser working in the Port Vila office and no other offices around the country.

[136] During my time working in the prosecution, I was often the only lawyer in the office and was given cases far beyond my level simply because there was no-one else. For example, despite the fact that I had never worked in the field of criminal law before, my first Supreme Court case was a triple homicide.

[137] Interview with a lawyer (Santo, 18 November 2004). This was also confirmed by my experiences working for a year in the Public Prosecutor's Office and by newspaper reports.

[138] Walter, Matthew 2005, 'Financial difficulties delay hearing of criminal cases', *Vanuatu Daily Post* (Port Vila), 3 August 2005, p. 4.

[139] Walter, Matthew 2004, 'Luganville judiciary team to visit Gaua', *Vanuatu Daily Post* (Port Vila), 22 September 2004, p. 6.

[140] Recently, the *Vanuatu Daily Post* reported that an officer from the Public Solicitor's Office had to meet clients outside the motel he was staying in due to the lack of an office, and an NGO was quoted as stating that 'the Vanuatu *Constitution* guarantees the protection of the law for every citizen and that they should not be discriminated against on the grounds of wealth, but the sad reality is that most times only people who have money can get good private lawyers'. See Binihi, Ricky 2006a, 'NGO wants government to inject more funds into Public Solicitor's Office', *Vanuatu Daily Post* (Port Vila), 13 June 2006, p. 6.

[141] Toa, Evelyn 2005, 'Hundreds of summons stranded with Public Prosecutor', *The Independent* (Port Vila), 8 March 2005, <http://www.news.vu/en/news/judicial/050308-summons-stranded.shtml>

[142] *Public Prosecutor vs Gideon*, 2002, VUCA 7, <http://www.paclii.org.vu>

[143] Informally, some officers in the prosecution have a 'no drop' policy, especially in relation to sexual offences, in that two legal officers told me that when someone tries to withdraw a case, they call her in and talk with her and try to persuade her to go ahead with the case.

[144] For general background, see Chapter 3 under 'Leadership structures in Vanuatu today'.

[145] *National Council of Chiefs (Organisation) Act* (Cap 183).

[146] Government of Vanuatu n.d., *Criminal Procedure Code*, Cap 136, Article 30(1).

[147] Malvatumauri, 'Kastom polisi blong Malvatumauri'.

[148] Lindstrom, 'Chiefs in Vanuatu today', p. 224.

[149] On file with author.

[150] On file with author.

[151] Garu and Yaken, *Chiefs' Legislation Project Report*, p. 9.

[152] Ibid., p. 7.

[153] For example, the report stated that 'the operations of customary dispute resolution mechanisms or custom courts are strong in rural Vanuatu. These custom courts are actively working, and this is due to two basic factors. First and foremost, is because the courts carry out their duties in a way that the people prefer it to the official justice system. Secondly the official courts are either not accessible, too difficult to access, too expensive to afford or simply too slow to act. In many communities only serious offences are referred to official courts. Even then custom courts continue to face a lot of challenges and chiefs who preside over the custom courts strongly request the government to give legal recognition to their roles and functions'. Garu and Yaken, *Chiefs' Legislation Project Report*, p. 14.

[154] Ibid., p. 22.

[155] Ibid., p. 29.

[156] Interview with Emeritus Professor Paterson, University of the South Pacific (Port Vila, 1 November 2005).

[157] Earlier drafts of this bill provided even more powers, including the immunity of members of councils of customary chiefs from prosecution for any decisions taken in the exercise of his office and the exclusion of jurisdiction of courts over appointment or disciplining of a chief and chiefly title disputes (Draft Bill for the National Council of Chiefs [Organisation] Act, copy on file with author).

[158] Bill for the National Council of Chiefs Act of 2006, Parliamentary Amendment, Section 2.

[159] Forsyth, *Report on the Vanuatu Judiciary Conference 2006*.

[160] For example, Sections 38 and 39 of the *Penal Code [Amendment] Act 2006*. Previously, Sections 118 and 119 of the *Criminal Procedure Code* (Cap 136).

[161] Svesson, 'Interlegality, a process for strengthening indigenous peoples' autonomy', pp. 51–2.

[162] Although there have been recent signs of more interest in engaging in such a dialogue. Thus, in the past five years, the Chiefs' Legislation Project, the Vanuatu Judiciary Conference on *Kastom* and the Law, the AusAID Malvatumauri Governance Project and the NZAID Corrections Project have all precipitated discussion between the two systems.

[163] von Benda-Beckmann and von Benda-Beckmann, 'The dynamics of change and continuity in plural legal orders', p. 241.

6. The problems of the existing relationship between the state and *kastom* systems

The previous chapter characterised the relationship between the state and *kastom* systems as fluid, informal and largely involving the two operating in parallel with each other rather than meaningfully interacting. This chapter examines the problems flowing from such a relationship, elucidating additional imperatives for reform to those identified in Chapter 5. The main focus of the chapter is a case study, *Public Prosecutor vs Agnes Kalo and Peter Obed*,[1] which concerns a conflict in Vila dealt with by both the state and the *kastom* systems. This case illustrates many of the problems within, and most importantly, *between*, the two systems. The approach adopted in this chapter thus highlights the types of conflicts that commonly arise between the two systems, following Shah's advice that 'it is essential to observe conflicts within legal pluralism, the better thereby to highlight and to manage them "wisely", and to address this from the subjective perspective of the recipient of legal pluralism'.[2]

Before beginning a detailed analysis of the problems of the current relationship between the two systems, its advantages should be acknowledged. There are five main advantages to the situation at present. First, the fluid nature of the current relationship allows it to adapt in response to the needs of each particular situation—a very important feature in Vanuatu where plurality is manifested in every sphere of life, as discussed in Chapter 1. Second, the *kastom* system is able to define its own norms and procedural framework, allowing it to remain a dynamic and legitimate grassroots justice system. Third, as it is based entirely on respect, there is considerable incentive for the chiefs to maintain their integrity and to work hard to gain community support. Fourth, from the standpoint of individuals, the possibility of resort to alternative legal regimes can at times be extremely helpful.[3] Finally, the *kastom* system provides access to justice in areas not serviced by the State and keeps a high percentage of cases out of the state system with no cost to the State.

Two features of the current situation in particular stand out as positive features that could be built on in developing a better relationship between the two. First, there is currently a great deal of respect in both systems for the other. Judges and police officers are therefore very positive about the advantages of the *kastom* system, and conversely chiefs are also respectful of state institutions. Second, there are some individuals with an official capacity in both systems, such as judges, lawyers and police officers, who are also chiefs, who facilitate a degree of mutual understanding and movement between the two systems.[4]

The facts of the case study

The second defendant, Agnes, is a forty-eight-year-old widow from North Santo with six children who was employed as a receptionist in a government department before the case. Agnes's deceased husband, a man from East Santo, had an adopted son, the first defendant, Peter, who was also from East Santo. Peter lived with Agnes as his 'mother' although he is forty-two years old, so they did not have the normal age difference between mother and son. Peter is a leader in the Church, a focal point of the East Santo community, and hence an important man. Both defendants currently live in Vila, although not in the same area. Peter and Agnes were charged with, respectively, attempted rape and rape and aiding attempted rape and aiding rape. The victim was Agnes's natural daughter and Peter's step-sister, Mary. She is nineteen years old.

The facts giving rise to the case as set out by the judge in his sentencing judgment were based on an agreed statement of facts made between the defendants and the prosecution. One day in May 2005, Peter came to Agnes's house and picked up Agnes and Mary in his truck and took them to a deserted area a little way out of town. Peter then took Agnes aside and told her to tell Mary that he wanted to have sex with her. Agnes came back to the truck and, crying, told Mary what Peter had said. Mary said no and then Agnes went to the back of the truck and continued to cry. Peter then came into the truck and tried to have sex with Mary in the truck, but after trying for 15 minutes eventually gave up. A week or two later, the same situation occurred, with Peter coming and picking up Agnes and Mary and taking them to a deserted area. This time, Agnes told Mary to get out of the truck and to go to talk with Peter. Mary reluctantly did so and was followed by Agnes, who gave her a cloth as the place was cold and 'because [Peter] had asked for a cloth to wipe blood on'. Peter then forced Mary to have sex with him. In later discussions with the parties, very different versions of the facts were given, as is discussed below.

The two incidents came to light a few months later after Mary had run away to live with her uncle, Paul. She told him what had happened and Paul then told Agnes and Peter that he knew what had happened and gave them two weeks to deal with the matter in *kastom*. In fact, he finally waited for a month and a week for the chiefs and community leaders to approach him and to say to him that they would deal with the case. When no-one came to him, he took Mary to the police to make a complaint. When Peter found out that the complaint had been made, he went to see the North Santo Town Council of Chiefs (NSTCC, the council of chiefs for the community of North Santo in Vila).[5] There then began a very public argument over the forum that should manage the conflict. Initially, there was a dispute as to whether the NSTCC or the East Santo Town Council of Chiefs had 'jurisdiction', but eventually the NSTCC was chosen. On 24 October, the chiefs of North and East Santo and church leaders wrote to the prosecution asking them to withdraw the case and to allow the NSTCC to deal with the matter in *kastom*. The letter set out a number of grounds to support their argument, including:

- sending the defendants to jail will not solve the differences that exist in the family
- the court will deal only with the criminal side of the case but the *'kastom side'* will not be dealt with (in other words, the necessary payments to be made to people other than the victim in order to mend relations fractured by the incident)
- if the court punishes the two defendants they will not suffer very much as life inside the prison today is *'an easy life'*
- if the defendants are sent to jail, Agnes's other children will be affected as well, especially the ones who are at school (for whom Peter has previously paid school fees) and whom Agnes still needs to look after
- the case and the ensuing dispute have also created a dispute over land in East Santo and therefore the matter should be dealt with in *kastom* because if the court deals with the case it will not deal with the issue of land and *'bambae hemi save stikim wan narafalla trabol bakeken long saed blong kraon, mo ol narafalla isiu bagegen long famili'* (it might create another land dispute and another issue among the families)
- in *kastom* it will be possible to unite Agnes with her children, brother and entire family again
- in *kastom* it will be possible to unite Peter with his children, wife and family again
- if the case is dealt with just in *kastom*, this will make sure that people have respect for *kastom* and show that they can deal with disputes *'witaot kot blong waetman'* (without 'white man's court').

The letter then explained that they wanted to deal with the matter in *kastom* by making the two defendants pay a number of heavy fines in order to *'putum bak olketa samting ia iko bak long road blong kastom blong mifala'* (put everything back onto a straight road again). In particular, it was specified that *'respek'* had to be given back by Peter to the following people: Mary, Agnes, the land, the grave of Agnes's deceased husband, Peter's uncles (Agnes's brothers), Mary's brothers, Peter's wife and their children and Peter's wife's family in West Santo. Agnes had to give back *'respek'* to Mary and to her brother, especially because in their *kastom* brothers do not have the right to hear things or be involved in disputes involving their sisters. The letter concluded by saying that Mary and Paul had agreed that the best forum for the dispute was the NSTCC.

About this time, Mary also went to the prosecution and asked to withdraw the case. The prosecutors who spoke with her reported that she told them that she was caught in the middle between the chiefs who were pressuring her to withdraw the case and her uncle who urged her to continue. In the event, the legal officers convinced her not to withdraw the case. At that stage, it was still not clear whether or not the two defendants were going to plead guilty. There was therefore a further dispute between the courts, the prosecution and the chiefs as to whether the *kastom* reconciliation that the chiefs wanted to perform could go ahead before the plea date.

Most unusually, this entire dispute over forum was widely publicised through the local newspaper and radio, drawing considerable public comment. In particular, the Vanuatu National Council of Women spoke out strongly against the move by the chiefs to stop the prosecution going ahead and was reported as stating that 'in a situation where chiefs are asked to intervene to stop the law from dealing with a criminal suspect through the courts, they should be careful as they could be seen as "hiding" an alleged criminal in the name of custom'.[6]

In a further attempt to stop the court case from going ahead, and in order to mend relations between the family, a 'preliminary' reconciliation ceremony was held on 26 October, presided over by the NSTCC, in which a pig's tusk and some mats were paid by Peter to Mary and her family and a kava ceremony was held. On 30 October, the NSTCC wrote to the prosecution informing them of what had been done and again asking that the case be withdrawn. The letter stated:

> The respondent of the ceremony [Paul] vowed their thanks and agreement to the ceremony and accepted the gifts and made a vow to withdraw the matter from the State Prosecution by sending them a letter of notification…The ceremony ended on a very peaceful manner and a kava ceremony was shared amongst the leaders with the victim's family to seal the agreement.

When discussing the case later with me, Paul said that he had never agreed to the case being withdrawn but had rather wanted there to be a *kastom* reconciliation before the court case was held. The prosecution refused to withdraw the case and the plea was finally held on 1 November when the two defendants pleaded guilty. The sentencing date was set for 25 November 2005.

The NSTCC then continued to negotiate with the court and the prosecution to be permitted to 'lay custom charges' against the two defendants without having to wait for the court case to be concluded. The court apparently agreed to this on the basis that the two defendants had pleaded guilty and agreed to take into account any *kastom* punishment ordered when sentencing.[7] Accordingly, a *kastom* reconciliation ceremony was held on 23 November. This ceremony involved the two defendants paying very heavy *kastom* fines to a wide variety of different people and groups, even extending to the payment of a rooster and a mat to the President of Vanuatu. The fines were paid in *kastom* objects, such as pigs' tusks, mats and kava, but their cash value was stated as amounting to vt474 000. Of this, only vt115 000 went to the victim.[8] The President of the NSTCC explained that the fines were so high because the case had been so widely publicised, meaning that more was needed to bring back respect for the defendants and that compensation was also needed because of the damage the case had done generally to the Church and the community. Agnes was of the more pragmatic opinion that the fines were so high so as to reduce the possible sentence the court would impose. Paul said that he had demanded these high fines in order to make sure that Peter really felt punished, and that Peter had agreed partly because Paul was threatening that he would go to the police and lodge complaints against Peter for having committed incest with his daughter as well.

On 25 November, the case came before the court for sentencing. As part of the sentencing process, the defence gave the court a letter from the NSTCC detailing the *kastom* reconciliation performed. The President of the NSTCC was in court but was not called on to speak. In his judgment, the presiding judge referred to the fact that the *kastom* payment had been made and its cash value, stating, 'The Defendant has taken part in a custom settlement to "clean face" and restore a sense of order and peace into the community and appease the victim and those associated as a result of the wrong he has done.' His Honour, however, also made the main consideration underpinning his sentencing decision clear, noting, 'It is of a very serious concern to note that rape has becoming [sic] a common offence in Vanuatu. This is unacceptable. Women and girls must be protected. The courts must set severe punishments to Rape offenders.'

When dealing with Agnes, in addition to the *kastom* payment and the fact that the victim had forgiven her, his Honour noted a number of other mitigating features.[9] Finally, the court awarded Peter a sentence of imprisonment for three years and Agnes a sentence of imprisonment for three years suspended for two years. Unfortunately, his Honour did not make clear in his judgment the weight he gave to the *kastom* payment, as opposed to other mitigating factors, in arriving at the final sentence. Peter and the President of the NSTCC believe that the sentence was reduced by one-third due to the *kastom* payment, but this is not at all clear from the judgment, which merely sets out the payment as one of many mitigating factors.

A week after the sentence was handed down, some members of Mary's family[10] went to see the President of the NSTCC to ask him to petition the President of the Republic to pardon Peter. The President of the NSTCC stated that this was symptomatic of the general feeling among everyone involved in the case that Peter should not have had to go to prison after having made such a heavy *kastom* payment. Paul, however, disagrees with this and says that his side of the family is very happy that there has been 'double punishment' and that Mary too is pleased that Peter has been sentenced to jail. The president refused to make the petition and today Peter remains in jail. Although not in prison, Agnes also is suffering from the consequences of the court case. She has been suspended from her job and is awaiting a decision about whether she will be terminated for misconduct. She also receives no money from Peter to support her children any more.

This particular case study had some unusual features, in that the case was very public and the fines paid were very high. The basic facts of how the case went backwards and forwards between the two systems and the problems and conflict this caused, are, however, typical of a significant number of cases in Vila and Santo.

Problems *within* the two systems demonstrated by the case study

In addition to demonstrating a number of difficulties with the present relationship between the state and *kastom* systems, discussed below, the case study also demonstrates problems *within* the two systems themselves, thus expanding on and supporting the findings in Chapters 4 and 5.

Problems within the state system

A significant problem raised by the case study is that some aspects of the current operation of the state system give rise to the risk that people prefer to plead guilty rather than face trial, even if they are innocent, due to shame and the wish to avoid the court process. This problem was raised by Agnes, who claimed that the facts set out in the judgment were not correct. According to her, Peter was known to have a tendency to make sexual overtures to young girls and indeed he had done the same thing to her in the past.[11] Agnes said, however, that Peter had said that he wanted to teach Mary how to drive and that was why they went out with him in the truck. On the first occasion, she had no idea what he was doing to Mary and, on the second occasion, she realised—'*hemi click*'—while he was trying to have sex with Mary. The reason that she did not try to stop him after she had realised what was going on was a mixture of shame and fear of his short temper.

This is a very different story to the one presented to the court, in which she is portrayed as actively helping to arrange for Peter to have sex with Mary. In her version of the facts, she did not commit any crime because she had in no way consciously aided Peter; quite the reverse: she was horrified and deeply upset by what he had done. Agnes explained that even though she knew she was innocent she had decided to plead guilty because she did not want to make her children, particularly her son, who would have been a witness, feel shame by having to testify in court.[12] She explained that in her *kastom*, for a brother to have something like that happen to his sister was very shameful. She said that she had not even read the agreed statement of facts because she was too upset and because of her high blood pressure could not deal with any more stress. It is possible that what Agnes told me was false and that she was just justifying her actions to me, but what she said did ring true. Even if the truth lies somewhere in between, what she said raises a serious concern that innocent defendants do plead guilty due to a desire to protect themselves or others from the shame of having to speak in court.[13] The Director of Youth and Sport raises a similar point when he states that often when young people go to the courts they are too afraid to speak and they cannot pay for a lawyer, so they are convicted.[14]

In contrast, only one respondent said that she felt publicly exposed in a *kastom* court, whereas numerous others reported fear of the courts and gave that as a reason for preferring the *kastom* system. It is interesting to consider why people feel shame in court and not in a *kastom* meeting, which similarly involves public scrutiny and questioning. I suggest the answer is related to the foreignness of the state system and to the fact that in the state system there are many people involved whom the defendants have no personal or familial relationships with, which in turn increases feelings of shame and alienation. In addition, the whole point of the *kastom* system is that it is about overcoming shame and putting back respect. Thus, the parties might start off feeling shame, but at the completion of the process they should feel that they have won back the respect of everyone affected by the conflict and thus become reintegrated back into the community. In contrast, the state system has no such restorative processes at present.

I also asked Agnes why she had performed the *kastom* ceremony even though she was not guilty. She said that she did it for two reasons: first, because as a mother she was responsible for her children, and second, because when her family and community got to know about the case they started avoiding her and were cross with her. So she made a *kastom* fine to five different groups of people: her relatives from East Santo, Paul, her husband's brother (for her husband's grave), Mary and finally Peter's wife. After this was done the relations with the families were mended and *'hat blong olgeta igud bakegen'* (everyone's heart was made good again), although relations with Peter's wife were still difficult. This illustrates the difference between the narrow focus of the state system on the complainant and victim to the exclusion of the other people involved in the conflict and the more holistic *kastom* approach that facilitates a mending of relationships. It also demonstrates the difference between agreeing to make a *kastom* payment and admitting guilt in the context of the state system.[15]

Problems within the *kastom* system

The case study also identifies some aspects of the present operation of the *kastom* system that are problematic.[16] Apparently, it was well known that Peter had committed similar offences on other girls, including, according to some reports, his own daughter, and the chiefs had tried to call meetings to deal with the issues on a number of occasions, but each time Peter had refused to come to the meeting so the issue was let slide. In the instant case, as mentioned above, once Mary had told Paul about the incidents, Paul waited for a month and a week for the chiefs and community leaders to approach him and to say to him that they would deal with the case before going to the police.[17] They, however, did nothing and it was only once the police had arrested Peter that the chiefs and church leaders came to see Paul. Paul explained that he was very frustrated at the chiefs for not dealing with the matter themselves, but that he also understood that they had no way of compelling defendants to attend meetings and that this was one of the weaknesses of the current situation.

The problem of chiefs not wishing or not being able to deal with matters that then eventually enter the state system has been referred to in other cases that have come before the courts in recent years. For example, in the case of *Public Prosecutor vs Niala* (2004, VUCA 25), involving two brothers killing a man who had been spying on their sister, the court stated: 'the matter had earlier been referred to the Chiefs but unfortunately no meeting was called to discuss and resolve the matter.'

Another problem with the *kastom* system illustrated by this case study is that sometimes the victim is marginalised as so much attention is paid to her family and to the community. For example, in this case study, the victim received only a fraction of the overall fine. As the fine was very large, this still amounted to a substantial payment in her case, but in other cases the necessity to take into account the whole community can make the amount received by the victim quite insubstantial. The focus on achieving community peace and harmony, and the desire not to 'stir up trouble', can result in the rights of victims being neglected by the *kastom* system—in terms of voice and repair.

Problems with the relationship between the two systems

In analysing the problems with the relationship identified through the case study, findings from earlier chapters and other material generated through fieldwork are also identified and discussed.

Uncertainty about where the conflict should be dealt with puts complainants in a vulnerable situation

The first, and perhaps most serious, problem with the current relationship between the two systems demonstrated by the case study is that the present perception that the forum for managing a particular conflict is open to negotiation puts a great deal of pressure on victims at a vulnerable time. In this case study, Mary faced pressure from her uncle, telling her the police should deal with the matter; from women's groups, telling her that as a woman it was important to use the courts and not allow 'chiefs to obstruct the rightful legal processes to deal with such high risk criminal suspects';[18] from the chiefs, telling her that she was betraying her culture by not withdrawing the case; from her church leaders, urging her to let the case be resolved in *kastom*; and finally from her own mother and step-brother, asking her to let the matter be dealt with in *kastom*. It was no wonder that, as she told the prosecution, she felt caught in the middle and behaved in an inconsistent manner, attempting to withdraw the case and then being persuaded to let it remain on two different occasions.[19]

Mary's situation is not unique; it is common for complainants, particularly women and children, to be pressured not to report crimes to the police or to withdraw complaints in order to allow the matters to be dealt with in *kastom*. A prosecutor said that often one of the reasons given for this pressure was that the defendant was a family member and so a 'gap in the family' would be created if the case went to court (the legal officer then said that she told the families who provided these sorts of explanations that the defendant should have thought about the potential gap before he or she engaged in the prohibited conduct). As well as trying to persuade the complainant to withdraw the case, the families might also use other tactics to try to stop her from testifying—for example, by not giving her money to travel to court.

Dispute and confusion over jurisdiction

Another issue raised by the case study is that there is a great deal of confusion and conflict regarding which system should deal with which types of cases. These disputes often involve a political element, as Franz and Keebet von Benda-Beckmann relevantly observe:

> As law provides an important legitimation for the exercise of power by social actors or organisations, the question [of] which is the proper law is frequently the object of political struggles. The invocation of the rules or the authorities of one law not only serve to settle a particular problem, but may also be treated as a *pars pro toto* for the relationship between the respective legal orders as a whole.[20]

As discussed in Chapter 5, the police have a vague and informal policy that encourages chiefs to deal with 'minor' offences, while referring 'serious' offences to the police.[21] The chiefs, however, expressed a wide range of opinions about the sorts of cases that they believed they could deal with themselves, ranging from petty theft to murder. Even when chiefs agreed that 'serious' cases should go to the police, it was clear that what they considered serious might not be considered serious in the state context and vice versa. For example, a resident linguist in Epi commented that he had attended many *kastom* meetings but the case that had really stood out in terms of a disproportionately heavy penalty (to him) was where a man had said to one of his relatives that to speed up the process of paying a bride price he should 'set up a brothel and sell his arse'. Such a statement would not even be prosecuted in the state system. There are also a whole variety of crimes in *kastom* that are not recognised as being crimes in the state system, such as women wearing trousers,[22] or those concerning correct behaviour towards people in certain types of relation to each other.[23] Conversely, serious crimes such as rape and indecent assault in the state system might be considered minor matters in the *kastom* system, where the issue of consent to sexual intercourse is not a central issue. A complicating factor as well is that in *kastom* a case is often judged serious or not depending on the consequences that flow from it. For example, a boy forcing a girl to have sex might not be considered serious unless it results in the girl getting pregnant.[24]

The lack of clear guidelines about which cases each system can deal with has caused confusion on the part of the general population and the chiefs. This confusion was demonstrated by the fact that a chairman of a council of chiefs said that a police officer had told the chiefs that now they could deal with cases of rape, although the officer in charge of the relevant police station denied this policy. Similarly, in Ambae, it was reported that there was a problem that people did not know what matters the police should deal with and which the chiefs were responsible for, so people went to the police and were sent back to the chiefs and this caused confusion for everyone. As a result, many chiefs are asking for a clear list to be drawn up of matters they can decide and matters they cannot. The serious/minor policy of the police also creates anger and frustration on behalf of the chiefs, who feel they are being told they cannot deal with matters that they have always dealt with—such as sexual offences and murder—and yet at the same time the State is not providing adequate access to justice, especially for rural communities.

This confusion sometimes leads to confrontation between chiefs and police officers and other state officials. For example, in Vila, the head of the Police Sexual Offences Unit says that she regularly has arguments with chiefs who come to try to 'take out' cases from the police to deal with them in *kastom*. She says that she tries to explain to them that the court must deal with these cases but many do not agree.[25] She provided many examples from her files of cases where women and youth had lodged cases involving serious sexual offences, which had then been cancelled after a request from the complainant or the complainant's family to deal with the matter in *kastom*.[26] In rural areas as well, chiefs often try to stop the police from becoming involved in matters that they have dealt with before the police investigate.[27] Although usually it is the police who must deal with chiefs claiming their right to deal with a particular case, sometimes this occurs in the Public Prosecutor's Office, and occasionally even in the court itself. A prosecutor commented that on one occasion a chief had come into the courtroom while the case was proceeding and tried to argue that the case should be given to him to handle. She stated, 'I was so mad!'[28]

A related issue is that there is general confusion about the powers of chiefs to make certain orders, particularly those that are perceived to be in conflict with the constitution. For example, in Santo in 2006, nine area chiefs ordered a family originating from the island of Paama, but residing in Santo, to leave within 72 hours, after allegations that they were behind a series of brawls that occurred during Independence Day celebrations.[29] For a number of days, there was a state of tension in Luganville, with residents erecting roadblocks and keeping their children home from school. Despite the fact that the uncertainty over the legality of the chiefly decision considerably heightened the tension, the only statement made by state officials concerning the actions of the chiefs was that 'while the chiefs have the right to make decisions the law also has its place and must be seen to prevail'.[30] This failure to clarify the legitimate boundaries of chiefly powers is symptomatic of the general confusion and unease regarding these issues.

Finally, there is the problem of cases that neither system wishes to deal with and which each system claims is the responsibility of the other. For example, in domestic violence cases, chiefs often send complainants to the police, saying they are unable to deal with them, and the police often send such cases back to the chiefs, on the basis that they are 'private' matters.[31] In Ambae, for example, the policy of the police is to send a woman back to the chiefs unless she has been beaten so badly she needs to be hospitalised or the man has done it many times. As a result, the victims are abandoned by both systems. Another situation where this occurs is cases involving 'big-men', such as politicians, where the police do not want to become involved. For example, in April 2007, a politician allegedly assaulted three men, but when they went to lodge a complaint at the police station they were advised to 'solve the matter according to the traditional way'.[32]

On some occasions, both systems blame each other for a particular situation and so try to avoid responsibility for fixing it. An example is the situation in South Santo where there is almost a vacuum of authority and increasingly serious law and order issues. The chief of the largest village in this area said that there were large groups of people fighting each other over land issues with weapons such as knives. The village chiefs and the area chiefly council have tried to stop the fights but they have not been able to do so because people do not attend the meetings called or pay the fines that are set. A village chief commented that the chiefs currently did not have much respect as they were seen as being biased. He said that he had asked the police to help support the chiefs but they refused to come. He commented, '[T]he police say that it is my work to make people pay the fines, but how can I when I have no power?'[33]

The police on the other hand state that they are refusing to deal with these cases because the fighting is due to disputes over land, which the chiefs should deal with. A senior police officer states that they tell the chiefs that they must deal with the underlying problem first, and until they do so there is no point in them taking the end situation (the fighting) to court. He commented that these sorts of situations arose when chiefs did not do their work properly, such as sorting out disputes over land. He further commented that a chief should set up a situation in which his community respected him so he could control his community.[34] It is clear that circular arguments such as these lead to the situation where the relevant community is unprotected by either system of law and order. Luckily, at present, this type of situation is not widespread, but it does show how there is a need for the state system to recognise that the *kastom* system today is facing serious challenges to and diminution of its abilities to enforce orders that need to be addressed in a more fundamental way than exhorting the community to respect the chiefs.

The problem of which system should deal with a case first

There are many times when the *kastom* system and the state system deal with different aspects of the same case. Even where both systems accept the right of the other system to be involved, however, there is often considerable difficulty about the order in which the *kastom* processes and the court processes should occur.

The problems with the *kastom* system dealing with a matter first

Under *kastom* there is an imperative to deal with a matter quickly—to restore relations between conflicting parties[35] and to prevent it leading to further disputes and getting out of hand.[36] The holding of a *kastom* ceremony before the court has dealt with a matter can, however, create serious difficulties for the state process. There is the risk that after the ceremony the victim will not want to proceed with the case or will be pressured to withdraw the case, as in fact happened in the case study, making it extremely difficult for the prosecution to go ahead. There is also a substantial risk that the witnesses in the state court case will have their evidence seriously interfered with by the *kastom* process, as the facts of the case will be discussed extensively during the *kastom* ceremony. In addition, in cases that are brought to the court because the defendant has not paid the fine the chief ordered, or the parties are dissatisfied with the chiefs' decision, there will often be a significant time lapse. This time lapse makes it very hard to investigate, especially as it precludes the possibility of getting a medical report.[37]

Finally, if the defendants plead not guilty, it will be very difficult to keep the judge from being aware that a *kastom* reconciliation has taken place, and this must inevitably have some effect on his or her determination of the guilt of the defendants. This raises the point that there might not be exact parity between a 'crime' in the *kastom* system and a crime in the state system. For example, in the case study, in *kastom* the 'crime' that was committed by Peter was not rape but incest, as he had sex with his 'sister'. It was this that he was atoning for in his *kastom* payment, as well as the consequent disruption he had caused to the community and his family, rather than the charges of rape.[38]

On a more symbolic level, there are also problems with the court proceeding occurring after a *kastom* payment has been made. These problems have been highlighted in a number of high-profile cases involving the government in recent years. The first case involved four high-ranking police officers who had committed mutiny. A public reconciliation ceremony negotiated by the Deputy Prime Minister and the police force was performed by the four men. After the ceremony, however, the men were prosecuted and subsequently found guilty of mutiny, incitement to mutiny, kidnapping and false imprisonment and were sentenced to imprisonment. An opinion article in the local newspaper argued:

> If the ceremony was to settle a quarrel or difference between the Police and Government then I suggest that prosecution should not have been brought in at all. Certainly the crime committed is very serious but if we are serious about custom being the basis of our position as a free people then custom power should also be allowed to prevail to forfeit such a crime with a reconciliation ceremony.[39]

In another case, the government performed a reconciliation ceremony with the paramount chiefs of Central Pentecost to apologise for the brutality of members of the police force who had been sent to the area to facilitate a peace process between factions in a land dispute. After the ceremony, the police involved were charged with criminal offences. The Secretary-General of the Malvatumauri commented that bringing proceedings after there had been reconciliation 'defeated the purpose for which it [the reconciliation] was organised' and degraded *kastom*. He further explained:

> A clear line has to be drawn to clearly state where and when *kastom* comes into play and where and when court comes into play…In *kastom*, when a person kills a pig or accepts one in a reconciliation ceremony, automatically he is saying 'Peace and unity returns. I declare that we forgive [each other] and forget [the suffering caused]'.[40]

For this reason, the Malvatumauri proposed that if there was a traditional reconciliation ceremony, it must take place after the investigations (and presumably the whole state process) were completed.

The knowledge that the state system will deal with the matter after the *kastom* system might even affect the ability of the chiefs to call a meeting in the first place. A youth observed that sometimes the chiefs called a meeting and said that they had passed a complaint to the police but they wanted to deal with the matter '*long level long kastom*' (at the level of *kastom*). He commented that no-one was very interested in this because there was no point if the case was already with the police.[41]

The problems with the state system dealing with a matter first

There are also problems with holding a *kastom* meeting after a case has passed through the state system. Significantly, if the *kastom* meeting is not held until after sentencing, the court cannot take any *kastom* payment made into account at all, increasing the problem of double jeopardy, discussed below.[42] Also, as Paul points out, if a *kastom* meeting is not held until after a person has been punished by the state system, the defendant will be likely to refuse to make a *kastom* payment, arguing that he or she has already been punished once. In such a situation, he opined that the *kastom* payment would never be made and relationships would not be able to be mended. This view is supported by many chiefs, who have commented that it is common for people to say they have already been punished by going to jail and therefore refuse to pay the *kastom faen* that will enable them to be reintegrated back into the community. A prisoner also supported this view, stating that he felt that he did not need to make *kastom* because the law would get him and put him in prison anyway. Some chiefs also mention that they feel they cannot make a party do *kastom* after the court has dealt with a case because there has been '*jastis finis*' (justice done already). This causes big problems because, as they ask, how can the conflicting parties live together in the same village when the case is finished if there is no *kastom* settlement?[43]

The various disadvantages of each system dealing with a conflict first can be summarised as in Table 6.1.

A possible way of overcoming most of these problems is to hold a *kastom* ceremony after the determination of guilt by the state system, but before sentencing. The problem of having to wait for the slow state processes, however, remains.

Table 6.1 Temporal ordering problems

Kastom system first	State system first
• The victim might not want to continue with the prosecution or might have pressure imposed to withdraw charges. • Evidence of witnesses potentially contaminated by kastom processes. • Time delay impedes police investigation. • Difficulties for judge if aware that defendant has made a kastom payment but pleaded not guilty. • State proceedings might undermine the benefits achieved by the kastom processes and make the kastom system look irrelevant.	• The court cannot take kastom payment into account when sentencing. • Offender might refuse to make a kastom payment meaning that relationships are not restored. • The conflict is not able to be resolved quickly, potentially leading to continuing avoidance (meaning ties of interdependence are fractured) and the risk of precipitating further conflicts.

The problem of 'double jeopardy'

A further problem raised by the case study is that of 'double jeopardy', meaning in this context that the defendant is seen to be punished twice for the same conduct—once by the chiefs and then by the courts. This issue was specifically raised by a number of people involved in the case study and by many other respondents as well. Thus, Agnes said that the punishment of her and Peter was a 'double judgment' that went 'over' the punishment required. She said that when Peter got out of prison, she and her family would have to pay kastom to him again to make up for the imbalance created by the jail sentence. The uncle, Paul, also referred to 'double punishment', but he insisted that he was not sorry for having gone to the police and told the relatives who were cross with him that at least he had accepted the kastom payment, thus reducing the prison sentence considerably.

The Chief Justice explains that the ordinary person does not see that their kastom payment is taken into account by the courts. He comments that every day people say 'be mi mekem long kastom finis!'. He explained that this was because 'in their own mind they are clean, they have paid out, and they do not understand why they are being punished again'.[44] A prisoner also expressed this view, explaining bitterly that although he had paid a high kastom fine he was still sent to prison, meaning in his understanding that the fine had not been taken into account. Even many respondents from the state sector commented that personally they believed that it was double jeopardy for the State to punish someone after they had sorted matters out in kastom and made kastom payments. For example, a judicial officer gave an example of a recent case he had dealt with in which a man had killed another man but had acknowledged his guilt by making a big kastom payment of 10 pigs and vt500 000 compensation to the widow as well as paying for the school fees of the deceased's children. This man was also the sole breadwinner in his family, with three children of his own to support. The judicial officer stated that at the moment there was no alternative but to send such a man to prison, but he asked what this would achieve. He observed that he would like to have some leeway in dealing with such cases.[45]

The operation of the state system creates feelings of disempowerment among the chiefs

Many chiefs state that they believe that the value of *kastom* is being undermined by the existence of the state system, leading to them feeling disempowered and demoralised. Often chiefs express frustration that they are not left to deal with matters themselves. Thus, the President of the NSTCC, who was involved in the case study, said that there was always the feeling of 'another superpower coming behind us'. He expressed disappointment that the court had not left the NSTCC to deal with the matter, stating that it was a 'waste' of *kastom* 'because at the end of the day the court rules'. Further, even if the sentence was reduced due to the *kastom* compensation, he said that it still 'undermines the value of what we believe in...[*kastom*] should be the final [word]'.[46] The secretary of an island council of chiefs similarly commented that the knowledge that chiefly decisions could be challenged in court was demoralising for chiefs, noting that if one of their decisions was challenged this undermined their decisions in the other 90 per cent of cases that were not challenged.[47]

The state system hinders the operation of the *kastom* system

It is common to blame the weaknesses of the *kastom* system on the personal failures of chiefs and on the youth of today for 'lack of respect'. The findings of this study, however, show clearly that the state system *itself* hinders the operation of the *kastom* system—directly and also indirectly by undermining its authority and enforcement capacity. First, we consider direct, and then indirect, hindering of the state system.

Direct hindering of the *kastom* system by the state system

On some occasions the state system directly hinders the operation of the *kastom* system. The first way it does this is by making orders contrary to chiefly decisions. Unfortunately, the lack of adequate records means that it is very difficult to determine what percentage of cases come to the courts because the parties are dissatisfied with the decision of the *kastom* system. All that can confidently be said is that this happens with some degree of regularity in communities with adequate access to state courts. It is also not possible to determine in what percentage of such cases the courts make decisions that contradict those of the chiefs. It can be assumed, however, that this occurs frequently, as the courts consider cases with no regard to how the *kastom* system might previously have dealt with the case and they are likely to approach the issues in a different way to the *kastom* system.

This has two consequences: first, it is clear from many respondents that the knowledge that the courts can change a chief's decision affects their view of chiefs. One respondent gave an example of where the chief had ordered that someone should go back to the island and then the court had said the man should not go, and they commented that this '*mekem oli luk daon long ol jif nao*' (makes people look down on chiefs now).[48] Other people made comments such as that 'people tend to drift away from chiefs when they see their decisions are overturned by the courts'.[49]

Second, it means that the work the chiefs have put into restoring peace in their community might be wasted and friction created again, making their work more difficult. For example, recently in North Pentecost, a fight between two men ended in one assaulting and killing the other with a piece of iron. The man paid compensation two times, each time with 10 pigs with rounded tusks, and there was harmony again in the community. Two to three weeks later, however, the victim's eldest brother reported the incident to the police[50] and the whole matter was stirred up again. The chief involved was extremely frustrated because there was nothing he could do to stop the police from becoming involved, but the effect of it was to undermine all of his work in trying to ensure peace in his community. The Secretary of the Malvatumauri summed up this problem by stating that 'when the hair of the pig has been smoothed down, it should not be rubbed up the wrong way again'.[51]

An interesting issue that has arisen in a number of cases is whether or not a claimant can petition the courts for remedies in situations where the *kastom* system has breached their constitutional rights. The constitution provides in Article 6(1) that 'anyone who considers that any of the rights guaranteed to him by the Constitution has been, is being or is likely to be infringed may…apply to the Supreme Court to enforce that right'. This provision does not specify whether or not the rights can be enforced horizontally—that is, against private bodies and individuals, including chiefs and chiefly councils—or just vertically against the State. On three occasions when the courts have considered this matter, they have found that there is horizontal enforcement, but a recent case held that there is only vertical enforcement.[52] Thus, there is an unresolved issue about whether or not the courts can in fact overturn decisions made by the *kastom* system on the basis that they have breached the constitutional rights of the parties, although the weight of authority seems in favour of the fact that they can.[53]

The state system also directly hinders the *kastom* system when the courts make orders that interfere with the ability of the chiefs to resolve conflicts. One example is the refusal of bail, which can in fact prevent a *kastom* payment being made before the courts deal with the case. For example, in the case of *Public Prosecutor vs Munrel*, the court stated in its sentencing decision, 'You wanted to undertake a custom settlement but your custodial arrangements have precluded that.'[54] Another very common example is a Domestic Violence Protection Order that prevents a person from going within a certain distance of a family member with whom they have had a disagreement. For example, the Acting Chief Registrar stated that a group of chiefs had visited him and expressed concern that the courts were making orders that were having an effect on their ability to hold *kastom* meetings. They explained that if there was an order that stopped someone from moving around or from coming into contact with other people then they felt paralysed and unable to do their work.[55]

Finally, the state system hinders the *kastom* system because in some instances the courts have found chiefs criminally liable for executing or authorising the execution of their decisions. The most famous example of this is the case of *Public Prosecutor vs Kota* (1989–94, 2 VLR 661), in which the court held that the chiefs' decision for a woman to be returned to her island was unlawful and the chiefs were guilty of inciting to commit kidnapping. In another case, several chiefs were reportedly put in jail for contempt of court when they went ahead with ordaining a chief contrary to a court decision.[56] Another example was recalled by a chief, who said that he had to spend two years in prison as a result of being found guilty of unlawful assembly as a consequence of holding a meeting to try to resolve a dispute over chiefly title in his community. He then commented:

> Before when the *kastom* court made a decision that people were wrong they just surrendered. But today it is not the same because the trouble-makers can put the chiefs in court together with their council. Respect has been lost. Lawyers can defend the trouble-makers. This sort of thing has weakened or damaged the energy of all *kastom* chiefs.[57]

Many other comments made by chiefs showed that there was a real fear, and also frustration, that they risked breaking state law by carrying out their chiefly duties.

Although these types of orders might not be made very often, the message they send out to chiefs and the community has far wider repercussions than the particular case in question. Effectively, the state courts are telling the chiefs that, whatever they do, they are at risk of having the state system contradict them, and in some instances perhaps imprison them. Given the chiefs' limited understanding of the legal system, and what must appear to them to be at times very arbitrary decisions, this understandably causes a great deal of unease and a consequent weakening of their confidence in their own powers and abilities—qualities that are needed in the role of community leader. [58]

Indirect hindering of the *kastom* system by the state system

The state system also hinders the *kastom* system indirectly, by undermining the authority of the chiefs and hence their enforcement capacity. One way it does this is through providing dissatisfied parties with a way of avoiding compliance, as they are able to say that they will 'appeal' to the state system. Numerous examples of this were given during the course of the fieldwork. For example, in one case, a man hit an old man with a piece of wood he was carrying and the old man fell over and was seriously injured. The old man was given a choice of whether to file a complaint with the police or lodge the case with the council of chiefs. He decided to give it to the council as the court would take a long time and he would have to go to Vila to attend court. The council ordered the man to pay a fine of five pigs. The man refused to pay the fine, however, justifying his actions by saying that he wanted to appeal to the court. Another example occurred in Vila, where the Port Vila Town Council of Chiefs fined a police officer for his role in a fight. He was reported in the newspaper stating that he would not pay but would 'use his constitutional right to challenge the decision in the court'.[59] This problem was also highlighted in a recent report by the Foundation of the Peoples of the South Pacific, which found that individuals felt free to decide which system to choose and often when unsatisfied by the decision of one to revert to the other. It further found that 'freedom to move [from the *kastom* system] into the formal system serves to undermine the authority and enforcement capacity of Chiefs'.[60]

Another way the *kastom* system is indirectly hindered by the state system is that people regularly challenge the chiefs on the basis either that they do not have power or that they are breaching the constitution. This also makes it difficult for chiefs to enforce their orders and wield authority effectively. For example, the chiefs might want to send a '*stronghed*' in Vila who has been punished two or three times already by the chiefs but still continues to cause trouble back to their home island. Often, however, people say to them, 'We have freedom of movement, you can't do this to us.' Even in remote islands such as Erromango, it is common for chiefs to complain that young people challenge their authority by saying that chiefs do not have the right to tell them what to do and that only the police have that authority.[61] They say that this is even more frustrating because of the fact that the police seldom come to the island.

In addition, sometimes people criticise the chiefs by comparing what they do with the state system. For example, people complain that the chiefs do not deal with the cases 'properly', as they do not use proof in the way the courts do, without realising the different basis on which the chiefly system works. As shown in Chapter 4, chiefs have started to try to adapt their system to meet these criticisms—for example, by writing laws and calling witnesses—but often these adapted procedures are difficult to implement in practice.

The fact that people are aware of the state system, but do not understand it properly, also leads to dissatisfaction with the *kastom* system, as people feel that they might have been able get a 'better' outcome in the state system. For example, a chief from Malekula explained that the big gap between *kastom* penalties and those imposed by the court was creating problems. He gave the example of a person who raped a woman, who would be made to pay a fine of a pig, kava and a mat in *kastom* but in the court would be sentenced to 12–13 years in jail.[62] He commented:

> People know about the system the court is exercising, like so much number years in jail [sic], and people will have the feeling that that punishment is bigger than this one, stronger…The woman's family will continue to have [a] bad feeling [if the matter is dealt with just in *kastom*] because they know the heavy penalty [in court].[63]

Due to the impression, however unfounded, that the complainant might have received a better deal if the state courts had dealt with the matter, one or both of the parties might feel resentment towards the other, thus undermining one of the main aims and benefits of the *kastom* system—that of reconciling the two parties. The same chief commented that the bad feeling this created could last a 'whole lifetime'.

Finally, the existence of the state system and the knowledge that the making of a *kastom* payment will reduce a criminal sentence have led some members of the community to adopt a cynical attitude towards such payments. There is a reasonably widespread concern that in some cases people just pay 'a mat and a few chickens' in order to lessen their criminal liability before the state system, when there is no accompanying true remorse or restoration of the relationship. This is especially a problem in Vila, where much of the cultural context of the *kastom* system, such as full community participation, is missing. For example, in the case of *Public Prosecutor vs Niala*, the court commented: 'In this case the compensation by custom was carried out expeditiously and genuinely…This is not a case where the compensation by custom took place near to the sentencing date in order to influence the result of such sentencing.'[64]

The existence of the *kastom* system hinders the operation of the state system

The undermining of one system by another works in both directions: the existence of the *kastom* system also undermines the state system, although not as significantly. There are a number of ways this occurs. First, because many people go first to the *kastom* system, complainants often bring their cases late to the state system. This makes it hard for the police to collect evidence and impossible to get evidence such as medical certificates that are often crucial in criminal trials.[65] Second, when people go to the state system first, they might subsequently withdraw their case after it has been settled in *kastom*, thus wasting the time and money that have been spent on investigations or prosecutions. This is reportedly very common—a prosecutor reports that this happens 'almost all the time, especially in rural areas'[66] —and police officers and legal officers in the prosecution office have reported high feelings of frustration about the fact that they put work into a case that then goes nowhere. The Commissioner of

Police stated that this had a demoralising effect on his officers and was a strong disincentive to work hard on a prosecution or investigation.

The existence of the *kastom* system also contributes to lessening the legitimacy of the state system, as people do not see it as 'belonging' to them, but rather as being foreign and imposed, regardless of the fact that the laws have been passed by the Parliament they elected. This is shown in the way people refer to the state system as '*loa blong waetman*' (white man's law) and the continual criticism that the state system does nothing to heal breaches of relationships in the community and that in the state system '*wan iwin, wan ilus*' (one wins and one loses).[67] For example, the police discovered an entire village in Malekula was growing marijuana and many people were arrested and brought to Vila. The leader of the operation (Pais) was reported to have asked 'whether the *nakamals/nasara* and their chiefs have any authority over their people at all' or whether it is 'foreign laws that have authority'.[68] This example shows how people try to manipulate public sentiment by arguing that the state laws are foreign and therefore not legitimate.

In addition, as for the *kastom* system, in the other system, the possibility of being treated better or getting a different outcome is a significant destabilising factor. For example, a former prime minister who was found guilty of forgery was able to undermine the strength of the judgment against him by claiming that he had not been found guilty by the chiefs. It was possibly this factor that led to him being pardoned (after serving only four months of his three-year prison term) and being elected back into Parliament. In a newspaper report, he is cited as saying, 'The public didn't agree. The President didn't agree, and the chiefs didn't agree either.'[69]

Conclusion

This chapter has demonstrated that in Vanuatu it is common for people to engage in 'forum shopping' and 'forum negotiation' at all stages of the process of managing a particular conflict. We have therefore seen that:

- complainants and their families pressure chiefs to deal with cases by threatening to lodge a complaint with the police if they do not
- chiefs pressure defendants to attend meetings and make *kastom* payments by threatening to go to the police if their orders are not obeyed
- complainants and chiefs attempt to withdraw cases from the state system at all stages of the criminal justice process
- there are negotiations over the temporal ordering of the processes of both systems when both systems deal with the same case.

Although some scholars argue that 'people should be allowed to shop for justice',[70] the data generated by this study suggest that the current freedom to do so is destructive as it generates a variety of problems. These problems can be classified into four groups: disempowerment problems, de-legitimation problems, destabilisation problems and individual justice problems. Disempowerment problems involve each system experiencing a loss of exercise of control over what it considers to be its legitimate work because of the actions of the other system. De-legitimation problems arise from each system undermining the authority and legitimacy of the other. Destabilisation problems include all the negative effects on society as a whole that flow from the tensions between the two systems and from the fact that they are not working well together. Finally, individual justice problems are those that particular individuals face as a result of the current relationship between the two systems. The various examples of these four classes of problems, which overlap to a certain extent, can be seen in Table 6.2.

We can see therefore that currently not only is each system missing out on the opportunity to be enriched by, and learn from, the other, each is actively competing with and undermining the other. These findings support Tamanaha's contention that:

> People and groups in social arenas with coexisting, conflicting normative systems will, in the pursuit of their objectives, play these competing systems against one another. Sometimes these clashes can be reconciled. Sometimes they can be ignored. Sometimes they operate in a complementary fashion. But very often they will remain in conflict, with serious social and political ramifications.[71]

Recognition of this is crucial in moving towards a better relationship between the two systems, as it involves acknowledgment that strengthening the *kastom* system cannot be done in isolation from a consideration of how it is affected by the state system, and vice versa.[72] As such, the current response to calls for assistance to shore up chiefly power of putting responsibility solely onto the chiefs is misguided.[73] Rather, what is required is a reform of the relationship between the two systems to encourage greater synergy between them, and it is the various possible models for this that is the concern of the next two chapters.

Table 6.2 Four classes of problems flowing from unrestricted forum shopping

Disempowerment problems	Chiefs feel disempowered because: • the State prohibits them from using coercive powers to enforce their orders • there is concern that their orders breach the constitution • the State makes orders that stop them from being able to hold *kastom* meetings (for example, custodial arrangements, protection orders) • defendants can refuse to make *kastom* payments by arguing they have already been dealt with by the state system • the State sometimes overrules chiefly orders • their authority and therefore enforcement capacity are affected by the de-legitimation problems. State system officials feel disempowered because: • complainants withdraw cases after they have already been actioned • complainants come to the state system too late for the best evidence to be collected.
De-legitimation problems	The *kastom* system is undermined because: • people challenge the authority of chiefs on the basis that their power is unconstitutional and their laws are not written 'in black and white' • chiefly orders are overridden by the State and prosecutions are made after *kastom* reconciliations, suggesting *kastom* processes do not 'really' count • people refuse to make *kastom* payments by claiming they will 'appeal' to the state system • people adopt a cynical attitude towards *kastom* payments, suggesting that people make them just to get a lesser sentence in the state system. The state system is undermined because: • people claim that the state system is foreign and that therefore its judgments do not 'really' count.
Destabilisation problems	• People emerge from prison resentful, creating tension in the community. • The feeling that a complainant could have received a better outcome with the 'other' system undermines reconciliation processes. • Neither system adequately supports the other, meaning that civil disturbances are not managed effectively (for example, the Vila riots discussed in Chapter 1 and the Santo tensions discussed above). • Community confusion and misinformation about which system is responsible for what undermine public confidence in using the two systems. • Both systems avoid taking responsibility for certain types of cases—for example, domestic violence cases—by claiming it is the responsibility of the other system. • State resources are wasted in processing cases that are later withdrawn, meaning less can be spent on effective law and order processes.
Individual justice problems	• Double jeopardy. • Complainants are susceptible to pressure from others to use a particular justice forum.

ENDNOTES

[1] This is a real case but the names of the parties and places have been changed to protect confidentiality. In addition, the identifying parts of newspaper article references have been deleted.

[2] Shah, *Legal Pluralism in Conflict*, p. 9.

[3] This point was made by Tamanaha, *Understanding legal pluralism*, p. 17.

[4] This was identified as a positive feature by the participants at the Vanuatu Judiciary Conference in 2006. See Forsyth, *Report on the Vanuatu Judiciary Conference 2006*.

[5] The real name of the council has been changed to this fictitious name.

[6] Garae, Len 2005, 'Ligo cautions Ambae chiefs not to interfere in alleged rape case', *Vanuatu Daily Post* (Port Vila), 27 October 2005, p. 3.

[7] Garae, Len 2005, 'Lakalakabulu allowed to punish Ambaeans', *Vanuatu Daily Post* (Port Vila), 21 November 2005, p. 2.

[8] The relative value of this payment is shown by the fact that both of the defendants' monthly incomes were approximately vt50 000.

[9] These were that at the time of the offences Agnes had been unwell as a result of diabetes and high blood pressure. Further, over a period of years, she had received considerable financial support from

Peter and his wife, which allowed her to pay for water, lighting, food and school fees for her children. The court found that as a result of her feelings of gratitude and obligation to Peter and his wife, she could not properly deal with the problem of Peter's feelings towards her daughter.

[10] One respondent said that Mary herself went as well, but another denied this. As I could not speak with her directly, I could not find out definitively.

[11] Another respondent had also stated that there was some type of sexual history between Peter and Agnes, which tended to confirm this part of the story.

[12] The concept of shame has very important cultural meanings in Vanuatu. See the discussion of this in Chapter 4 under 'The restorative nature of the *kastom* system'.

[13] This is related to the idea that people's identities are relational (to family and relatives) just as much (or more so) as individual. Strathern terms this notion of Melanesian personhood 'dividuality', emphasising that '[f]ar from being regarded as unique entities, Melanesian persons are as dividually as they are individually conceived. They contain a generalized society within. Indeed, persons are frequently constructed as the plural and composite site of the relationships that produce them.' Strathern, Marilyn 1988, *The Gender of the Gift*, p. 13. Hess (Person and place on Vanua Lava, Vanuatu, p. 76) discusses the fact that in Vanua Lava the blood of a person is seen not as an individual's property, but as belonging to the whole matrilineal group, and explains that therefore when it is spilt the person who did so must pay a small fine to the group.

[14] Interview with the Director of Youth and Sports (Port Vila, 11 June 2004).

[15] Discussed further under 'Dispute and confusion over jurisdiction'.

[16] See further Chapter 4 under 'Challenges for the *kastom* system today'.

[17] He said that he waited for them to come to see him, rather than approaching them himself, because in the *kastom* of East Santo a brother should not be involved in affairs concerning his sister and that they should have known this and come to take the matter off his hands.

[18] Garae, Len 2005, 'Court proceeds with rape case despite chief's appeal', *Vanuatu Daily Post* (Port Vila), 2 November 2005, p. 1.

[19] I did not speak to Mary as I was told that she did not want to speak about it and was not a communicative type of woman.

[20] von Benda-Beckmann and von Benda-Beckmann, 'The dynamics of change and continuity in plural legal orders', p. 25. Santos also argues, in the context of discussing traditional authorities in Mozambique, that '[w]hat is at stake is, once again, the relationship between the political control and the administrative control of populations and their territories, and particularly the question of the legitimacy of the power needed to secure either form of control'. Santos, 'The heterogeneous state and legal pluralism in Mozambique', p. 68.

[21] See Chapter 5 under 'The relationship between the police and the *kastom* system'.

[22] Hess, Person and place on Vanua Lava, Vanuatu, p. 73.

[23] For example, in some areas, it is a very serious breach of *kastom* for a brother to speak about his sister's personal life, as discussed in the case study.

[24] See a further discussion of this in Chapter 4 under '*Kastom* procedures and *kastom* law'.

[25] Interview with Head of Sexual Offences Unit (Port Vila, 23 May 2003).

[26] Copies of police reports on file with the author.

[27] I describe one instance of this that I witnessed in the Prologue.

[28] Interview with a legal officer, Public Prosecutor's Office, Santo (Santo, 17 November 2004).

[29] Binihi, 'Family Ulas prepared to leave Luganville'.

[30] This statement was made by the First Political Advisor in the Ministry of Home Affairs. See Garae, 'Police arrest five in tense Luganville'.

[31] The Church also often becomes involved in such cases, mostly in terms of 'witnessing' and 'counselling' families, offenders and victims before or instead of them ever reaching a *kastom* or state stage.

[32] 'Three VRP members assaulted by UMP leaders', *Vanuatu Daily Post* (Port Vila), 21 April 2007, p. 8.

[33] Interview with a chief (Santo, 17 November 2004) (my translation from Bislama).

[34] Interview with a senior police officer (Santo, 18 November 2004).

[35] In particular, it is important that the ties of interdependence can continue (for example, in the case study, many of Agnes's children and even Mary were dependent on the support of the first defendant and his family).

[36] For example, in the case study, there was the threat that disputes over land in East Santo would flare up and create further divisions.

[37] Interview with the Head of the Sexual Offences Unit, Vanuatu Police Force (Port Vila, 23 May 2003).

[38] According to the President of the NSTCC, the sex had not in fact been forced; rather, Mary had agreed to it in exchange for money. Whether these facts are true or the ones set out in the judgment are true is not clear, but certainly in the president's mind, and most likely in the minds of many of the participants, the *kastom* payment is not concerned with the question of rape. See also below under 'Problems within the *kastom* system'.

[39] Garae, Len 2003, 'Where custom seems to lack value', *Trading Post* (Port Vila), 15 May 2003, p. 4.

[40] Garae, Len 2003, 'Chiefs urge investigation before reconciliation', *Vanuatu Daily Post* (Port Vila), 20 August 2003, p. 4.

[41] Interview with members of Wan Smol Bag Theatre Group (Port Vila, 15 April 2004).

[42] Although Section 39 of the *Penal Code (Amendment) Act 2006* does permit a court to postpone sentencing to allow a *kastom* payment to be made 'if satisfied that it will not cause undue delay'.

[43] Interview with chairman of an island council of chiefs (Santo, 18 November 2004).

[44] Interview with Chief Justice Lunabek (Port Vila, 5 September 2003).

[45] Anonymous interview.

[46] Interview with a chief (Port Vila, 28 February 2005).

[47] Interview with a chief (Port Vila, 31 March 2004).

[48] Interview with Port Vila Town Council of Chiefs (Port Vila, 26 May 2004).

[49] Interview with Legal Officer, Sanma Provincial Council (Santo, 15 November 2004).

[50] The respondent did not know why the brother did this.

[51] Selwyn Garu, Secretary of the Malvatumauri (Author's notes from the Vanuatu Judiciary Conference, University of the South Pacific, Emalus Campus, Port Vila, Vanuatu, 26 August 2006).

[52] For an in-depth discussion of these cases, see Forsyth, Miranda 2005, 'Is there horizontal or vertical enforcement of constitutional rights in Vanuatu? *Family Kalontano v Duruaki Council of Chiefs*', *Journal of South Pacific Law*, vol. 9, no. 2, <http://paclii.org.vu/journals/fJSPL/index.shtml> See also New Zealand Law Commission, *Converging currents*, pp. 212–16, for a discussion of the approach taken in other countries in the region. The New Zealand Law Reform Commission, *Report of Proceedings*, p. 216, concludes that '[c]ustom and human rights can be better synthesised by constitutional or statutory provisions for the horizontal application of human rights, so that they come to apply between individuals, including between customary leaders and their people'.

[53] In any event, the issue is largely a technical one because, as already discussed, the decisions made by the *kastom* system are unenforceable and so the complainant can just refuse to comply with the order. If the order is enforced through force then criminal proceedings can be brought, as occurred in the case of *Public Prosecutor vs Kota and Others* (1989–94, 2 VLR 661). It would become more of an issue if the *kastom* system had formal recognition by the State, although then it might be possible to argue that in fact the *kastom* system is part of the state system for these purposes anyway.

[54] *Public Prosecutor vs Munrel*, 2005, VUSC 75, http://www.paclii.org.vu

[55] Interview with Acting Chief Registrar (Port Vila, 5 April 2004).

[56] Garae, Len 2005, 'North Efate chiefs in prison after losing court case', *Vanuatu Daily Post* (Port Vila), 9 May 2005, p. 6.

[57] Interview with a chief (Port Vila, 22 September 2004).

[58] The level of concern about this is shown by the fact that in one of the earlier drafts of the Bill for the National Council of Chiefs (Organisation) Act, the following provision was included: 'Immunity of members of Councils of Customary Chiefs. No member of any councils [sic] of customary chiefs may be arrested, detained, prosecuted or proceeded against in respect of opinions given, or votes cast, or decisions taken by him in the customary council in the exercise of his office.' This provision was not present in the bill that was in fact presented to Parliament on 14 June 2006, presumably due to the advice of the State Law Office.

[59] 'No faen i go long PVTCC—kot i mas harem Apil: bong i talem', *The Independent* (Port Vila), 14 August 2005, p. 4.

[60] Kalontano et al., *Assessing Community Perspectives on Governance in Vanuatu*, p. 121.

[61] Interview with chief's son (Erromango, 18 May 2004).

[62] Actually this is much higher than the usual rape sentence, which averages about seven years.

[63] Interview with a chief (Port Vila, 14 April 2004).

[64] *Public Prosecutor vs Niala*, 2004, VUCA 25, <http://paclii.org.vu>

[65] Especially because the corroboration rule still exists in Vanuatu for sexual offences. See, for example, *Public Prosecutor vs Mereka* (1992, VUSC 10, http://www.paclii.org.vu).

[66] Interview with a legal officer in the Public Prosecutor's Office (Port Vila, 11 May 2004).

[67] In other words, it is not a win-win situation, such as the *kastom* system is widely perceived as being.

[68] Garae, Len 2006, 'Pais hits out at police over arrests', *Vanutau Daily Post* (Port Vila), 26 October 2006, p. 3. Interestingly, apparently the chief of the village had said himself that he had no control in the village and that no-one listened to him, and the reply given by Pais was that this was because the chief adhered to foreign authority.

[69] Bohane, Ben 2002, 'The boxer: Barak Sope, ex Prime Minister and political maverick', *Pacific Weekly Review*, 25 November – 1 December 2002, p. 6.

[70] Penal Reform International, *Access to Justice in Sub-Saharan Africa*, p. 169.

[71] Tamanaha, *Understanding legal pluralism*, p. 60.

[72] Such an argument is also made in a development context in Boege et al., *States emerging from hybrid political orders*.

[73] This response was illustrated by the recent refusal of Parliament to legislate for chiefly jurisdiction over conflict management when the Bill for the National Council of Chiefs Act (2006) was presented to Parliament. See Chapter 5 under 'The Malvatumauri'.

7. A typology of relationships between state and non-state justice systems

We have seen in the past three chapters that there are significant problems with the current relationship between the *kastom* and state systems in Vanuatu. Therefore, the final questions posed by this study concern an inquiry into other types of relationship that might enable the two systems to work together better, and how such a new relationship could be chosen and implemented. As discussed in Chapter 2, however, to date there has not been a serious attempt to create a framework for a comparative study of relationships between state and non-state justice systems. Further, although in much of the relevant literature there are references to the need to 'recognise', 'empower' and 'harmonise' relations between state and non-state systems, as yet there has been limited inquiry into what exactly is meant by these terms. One explanation for this is the connection of this inquiry with sensitive issues concerning state sovereignty. While it is easy to agree in theory with broad statements about the need for recognition of non-state systems, once the real detail is broached, significant levels of disagreement emerge.[1] This could be due to what Blagg calls the 'meticulously embroidered fiction that it is possible to both "empower" communities and not to give up any of one's own' power.[2] Another reason is that issues of normative recognition and institutional recognition have tended to be conflated.[3]

The aim of these final two chapters is therefore to develop a framework that facilitates the investigation of the range of possible relationships between state and non-state systems, the specific details that differentiate one model of relationship from another, the potential advantages and disadvantages of the different models and the situations in which these models are working or not working and why. It does this through a comparative analysis of the literature on non-state justice systems from more than 20 jurisdictions.[4] In addition, it also considers the internal changes each system could make to develop a more collaborative and closer relationship with the other system. The process advocated thus involves a three-pronged approach. The final chapter is concerned with outlining a methodology of how to use the typology and mutual-adaptation suggestions set out in this chapter to go about restructuring and reforming the relationship between state and non-state justice systems.

One of the key questions this chapter is concerned with is whether it is possible to have the state and non-state justice systems working 'side by side' in a situation of mutual respect and recognition as advocated by many indigenous groups and, if so, what such a situation would look like.[5] Other important questions are whether, and if so, how, a non-state justice system can retain its integrity and wholeness while working together with a state system; and to what extent a state can legitimately empower a non-state justice system to exercise adjudicative power, while respecting the State's constitutional obligations to ensure everyone a fair trial. A strong thread running throughout these two chapters is the emphasis on the need to think less about hierarchy and rules and more about flexible, responsive partnerships and collaborations. In other words, there needs to be both 'bottom-up' and 'top-down' initiatives, as well as continuing dialogue between the two systems about how their relationship can be restructured and renewed to allow each system to support the other in working towards those goals that are common.

In Vanuatu, and in the majority of countries surveyed for this book, there are only two major legal orders: most commonly, the state and a customary justice system. There are, however, other jurisdictions where there are three, and possibly even more, main legal orders. The most common types of non-state legal systems, in addition to customary law systems, are religious-based legal systems, such as the sharia courts in Nigeria,[6] and it is also increasingly recognised that there are transnational legal systems.[7] Although the focus of these two chapters is on a situation involving two types of system only, the same general approach could be adapted to fit a situation where three or more types of legal systems must be accommodated.[8]

A framework for analysing different types of relationship between non-state and state justice systems

Given the lack of an existing framework to analyse different types of relationship between state and non-state justice systems, I propose a framework that conceptualises various types or models of relationship as existing along a spectrum of increasing state acceptance of the validity of the exercise of adjudicative power by the non-state justice system. At one end of the spectrum, the model of relationship involves the State outlawing and suppressing the non-state justice system, while at the other end the model involves the State incorporating the non-state justice system into the state legal system. The proposed framework can be diagrammatically represented as in Figure 7.1.

There are a number of general points to be made about this framework before a detailed description of the different models included in it is entered into. First, many of the models discussed contain *within themselves* a significant range of relationships. It is for this reason that they should be viewed as existing on a spectrum, where one model gradually fuses into another as the detail of the real operation of the relationship is worked out. That said, there are some places along the spectrum where clear lines *can* be drawn and it is possible to say that a fundamentally different approach has been adopted.

Figure 7.1 Typology of relationships between the different systems

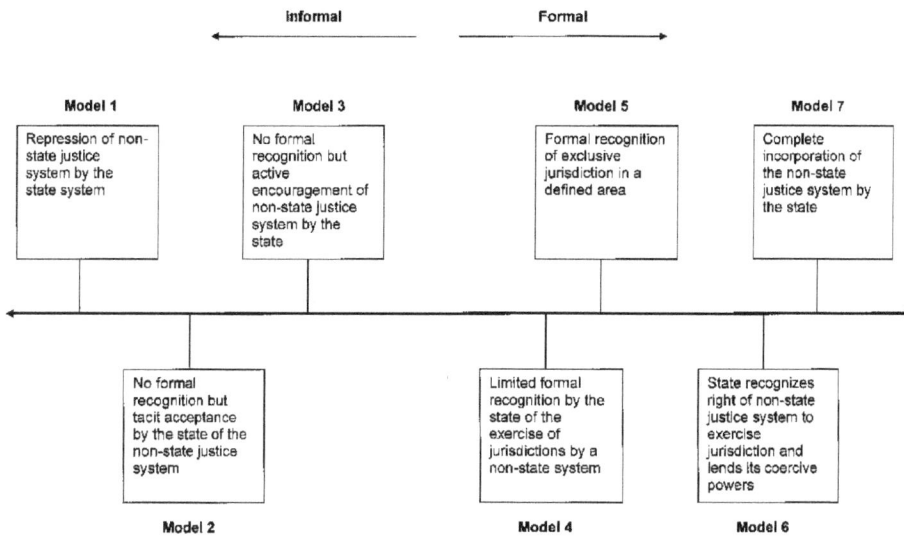

The first of these points is the decision by the State to formally recognise the legitimacy of the exercise of adjudicative power by the non-state justice system. This step changes the relationship from one of informality to one of formality, thus radically altering the nature of the linkages required between the two systems—for example, by introducing questions of supervision and appeal. The importance of this distinction should not, however, be overstated. Bouman argues, 'It is a mistake to equate recognition with active, explicit national regulations.' He observes that in Botswana the unwarranted and non-formally recognised customary courts are by no means autonomous but are controlled indirectly by the State.[9] This suggests the necessity to recognise that even an informal relationship might allow the State to exercise a degree of control over a non-state justice system. Further, this regulation could in fact be as effective in supporting/regulating non-state justice systems as formal recognition. This could also work in the opposite direction. Tamanaha notes, 'The private arbitration tribunals of the *lex mercatoria*, for example, constitute an avoidance of state legal systems, yet state legal systems bolster this putative rival every time judges pay deference to or enforce arbitration decisions.'[10]

A further point where a distinctly different type of relationship arises is where the State lends its coercive powers to the non-state justice system, thus allowing the latter to enforce its decisions by force if necessary and to compel attendance before it. This also has a considerable effect on the relationship as it alters the degree of independence of the two systems from each other, resulting in far more regulation by the State of the non-state justice system and a fundamental change for the non-state justice system of the basis of its authority.

A second general point about the framework is that it considers the response of the State towards the non-state justice system as the defining feature of the relationship, and is thus based on the assumption that there will always be a state system and this will always be important. Of course, there were periods of history (especially before the Treaty of Westphalia in 1648) when this was widely not true, and Chanock argued that even today in many countries state law had a limited role—'not only in the normative universe, but also in its use as a means of settling disputes'.[11] Because of the way the international system of granting states sovereignty over law making works today, there is, however, no jurisdiction where state law does not have at least *theoretical* capacity to regulate local disputes. As Santos argues, 'The nation state and the inter-state system are the central political forms of the capitalist world system, and they will probably remain so for the foreseeable future.'[12]

The approach that is taken in the framework could nonetheless be criticised as privileging the state over the non-state justice system, and thus falling into the ideology of legal centralism.[13] As discussed in Chapter 2, however, it is legitimate (and pragmatic) to recognise that state justice systems in general have certain features that non-state justice systems often do not have, such as a monopoly on the legal use of force, access to state funding and resources, a coherent national structure and, in many countries at least, transparency and institutional structures requiring respect for human rights. Many of these structural characteristics give the State a normative advantage in implementing reforms.[14] In contrast, authority is often dispersed in non-state justice systems, making it difficult to obtain leverage for substantial changes, and funding is often extremely limited. It is not, however, legitimate to treat state law differently merely because it is state law, so once the discussion moves away from the typological framework and into a more normative theory discussion in the next chapter, attempts are made to rebalance this state-centred approach by considering creatively how a non-state justice system might recognise and regulate a state system.

The focus of the framework on the State and its relationship with other systems is also based on a presupposition that there is a separation between state and non-state organs. Given the increasingly elastic boundaries between state and non-state institutions, this is a limitation of the framework that it is hoped future work might overcome. In particular, it means that hybrid legal structures, such as the Village Courts in Papua New Guinea or the Island Courts in Vanuatu, do not fit comfortably into the spectrum. They are, however, discussed in this chapter (under 'Mutual adaptations/innovations by state and non-state systems'), along with a consideration of other adaptations/innovations by both systems.

The third general point to be made about the framework is that it is concerned with what Woodman has termed institutional pluralism, which involves recognition of the structures, institutions and processes of other legal systems, rather than legal norms.

A fourth observation is that it is possible that there might be two or more different models of relationship in existence in the one country at the same time. For example, in Bangladesh, the *shalish* system of dispute resolution exists in three ways: as traditionally administered by village leaders; as administered by a local government body; and in a modified form introduced and overseen by NGOs.[15] Indeed, the research suggests that it is likely that if a state coopts the non-state justice system in a way that limits, rather than increases, effective access to justice, a non-state-authorised version of the same system will develop and exist simultaneously with the state form. For example, in Nigeria, although there are state customary courts, local people prefer to use the non-state traditional courts as these are seen as being not imposed by the government, as the customary courts are.[16] In situations where there are two different types of non-state justice system in one jurisdiction, such as a customary system and a religious-based system, it is also possible that there will be different relationships between the state and the different non-state justice systems.

Finally, it is not necessary for there to be a uniform relationship between the state and non-state justice systems throughout the jurisdiction, but different relationships can be formed depending on the various needs and resources in particular localities. For example, the Northern Territory Law Reform Commission in its *Report of the Committee of Inquiry into Aboriginal Customary Law* recommended that each Aboriginal community should be assisted to develop its own plan to incorporate traditional law into the community *'in any way the community thinks fit*. The inquiry's general view is that *each Aboriginal community will define its own problems and solutions'*[17] and draw up a 'law and justice plan' that will appropriately incorporate or recognise Aboriginal customary law as a method of dealing with issues of concern to the community.[18] The Australian Human Rights and Equal Opportunity Commission has also recognised that 'it is reasonable to expect that one size will not fit all and a variety of forms of modelling and agreement-making could be pursued in regard to community justice'.[19]

Models of relationship

This section analyses seven different types of relationship between state and non-state justice systems. The models that involve *informal* state recognition are analysed in terms of the extent of support given by the State to the non-state justice system. The models that involve *formal* recognition of the non-state justice system by the State are analysed in terms of the extent of the recognition of jurisdiction and its degree of exclusivity, the types of regulation or supervision the State exercises over the non-state justice system and the linkages between the systems in terms of referral and appeals. For all models, examples are given of where they have been used, an assessment is made of the advantages and disadvantages of each model and finally suggestions are made as to the circumstances in which the model should be considered by a particular jurisdiction. It must be noted that these models, and this framework, are very much a beginning rather than a finished product, and are based on data that are often incomplete.

Model 1: Repression of a non-state justice system by the state system

Table 7.1

Significant features	A non-state justice system is actively suppressed by the State—for example, by prosecuting those who administer the system.
Advantages	Ideally ensures a homogenous legal system with no competing systems undermining each other (assuming there are no other non-state justice systems in the country).
Disadvantages	• Might not work in practice but merely force non-state justice systems to go underground. [20] • Breaches of natural justice and human rights of parties much harder to remedy if the system is operating in secret. • The benefits of non-state justice systems such as speed, local presence and easy accessibility are lost. • May in fact alienate those who wish to use the non-state justice system even further from the state system.
Circumstances in which the model should be considered	If the non-state justice system(s) were completely dysfunctional, abuses of human rights were pervasive and these problems were so entrenched as to be incapable of being fixed (for example, the Klu Klux Klan's justice system or that of the Mafia or Colombian bandits) [21] while the state system ensured access to justice for everyone.

This model involves the State actively repressing a non-state justice system by making it illegal for it to deal with cases (rather than by merely outlawing the use of coercive force by the non-state justice system). It is not common, but exists formally in Botswana. As discussed below in Model 7, Botswana has attempted to incorporate its customary justice system almost entirely into its state system, and perhaps as a result has tried to ensure that there will be no 'non-state' customary justice system to compete with its 'state' customary justice system. Thus, Section 33 of the *Customary Courts Act* (Chapter 04:05 [Botswana]) provides that any person who attempts to exercise judicial powers within the jurisdiction of a duly constituted customary court or knowingly sits as a member of such a court is guilty of an offence. In reality, Bouman states that unwarranted and not formally recognised chiefly courts are in fact tolerated, or even supported, by the official police forces, although their adjudication activities are in violation of various national laws. [22] This suggests that enforcement of this model might be problematic. Tamanaha also comments on the possibility of a state system suppressing contrary norms and practices, and notes that '[w]hen the competing system is longstanding or deeply entrenched, the official legal system is confronted with a formidable task, which it often falls short of achieving'. [23]

Model 2: Formal independence between the systems but tacit acceptance by the State of a non-state justice system

In the majority of countries in the world where there is a weak state and a non-state justice system of some sort, there is no formal recognition given to a non-state justice system, but the State turns a 'blind eye' to the fact that the non-state justice system processes the majority of disputes, and state actors often unofficially encourage reliance on the non-state justice system. The literature suggests that this model of relationship exists in: Timor Leste,[24] Lesotho,[25] Malawi,[26] Zambia,[27] Mozambique,[28] Kiribati,[29] Ghana,[30] Nigeria,[31] Solomon Islands[32] and, of course, in Vanuatu. For example, in relation to Timor Leste, Mearns notes:

> Police are acting pragmatically at the village level by encouraging some (often most) situations to be resolved through the village chief (*Chefe de Suco*) and a village council. Like it or not, the local justice system is operating and appears to be the preferred system.[33]

In this model, while the State does not actively suppress the non-state justice system, neither does it support it in any way. The advantages and disadvantages of this model in respect of Vanuatu have already been discussed in full in the previous three chapters. Some of these problems have also been noted in the literature discussing the operation of this model in other jurisdictions. For example, the problem of enforcement of orders that is troubling the chiefs in Vanuatu is also apparent in Malawi:

> [T]he chiefs lamented that because they function outside the constitutional and legal framework they find it difficult to have their judgements enforced. The chiefs demanded that they be given back their powers, particularly their former powers to order detention and the power to impose community service orders, since people are now often likely to ignore their decisions, advice and directives.[34]

One of the other problems of this model highlighted by this study is the lack of mechanisms for controlling abuses of power and breaches of human rights by non-state justice systems. Such problems also appear to exist in other jurisdictions. For example, Mearns notes that in Timor Leste, 'local patterns of dispute resolution certainly do not always accord with ideas of equality, democracy and international human rights'.[35]

In some countries where this model exists, the State does formally recognise the non-state justice system in a very limited way, such as in Vanuatu, where state courts are required to take into account any customary settlement that has been made when sentencing.[36] The courts are not, however, allowed to dismiss a case on the basis that it has been already dealt with by the non-state justice system[37] and, in Vanuatu at least, the customary settlement affects only the quantum and not the nature of the sentence given by the State.[38]

Table 7.2

Significant features	• No formal recognition of right of non-state justice system to exercise adjudicative power. • Allowance by the State of informal relationships between the two systems.
Advantages	• The linkages between the two systems remain flexible and dynamic. • The non-state justice system is able to define its own norms and procedural framework, thus allowing it to meet the changing needs of the community. • It keeps cases out of the state system with minimum cost to the State. • It provides people living in weak states with access to justice they might not have if they rely entirely on the State. • Leaves space for innovation. • It means the non-state justice system must continue to meet community needs and expectations to remain utilised.

Disadvantages	• Temporal ordering problems (see Table 6.1).
	• Problems flowing from unrestricted forum shopping:
	  • disempowerment
	  • de-legitimation
	  • destablisation
	  • individual justice (see Table 6.2).
	• Could be problems of unregulated bias or discrimination against women and youth in the non-state justice system.
	• Non-state justice system could face difficulties with enforcement of orders.

Circumstances in which the model should be considered	If the non-state justice system is very strong with no need of state assistance; its own regulatory processes effectively do or could prevent abuse of human rights; and the informal links with the state system are clear, and do not lead to the undermining of each system and are not subject to abuses of power.

Model 3: No formal recognition but active encouragement of a non-state justice system by the State

This model involves the State fostering and supporting a non-state justice system at an informal level, but stopping short of endorsing its exercise of adjudicative power. Such a relationship exists in many countries throughout the world, particularly where governments are becoming increasingly aware of the limitations of the state justice system and the value of non-state justice systems to overcome some of these limitations. Vanuatu is in fact drifting closer to this model as the State is beginning to support the training of chiefs in dispute-resolution practices, good governance and human rights.[39]

An example of this model is the Zwelethemba Model of Peace Committees in South Africa.[40] This is a pilot project in a poor black community, the aim of which is to improve security for members of the community by using the ability and knowledge of those members. The program was initiated with the support of the national police and the Ministry of Justice. In essence, the Peace Committees receive complaints and then convene 'gatherings' of members of the community who are thought to have the knowledge and capacity to solve the disputes. The Peace Committee members facilitate the process whereby those invited help to outline a plan of action to establish peace. If one of the parties wishes to go to the police then the Peace Committee members facilitate this. No force is used or threatened to ensure compliance. The issue of remuneration for the Peace Committee members is solved in an ingenious way: committees earn a monetary payment for every successful gathering held.[41]

Initial reviews of this pilot project were promising: it was found that commitments to plans of action took place in more than 90 per cent of gatherings, that the process was fast, that women and young people played a major role in the processes and that the Peace Committees dealt effectively with serious problems such as domestic violence that might not have been dealt with by the police. In discussing the approach of the Zwelethemba Model of Peace Committees, Johnston and Shearing comment that 'it does not subscribe to a neo-liberal strategy whereby the state "steers" and the community "rows". On the contrary, the model is based on a process in which governments provide support to local people who, themselves constitute a significant node in the governance of security.'[42]

In Australia, there are a number of ways in which the State is working informally with various Aboriginal communities that also fit this model. Examples are the Community Justice Groups in Queensland and Law and Justice Committees in the Northern Territory. Neither has any statutory authority, but they enter into various agreements with government and community agencies and work together with courts and police in a variety of ways, including diversion programs, pre-court sentencing and community service orders.[43]

There are a number of advantages with such a relationship. Significantly, this model allows the State to support the non-state justice system and also to exercise a degree of *informal* regulation over it, while permitting it to develop through its own processes. It also develops clearer pathways between the systems, reducing confusion about different roles and also ideally reinforcing each other's legitimacy, as they are perceived as working together rather than in competition with each other. Such initiatives have, however, also been criticised as having significant long-term flaws. For example, an Australian Human Rights and Equal Opportunity Commission report states:

> Such community-based processes are generally an add-on to the existing system—tolerated and allowed to operate in tandem with the mainstream system, yet not given the legitimacy or support necessary for them to challenge the fundamental basis of the mainstream system or result in any reconfiguration of relationships and responsibilities. Power is ultimately retained by the relevant authorities within the formal system.[44]

Many of the problems associated with Model 2 also exist in this model, although there is more opportunity for them to be managed by establishing an active dialogue between the two systems.

Table 7.3

Significant features	• No recognition of right of non-state justice system to exercise adjudicative power. • Active encouragement of the non-state justice system by the State. • Informal partnerships with government agencies.
Advantages	• Allows the non-state justice system to remain as close to existing cultural practices as possible, and to develop organically, while assisting with the gradual process of reform. • Prevents the State from dominating the non-state justice system, thus preserving its integrity. • Leaves space for justice innovations. • Close links with state institutions facilitate mutual learning about the two systems. • The ability to refer cases to the state system might provide an extra degree of legitimacy and power to the non-state justice system. [45]
Disadvantages	• Does not provide support for the non-state justice system in terms of enforcement of orders. • Might not provide an effective means of regulating non-state justice systems to prevent possible abuses of power. • Temporal ordering problems and the four categories of problems flowing from unrestricted forum shopping (see Table 7.2) might still exist although these might be able to be negotiated more readily. • Heavily dependent on individuals working in the various systems and therefore susceptible to being short lived.
Circumstances in which the model should be considered	If the non-state justice system is very strong, effectively self-regulating, with no need of state assistance and all that is needed to ensure compliance with constitutional principles and fundamental human rights is some training and better linkages with the state system.

The sorts of questions states considering such a model would need to think about are:

• What kind of informal relationships should be fostered and with whom—that is, who are the people/institutions with the best potential to act as bridges between systems?
• What level of formality should there be in the regulation of those relationships or linkages—that is, a written policy or left to the discretion of people in the position of 'gate-keepers', for example, the police?
• Would people working for the non-state justice system be financed by the State and, if so, how?

Model 4: Limited formal recognition by the State of the exercise of jurisdiction by a non-state justice system

This model involves the State giving limited legislative recognition to a non-state justice system, but no exclusive jurisdiction, no coercive powers and, often, very little in the way of state resources and support. An important feature of this model is that the non-state justice system is also able to make rules or by-laws for the communities it governs, although this might be limited by the requirement that such laws must be in accordance with 'custom and usage'.[46] This feature is due to the recognition that in many customary governance systems there is no distinction drawn between the exercise of legislative and adjudicative powers. The other significant feature of this model is that the State does not seek to exercise much regulatory power over the non-state justice system. In many ways, this model resembles the relationship between equity and the common law before the *Judicature Acts* in the late 1800s.[47]

An example of jurisdiction with this model is the Samoan village *'fono'*.[48] The *Village Fono Act* is relatively recent—passed only in 1990, shortly after the Samoan people had voted in favour of universal suffrage (previously only the *matai* or title-holders were eligible to vote). The act, introduced as 'a move to reinforce and strengthen rural self-reliance'[49] and also possibly as a sweetener to the *matai* as compensation for their loss of political monopoly, confirms the authority of the village *fono* (or council) 'to exercise power or authority in accordance with the custom and usage of that village' (Section 3[2]).[50] Section 6 provides that the village *fono* may impose punishment in accordance with the 'custom and usage of its village' and it specifies a number of punishments, including the power to impose fines and work orders. The Samoan Supreme Court recently held that village *fonos* were not entitled to make an order of banishment and may only petition the Land and Titles Court (a state court) to make such an order.[51] The punishments given by the village *fonos* must be taken into account by a court in sentencing if the person is subsequently found guilty of the same matter (Section 8). The act also provides that there may be an appeal from decisions of village *fonos* to the Land and Titles Court, which may allow or dismiss an appeal or refer the matter back to the *fono* for reconsideration. In the last case, there is no further right of appeal. The Supreme Court has jurisdiction to hear appeals from the Land and Titles Court in relation to alleged infringements of fundamental rights under the constitution.[52]

Another example of this model is the proposed Community Justice Groups (CJGs) recommended by the WA Law Reform Commission in its final report into Aboriginal customary law.[53] The proposal allows Aboriginal communities to apply to the minister to be recognised as CJGs. Those communities with identifiable physical boundaries should then be able to set their own community rules and sanctions to apply to everyone in that particular area. In order to avoid the problems of codification, the communities are free to decide for themselves the rules and sanctions and these may include the incorporation of matters that are offences against Australian law and offences against Aboriginal customary law.[54] This 'untethering' of a non-state justice system from being limited to rules based on custom and tradition is a step that should be applauded as it recognises that indigenous communities need to have laws and procedures that change and develop to meet their needs.

In order to be consistent with 'the aim of facilitating the highest degree of autonomy possible', there are no limits on the matters that may be considered by the CJG, other than the constraints of Australian law.[55] The use of physical force by the CJG is prohibited, as is the power to detain someone, but the communities are given the power to refuse to allow someone to remain in the community for a specified period.[56] An underlying principle of the proposal is that no person may be forced to submit to sanctions imposed by a community. Consequently, the discussion paper noted that enforcement of the orders of the CJG 'will depend primarily on the cultural authority it exerts and the support for the establishment of community rules and sanctions within the community itself'.[57]

In terms of linkages with the state system, the proposal states that it is the responsibility of the CJG to decide whether it should deal with a matter or refer it to the police. It also provides, however, that '[t]he rules set by a community justice group do not replace mainstream law and the police retain full discretion about whether they charge an offender'.[58] In addition, the CJGs are envisaged as playing a crucial role within the state system.[59] The final report stated explicitly that it was for this reason that the commission concluded that it was necessary for CJGs to be formally established.[60]

The only regulation of the CJG is in terms of its composition. It is required to include a representative from each different family, social or skin group within a community and to comprise equal numbers of men and women.[61] In addition, it must be shown that there has been adequate consultation with the members of the community and that a majority of the community members support the establishment of a CJG and its power to set rules and sanctions.[62] There is no appeal from the CJG to the state courts. One way the State is envisaged as supporting CJGs is the establishment of an Aboriginal Justice Advisory Council with the role of providing support and advice to communities who wish to set up a CJG. The State will also provide adequate resources and continuing funding.

This type of model is the preferred model for Penal Reform International, which argues that

> traditional and informal justice forums should be allowed a wide jurisdiction in terms of both civil and criminal matters save only in cases involving the most serious offences such as murder and rape. The broad jurisdiction must go hand in hand with the absence of physically coercive measures.[63]

This view is, however, based on the premise that such forums have the power of social pressure to secure attendance and compliance with an agreement. This premise is, however, not always well founded, as in Vanuatu, as discussed in Chapter 4.

One problem with this model is that it does not overcome the problem of double jeopardy because a person may be found guilty by the non-state justice system *and* the state system. Another concern is that there are not enough checks on the power of the non-state justice systems. For example, in Samoa, it has been argued that the *Village Fono Act* 'entrenches patriarchal and status based norms of customary law, and that these powers have been abused by traditional leaders'.[64] There have been a number of cases where the *fonos* have ordered people to be banished and, in the most extreme of cases, village *fonos* have ordered people to be 'roped to large sticks like pigs' and even, on one occasion, killed.[65] In light of such cases, there have been a number of scholars who have forcefully criticised the act. For example, Meleisea argues that the act 'has in fact formalised the power of the *matai* and local hierarchies. The act allows *matai* to force compliance with their dictates through fines or even expulsion from the village. Increasingly rural people see *fa'a Samoa* as another word for oppression.'[66]

Although these excesses are to an extent checked through the appeal process, often by the time the case finally emerges from the court system the consequences for the victim—banishment, destruction of property, bodily injury—are not easily mended. Another problem with the village *fono* system noted by scholars is that the legislation restricts the powers of the *fono* rather than enhancing them.[67] The removal of the traditional power of banishment is a prime example of this. Corrin Care argues:

> The possibility of mutual support and cross-fertilization of ideas for culturally appropriate penalties held out by earlier decisions on banishment in the formal courts of Samoa has gradually diminished. In Samoa, ownership has been taken from the indigenous forum on the grounds that only the formal courts guarantee the offender due process; a stance that ignores the cultural context of local sanctions.[68]

Among the questions that states considering such a model would need to think about are:

- Should there be some regulation of the composition of the non-state justice system tribunals or procedures and, if so, what?
- What limitations, if any, should there be on the types of matters the non-state justice system can deal with?
- What limitations, if any, should there be on the types of orders the non-state justice system can make?
- Should the non-state justice system be funded in any way by the State?
- What degree of recognition should the State give to a decision made by a non-state justice system (that is, just a mitigating factor in sentencing or should it allow a state court to dismiss a matter entirely)?
- Should there be appeals, or restricted appeals, to the state courts?
- If so, what powers should an appellate court have?
- What should the geographical boundary of the non-state justice system be?

Table 7.4

Significant features	• State recognises validity of exercise of adjudicative power by non-state justice system. • State leaves enforcement to the non-state justice system. • No exclusive jurisdiction given to the non-state justice system. • Very limited regulation of non-state justice system. • Non-state justice system has power to implement its own procedures and substantive laws.
Advantages	• Non-state justice system retains a high degree of autonomy. • Helps to build pride and respect for non-state justice system. • Non-state justice system is not an expense for the State as it operates independently on the basis of voluntary work (note the WA model proposes payment for non-state justice system). • Non-state justice system not subject to challenges to the legitimacy of their exercise of power by the State or the community. • Legal pluralism is formally embraced by the State, which increases the likelihood that the State will work together with the non-state justice system. • Possibility of appeal (if it exists) provides an extra safeguard for ensuring respect for human rights and fair process by the non-state justice system. • Enhances the cultural authority of traditional leaders. • Greater clarity in the jurisdiction of each system and the pathways between the two systems.
Disadvantages	• Does not deal with problem of double jeopardy. Does not assist the non-state justice system with enforcement or resources. • Can lead to abuse of human rights and natural justice in the name of 'tradition'. • Appeals might not always be an option in small communities where people might fear upsetting powerful traditional authorities. • There could still be unregulated 'forum shopping' and related problems.
Circumstances in which the model should be considered	If the non-state justice system is very strong with no need of state assistance, but its own regulatory processes need some state regulation in order to ensure human rights are protected.

Model 5: Formal recognition of exclusive jurisdiction in a defined area

This model involves the State recognising the legitimacy of the non-state system exercising *exclusive* jurisdiction within a defined area. This area might be either a specific geographical location, such as a village or a reserve, or a specific type of subject matter, such as family law or minor criminal matters. It could also involve a separate system for members of a particular ethnic group, even where there is no discrete geographical boundary for that group. What is crucial in this model is that the non-state justice system makes the final decision in a particular case. In many ways, this model is similar to that which exists in federations where each state or province has limited exclusive jurisdiction over certain matters occurring within its geographical boundaries.[69] In this model, each system exists separately from the other and exclusive jurisdiction over particular cases is determined through an agreement that might take the form of legislation or of contract. This model has also been described as involving 'parallel justice systems'.[70]

An example of a situation where jurisdiction is shared on the basis of subject matter is Nigeria, where cases involving Islamic personal law are dealt with in the sharia court system.[71] This is also common in other countries with a large minority Muslim population.[72] An example of a situation where jurisdiction is shared on the basis of geography is Panama, where the Kuna Indians live in internally regulated administrative territories, although this is under the jurisdiction of the national government.[73] Another example is the Tribal Courts in the United States, which have coercive powers and are highly autonomous,[74] although often they are patterned on non-indigenous courts and so can be said to be more hybrid structures than indigenous institutions. Finally, an example of where jurisdiction is based on ethnicity is the situation in many Latin American countries where a significant number of constitutions have recently been amended to recognise the right of indigenous peoples to apply their own customary laws.[75] For example, Article 246 of the *Constitution* of Colombia provides that:

> The authorities of the indigenous peoples may exercise jurisdictional functions within their territories in accordance with their norms and procedures, provided they are not inconsistent with the Constitution and the laws of the Republic. The law shall regulate the way this special jurisdiction will relate to the national judicial system.[76]

It appears, however, that in many states these constitutional provisions have not yet been implemented in practice.[77] Faundez explains:

> Courts in Latin America, however, have a unique problem because, although most constitutions today recognise multiculturalism and legal pluralism, legislatures have failed to address the crucial question as to how indigenous or other non-state forms of law are related to state law. As a consequence, courts have no substantive legislative guidelines on how to respond to their activities or decisions of non-state justice systems. Not surprisingly, in the case of Peru, the response of the courts to the non-state justice system has generally been hostile.[78]

A slightly different picture in relation to Colombia is presented by Assies, who observes that it has taken two important steps to progress the constitutional provisions.[79] The first is the commissioning of a study of indigenous legal systems and the second is the creation of a new constitutional court. He states that this court appears in some cases to have extended 'a large degree of autonomy to a relatively acculturated community'.[80] He concludes, 'An outstanding feature of the Constitutional Court verdicts is that they seek to promote intercultural dialogue rather than to resolve all conflicts of jurisdiction through the usual means of state intervention based on the unilateral imposition of a unified body of positive law.'[81]

In the absence of more detailed information about the real workings of these systems, it is impossible to determine whether they fit exactly into this model or whether the State in fact remains the final arbiter, thus bringing them closer to the previous model.[82] In most countries, it would seem that the State keeps at least a small degree of control over the non-state justice systems, thus making this model more of an ideal than a reality experienced in any jurisdiction.[83]

The principal advantage of such a system is that it allows non-state systems to function without interference from the state system, which might distort them, undermine their effectiveness or interfere with their integrity. For example, Webber argues that such a system might be required in Canada because a measure of separation is needed if distinctively aboriginal approaches and procedures are to be re-established. He states that this approach 'allow[s] the administration of justice in Aboriginal communities to take into account the experience of Aboriginal peoples...rather than baldly imposing the language and forms of non-Aboriginal traditions'.[84] A second advantage is that this model stops forum shopping and its associated problems, as matters will be able to be dealt with in only one system. Dewhurst therefore argues, also in the context of advocating such a model for aborigines in Canada, that '[i]f Aboriginal systems are considered to be alternative, preliminary, of lower authority, or unofficial, their opponents will resort to the more "final" or "official" adversarial system...Instead, Aboriginal justice systems must be designed as authoritative and parallel models of justice'.[85]

Further, as Oba argues in the Nigerian context, having appeals from a non-state system to a state system could in fact create injustice, as the state system might be ill equipped to deal with the law and procedures of the non-state system. He therefore argues that '[i]t is definitely unacceptable to Muslims that someone who is not subject to Islamic law, who may be totally bereft of any knowledge of Islamic law and may even have an aversion to it be engaged in its administration'.[86] He concludes that a parallel series of courts is the most feasible option for Nigeria.[87]

There are, however, a number of problems with such a system. First, separation on the basis of geography brings up very visibly problems of equality before the law. These arguments have been dealt with exhaustively by Webber, and for reasons of space his arguments will not be repeated here.[88] He concludes that 'when one thinks more carefully about freedom, equality, and the relevance of culture for law, there are circumstances in which parallel systems of Aboriginal justice are both acceptable and appropriate'.[89] Dewhurst suggests that such concerns can be overcome by allowing all accused, aboriginal and non-aboriginal alike, to elect the system under which they will be tried. Second, the absence of any degree of regulation by the state system means there is the possibility that there will be abuses of power that will go unchecked, particularly in sensitive areas such as cases involving women and children. Webber suggests that such concerns raise the more general issue of trust in non-state institutions, observing that overcoming this might require that these institutions are 'reinvented' in a way that allows for a system of checks such as did not exist, or existed in a different form, before the imposition of non-indigenous institutions.[90] Horton raises a third concern, arguing that indigenous territorial and political autonomy might be used to justify state neglect and abandonment.[91]

Among the questions that states considering such a model would need to think about are:

- Would parties be required to elect at the outset which system to use? What would happen if they disagreed?
- What should a system do if a case comes before it that has already been adjudicated by another system?
- Should the division in jurisdiction be on the basis of subject matter, territorial reach[92] or ethnicity of parties?
- Should the State have control over any procedural elements of the non-state justice system (for example, to reduce the likelihood of bias or abuses of power, and so on) as an initial prerequisite for recognition?[93]
- If there are constitutional guarantees about justice, how can these be accommodated and which system will adjudicate on potential breaches?

Table 7.5

Significant features	• Non-state justice system is given exclusive jurisdiction that is limited on the basis of territorial reach, subject matter or ethnicity of users. • State does not provide enforcement mechanisms or regulate non-state justice system.
Advantages	• Non-state justice systems allowed to function independently and autonomously. • No forum shopping allowed. • Non-state justice system recognised as being fully equal with state system (consequently empowers and legitimises customary justice system). • Only administrators skilled in the system have the right to make decisions concerning the implementation of its norms. • Helps to build pride and respect for non-state justice systems that might have been historically marginalised.
Disadvantages	• No facilitation of cross-fertilisation between the two systems. • No ability for the State to control abuses of power, bias, discrimination against women, and so on. • Non-state justice system not supported by state resources or coercive powers. • State might be able to justify abandonment and neglect of areas regulated by non-state justice system. • Concerns about equality before the law.
Circumstances in which the model should be considered	Where there are discrete groups of people within a state with very different justice needs that can be met completely by a non-state justice system and are not being met by the state justice system.

Model 6: Formal recognition and the giving of state coercive powers to a non-state justice system

In this model, the State recognises the right of a non-state justice system to exercise jurisdiction and also provides support in terms of using its coercive powers to enforce decisions made by a non-state justice system. The exercise of jurisdiction is exclusive in that a person who has been dealt with by one system cannot go afresh to the other system. It is not, however, exclusive in that a person may appeal from the non-state justice system to the State. It responds to the situation where there are a number of competing requirements: state support for a non-state justice system in terms of resources and enforcement; the need for a non-state justice system to operate within the values underlying the constitutional framework of the State; and the desire to maintain a non-state justice system in a form that is as unchanged as possible so as to preserve its advantages in terms of accessibility, legitimacy, speed, simplicity, informality, holistic approach and cultural relevance. The continuing challenge with a model such as this is to provide sufficient support to a non-state justice system while resisting the temptation (and political pressure) to overregulate and modify it.

An example that fits this model and comes close to successfully managing all of these criteria is the South African Traditional Courts. These courts are based on a proposal developed by the South African Law Commission (SALC) and the South African Department of Justice and Constitutional Development.[94] The general approach adopted was to regulate non-state justice systems rather than incorporate them and to generate clear and easy links between state and non-state systems while ensuring that they operated within the law.[95] Based on a long and extensive discussion process, the SALC produced a *Report on traditional courts and the judicial function of traditional leaders* (2003) and also a draft Customary Courts Bill (2003). The bill was finally introduced, after modifications, into Parliament in May 2008 as the Traditional Courts Bill.[96]

The preamble to the bill explains that its purpose is to 'provide for the structure and functioning of Traditional Courts in line with constitutional imperatives and values'. The courts are recognised by the State through the minister designating a senior tribal leader as presiding officer of a traditional court for his or her area of jurisdiction.

The courts are given jurisdiction over civil disputes arising out of customary law and custom, although there is a list of matters the courts do not have jurisdiction over. The courts are also given jurisdiction over a limited range of minor criminal offences, including theft, malicious damage to property, assault and *crimen injuria* (Sections 5 and 6 and Schedule 1).

The courts are specifically enjoined to resolve disputes in accordance with custom and to follow customary procedures (Sections 7, 8). There are, however, also very detailed provisions requiring the courts to resolve disputes 'in accordance with the norms and standards reflected in the Constitution' and also to ensure that the Bill of Rights is followed during hearings (Sections 7, 9). There is no acknowledgment, in the legislation at least, that there might be a conflict between resolving a dispute in a customary manner and applying constitutional norms. This could lead to some difficulties for traditional leaders when dealing with such conflicts.

The bill gives fairly significant powers to the Traditional Courts, providing that a Magistrate's Court must enforce a decision made by a customary court if the decision is not followed within the time specified (Section 11). The courts have powers to fine people, make orders of compensation, make orders to give an apology, make an order directing a matter be submitted to national prosecuting authorities and to order a person to do community service (Section 10).

There are a number of ways in which the State regulates the Traditional Courts. It requires that all fines are to be paid into a special account, that the courts are to keep written records of certain basic information concerning the cases they deal with and there is a system of appeals to the state courts (from orders to pay fines and compensation and an order that deprives a person of benefits accruing under customary law only) (Section 13), as well as procedural review by Magistrates' Courts.[97] A proposal from the SALC that did not make it into the final bill was to have a registrar for the courts whose general role was to guide and supervise the courts and to transfer cases to the state system where it was appropriate. The report explains that:

> The preponderant view was that keeping the supervision and monitoring of customary courts away from magistrates courts and leaving the process to a dedicated office would insulate customary law and adjudicatory procedures from encroachment by the common law through too much association with magistrates' courts.[98]

A further type of control over the courts is the section that penalises members of the court who are incompetent or engage in misconduct (Section 16).

The relationship between the two systems is very clearly regulated in this model. In addition to the appeal procedures, there are detailed provisions relating to the transfer of cases between the different systems (Section 19). The SALC proposal provides that in all criminal cases the accused person has the right to demand that the case be transferred to another court of competent jurisdiction, but this has not been included in the final bill.

Another example of this model, in an economic context, is where the state legal system recognises and encourages parties to reach private arbitration decisions and then enforces them.[99]

One of the issues of such a model is how to ensure that constitutional guarantees of natural justice and human rights are protected by the non-state justice system. The rules of natural justice, which underpin the right to a fair hearing that is included in many constitutions and is embodied in Article 14 of the *International Covenant on Civil and Political Rights*, require that people exercising judicial power should be seen to be impartial and without a personal interest in the outcome, and also that a person is present at the hearing of the matter. Some features of some non-state justice systems can compromise these principles—for example, by having as judges people who are related in some way to the parties.

Such concerns can, however, be managed. First of all, there should be an inquiry into what sort of constitutional breaches are likely to occur, based on empirical evidence rather than non-factually based assumptions, and then mechanisms developed that can manage these in the least intrusive way possible. Thus, the Australian Law Reform Commission has said: 'It cannot be argued that the establishment of local "traditional courts" or similar mechanisms will necessarily involve breach of the Convention [*International Covenant on Civil and Political Rights*] standards, provided appropriate procedural safeguards are established.'[100]

One procedural mechanism that can be used, and has been used in the South African Traditional Courts and also in the Samoan village *fonos*, is that of appeal. The European Court of Human Rights has held that procedural or other defects at first instance can be cured on appeal.[101] This approach has also been suggested by the New Zealand Law Reform Commission, which argues, 'The principles of natural justice may be maintained, however, through adequate appeal rights, in the case of those community justice bodies now provided for by statute.'[102] When considering the types of appeals possible, it suggests that the courts could adopt a policy of not overturning non-state justice system outcomes without good reason, and where these exist the court may go further and suggest guidelines to prevent further prejudice in future. The courts may also consider referring the matter back to the non-state justice system for reconsideration.[103] It in fact concludes that '[u]ltimately, the recognition of community justice bodies may best advance the constitutional objectives of respecting both human rights and the inherited wisdom of the Pacific'.[104]

Among the questions states considering such a model would need to think about are:

- Will the State enforce the orders of the non-state justice system in terms of punishments and in terms of orders to attend hearings? If so, how? By state authorities? Or will it give immunity to officials of the non-state justice system in the usage of reasonable force? Or assist in establishing a special police force for the non-state justice system?[105] Or should the parties have to sign an agreement that they will abide by the decision of the chiefs at the end of the meeting?
- How many layers of non-state justice system courts should there be?
- Should there be a non-state justice court of appeal or should a state court be the appeal court? On what grounds could there be an appeal?
- To what extent should the composition of non-state justice system courts be regulated by the State?
- Should the State mandate that women also serve judicial roles in the non-state justice system courts?
- When a party is outside the non-state justice system (for example, from a different custom area), what procedures should apply?

Table 7.6

Significant features	• State formally recognises validity of the exercise of jurisdiction by non-state justice system. • State lends its coercive powers to the non-state justice system. • Clear linkages and pathways for the transfer of cases between systems. • Non-state justice system free to apply its own norms and procedures.
Advantages	• Balances state support for the non-state justice system in terms of resources and enforcement; the need for the non-state justice system to operate within the values underlying the constitutional framework of the State; and the desire to maintain the non-state justice system in as unchanged a form as possible so as to preserve their various advantages. • Pathways can be instituted to avoid double jeopardy and duplication/waste of resources. • Forum shopping is limited.
Disadvantages	• The non-state justice system aligns itself very closely with the State and thus fundamentally alters the basis on which it gains its power and legitimacy. • As the chiefs are no longer dependent on the community for support, they might be less inclined to look after their community and thus become less accountable at a local level than if they need to continually maintain their community's support. • The State would have to expend resources on the non-state justice system. • Might require traditional leaders to administer state laws, which they might not be equipped to do. • Limits space for innovation for the non-state justice system. • There might be a lack of political will to introduce such a model.
Circumstances in which the model should be considered	Where the non-state justice system requires assistance from the State in terms of enforcement of orders and where some degree of regulation from the State would better ensure human rights are not being breached, and limits can be placed on the power of the State in its regulation of the non-state justice system.

- What should be the jurisdiction of the non-state justice system? How should it be determined? By agreement between parties? By limits set by regulations? Should one or either party be able to opt out of the jurisdiction of the non-state justice system?
- Should the non-state justice system be given jurisdiction over state crimes as well as customary offences?
- If criminal jurisdiction is given, what should be the rules about which non-state justice system court has jurisdiction (that is, should it be where the crime is committed)?
- Should any particular procedural requirements be mandated by the State—for example, the right of women and youth to have a voice?
- What rules, if any, should there be about the making of notes of proceedings and the keeping of such records?
- Should legal or other representation be allowed?
- Should there be any limitations on the types of orders that can be made?
- Should there be fixed fees the non-state justice system can charge? If so, should there be rules about what can happen to these funds?
- Should the members of the courts be paid?
- What safeguards should be created to guard against abuse of power in the non-state justice system?
- Should there be supervision of the non-state justice system? If so, by whom—magistrates or a special body?

- Should there be a special office, such as a secretariat, created to manage the non-state justice system and its relationship with the state system?

Model 7: Complete incorporation of the non-state justice system by the State

The last model involves incorporating the non-state justice system entirely into the state system by 'bureaucratising and "civilising" [it and] embracing [it] as the lowest tier into the family of courts under the Constitution'.[106] This model has been adopted in some African countries—for example, Botswana[107] and Nigeria.[108] It is also very similar to the chiefs' courts or customary courts in countries where the policy of indirect rule was used during colonial times.[109] This model is in many ways very close to the 'hybrid' structures of Village Courts discussed below, but is different in principle, even if not in practice, because the idea is to draw the non-state justice system into the state system, rather than to create a new hybrid system from the start.[110] Of course, the various regulations the State may impose on a non-state justice system as part of the incorporation might mean that in practice it ends up looking just as much a hybrid system as one that has been crafted as such initially. It is also similar to Model 6, but differs from it in that the non-state justice system is conceived as part of the state system, uses state norms and procedures and has little room to develop itself organically. This demonstrates that the intention and philosophy behind a reform agenda can often be just as important as the substantive content.

In Botswana, the two highest levels of customary courts were incorporated into the state system during the colonial period through a long process that began in 1934.[111] Today, the relationship between the two systems is governed by the *Customary Courts Act*, which allows a chief to submit to the minister a recommendation for the recognition, establishment or variation in jurisdiction of customary courts within his area (Section 7[1]). The minister may then recognise or establish the court and define its jurisdiction, prescribe the constitution of the court and the powers of the members of the court (Sections 7[2], 8). Through the act and the rules made under the act, the customary courts are very significantly controlled by the State. The courts are required to use state law rather than customary law in the area of criminal law, as Section 12(6) provides that 'no person shall be charged with a criminal offence unless such offence is created by the Penal Code or some other law'. An example of the consequences of this is the case of *Bimbo vs State*, in which the accused was convicted of adultery by a customary court, however, the High Court quashed the conviction on the grounds that adultery was not an offence created by the Penal Code or other written law.[112] Further, customary courts are required to follow the provisions of the *Customary Courts (Procedure) Rules* in criminal cases, meaning that even their procedural flexibility is curtailed (Section 21). The courts are, however, given considerable power, including the power to compel attendance (Section 29), to imprison and even to impose corporal punishment (Section 18).

The relationship between the two systems on an institutional level is very close. The act provides for appeals to the state courts from the customary courts (Section 42) as well as supervisory provisions (by chiefs) (Section 40) and 'revisory' provisions by magistrates (Section 39). There are also complex transferral procedures between the two different sorts of courts (Section 37). Griffiths comments that the closeness of the two courts is not merely determined by these institutional links, however, but that '[t]he personnel themselves view their role and that of their institution as part of a larger whole, an overall system in which these institutions have their place'.[113] There is even some suggestion of a real change of personnel within the two systems. For example, Schärf reports that although the Customary Court of Appeal is in theory staffed by chiefs, in practice, it is sometimes staffed by non-chiefly bureaucrats.[114]

The significant advantage of this model is that it allows, indeed fosters, a cross-fertilisation of ideas and procedures between the two systems. Schärf notes that 'the literature reveals an active dialogue between customary courts and magistrates' courts and equally that in this situation neither legal system remains pure.[115] In other words customary law is increasingly incorporating aspects of general law and vice-versa.' Griffiths similarly finds that it is no longer possible in Botswana to see the customary system as 'representing something "other" than state justice, as more egalitarian and from which considerations of power and status [are] absent', but also that neither can the Magistrate's Court be seen as 'representing an inaccessible and inflexible rule based system of justice'.[116] (A negative consequence of this, as Griffiths points out, is that women might not be able to rely on the state system for equality and neutrality, but might find that there, too, 'gender cuts across social and economic divisions...to place women generally at a disadvantage when it comes to negotiating their status with men'.)[117] Some of the other advantages of this model are that it brings non-state justice systems into conformity with state constitutions, it provides enforcement mechanisms for the non-state justice system, it makes non-state justice system officials more accountable and it prevents there being two or more conflicting systems of justice in operation. Schärf concludes that '[b]oth warranting and recognizing customary courts appears to have reduced the worst excesses of such courts'.[118]

There are, however, also a number of disadvantages with the model. First, it has been argued that the dominance of the State undermines the non-state justice system. Otlhogile states that '[a]lthough the relationship between these two legal regimes could have been mutually enriching, the inevitable precedence of general law over customary law has served to undercut the legal and moral authority of both institutions'.[119] Schärf similarly comments that the magistrates can and do overturn the judgment of chiefs and thereby undermine the influence of chiefs and headmen.[120] Elechi states that in Nigeria the Customary Courts

> are accused of being unnecessarily formal and rigid, employing a coercive rather than a persuasive approach. Even though the Customary Courts are staffed by indigenous people, they are employed by and are accountable to the central government. The delivery of justice in the customary courts is hampered by a bureaucratic structure and corruption.[121]

Penal Reform International similarly argues that the experience of many African countries in incorporating existing non-state justice systems into the state system has tended to undermine the positive attributes of the informal system, noting:

> The voluntary nature of the process is undermined by the presence of state coercion. As a result, the courts no longer rely on social sanctions and public participation loses its primary importance. At the same time, decisions which do not conform to procedural requirements, or which deviate from the strict law in the interests of reconciliation may be reviewed and overturned on appeal to the higher courts. Procedural requirements invariably become greater and public participation is curtailed.[122]

A more optimistic picture is provided by Fombad, who argues that '[a]lthough process-wise and even rule-wise, today's customary law may not always correspond exactly with that of the pre-colonial past...value-wise, it has retained its distinctive communal nature'.[123]

Boko discusses another problem with this model.[124] He points out that although judges in the customary courts are untrained, and some are barely literate, they are nevertheless expected to interpret and apply provisions of written penal laws, none of which has been translated into the vernacular. These courts can sentence people to custodial sentences of more than five years. He argues:

> The only feature of the customary courts which endears them to the government is that they dispose of their cases quickly and swiftly. But the quality of the justice they dispense is highly questionable. Perhaps it is time note was taken that justice rushed may also be justice denied.[125]

This is of significant concern, especially given Fombad's observation that in some towns almost 75 per cent of those in prison are serving sentences handed down in customary courts.[126]

A final problem is that in the context of existing local power struggles, such as between traditional elites and commoners, state incorporation of traditional chiefly tribunals might give a considerable advantage to one side.[127]

The sorts of questions that a state considering such a model would need to consider are similar to the ones discussed for Model 6 above. If this model were considered in a three-systems jurisdiction, the State could either incorporate both non-state justice systems, on similar or different bases, or incorporate one and develop a different relationship with the other. In the former case, there would be additional questions concerning pathways between the two non-state justice systems. In the latter case, the non-state justice system that had been incorporated would need to develop a relationship with the other non-state justice system in line with the relationship the State had adopted, as it would be almost entirely under the control of the State.

Table 7.7

Significant features	• Incorporation of non-state justice system into state system. • Non-state justice system follows state procedural and substantive laws.
Advantages	• Fosters a cross-fertilisation of ideas and procedures between the two systems. • It brings the non-state justice systems into conformity with state constitutions. • It provides enforcement mechanisms for the non-state justice system. • It makes the non-state justice system officials more accountable. • It prevents there being two conflicting systems of justice in operation, which alleviates the problems of undermining, double jeopardy and forum shopping.
Disadvantages	• State has to invest considerable resources. • Untrained judicial officers are required to administer state legislation. • Traditional leaders might feel they are being dominated by the state system and refuse to cooperate. • Many of the advantages, such as informality and flexibility, of the non-state justice system would be reduced. • Changes the basis on which the non-state justice system wins its legitimacy and support. • Payment of people involved in the non-state justice system could lead to jealousy, division and corruption in the non-state justice system. • Could stifle the dynamism of the non-state justice system. • Problem of 'creeping procedural formalism'. • Could make the non-state justice system less accessible to the public. • There could still be 'non-state' non-state justice systems competing with and undermining the 'state' non-state justice systems. • The basic principles of decision making of the non-state justice system are likely to be substantially modified.
Circumstances in which the model should be considered	Where the non-state justice system has already adopted many features of the state system and has lost its traditional basis of legitimacy (for example, by being used by colonial governments in a system of native rule such as in many African countries)[128] and there is a need for more grassroots courts.

Mutual adaptations/innovations by state and non-state systems

This section examines a number of reforms that can be made to state and non-state systems to help to strengthen the links between them and to enable them to work in a more supportive relationship with one another. In addition, these changes could also improve each system, as each would be learning from, and adapting, positive aspects of the other system(s).[129] This kind of two-way dynamic process might be one of the best ways of allowing the systems to deal more successfully with new and existing challenges. Most of these changes could be made within any of the models of relationships, although a few are not so flexible.

The changes discussed in this section are considered in the context of a state and a non-state customary justice system. If the non-state justice system under consideration is not a customary justice system but another type of legal order (for example, one based on religion), different adaptations/innovations might be necessary. The general approach proposed, however—to mirror the changes made by each so that they grow towards each other and learn from each other—remains applicable.

Table 7.8: Summary of mutual adaptation possibilities by state and customary justice systems

Areas of mutual adaptation	State	Customary justice system
Mutual learning	Learn about the customary justice system's institutions, principles and procedures.	Learn about the state justice system's institutions, principles and procedures.
Sharing of procedures	Use of more customary procedures in state courts—for example, by creating hybrid institutions such as Village Courts in Papua New Guinea.	Consideration of the utility of introducing good management initiatives from the state system.
	Adoption of a less adversarial approach.	Awareness programs about different types of decision-making procedures, especially in areas where there is domination by traditional leaders.
	Reform the laws of evidence to make them less complex and more culturally relevant.	Learn about the State's rules of evidence that might be useful.
Sharing of substantive laws/principles	Use of substantive customary law in state courts—for example, mandating its use, as in Papua New Guinea.	Use of human rights principles from the state system.
Use of key players/institutions from the other system(s)	Use of chiefs/traditional leaders in state courts.	Use of state officials by the customary justice system.
	Referral of issues/cases to the customary justice system.	Referral of cases to the state system.
	Involve traditional leaders in judicial appointments committees (might not exist in some/all state systems—for example, where the appointments are the prerogative of the Executive).	Involve a member of the state judiciary in highest levels of the customary system, either by involvement in appointments or as a member.

One of the major challenges in this area is identifying *how* change can be brought about in customary justice systems, especially in those with a decentralised administration and limited resources. Woodman has highlighted this issue, noting that '[a]lmost every set of development proposals and even general discussions of development assume that the type of activity that potentially can assist development is action by or within the institutions of the state'.[130] Given the practical realities surrounding most customary justice systems, apart from programs generated within the customary justice system itself (that are likely to be restricted in scope due to funding and organisational limitations), it is likely the State will be involved to an extent in any reform program.[131] The challenge is therefore to limit the opportunity for the State to dominate the reform agenda. One possible way to achieve this is to establish an office with specific responsibility for assisting customary justice systems with reform initiatives, with as much control as possible over the office given to the customary justice system. Such an office might also ensure that much of the empowerment of the customary justice system occurs at local levels outside the State, with local leaders given control over the priorities and directions of reform.

The four areas of adaptation that should be considered are set out in Table 7.8. It must be highlighted that what is presented are merely suggestions and their main use is in exposing the range of possibilities available. Depending on the particular situation of the customary justice system, some might not be helpful.

Mutual learning

One of the easiest, but most important steps for the two systems to work together well is for each to have a sound understanding of the other. Such an approach was supported by an Australian Law Reform Commission report in 1986 that recommended that judges, lawyers and others involved in criminal justice all needed better information and education about Aboriginal customary laws, noting that '[m]uch can be achieved towards the recognition of Aboriginal customary laws and satisfying Aboriginal demands in this regard by simple administrative measures of this kind'.[132] Similar comments were made at a workshop conducted by the New Zealand Law Reform Commission on Custom and Human Rights in the Pacific, at which some participants observed that rather than having more *supervision* of community justice mechanisms by formal courts and central government, what was needed was greater *respect, understanding and collaboration* between the different systems.[133]

Just as there is an obligation on the State to understand more about the customary justice system, it is important for those in the customary justice system to understand the approach and procedures of the state system. At the Vanuatu Judiciary Conference in 2006, one of the important points to emerge was that many chiefs were not aware of the mechanisms that currently existed for the two systems to work together, such as the power given to courts to take into account customary compensation when sentencing.[134] Many were pleased to discover that this procedure existed, as it made them feel that the *kastom* system was given more importance by the State than they had previously thought. Following from this, one of the major ways identified to move the relationship between the two systems forward was thus that the Malvatumauri should 'ensure that the chiefs are provided with more training and awareness about the existing state legal structure and laws'.[135] This learning could be facilitated through workshops, conferences and training programs and also through indirect means such as through the use of assessors, as discussed below. It might also be a useful idea to have certain people trained as 'justice advocates' who can act as resources for their fellow community members about the state system.

Sharing of procedures

Changes the state system could make to its procedures

Creation of hybrid institutions

The first reform that the state system can make on a procedural level to bridge the gap between it and the customary justice system is to create a lower level of courts or dispute-resolution scheme modelled to a degree on the customary justice system. These schemes have the potential to deliver many of the same benefits of a customary justice system, as they are based on tradition, are far less costly than the state courts and generally much quicker as well. They also tend to be more informal than higher courts, are staffed by judicial officers with no formal training in law, may exclude lawyers and employ a less-adversarial approach. Importantly, however, these schemes are really state institutions as they are created by statute and have their parameters set by statute. Examples of such schemes are the Village Courts in Papua New Guinea, local courts in Solomon Islands, the Island Courts and Customary Land Tribunals in Vanuatu and the Barangay Justice System in the Philippines.[136]

There are two main areas of concern with the workings of such hybrid schemes. The first is that they are susceptible to domination by local 'big-men' and can in fact perpetuate power imbalances, such as those between women, youth and men. For example, Dinnen argues that the PNG Village Courts 'reinforce the subordination of women by condoning "domestic" violence and other abuses, and regularly exceed their powers'.[137] He concludes:

> The broader policy challenge is how to avoid the capture of such institutions by sectional interests [or indeed domination by power inequalities] while allowing them to remain responsive to local circumstances. Part of the institutional solution in the case of the village courts is to ensure effective supervision as provided for under their enabling legislation.[138]

It should be noted that the view that women are not given a voice in PNG Village Courts has recently been challenged by Goddard, who argues that the literature that espouses this view is not based on rigorous research 'but by an *a priori* position that the male-dominated courts necessarily impose indigenous patriarchal forms of social control'.[139] He states that he 'remain[s] unconvinced that women are not generally confident and reasonably successful users of the village courts'.[140]

A second problem is that there is often a 'creeping formalism' in such courts. For example, Goddard notes that although the court magistrates in Papua New Guinea are elected based on their status as customary experts, in fact they rigidly apply, and are constrained by, state law as well as procedures.[141] It is also often the case that, although such courts are mandated to apply customary law and employ customary processes, in reality they may choose not to do so or, as with the Island Courts in Vanuatu, might not be able to due to the limits of their warrant.[142] Concerns such as these led the Law Reform Commission of Western Australia to consciously reject the creation of hybrid institutions. It concluded that 'an attempt to create an Aboriginal-controlled court which is partly based on Aboriginal customary law and partly based on general legal principles is fraught with difficulty'.[143]

A variation on village courts has been proposed recently to the Fijian Law Reform Commission. The proposal is essentially to allow villages to make their own by-laws and for these to be administered by magistrates who will sit frequently in the provinces. These courts would be conducted in local languages and the magistrates would have flexibility in dispensing justice, particularly with regard to alternatives to custodial sentences.[144] A similar scheme exists in Western Australia under the *Aboriginal Communities Act 1979* (WA), whereby certain approved Aboriginal communities can make by-laws controlling behaviour on their community lands that are enforced by the police and Magistrates' Courts.

There are, however, some concerns about the viability of such by-law schemes. In its review of the WA scheme, the Law Reform Commission of Western Australia found many problems, including issues with enforcement (police had the responsibility for enforcing the by-laws but were often not present in the communities), the fact that the by-laws did not reflect Aboriginal customary law and the fact that they were not necessarily controlled by traditional authority structures. It concluded that '[t]he by-law scheme...has done little to improve the justice-related outcomes for Aboriginal people or to allow Aboriginal people to practice customary law'.[145] It also noted that 'what commenced as a consultation process with consideration to the application and process of traditional law within the communities, resulted in a process, application and interpretation of rules and regulations based entirely on [the state] laws and legal system'.[146]

Adoption of a less adversarial approach

Many aspects of customary justice systems are far closer to the procedures and approaches of the inquisitorial system used in many civil law countries than the adversarial approach used in common law countries. The key characteristic of such an approach is that the judge or magistrate has far greater control over the course of the proceedings and does not rely on the parties to bring arguments and evidence before them. It could therefore be helpful for state systems in common law countries to move towards the adoption of some aspects of the inquisitorial approach, such as greater judicial control, less emphasis on the role of lawyers and less complicated procedural rules. While a complete reform of the state system is probably unrealistic, an incremental approach could be adopted, whereby when a particular aspect of the state system needs to be changed (for example, new rules of civil or criminal procedure need to be drafted) then consideration can be given to how a more inquisitorial approach can be adopted.[147]

Reform the laws of evidence

A third change that could be considered is to reform the laws of evidence to make them less complex and more culturally relevant. The laws of evidence are confusing and frustrating even for those trained in the common law, and for those participants used to a customary justice system they often appear to be arbitrary and unfair. In Vanuatu, the rules that seem to cause the most concern are those preventing the court from looking at material that is not relevant (compared with the holistic approach taken in most customary justice systems) and the rules requiring corroboration. In many of the hybrid courts discussed above, there are provisions allowing for the rules of evidence to be largely overlooked.[148] Again, it is not suggested that the entire system of evidence needs to be reformed, but that consideration is given to which rules of evidence really serve a relevant purpose in today's courts, rather than merely being a historical relic. For example, in Vanuatu, the common law rules of evidence that were developed largely in the English context of trial by jury still apply even though there are no juries in Vanuatu. This reform also involves learning from the simpler approaches to the laws of evidence from civil law jurisdictions.

Changes the customary justice system could make to its procedures

Introduction of good management initiatives

There are a number of good management initiatives that customary justice systems can consider adopting, including the introduction of record and account keeping, training in the management of meetings and the writing down of oral laws.[149]

The benefits of record keeping for a customary justice system are that it helps to ensure consistency of decisions and also might be needed during appeals or reviews by overseeing courts in jurisdictions where there is partial or complete integration. In designing a record-keeping system, one donor organisation advises that it is important 'to identify what the recorded information will be used for, how the system will be maintained and what linkages with the formal system are envisaged'.[150] The benefits of record keeping are shown by the situation in Bangladesh, where some NGOs have started working with the traditional customary justice system, known as *shalish*, to facilitate its use, but also to modify some aspects. The research has shown that the introduction of basic record keeping so that agreements and other key proceedings are documented, together with other factors,[151] have made this the most effective form of *shalish* in delivering a degree of justice and alleviating poverty.[152] An associated reform is training in account keeping, especially for customary justice systems that use monetary penalties and charge fees to hear cases.

In regard to meeting-management training, it has been noted that many of the benefits of the customary justice system stem from its holistic approach and ability to include the entire community in the process. One of the challenges that customary justice systems might face in the future, however, is a lessening of the tolerance of community members for long, drawn-out and repetitive cases or meetings. This is likely to be especially the case in peri-urban and urban areas where community members have work or other commitments they also need to attend to. This suggests that if customary justice systems wish to remain relevant and respected by their communities they might need to consider training in more effective means of time management and keeping cases 'on track'. Such reforms will also be useful in developing linkages with the state system as the State will be more likely to enter into relations with systems that use time and resources efficiently. The challenge, of course, will be to find a balance between these aims and the need to keep the courts open to community participation and holistic in nature.

A final reform to be considered is the recording of substantive customary laws. This is a controversial reform, which was pursued by many colonial governments, but more recently has been criticised on the basis that codifying custom effectively 'freezes' it, thus losing its dynamism and flexibility.[153] Such moves also risk customary law starting to be used more as state law, rather than as principles that are applied in regard to the context of a particular situation. As discussed in Chapter 4, however, in Vanuatu, it is the chiefs themselves who are leading the movement to write down their laws in an attempt to give them greater legitimacy and permanency in response to the challenges of educated youth and the threats of an increasingly mobile and disparate community. This suggests that the recording of customary laws might be a useful exercise in itself, especially for communities in which their customary law is under threat from the state system, as it will promote community discussion and involvement in the customary justice system. Further, the problems of 'freezing' customary law by writing it down are not as great as first appear: first, it is largely the customary justice system that will be using it, and not the courts, so it is not likely to be used in as rigid a way as it would by those who come from a state law background; and second, there is no reason why written customary law cannot be amended when necessary just as written state law is. The New Zealand Law Reform Commission offers another way around this potential problem with its suggestion of codifying customary *values* rather than customary *law*.[154]

Awareness programs about different types of decision-making procedures

Another possibility is awareness raising for leaders of customary justice systems about different types of decision-making procedures, with particular focus on those involving a more participatory and conciliatory approach. This could involve learning about approaches developed by the state system, such as mediation and arbitration, but also could involve learning about the ways that other customary justice systems, or parts thereof, make decisions. For example, in those areas of Vanuatu where the decision-making style is very chief dominated, such as in North Pentecost, there could be a program whereby chiefs from more southern areas (where there is a more mediation-style of decision making) come to provide information and training.

Learn about the rules of evidence

While it is noted above that many rules of evidence might be due to historical factors and do not serve an important purpose in the court systems today, it is also true that many rules are useful. It is likely that, as has happened in Vanuatu, the influence of the state system has meant that many customary justice systems are starting to face pressure from communities to incorporate concepts such as proof in their determination of cases. In countries where this occurs, it might be useful for customary justice systems to learn about the basic rules of evidence that might be helpful, such as the rules against leading questions and hearsay.

Sharing of substantive laws/principles

Use of substantive customary law by state courts

The focus of this study has been largely on institutions and processes rather than substantive law, but this should not be taken to mean that substantive law is not important as well. Many countries recognise that it is important for state courts to use substantive customary laws in their decision making, but the implementation of this has proven to be difficult in practice. Some countries such as Vanuatu and Solomon Islands have provisions in their constitutions stating that customary law is a source of law. There has, however, not been consideration of how the courts are to go about treating customary law and, as a result, it is not often used.[155] A number of countries have gone further than this and attempted to deal with this question through legislation, such as: the PNG *Customs Recognition Act 1963*,[156] the PNG *Underlying Law Act 2000* (which imposes on legal counsel an obligation to plead custom where it is relevant),[157] the Solomon Islands *Customs Recognition Act*[158] and the Australian draft *Aboriginal Customary Laws (Recognition) Act 1986* (which has never been implemented).[159]

It does not appear that any of these pieces of legislation have been particularly successful, although some developments in the *Underlying Law Act*, such as treating custom as law instead of fact—allowing courts to declare customary law by judicial notice and providing guidelines for choosing which customary law to apply to particular proceedings—have been favourably commented on.[160] The most significant problem, as pointed out by Corrin Care and Zorn is that the *Underlying Law Act* still leaves the recognition of custom essentially to counsel and the courts, which, given the common law bias of the judiciary, could mean that the mandate to use custom remains unfulfilled.[161]

These reflections suggest that, in addition to such legislation, the knowledge and the will of all the judges and lawyers involved with the system are needed to bring such ideals into practice. Combining some of the methods suggested in this section might be a way of creating such knowledge and will. A final suggestion, made by the New Zealand Law Reform Commission, is for a country to 'develop non-prescriptive custom law commentaries to give judges, officials and others insight into the nature of the custom law(s) operating in its territory'.[162]

Use of human rights principles

Human rights law is an area where the customary justice system could learn a great deal from the state system, in particular in relation to principles of natural justice. Although there has been a considerable literature written on the supposed 'conflict' between human rights and custom,[163] a recent study by the New Zealand Law Reform Commission has found that this conflict has been exaggerated, stating:

> [T]he human rights framework's focus on individual rights is said to be in conflict with the customary focus on the individual's duties to the group. However, human rights are also concerned with groups. In addition, with every right there is a duty and with every duty a right. Whether more stress is given to one or the other depends on the problem in question.[164]

It recommends that a harmonising approach be adopted when dealing with human rights and custom. Such an approach draws on the values of custom *and* human rights to enhance custom and advance the application of human rights. This harmonising approach could usefully be adopted in areas where there is likely to be some disparity between the approaches of the customary justice system and the state system, such as issues concerned with:

* tensions between individual rights and community interests—for example, freedom of religion and freedom of movement
* fair process and bias, partiality and conflict of interest
* punishment—for example, banishment
* women, young people and other vulnerable groups.

Ibhawoh similarly advocates giving cultural communities within the state some latitude over how to put human rights into practice.[165] She suggests that one approach that has worked in some African countries to help achieve this congruence is to involve the community in advocacy, information, education, legislation and policy formation.[166] She also argues that the dialogue about human rights should be a two-way process, because 'a complementarity if not an absolute congruence of state laws and cultural norms is required if national human rights regimes are to gain grassroots acceptance'.[167] Faundez also observes:

> It is not necessary to adhere to any form of moral relativism to realise that it is often impossible, unwise and even counter-productive to attempt to remedy at once all the human rights shortcomings of the non-state justice systems. It must also be borne in mind that many non-state justice systems come into existence precisely because the official legal system tramples or ignores the rights of members of remote or marginal communities.[168]

Bringing these ideas together, it is suggested that customary justice systems investigate developing a dialogue with the State over human rights standards and develop training programs in human rights that draw on customary principles, and also take into account *why* customary justice systems operate in certain ways, given cultural, political, institutional, economic or security constraints.[169] It must be acknowledged, of course, that it might be difficult to identify who exactly will be the actors to do this and how it can be done given the problems in some societies of determining who is entitled to speak on behalf of customary systems. A national customary organisation—for example, the Malvatumauri in Vanuatu—is one such institution that could be used to coordinate such a dialogue.

Another way for customary justice systems to develop human rights is through the creation and dissemination of handbooks for customary justice system officials that clearly state what types of standards should be applied. For example, the PNG *Village Courts Handbook* contains information for Village Court officials such as, '[i]t is the new custom of all people in Papua New Guinea that women have the same rights as men. No one can argue with this' and '[w]hen dealing with disputes involving children such as a custody matter, custom cannot be applied if the result will not be [in] the best interests of the child'.[170]

A final way to improve the compliance with human rights standards for customary justice systems is to introduce positive measures to ensure greater participation by women in the customary justice system, as decision makers and, where appropriate, as lay advocates or customary law advisers.[171]

Use of key players/institutions from the other system

Use by the state system

Use of chiefs/traditional leaders in state courts

A further measure to strengthen the linkages between the two systems is the adoption of a system of assessors in the state courts. The role of assessors would be to sit with state court judges and assist them to reach a decision on the facts in the cases that come before them, or else to help the judge in accessing and understanding customary law.[172] The assessors could be leaders of the customary justice system and would thus be able to act as an important bridge between the two systems as they would pass knowledge about the substance and processes of each system back and forth. For example, the position of assessors was included in the new judicial system of Bougainville in order to assist formal courts to understand *kastom* and customary practices.[173] Assessors could be used just for sentencing or for a determination of guilt in criminal cases. Other areas of law where they would be particularly useful are family law and land cases. Consideration would need to be given to what sorts of powers the assessors have (advisory only or with a power of veto)[174] and who should be the assessors for particular cases. This latter question is particularly vexed in countries where there is a great deal of diversity in custom throughout the jurisdiction. Decisions need to be made about where the balance should be found between ensuring the assessors are familiar with the relevant customary practices and ensuring that there is not a problem of perceived bias or conflict of interest.

Another adaptation that would use traditional leaders is the development by state courts of restorative justice initiatives, such as circle sentencing programs, which draw on customary ideas of reconciliation rather than retribution.[175] These courts might include members of indigenous groups to advise magistrates on sentencing options, and the aims might include involving the community as much as possible in the court process and using the courts as the gateway to treatment for the offender.[176] For example, in Australia, various states and territories have introduced their own 'Aboriginal courts', although it should be noted that these courts 'operate within the boundaries of the Australian legal system and in no case does an Aboriginal Elder have authority in the Australian legal system to decide a case or impose punishment'.[177] Examples are the Koori Court in Victoria, the Murri Court in Brisbane, the Nunga Court in South Australia, Circle Sentencing in New South Wales,[178] the Ngambra Court in the Australian Capital Territory and the Darwin Community Court in the Northern Territory.[179] The key features of these courts are that they use informal procedures and communication, involve Aboriginal elders in the sentencing process (although only in Queensland are magistrates obliged to consider what these elders have to say)[180] and they allow all parties to speak about the crime and approach the issue of sentencing, taking a holistic account of the offender's circumstances. Appraising the effectiveness of these courts, the Law Reform Commission of Western Australia states: 'While it is still too early to judge the success of Aboriginal courts, especially in terms of recidivism, there are positive signs that these courts have achieved significant gains in terms of justice outcomes for Aboriginal people.'[181]

A review of the NSW Circle Sentencing program found that it had considerable advantages, including breaking the cycle of recidivism, promoting healing and reconciliation and reducing the barriers between the courts and Aboriginal communities.[182]

Finally, other ways such key players could be used are as expert witnesses who would come to court to provide evidence about customary law or by customary institutions providing *amicus curiae* briefs to the court.[183]

Referral of issues/cases to customary justice systems

It might be possible to explore avenues for referring cases or parts of cases to the customary justice system for matters such as mediation and conciliation, for advice on a point of customary law[184] or even for diversion before a case gets to court.[185] Such proposals could be considered along with the adoption of a policy of 'judicial deference' proposed by the New Zealand Law Reform Commission.[186] This involves state judges respecting and deferring to the specialist skills and local knowledge of customary justice systems. In many respects, such involvement is likely to be far less controversial and political than the relinquishing of absolute control over judicial power. The Australian Law Reform Commission has noted that proposals that 'focus on mediation and conciliation and a greater voice for Aborigines in the existing criminal justice system pose fewer problems of implementation than proposals for "Aboriginal courts"'.[187]

Involve traditional leaders in judicial appointment committees

The idea of involving traditional leaders in judicial appointment committees comes from Bougainville, where the new constitution provides that a traditional chief or other leader should be included in the membership of such a committee.[188] In addition, it provides that one consideration the committee should have when making appointments is the 'extent of a person's knowledge of the Bougainville situation and of Bougainville *Kastom*'.[189] The *Report on the Bougainville Constitution* notes that these provisions 'ensure that the importance of *kastom*, in particular, and its roles in the law and justice system must be kept well and truly in mind when all judicial appointments are being made'.[190]

Use of key players by the customary justice system

Use of state assessors, kiaps or state police

During the period of colonialism in Vanuatu and Papua New Guinea, there was a system of assessors and *kiaps*, respectively. The role of these institutions was roughly similar: they involved investing state officials with power in a range of matters, including local dispute resolution, and sending them on regular patrols of rural communities.[191] The *kiap*, for example, could 'link dispute resolution to the provision or withdrawal of various "government" services and facilities. He could persuade and reward, as well as punish. He could address remedies to either individuals or groups.'[192] In relation to the *kiap* system, Dinnen comments that '[i]n practice, if not necessarily by design, kiap justice allowed for a high degree of articulation between formal and informal fields of justice'.[193]

Consideration could be given to developing a similar mechanism today, whereby a person with access to state resources is used by the customary justice system as a bridging point and also a support. Such a person could be in the form of a 'justice advocate', mentioned earlier under 'Mutual learning', a probation officer or even a police officer.

Another way to use state officials is to establish a 'dial-a-judge' (or retired judge) service to assist the administrators of the customary justice system to have a better understanding of how the state system would really operate in a particular case. The rationale for this is that if they were able to have regard to what decision a state court would make when faced with similar facts, they might make decisions that are less disparate than they would without such information. This might in turn reduce the likelihood of forum shopping and the associated problems such a practice creates.[194] If a customary justice system decides to make a decision that is very different to what a state court would decide, it would be better for this to be discussed openly, and the reasons for the decision justified, rather than people speculating about it on the basis of what is likely to be inaccurate information.

Referral of cases to the state system

The customary justice system (as a whole or in different parts) could develop a policy concerning the types of cases it considers the state system should handle and inform the relevant community about the policy and refer such cases to the state courts when they arise. This could be done in conjunction with the relevant officials from the state system. Such a measure would build linkages with the state system, reduce any potential conflicts over the exercise of jurisdiction and assist in dispelling community confusion about which system to put which cases before.

Involve a member of the state judiciary in the customary justice system

The final proposal is to involve a member of the state judiciary in the top levels of the customary system, either as a decision maker (for example, as a special member who could be brought in to deal with certain important cases) or by involvement in decisions regarding the composition of this highest level. For example, in Vanuatu, a member of the judiciary (one with a track record of a respectful dialogue with *kastom*) could be involved at island or provincial levels of the *kastom* system at various times. This would be important on a symbolic level and also would provide considerable opportunity for cross-fertilisation of ideas in the context of specific situations.[195]

Conclusion

The aim of this chapter was to unpick terms such as 'recognise' and 'harmonise' by exploring in detail as many different types of relationship state and non-state justice systems could have with each other as possible. These were conceptualised as existing along a spectrum of increasing state recognition of the non-state justice system and specific features of their relationship were highlighted. The dimensions of variation that underpin the typology are as follows:

- the extent of repression of a non-state justice system by the State
- the extent of informal support and regulation of a non-state justice system by the State
- the existence and operation of informal relationships between stakeholders in the two systems
- whether there is constitutional recognition of non-state justice systems
- the extent of formal recognition of the exercise of adjudicative power by a non-state justice system, and the exclusivity or otherwise of that jurisdiction
- the extent of formal regulation of a non-state justice system by the State (appeals and supervision)
- the extent to which a non-state justice system is free to follow its own procedures and substantive laws
- the extent to which a state funds a non-state justice system
- the extent to which a state enforces decisions made by a non-state justice system
- the availability and type of appeals from a non-state justice system to the State.

In addition, this chapter developed a range of mutual-adaptation options for states and customary justice systems to assist them to work together in more supportive ways. The main areas identified were:

- mutual learning about the other system's or systems' principles, institutions and procedures

- adoption of procedures from the other system(s) to facilitate pathways between the two systems that might offer improvements to the other system(s)
- more use of substantive laws and principles from the other system(s) to improve each system and to lessen any substantive differences between them
- use of key players and institutions from the other system(s) to facilitate mutual learning, aid cross-fertilisation of ideas in the context of specific cases and for symbolic purposes to demonstrate the closeness of the relationship between the two systems.

It has been shown that what is important in this exercise is for both systems to make changes so that the bridge starts to be built on both sides of the river.

Through surveying literature from many different jurisdictions, we found that in the majority of jurisdictions relationships between state and non-state justice systems were not mutually supportive, and even the more 'successful' examples had problems that we identified. These findings suggest that for many jurisdictions what is required is reform of the relationship between the state and non-state justice systems to maximise the chances of the systems cooperating with each other, performing to their fullest potential the tasks for which they are best suited and covering each other's weaknesses with their own strengths. The final chapter of this study proposes a method for a jurisdiction wishing to undertake such reforms, using the typology and mutual-adaptation suggestions developed in this chapter.

ENDNOTES

[1] For example, Fitzgerald argues that '[t]here is a significant body of literature in Australia around the well-recognised imperative to recognise customary law, and significant disagreement as to what this term means in practice.' Fitzgerald, *The Cape York Justice Study Report*, p. 112.

[2] Blagg, *A New Way of Doing Business?*, p. 340.

[3] Woodman coined these terms, as discussed in Chapter 2 under 'The possibilities and limitations of legal pluralism for Melanesia'.

[4] These countries were: Australia, New Zealand, Samoa, Kiribati, Timor Leste, Vanuatu, Fiji, Papua New Guinea, Solomon Islands, Tuvalu, Tokelau, South Africa, Malawi, Nigeria, Zambia, Mozambique, Lesotho, Botswana, Bangladesh, Philippines, Peru and Colombia.

[5] Blagg reports that this is what many Australian Aboriginal elders reportedly wish to see, and such comments have resonance with those expressed during this study about the wish to 'marry' the two systems. Blagg, *A New Way of Doing Business?*, p. 319.

[6] Oba, Abdulmumini 2004, 'Lawyers, legal education and the Shari'ah courts in Nigeria', *Journal of Legal Pluralism*, vol. 49, p. 113. Another example is in Western Sumatra, where there are *adat* courts, Islamic courts and state courts. See von Benda-Beckmann and von Benda-Beckmann, 'Changing one is changing all'.

[7] Such as international law, EC law and *lex mercatoria*. See, for example, Twining, 'A post-Westphalian conception of law', p. 199; Santos, 'The heterogeneous state and legal pluralism in Mozambique', pp. 50–1. Santos argues elsewhere (*Toward a New Legal Common Sense*, p. 92) that we are now entering the third phase of legal pluralism that is concerned with 'suprastate, global legal orders coexisting in the world system with both state and infrastate legal orders'. See also Tamanaha, *Understanding legal pluralism*, p. 39.

[8] Although during the time of the Condominium in Vanuatu there were two *state* systems—the English and the French—this situation was so particular that no consideration will be given to the possibility of two state systems existing in a particular jurisdiction.

[9] Bouman, 'A note on chiefly and national policing in Botswana', p. 289.

[10] Tamanaha, *Understanding legal pluralism*, p. 52.

[11] Chanock, 'Customary law, sustainable development and the failing state', p. 366.

[12] Santos, *Toward a New Legal Common Sense*, p. 94.

[13] See the discussion concerning this issue in Chapter 2 under 'Theoretical issues'.

[14] Tamanaha (*Understanding legal pluralism*, p. 62) argues, '[O]fficial state legal systems, at least those that function well, have a distinctive instrumental capacity that enables them to be utilized to engage in a broad (potentially unlimited) range of possible activities.'

[15] Golub, Stephen 2003, Non-state justice systems in Bangladesh and the Philippines, Paper presented at the Workshop on Working with Non-State Justice Systems, UK Department for International Development, 6–7 March 2003. The position is perhaps even more complicated in Botswana where there are warranted customary courts, unwarranted recognised customary courts (that are permitted to engage in reconciliation) and unwarranted, not formally recognised courts and unwarranted, not recognised courts. See Bouman, Marlies 1987, 'A note on chiefly and national policing in Botswana', *Journal of Legal Pluralism*, vols 25–6, p. 279.

[16] Elechi, Ogbonnaya Oko 1996, 'Doing justice without the State: the Afikpo (Ehugbo) Nigeria model of conflict resolution', *International Journal of Comparative and Applied Criminal Justice*, vol. 20, no. 2, p. 344.

[17] Northern Territory Law Reform Commission 2003, *Report of the Committee of Inquiry into Aboriginal customary law*, Report No. 8, p. 6.

[18] The report did not provide any detail about how this general system would be established, other than noting that it would need to be carefully designed, developed and adequately resourced.

[19] Human Rights and Equal Opportunity Commission 2003, Submission to the Northern Territory Law Reform Committee Inquiry into Aboriginal Customary Law in the Northern Territory, Aboriginal and Torres Strait Social Justice Commissioner of the Human Rights and Equal Opportunity Commission, p. 29.

[20] For example, in relation to Timor Leste, Mearns states: 'It was put to me in several different contexts that the local systems of resolving disputes and punishing crimes will go underground and act as a clandestine and preferred alternative to the formal system unless they are given recognition and [are] regulated.' Mearns, David 2002, *Looking Both Ways: Models for justice in East Timor*, Australian Legal Resources International, p. 54.

[21] *Toward a New Legal Common Sense*, pp. 92–3.

[22] Bouman, 'A note on chiefly and national policing in Botswana', p. 291.

[23] Tamanaha, *Understanding legal pluralism*, p. 50.

[24] Mearns, *Looking Both Ways*, p. 26.

[25] Schärf, Wilfried 2003, Non-state justice systems in southern Africa: how should governments respond?, Paper presented at the Workshop on Working with Non-State Justice Systems, UK Department for International Development, 6–7 March 2003, p. 18.

[26] Schärf, Wilfried et al. 2003, *Access to Justice for the Poor of Malawi? An appraisal of access to justice provided to the poor of Malawi by the lower subordinate courts and the customary justice forums*, Malawi Law Commission.

[27] Schärf, Non-state justice systems in southern Africa, p. 50.

[28] Ibid., p. 59.

[29] My knowledge of the situation in Kiribati comes from unpublished research papers written about the customary legal system there by some of my students.

[30] Government of South Africa 2008, *Policy Framework on the Traditional Justice System Under the Constitution*, Department of Justice and Constitutional Development, South Africa, p. 16.

[31] Elechi, 'Doing justice without the State'.

[32] Corrin Care, Jennifer 2002, 'Off the peg', *Alternative Law Journal*, vol. 27, no. 5, p. 210.

[33] Mearns, *Looking Both Ways*, p. 26.

[34] Schärf, Non-state justice systems in southern Africa, p. 39.

[35] Mearns, *Looking Both Ways*, p. 54.

[36] Section 39 of the *Penal Code (Amendment) Act 2006* (Vanuatu). It is also a common law requirement in Solomon Islands.

[37] In *Regina vs Funifaka* (1997, SBHC 31), Palmer, J held: 'The payment of compensation or settlements in custom do not extinguish or obliterate the offence. They only go to mitigation. The accused still must be punished and expiate their crime.'

[38] *Public Prosecutor vs Gideon*, 2002, VUCA 7, <http://www.paclii.org.vu>

[39] For example, the Chiefs' Capacity Building project currently being run by AusAID, the Malvatumauri and the Australian Centre for Peace and Conflict Studies at the University of Queensland.

[40] Johnston, Les and Shearing, Clifford 2003, *Governing Security: Explorations in policing and justice*, p. 151. A similar, although less developed, program is the Restorative Justice Peace Mediation process used by the Saraga Peace, Good Order and Community Development Association in some urban parts of Papua New Guinea. See Wai, Isaac and Maia, Paul 2005, 'What we do in Saraga: building community peace and harmony', *Development Bulletin*, vol. 67, pp. 53–5.

[41] Success is defined as meaning that a particular case has conformed with the principles and procedures to which the committee members have subscribed. Sixty per cent of this money goes into a community fund for local development projects, 10 per cent supports the administrative expenses of the committee and 30 per cent goes to the committee members who were involved in facilitating the gathering.

[42] Johnston and Shearing, *Governing Security*, p. 157.

[43] Human Rights and Equal Opportunity Commission, Submission to the Northern Territory Law Reform Committee Inquiry into Aboriginal Customary Law in the Northern Territory, pp. 31–50.

[44] Ibid., p. 28.

[45] For example, Bouman ('A note on chiefly and national policing in Botswana', p. 291) explains that in Botswana one reason why local people hold the unwarranted customary courts in awe is because of their informal links with the state courts that allow them to refer cases to the state system and threaten the offenders with punishments. See also Greenhouse's comments about the importance of external relationships discussed in Chapter 2 under 'General principles'.

[46] Chanock argued that in Africa the imperial view of custom requiring it to be static and fixed in order for it to have legal force came from the beliefs that African societies were static in nature 'because of a cultural judgment that was made about African societies, which were seen as having failed to be "progressive"'. Chanock, Martin 2005, 'Customary law, sustainable development and the failing state', in Peter Orebech et al. (eds), *The Role of Customary Law in Sustainable Development*, pp. 342–3. Unfortunately, such beliefs seem to have transcended the end of colonialism and have been perpetuated by independent states such as Samoa.

[47] Dewhurst, Dale 2004, 'Parallel justice systems, or a tale of two spiders', in Catherine Bell and David Kahane (eds), *Intercultural Dispute Resolution in Aboriginal Contexts*, p. 225. Under the *Judicature Acts*, where any conflict exists between common law and equity the principles of equity prevail.

[48] Other examples are the Tuvaluan *falekaupule* (see the *Falekaupule Act 1997*) and the Tokelauan *taupulega* (see the *Taupulega Act 1986*).

[49] Meleisea, M. 2000, 'Governance, development and leadership in Polynesia', in E. Huffer and A. So'o (eds), *Governance in Samoa*, p. 197.

[50] Lawson, Stephanie 1996, *Tradition Versus Democracy in the South Pacific: Fiji, Tonga and Western Samoa*, p. 156.

[51] *Leituala vs Mauga*, 2004, WSSC 9, http://www.paclii.org.vu

[52] *Sefo vs Attorney-General*, 2000, WSSC 18, http://www.paclii.org.vu

[53] Law Reform Commission of Western Australia 2006, *Aboriginal customary laws*, Report Project No. 94, p. 97.

[54] Ibid., p. 105.

[55] Ibid., p. 104.

[56] There are some conditions attached to this; see ibid., p. 109. This allowance of banishment, however, is an interesting contrast to the position taken in Samoa with regard to the village *fonos*, and could perhaps come from the fact that Australia, unlike Samoa, does not have a list of fundamental rights and freedoms in its constitution.

[57] Law Reform Commission of Western Australia, *Aboriginal customary laws*, Discussion Paper Project No. 94, p. 136.

[58] Law Reform Commission of Western Australia, *Aboriginal customary laws*, Report Project No. 94, p. 106. This makes it clear the jurisdiction given to CJGs is not exclusive.

[59] By providing information about customary law and culture to the courts, presenting information about offenders at sentencing and bail hearings, participating in diversionary programs and in the supervision of offenders who are subject to court orders.

[60] Law Reform Commission of Western Australia, *Aboriginal customary laws*, Report Project No. 94, p. 97.

[61] Ibid., p. 104.

[62] Ibid., p. 105.

[63] Penal Reform International, *Access to Justice in Sub-Saharan Africa*, p. 139.

[64] Corrin Care, Jennifer 2006, 'A green stick or a fresh stick?: locating customary penalties in the post-colonial era', *Oxford University Commonwealth Law Journal*, vol. 6, no. 1, p. 32.

[65] Unfortunately, many of these decisions are not readily available. They are, however, discussed in Va'a, U. 2000, 'Local government in Samoa and the search for balance', in Elise Huffer and A. So'o (eds), *Governance in Samoa*, pp. 156–60. An initial decision in the murder case is available; see *Police vs Afoa*, 1994, WSSC 3, http://www.paclii.org.vu. See also Forsyth, Miranda 2004a, 'Banishment and freedom of movement in Samoa', *Journal of South Pacific Law*, vol. 8, no. 2, <http://paclii.org.vu/journals/fJSPL/index.shtml>

[66] Meleisea, 'Governance, development and leadership in Polynesia', p. 198.

[67] Corrin Care, 'A green stick or a fresh stick?', p. 32.

[68] Ibid., pp. 58–9.

[69] Webber argues, 'The very existence of federalism is premised on the idea that variation in law from one part of the country to another is legitimate. This variation even affects the criminal law, though indirectly, through provincial control over policing, prosecution, the establishment of courts, some elements of the corrections system, and such other associated measures.' Webber, Jeremy 1993, 'Individuality, equality and difference: justifications for a parallel system of Aboriginal justice', in Royal Commission on Aboriginal Peoples (ed.), *Aboriginal Peoples and the Justice System: Report of the National Round Table on Aboriginal Justice Issues*, p. 152.

[70] Dewhurst, 'Parallel justice systems, or a tale of two spiders'; Webber, 'Individuality, equality and difference'.

[71] Oba, 'Lawyers, legal education and the Shari'ah courts in Nigeria', p. 130. Also in Medieval Europe, including England, it used to be the case that certain matters, such as marriage and inheritance (other than land subject to feudal relations), were left to ecclesiastical courts.

[72] Berman, 'Global legal pluralism', p. 1206.

[73] Horton, Lynn 2006, 'Contesting state multiculturalisms: indigenous land struggles in Eastern Panama', *Journal of Latin American Studies*, vol. 38, p. 830. Raja Roy notes that among notable examples of autonomy arrangements in formally unitary states are South Tyrole (Italy), Catalonia (Spain), Isle of Man (United Kingdom) and Northern Ireland (United Kingdom). Among the highest forms of autonomy exercised in indigenous peoples' territories are Greenland (Denmark), Mizoram and Nagaland (India) and Kuna Yala (Panama). Roy, Raja 2004, 'Challenges for juridical pluralism and customary laws of indigenous peoples: the case of Chittagong hill tracts, Bangladesh', *Arizona Journal of International & Comparative Law*, vol. 21, no. 1, p. 124.

[74] Berman ('Global legal pluralism', p. 1206) notes that the US Supreme Court has at times deferred to these courts (*Santa Clara Pueblo vs Martinez* [1978, 436 US 49]).

[75] The reason for the introduction of such constitutional provisions can most likely be found in the International Labour Organisation Convention 169 concerning indigenous and tribal peoples, which provides: 'Article 8(2): These peoples shall have the right to retain their own customs and institutions, where these are not incompatible with fundamental human rights defined by the national legal system and with internationally recognised human rights.'

'Article 9(1): To the extent compatible with the national legal system and internationally recognised human rights, the methods customarily practiced by the peoples concerned for dealing with offences committed by their members shall be respected.'

[76] Article 149 of the Peruvian *Constitution* contains a similar provision.

[77] Faundez, Julio 2003, Non-state justice systems in Latin America—case studies: Peru and Colombia, Paper presented at the Workshop on Working with Non-State Justice Systems, UK Department for International Development, 6–7 March 2003, p. 9.

[78] Ibid., p. 57.

[79] Assies, Willem 1999, 'Multi-ethnicity, the State and the law in Latin America', *Journal of Legal Pluralism*, vol. 43, p. 145.

[80] Ibid., p. 154.

[81] Ibid., p. 157.

[82] My research in this area has been hampered by my lack of Spanish.

[83] A parallel system of justice for the Maori in New Zealand was also proposed in Jackson, Moana n.d., *The Maori and the criminal justice system He Whaipaanga Hou—a new perspective. Part 2*, Study Series 18, Department of Justice, New Zealand. This report and the responses it has provoked raise many of the issues involved in such a system, as well as demonstrating the sensitivity of the political issues involved.

[84] Webber, 'Individuality, equality and difference', p. 138.

[85] Dewhurst, 'Parallel justice systems, or a tale of two spiders', p. 213.

[86] Oba, Abdulmumini 2004, 'The Shariah court of appeal in Northern Nigeria: the continuing crisis of jurisdiction', *American Journal of Comparative Law*, vol. 52, p. 899.

[87] Ibid., p. 900.

[88] Webber, 'Individuality, equality and difference', pp. 147–55. These issues are also discussed in the conclusion to Chapter 8.

[89] Ibid., p. 134. See also Crawford, James, Hennesy, Peter and Fisher, Mary 1988, 'Aboriginal customary laws: proposals for recognition', in Bradford Morse and Gordon Woodman (eds), *Indigenous Law and the State*, pp. 40–3. Steiner points out the paradox that 'autonomy regimes, or some forms thereof, find indirect but significant support in several prominent norms of the human rights movement. Moreover, they can be understood to reinforce some underlying ideals of that movement as a whole. On the other hand, these regimes can undermine other powerful human rights ideals, and to that extent embody a morally problematic counter-ideal.' Steiner, Henry 1991, 'Ideals and counter-ideals in the struggle over autonomy regimes for minorities', *Notre Dame Law Review*, vol. 66, p. 1539.

[90] Webber, 'Individuality, equality and difference', p. 147.

[91] Horton, 'Contesting state multiculturalisms', p. 835.

[92] Conflict-of-laws rules could be useful in working out the specific details of such an arrangement.

[93] Webber ('Individuality, equality and difference', p. 147) comments that '[a]cceptance of the general principle may depend upon the detailed justification of very specific institutional arrangements'.

[94] Government of South Africa, *Policy Framework on the Traditional Justice System Under the Constitution*.

[95] Schärf, Non-state justice systems in southern Africa, p. 35.

[96] It looks unlikely to be finalised before the end of the parliamentary session and has a start date of December 2009 (Email from Michael Palumbo, Deputy Chief State Law Adviser, Law Reform, South Africa, 14 November 2008).

[97] See a discussion of the issues involved in determining the appeal structure in Chapter 8 of South African Law Commission, *Report on traditional courts and the judicial function of traditional leaders*.

[98] Ibid., p. 30.

[99] Tamanaha, *Understanding legal pluralism*, p. 50. See also the controversy over the *Arbitration Act* (Ontario) that for a time permitted its structure for private arbitration, including the enforcement of arbitration awards, to be used for the arbitration of family disputes by religious authorities under religious law. An extensive report on this issue argued that '[u]se of the Arbitration Act by minority communities is a way of engaging with the broader community by formalizing a method of decision-making which currently occurs in an informal manner'. Boyd, Marion 2004, *Dispute Resolution in Family Law: Protecting choice, promoting inclusion*, Ministry of the Attorney-General, Ontario, Canada, p. 1. That report's recommendations were not accepted by the Ontario legislature, however, and the Act was amended in order to restrict the use of the regime for the adjudication of family matters.

[100] Australian Law Reform Commission, *The recognition of Aboriginal customary laws*, p. 74.

[101] *Adolf vs Austria*, 1982, ECHR, Ser. A, vol. 49, cited in ibid.

[102] New Zealand Law Reform Commission, *Report of Proceedings*, p. 160.

[103] Ibid., p. 165.

[104] Ibid.

[105] For example, in Botswana, the duties of the Local Police (an unofficial police force) are 'to assist the Chief in the exercise of his lawful duties, preserve the public peace, prevent the commission of offences,

apprehend offenders, execute orders (in particular administering corporal punishment) and warrants, and act as a messenger in Customary Court matters'. Bouman, 'A note on chiefly and national policing in Botswana', p. 284.

[106] Schärf, 'Policy options on community justice'.

[107] Bouman, 'A note on chiefly and national policing in Botswana'.

[108] Elechi, 'Doing justice without the State'.

[109] Government of South Africa, *Policy Framework on the Traditional Justice System Under the Constitution*, pp. 10–11.

[110] For example, Galanter and Krishan argue that the Lok Adalats in India 'are distinct from traditional panchayats in virtually every respect: they operate in the shadow of the official courts; they are staffed by official appointees rather than communal leaders; they apply some diluted version of state law rather than local or caste custom; they arrange compromises instead of imposing fines and penances backed up by the sanction of excommunication'. Galanter, Marc and Krishnan, Jayanth 2004, '"Bread for the poor": access to justice and the rights of the needy in India', *Hastings Law Journal*, vol. 55, p. 789.

[111] Roberts, Simon 1972, 'The survival of the traditional Tswana courts in the national legal system of Botswana', *Journal of African Law*, vol. 16, p. 106.

[112] This case is discussed in Otlhogile, Bojosi 1993, 'Criminal justice and the problems of a dual legal system in Botswana', *Criminal Law Forum*, vol. 4, p. 532.

[113] Griffiths, Anne 1996, 'Between paradigms: differing perspectives on justice in Molepolole Botswana', *Journal of Legal Pluralism and Unofficial Law*, vol. 36, p. 203.

[114] Schärf, Non-state justice systems in southern Africa, p. 63.

[115] Ibid., p. 66.

[116] Griffiths, 'Between paradigms', p. 212.

[117] Griffiths, Anne 1998, 'Legal pluralism in Botswana: women's access to law', *Journal of Legal Pluralism and Unofficial Law*, vol. 42, p. 136.

[118] Schärf, Non-state justice systems in southern Africa, p. 68.

[119] Otlhogile, 'Criminal justice and the problems of a dual legal system in Botswana', p. 532.

[120] Schärf, Non-state justice systems in southern Africa, p. 66.

[121] Elechi, 'Doing justice without the State', p. 344.

[122] Penal Reform International, *Access to Justice in Sub-Saharan Africa*, p. 129.

[123] Fombad, Charles 2004, 'Customary courts and traditional justice in Botswana: present challenges and future perspectives', *Stellenbosch Law Review*, vol. 15, no. 1, p. 191.

[124] Boko, Gideon 2000, 'Fair trial and the customary courts in Botswana: questions on legal representation', *Criminal Law Forum*, vol. 11, no. 4, p. 445.

[125] Ibid., p. 460.

[126] Fombad, 'Customary courts and traditional justice in Botswana', p. 181.

[127] I am grateful to Gordon Woodman for this point (Email from Gordon Woodman, <G.R.Woodman@bham.ac.uk>, 25 May 2007). Franz von Benda-Beckmann has similarly commented that '[s]tudies critically examining local traditional laws, focussing on class, caste, gender and age differences, have shown that "folk law" often turns out to be the law of local elites and/or the senior male population...Recourse to state law and its "non-traditional" values can be an important resource in the struggle for emancipation.' von Benda-Beckmann, Franz 2001, 'Legal pluralism and social justice in economic and political development', *IDS Bulletin*, vol. 32, no. 1, p. 50.

[128] Santos ('The heterogeneous state and legal pluralism in Mozambique', p. 64) refers to the fact that after independence in Mozambique, traditional authorities were '[s]een as obscurantist remnants of colonialism'.

[129] The importance of considering such changes in conjunction with the adoption of a model of relationship between a non-state justice system and a state system has recently been highlighted by the Law Reform Commission of Western Australia, which recommends the establishment of Community Justice Groups (discussed in Model 4) and Aboriginal sentencing courts (within the state system), commenting that these two proposals 'although capable of operating independently from one another, together offer a system where the Aboriginal people of this state can practise their own customary laws with as little interference as possible, while at the same time providing a more meaningful and effective criminal justice system'. Law Reform Commission of Western Australia 2006b, *Aboriginal customary laws*, Discussion Paper Project No. 94, p. 157.

[130] Woodman, Gordon 2001, 'Customary law in common law systems', *IDS Bulletin*, vol. 32, no. 1, p. 32.

[131] As Woodman points out (ibid.), even NGOs are required to work through governments to secure the conditions necessary for them to operate.

[132] Australian Law Reform Commission, *The recognition of Aboriginal customary laws* , p. 89.

[133] New Zealand Law Reform Commission, *Report of Proceedings*, p. 11.

[134] Forsyth, *Report on the Vanuatu Judiciary Conference 2006.*

[135] Ibid.

[136] Golub, Non-state justice systems in Bangladesh and the Philippines, p. 13.

[137] Dinnen, Sinclair 1999, 'Violence and governance in Melanesia', *Pacific Economic Bulletin*, vol. 14, no. 1, p. 71.

[138] Ibid. See also Dinnen, *Building bridges.*

[139] Goddard, Michael 2004, *Women in Papua New Guinea's village courts*, Discussion Paper 2004/3, State Society and Governance in Melanesia Research Paper Series, The Australian National University, viewed 31 May 2007, <http://rspas.anu.edu.au/melanesia/discussion.php>, p. 6. Goddard's arguments, however, have in turn been criticised by Slatter, who argues that none of the cases analysed by Goddard relates to sexual abuse, rape or other offences for which village courts have gained notoriety for discriminatorily penalising or shaming women. She argues that his research does not 'invalidate the analyses of other (mainly women) researchers and activists whose highlighting of "worst practice" cases of gender-discrimination have put village courts on notice'. Slatter, Claire 2007, Gender and custom in the South Pacific, Paper presented at the Tuhonohono Symposium: State and Custom, Waikato Endowed College, New Zealand, pp. 10–11.

[140] Goddard, *Women in Papua New Guinea's village courts*, p. 6.

[141] Ibid., p. 3.

[142] See Chapter 5 under 'The relationship between the courts and the *kastom* system'.

[143] Law Reform Commission of Western Australia, *Aboriginal customary laws*, Discussion Paper Project No. 94, p. 145.

[144] Filimone, *Problem Solving* , p. 7.

[145] Law Reform Commission of Western Australia, *Aboriginal customary laws*, Discussion Paper Project No. 94, p. 120.

[146] Ibid., p. 120. In its final report, the Law Reform Commission of Western Australia also criticised the scheme, although it finally did not recommend its abolition as it had originally done in its discussion paper. It commented that it had received a number of responses from Aboriginal communities in response to its proposal to abolish the scheme who 'have a strong sense of "ownership" of their by-laws and believe that they are an effective way to control behavior in their communities' (p. 115).

[147] A similar suggestion was recently made by the New Zealand Law Reform Commission (*Report of Proceedings*, p. 195), which observed that the adversarial system tended to break down in situations where parties did not have equal opportunity to present their case.

[148] For example, Section 25 of the *Island Courts Act* (Cap 167 [Vanuatu]) states that '[i]n any proceedings before it, an island court shall not apply technical rules of evidence but shall admit and consider such information as is available'.

[149] These suggestions might be of use only for a limited number of customary justice systems as they carry with them a considerable amount of work and the risk that they will cut into some of the advantages of the systems such as speed and lack of formality.

[150] Government of the United Kingdom, *Non-State Justice and Security Systems*, p. 14.

[151] Including participation of women as *shalish* panel members and as disputants who speak up during sessions, and training panel members in mediation.

[152] Golub, Non-state justice systems in Bangladesh and the Philippines, pp. 10–11.

[153] See discussion in Forsyth, Miranda 2004b, 'Beyond case law: kastom and courts in Vanuatu', *Victoria University of Wellington Law Review*, vol. 35, no. 2, p. 427. Gordon and Meggitt (*Law and Order in the New Guinea Highlands*, p. 204) argue that 'we must be acutely conscious of the possibility of customary law being transformed into a neocolonial fraud in the centers of government and then imposed upon the village periphery with the aid of the administrative petty bourgeoisie'.

[154] See the discussion in New Zealand Law Commission, *Converging currents* , pp. 190–6. See also Note 148 above.

[155] This issue is discussed in detail in New Zealand Law Commission, *Converging currents* , in relation to Vanuatu in Chapter 6, Section 1.2.1, and in the context of the Pacific generally in Chapter 13.

[156] Although Roebuck was sanguine about the application of custom by the state courts of Papua New Guinea, later writers painted a more muted picture. Roebuck, D. 1985, 'Custom, common law and constructive judicial lawmaking', in R. De Vere, D. Colqhoun-Kerr and J. Kaburise, *Essays on the Constitution of Papua New Guinea*, Tenth Anniversary Advisory Committee, Port Moresby, pp. 127–45. See also Jessep, O. and Reagan, A. 2001, 'Developing a coherent underlying law—interpreting custom and common law', *Twenty Years of the Papua New Guinea Constitution*, pp. 114–58; Kwa, E. L. 2001, *Constitutional Law of Papua New Guinea*, pp. 44–52.

[157] Whether that act has made any significant change to the extent to which state courts rely on custom is at this stage too early to judge.

[158] This act is basically a copy of the *Customs Recognition Act* enacted in Papua New Guinea in 1963. As observed above, this seemed to have little effect in the application of custom by the state courts in Papua New Guinea, and doubts have been expressed about the likelihood of it being any more effective in Solomon Islands in facilitating the application of customary law by the state courts. Perhaps because of such concerns, the act has not in fact come into force yet. See Corrin Care, 'Customary law in conflict'.

[159] In New Zealand, there are some pieces of legislation, such as the *Resource Management Act 1991*, that aim to bring Maori principles into the law in general. See, for examples, Sections 6(e), 7(a) and 8 of that act. See further Joseph, Robert 2007, The interface between Maori custom and state regulatory systems—Tikanga Maori consultation under the *Resource Management Act 1991*, Paper presented at the Tuhonohono Symposium: State and Custom, Waikato Endowed College, New Zealand. In Hawai'i as well, the concept of '*aloha*' has been introduced into state legislation. See MacKenzie, Melody 2007, Hawaiian values in state legislation, Paper presented at the Tuhonohono Symposium: State and Custom, Waikato Endowed College, New Zealand.

[160] Corrin Care and Zorn, 'Legislating pluralism'.

[161] Ibid., p. 97.

[162] New Zealand Law Commission, *Converging currents*, p. 193. Te Matahauriki Research Institute 2007, *Te Matapunenga: A compendium of references to the concepts and institutions of Maori customary law*, Te Matahauriki Research Institute, University of Waikato, New Zealand, is an excellent example of how this can be done.

[163] Brown, Ken and Corrin Care, Jennifer 1998, 'Conflict in Melanesia: customary law and the rights of women', *Commonwealth Law Bulletin*, p. 1334; Corrin Care, 'Customary law and human rights in Solomon Islands' ; Corrin Care, Jennifer 2003, 'Reconciling customary law and human rights in Melanesia', *Hiberian Law Journal*, vol. 4, p. 53; Farran, Sue 1997, 'Custom and constitutionally protected fundamental rights in the South Pacific region—the approach of the courts to potential conflicts', *The Journal of Pacific Studies*, vol. 21, p. 103; Elechi, Oko 2004, Human rights and the African indigenous justice system, Paper presented at the Eighteenth International Conference of the International Society for the Reform of Criminal Law, Montreal, Quebec, Canada, 2004.

[164] New Zealand Law Commission, *Converging currents*, p. 76.

[165] Ibhawoh, Bonny 2001, 'Cultural tradition and national human rights standards in conflict', in K. Hastrup (ed.), *Legal Cultures and Human Rights: The challenges of diversity*, p. 99.

[166] Ibid., p. 99.

[167] Ibid., p. 86.

[168] Faundez, Non-state justice systems in Latin America, p. 61.

[169] NGOs or other donors could provide funding for such a program.

[170] New Zealand Law Commission, *Converging currents*, p. 151.

[171] See further ibid., p. 164.

[172] For a discussion of this type of assessor, see ibid., pp. 198–9.

[173] Bougainville Constitutional Commission 2004, *Report on the Third and Final Draft of the Bougainville Constitution*, p. 198.

[174] In terms of powers, two different approaches are shown in Fiji and Samoa. In Fiji, the role of the assessors is advisory in nature only, but where the decision of the judge is contrary to the majority opinion of the assessors, the judge is required to give his/her reasons for disagreeing (*Criminal Procedure Code* [Fiji], Section 299). In Samoa, in contrast, no person can be convicted of any offence unless the conviction is concurred in by not less than three of the assessors where there are four, and by not less than four of the assessors where there are five assessors (*Criminal Procedure Act* [Samoa], Section 99).

[175] S ee Braithwaite, John 1999, 'Restorative justice: assessing optimistic and pessimistic accounts', *Crime and Justice*, vol. 25, p. 1 ; Crnkovich, Mary 1996, 'A sentencing circle', *Journal of Legal Pluralism*, vol. 36, p. 159.

[176] Tomaino, John 2006, *Aboriginal (Nunga) courts*, Information Bulletin No. 39, Government of South Australia, viewed 20 July 2006, <http://www.ocsar.sa.gov.au/docs/information_bulletins/IB39.pdf>

[177] Law Reform Commission of Western Australia, *Aboriginal customary laws*, Discussion Paper Project No. 94, p. 142.

[178] Potas, Ivan et al. 2003, 'Circle sentencing in New South Wales: a review and evaluation', *Australian Indigenous Law Reporter*, vol. 2004, p. 16, <http://www.austlii.edu.au/au/journals/AILR/2004/16.html>

[179] Law Reform Commission of Western Australia, *Aboriginal customary laws*, Discussion Paper Project No. 94, pp. 146–52.

[180] Ibid., p. 149.

[181] Ibid., p. 155.

[182] Potas, 'Circle sentencing in New South Wales'.

[183] New Zealand Law Commission, *Converging currents*, pp. 199–201.

[184] The Vanuatu Supreme Court has done this occasionally in relation to determination of chiefly title (*Tenene vs Nmak* [2003, VUSC 2, <http://www.paclii.org>]) and customary adoption (*M vs P, Re the child G* [1980–94, Van LR 333]).

[185] Relevant considerations in the decision about referral will include whether the parties agree to the referral and whether individual rights and interests can be protected.

[186] New Zealand Law Reform Commission, *Report of Proceedings*, p. 179.

[187] Australian Law Reform Commission, *The recognition of Aboriginal customary laws* , p. 834.

[188] Government of Autonomous Region of Bougainville 2004, *The Constitution*, Section 121.

[189] Ibid.

[190] Bougainville Constitutional Commission, *Report on the Third and Final Draft of the Bougainville Constitution*, p. 197.

[191] Originally in Papua New Guinea, all *kiaps* were expatriates but locals were introduced to the role by the 1960s (Gordon and Meggitt, *Law and Order in the New Guinea Highlands* , p. 47).

[192] Dinnen, 'Violence and governance in Melanesia', p. 5.

[193] Ibid. See also Dinnen, Sinclair 2001, *Law and Order in a Weak State*, pp. 23–9.

[194] It should be noted that Penal Reform International (*Access to Justice in Sub-Saharan Africa*, p. 169) argues that people should be able to 'shop for justice' by moving freely between the various systems as suits themselves.

[195] The danger of judicial domination of *kastom* proceedings could be avoided by making sure the judge is in the minority, not giving him/her a power of veto or ensuring that he/she attends by invitation only.

8. A new method of legal pluralism

It has been pointed out by many scholars that in today's Western world the State is becoming increasingly 'hollowed-out', meaning that more and more state functions are being devolved to non-state actors.[1] In Vanuatu and many other developing countries, however, the opposite of this has occurred: the State has engaged in a process of *taking over* more and more of the functions traditionally performed by community leaders in stateless communities. This has particularly been the case in countries emerging from periods of weak or scattered government (such as those emerging from civil war) to a stronger state. In these countries, it is the village or traditional levels of government that have been hollowed out, creating deepening problems of a variety of kinds, such as the governance of growing numbers of unemployed youth. This suggests that at any given period in any particular jurisdiction, there is likely to be flux in the division of functions between state and non-state actors. In the context of developing countries, although there has recently been a degree of recognition of this—and of the consequent need to develop capacity at state and non-state levels, and effective linkages between these levels[2] —there is currently a lack of a methodology for *how* to go about doing this.[3]

This chapter therefore takes the next step by devising a seven-step methodology for managing a shift in functions between state and non-state, so that each performs the jobs that it can do best and the weaknesses of one are covered by the strengths of the other. It does this by reflecting on a method that has proved useful in Vanuatu, drawing out its systemic features and offering it as a starting point for any jurisdiction investigating policy options for relating their different legal orders to each other. Although this chapter is concerned with just the legal aspect of this division of functions between state and non-state actors, it is hoped that the general approach outlined will have a broader application and apply to any situation where there is controversy about, or a shift in functions between, state and non-state bodies. Of course, it is important to note that the method proposed here has been tested only in one country and it is expected that each jurisdiction will need to make its own adaptations. Indeed, an important part of the method is feeding back into it lessons learnt and useful alterations developed during the implementation stages (Step 7 below).

The methodology this chapter proposes is one of how to grasp the holistic quality of a nation's legal system, how to pull it apart and then how to identify the complete range of options for recombining them (actually steering the process of their recombination), while the normative part of the method helps us to think more clearly about the strengths or weaknesses of that option in that context. There are two principles that are at the centre of the proposed method. The first is the principle of not privileging the state over the non-state system. In Chapter 2, we saw that legal pluralists demonstrated how treating the state as superior to other types of legal order with no justification for doing so forced non-state justice systems into a subordinate position, thus limiting the possibilities for them to operate to their maximum potential and for a situation of true legal pluralism to flourish. In this method, there is therefore a constant refusal to treat the state system in a more advantageous way than the non-state system, such as in regulation and oversight, merely because 'it is the State'. As discussed in the previous chapter, however, where the State's structural characteristics provide a normative advantage in making reforms, this should be capitalised on. The second principle is what Braithwaite refers to as 'incremental transition' and defines as 'experimentation…[and] innovation combined with evaluation'.[4] This principle means that all change should be viewed as being progressive and as being linked with the obligation to carry out empirical research designed to test the extent to which the changes are working and why this is or is not happening. In other words, the approach is explanatory/empirical as well as normative.

The proposed methodology is described in the remainder of this chapter, with Vanuatu used to illustrate how it could be applied in practice. Thus, although this study does not provide 'the solution' to the problems it raises, which would be not only impossible but inappropriate for a single, foreign scholar, it does provide a methodology the country can implement itself in its search for the solution. It should also be acknowledged that in many ways the process that is suggested is an ideal one, in that there might be resource issues, time constraints and problems such as lack of political will that will impact on the ability of Vanuatu, or any other jurisdiction, to carry out all seven steps. It is for this reason that the proposed method is an incremental one, to be implemented over time, when the conditions are ready. Finally, although Vanuatu has two major legal systems, the methodology can apply equally where there are three or more.

Step 1: Analyse the operation of the state and non-state systems

Step 1 of the method is to do 'whole-of-society' fieldwork, focusing on the different systems of legal ordering. The aim is to discover what systems operate in a particular jurisdiction, their norms, fundamental principles, procedures and key institutions; their strengths and weaknesses; and their formal and informal relationships with each other. The central approach is to interview key players within the systems referred to by other key players about their individual contribution to how the system works and how they see the system working overall. Put another way, it is interviewing with a micro–macro orientation. The interviewing continues until there are more and more informants who are saying the same thing that has been said many times before. This method should be triangulated with other research methods, such as participant observation and documentary analysis of primary and secondary sources. The importance of this step cannot be overemphasised, but it is frequently neglected. For example, Galanter and Krishnan comment that in India both sides in the debate about the development of Lok Adalats (hybrid local courts) base their arguments on supposition rather than investigation.[5]

This process was carried out in Vanuatu, in the domain of criminal law. The detailed results are discussed in Chapters 4 and 5. Some of the key findings are that:

- the State is weak and under-resourced and this is not likely to change in the near future
- the *kastom* system is currently managing a large percentage of conflicts in the country, which is saving the state judicial system from being completely overburdened
- there is enormous community support for the *kastom* system, which is seen as more legitimate than the state system in certain contexts
- there is support for the state system and recognition that it has an important role to play, but frustration with its inadequacies
- the *kastom* system faces significant and growing problems with enforcement of decisions and compulsion to obey calls to meetings
- the *kastom* system has problems of chiefly bias, unenergetic chiefs, discrimination against women and children and chiefly disputes, all of which significantly affect its capacity to deliver effective justice but for which there is currently no system of regulation
- the chiefs are becoming increasingly frustrated by the demands the State places on them in regard to maintenance of law and order in their communities and the denial of any sort of state power or aid to assist them in carrying out their functions.

Step 2: Consider the aims of the overall justice system

The second task is to develop a national dialogue to consider the aims of any reforms of the overall system. In every jurisdiction there will be different priorities, constraints and problems that affect the final system chosen: some might be concerned more with ensuring access to justice for all than with a geographical minority; others with preventing human rights abuses; others with dealing with specific problems related to a breakdown of traditional communities; and yet others with decongesting state courts. For example, the aim of the Zwelethemba Model of Peace Committees is to improve security,[6] whereas for many projects sponsored by the UK Department for International Development it is to improve access to justice.[7] That said, many countries will no doubt share a number of general aims, such as one suggested by Braithwaite:

> [T]he long-run hope is for a radical redesign of legal institutions whereby the justice of the people will more meaningfully bubble up into the justice of the law and the justice of the law will more meaningfully filter down to place limits on the justice of the people.[8]

It could be that in a particular jurisdiction there are a number of competing aims, in which case it is necessary that these are clearly articulated and there is full community participation in the decision about which aims to pursue, or what sorts of compromises should be made. For example, there might need to be choices made between preserving traditional aspects of a customary justice system, such as the exclusion of women, with the desire to develop a greater role for women in the administration of justice.

Working out the aims or goals for every jurisdiction should involve stakeholders in both systems, as well as broad community consultation. It is essential that the key actors in both systems, as well as the general public, broadly agree on the foundational principles of the new structure.

In Vanuatu, it is still too early to say what the aims of the overall justice system are, as there has not been the kind of national debate that is necessary to identify these with certainty. On the basis of what has been discovered during the fieldwork, however, it is possible to hazard a guess as to what factors might go into a desired justice system for Vanuatu. It is likely to be a system that maximises the ability of everyone to have effective access to a conflict-management system that everyone affected by the conflict considers fair and legitimate. There is also likely to be pressure for the system to be consistent with international human rights standards. These aims incorporate, and juggle, three main ideas.

First, the idea of effective access to a conflict-management system requires that the access is not merely theoretical and involves considerations such as geographical accessibility, financial accessibility and that the institutions themselves (and the processes they use) are understandable to the people who use them. Second, there is a subjective requirement—namely, that the conflict-management system must be considered fair and legitimate by the parties to the conflict, as well as those affected by it, such as families or communities of the parties. This requirement in the context of situations of legal pluralism means that parties should be free to choose the system that they consider to be a fair and legitimate forum. There will, of course, need to be some regulations to deal with a situation where one party considers one legal system legitimate but not the other.

The third part to the aim is the objective requirement that the conflict-management system conforms to certain international human rights standards, such as those ensuring freedom from discrimination and the rules of natural justice. Such a requirement is necessary in addition to the two above to deal with situations where the *parties* to conflicts consider the processes fair and legitimate, but they are in fact being dominated in some way by an oppressive force. An example of such a situation is a case where a husband beat his wife because she did not have his dinner warm for him when he came home. In a heavily patriarchal community, such as exists in some parts of Vanuatu, the response of the chief to a complaint by the woman might be that the man is entitled to do this and the woman might accept this due to her customary upbringing.[9] In such a situation, the conflict-management system must be changed because otherwise it reinforces the domination of women by men, which is slowly becoming less acceptable in Vanuatu, and is contrary to the constitution and the various international agreements that Vanuatu has ratified.[10] This aim is also responding to the fact that the *kastom* system is increasingly seen as a justice or rights system, as discussed in Chapter 4. In addition, as a practical matter, it is unlikely that Vanuatu would receive donor support for any reforms that would significantly limit international human rights standards. This is an example of a way in which particular aims might need to be the process of discussion and compromise.

Step 3: Examine the current positive and problematic features in the relationship between the systems

This next step[11] requires fieldwork into the operation of the state and non-state systems and those areas where they interact to discover the positive and negative features of their relationship. Key players in the systems, and especially those who act as 'gatekeepers' between the systems, must be interviewed. Identifying these gatekeepers is an important step also because they are the people who are most likely to be instrumental in building bridges between the systems. In addition, case studies should also be done where possible to demonstrate the real relationship between the two systems and the strengths and weaknesses of that relationship. The advantage of combining case studies with in-depth interviews is that it is possible to understand how people would like to see the systems working in practice (which often comes through in interviews) and also how they really do operate in reality (which comes through in case studies).

This step has been carried out in Vanuatu and the results are discussed in Chapters 5 and 6. The relationship between the two systems was found to be, for the most part, informal and undefined, continuously shifting in response to local conditions and individual relationships. One of the important variants was the strength of the state system in a particular area—in terms of manpower and other resources available. The strengths of the relationship were found to be its fluid nature, allowing it to adapt in response to the needs of each particular situation, the fact that the *kastom* system was able to define its own norms and procedural framework, allowing it to remain a dynamic and legitimate grassroots justice system, the fact that it was based entirely on respect and so dependent on the community for support and, finally, the *kastom* system provided access to justice in areas not serviced by the State and kept a high percentage of cases out of the state system at no cost to the State. An additional important strength of the current situation is that some people have roles in both systems, such as chiefs who are also police officers, and are able to act as links between the two systems. These are the people who, according to Putnam, are crucial to building social capital because they not only share bonding capital within these groups but bridging capital between groups.[12] As Granovetter points out, even if the bridges are shaky, there can be great strength in weak ties.[13] In Vanuatu, the Church, the Malvatumauri and the police officer chiefs provide much of this bridging capital.

A significant number of tensions and problems have also been found to exist in the relationship, the principal ones being:

- the ability to engage in unregulated 'forum shopping' leads to destabilisation and undermining of both systems and places vulnerable complainants under considerable pressure
- there is confusion and misinformation about which system has responsibility for dealing with different types of cases
- this confusion leads to confrontations between chiefs and state officials and considerable frustration on both sides
- this confusion also leads to both systems avoiding responsibility for dealing with domestic violence cases and refusing to take responsibility for fixing certain breakdowns in law and order
- there are no clear pathways for how a particular matter should move between the two systems; this means that in cases where the state system deals with the matter first this has consequences for the ability of the *kastom* system to deal effectively with the matter and vice versa
- when a case is dealt with in both systems, many defendants feel they are being punished twice for the same offence
- the operation of the state system disempowers and demoralises chiefs
- the operation of the *kastom* system undermines the effective operation of the state system—for example, by creating a competing forum that might be considered more legitimate and by delaying the reporting of cases and causing people to withdraw cases from the police when they have not been fully processed, thus wasting state time and resources
- the state system hinders the operation of the *kastom* system by prosecuting chiefs for enforcing their orders, making orders that contradict those of the *kastom* system and making orders that interfere with the ability of the chiefs to operate.

Step 4: Consider the applicability of the different models of relationship to this context

The next step is to establish a national dialogue to determine which of the seven models set out in the previous chapter comes the closest to overcoming the problems identified in the relationship between the systems, as well as the problems *within* the systems, without disproportionately jeopardising the existing advantages.

Taking this step involves looking at the tables in the previous chapter, especially the column that sets out 'circumstances in which this model should be considered' and analysing whether or not these particular circumstances apply. The consideration of possible models should also take into account factors such as whether or not certain models have already been tried and failed, and any particular cultural or historical reasons that would make a particular model impossible.[14] It is also possible that a particular jurisdiction might choose to combine various features from a number of different models to create a new model. For example, a jurisdiction might feel that having completely parallel justice systems might not work and so could give a limited right of appeal to state courts, thus combining Models 4 and 5.

In selecting a model, the main questions to be decided are whether or not the State will formally recognise the validity of the exercise of adjudicative power by a non-state system and, if so, the extent of that jurisdiction, and the State's powers of regulation and whether or not the non-state system will be able to use coercive power. The other questions or details that should be considered are set out under each of the models in the previous chapter.

The practical way the task of choosing a model can be implemented will vary from country to country, but a possible option is the establishment of a task force with equal representation of key players from the state and non-state systems, as well as other interest groups such as women and youth groups. This task force could hold focus groups to debate particular issues and also regular public briefings to discuss findings and gather feedback throughout the jurisdiction (importantly, paying as much attention to rural areas as to urban ones). It might also be advisable to hold at least one national summit on the issue to which a wide range of stakeholders is invited, as this might focus the national attention on the issues involved and generate a degree of unanimity in the direction to be followed. Particularly in countries where there is limited scope for dissemination of written materials, the importance of utilising avenues such as public meetings and even the radio for debates and discussions cannot be overemphasised.

This step is yet to be taken in Vanuatu. From the basis of this study, the possible models to consider are Models 4, 5 and 6, as the informal relationship that currently exists is becoming increasingly unviable. It could be, however, that for political reasons (the reluctance of the State to empower the chiefs), consideration should also be given to Model 3, particularly if a focus is given to establishing more structured relationships such as the Zwelethemba Model of Peace Committees in South Africa. Some of the issues involved in making the choice of model were discussed at the Vanuatu Judiciary Conference in 2006 and there was considerable disagreement between the different stakeholders—chiefs, judiciary, police—about most of them, thus illustrating the need for a slow and open process of discussion and negotiation in the future.[15]

Step 5: Develop the chosen model so that it becomes one of mutual adaptation, mutual recognition and mutual regulation

The previous step largely involves the State determining what relationship it will have with a non-state system and how it will recognise and regulate it, although its approach to this will be informed very much by the attitudes of the key actors in the non-state justice system. One of the principles at the centre of this proposed methodology, however, is not to privilege the state over the non-state system without good reason. This step therefore aims to remedy the state bias of Step 4 by modifying the model selected so that it becomes balanced in terms of responsibility and direction between the state and non-state systems—in other words, so that they are both (all) 'steering the boat'. In effect, this means that for every step taken by the State towards learning about, adapting to, recognising and regulating a non-state system, consideration should be given to how a reciprocal measure could be taken by a non-state system towards the state system. In order for such reforms not to create duplicate structures, it will be important for the efficiency capacity of both systems to be strengthened. This, together with prudent rules about when one system should defer to the other, should result in each steering the efficiency out of the other. As discussed in Chapter 7 (under 'Mutual adaptations/innovations by state and non-state systems'), there are considerable difficulties associated with the practicalities of implementing reforms in non-state justice systems. Many of the steps in this section therefore require the non-state justice system to form partnerships with either the State or donor organisations.

To apply this to Vanuatu it is necessary to first choose the model, which as explained above has not yet been done. For the purposes of this exercise, however, Model 6—in which the State formally recognises the *kastom* system and enforces its judgments, if necessary, with the use of state force—will be used. For reasons of space, this discussion will be limited to its essentials, as its purpose is not to provide a blueprint for Vanuatu but rather to illustrate the approach of integral plurality that is being advocated.

Internal adaptations

This step involves each system considering ways it can adapt or reform *itself* so it can strengthen the links between, and work together better with, the other system. A non-legal example of this occurring successfully in Vanuatu is the relationship of Christianity and *kastom*, where both have adopted elements of the other and today they are perceived as coexisting harmoniously and supporting each other.[16] The systems might draw from the mutual adaptation suggestions set out in Chapter 7 (under 'Mutual adaptations/innovations by state and non-state systems') or develop new ideas.

The state system

In Vanuatu, the simplest first steps to take to move in this direction are:

- to formalise a way to facilitate learning about the *kastom* system (such as through a series of workshops)
- reintroducing assessors, at least into the Supreme Courts if not the Magistrate's and appeal level as well
- making greater use of the *kastom* system in terms of diversion and sentencing.

In addition, consideration should be given to an idea that emerged from the Vanuatu Judiciary Conference, which is that there should be an office established within the government to ensure that the state system uses the *kastom* system as much as possible. It was suggested that this office could be established within the Ministry of Justice and its role would be to monitor and ensure coordination of projects and the two systems and provide funding, training and consultation.[17] Many of these steps would, in fact, be mutually supportive—for example, the inclusion of assessors in state courts would open paths of mutual learning.[18]

The *kastom* system

As for the state system, one of the most fundamental steps for the *kastom* system to take is to educate the chiefs about the workings of the state system and their role, such as it is, in it. There is also a good deal of scope for the *kastom* system to make changes to accommodate some human rights and natural justice issues, such as the right for all parties, regardless of gender, to be allowed to speak and the right for parties to have an unbiased panel of decision makers (and processes to ensure these rights can be exercised).[19] It is important that such reforms are seen to be warranted and necessary by the key actors in the *kastom* system, so that ownership of them is felt at a grassroots level and they are not seen as something that is being imposed on them.

A particular approach to advancing such reforms in Vanuatu is to find places where communities have already successfully implemented such measures (for example, the chiefly council in Erromango that includes a woman) and then to use that as a role model for other communities. Vanuatu Cultural Centre fieldworkers could carry out this initial research in conjunction with local scholars or donor organisations. Such an approach is similar to Parker's concept of 'triple-loop learning', which involves a successful development at a local level being replicated at successively higher levels of an organisation or structure—for example village, island, nation.[20] An important part of each 'loop' of the learning cycle is reflecting on how the diversity in the different levels can be accommodated and managed (for example, if a procedure is taken from a village-level council and applied to an area-level council), as well as the experiences from the previous level. This approach ensures that indigenous solutions are being used, rather than introduced ones.[21] An issue that might need to be overcome with this approach if it is used across islands is the risk that people from other communities might say in response to the suggested reform 'that is their *kastom*, this is ours'. With appropriate leadership, however, from non-state justice system leaders committed to the reform agenda, these sorts of attitudes should be able to be overcome.

Recognition

State recognition of the *kastom* system

The model chosen involves the State recognising the legitimacy of the *kastom* system to exercise adjudicative power. Two questions to be answered initially are: how will the State determine who are the legitimate administrators of the *kastom* system and what should be the extent of the recognition?

In terms of the first question, there are three possible approaches. The first is not to prescribe what the *kastom* system is or who can legitimately operate it, but to leave the issue to be dealt with on an individual basis (such as when a chief comes to a court asking for a judgment to be enforced). Given the existing level of disputes over chiefly title, this is unlikely to be a workable strategy and runs the risk of the courts being coopted into local power struggles. The second, and most preferable, approach is that taken in Botswana, where the chiefs apply to the State for recognition of their court. A possible refinement of it could be for the minister to impose certain criteria on the recognition of such a court, such as that the court has a certain proportion of women as members and provides guarantees about the right of women and children to speak. Such a system would leave to the individual community the decision about whether to form a relationship with the State and have access to its coercive powers in return for submitting to a degree of regulation or to remain alone and rely on the strength of *kastom* and respect to enforce orders. Importantly, in making such a decision, the community as a whole is likely to be involved in a discussion of the issues, which will have an invaluable educative effect about the roles and limits of each system.

The question about the extent of jurisdiction involves further questions, such as: should *kastom* courts have jurisdiction over *kastom* and state offences and matters, or just *kastom* ones? Should there be a list of offences or matters that the *kastom* system should not deal with? Should the *kastom* system have exclusive jurisdiction over any matters or offences? Should there be cross-referral provisions to ensure that only one system can deal with the conflict? Answering these questions is beyond the scope of this book, but the problems in Botswana (where the non-state system exercises jurisdiction over state matters)[22] suggest that the *kastom* system should deal only with *kastom* offences, as in South Africa.[23]

Kastom system recognition of the state system

The decision by the *kastom* system to recognise the state system involves the *kastom* system determining what offences or matters can legitimately be determined by the state system and whether there should be any areas where the State should exercise exclusive jurisdiction. It is likely that there will be broad agreement that the state system has exclusive jurisdiction over non-customary matters, such as taxation, customs and other laws that are essentially part of a modern nation-state. The difficult areas are likely to be in the area of criminal law, particularly sexual offences and serious assault and murder cases, which have been shown by this study to be contested areas. It could be that different parts of the *kastom* system throughout the country might choose to recognise the state system differently—and this is something that will need to be discussed and negotiated. For example, it might be that in areas where there is no police post, the *kastom* system will recognise the State's right to exercise jurisdiction in a more limited way than in urban areas.

In terms of implementation of these decisions, written policies might be drawn up or oral agreements made and publicised by various levels of the *kastom* system about what to do when particular cases arise over which the state system is recognised as having either exclusive or shared jurisdiction.

Regulation

State regulation of the *kastom* system

We saw in Chapter 7 that the issue of regulation of non-state justice systems was one of the most controversial and complex in the reform of pluralist relationships. The amount and type of regulation are very much dictated by the type of relationship adopted. For example, it is apparent that when the State is using its own coercive powers to enforce decisions made by non-state justice systems there is a need for some type of regulation. As Blagg comments, 'There is an inherent tendency for coercive policing powers to be misused unless restrained by oversight, visibility and mechanisms of accountability.'[24] If there is too much regulation, however, the non-state system risks losing its integrity and those very features that distinguish it from the state system and make it so valuable: accessibility, adaptability, legitimacy, familiarity and timeliness. One way to find the balance between over and under regulation is to adopt a policy of minimal intervention—that is, to intervene only in the substantive and procedural organisation of the non-state justice system where empirical research has shown that constitutional or human rights breaches have occurred or are likely to occur. The Traditional Courts model in South Africa demonstrates that it is theoretically possible to have such a 'hands-off' approach and yet be confident that citizens will still be assured of their rights to a fair trial.

The two main options for regulation of the *kastom* system by the State are appeals and supervision. One way to apply the principles of minimal interference to appeals is to have the appeal structure limited in various ways. For example, in Samoa, there are limited grounds of appeal to the Supreme Court, thus ensuring that the state courts (except for the Land and Titles Court, which is a hybrid customary system) become involved only when there are allegations of breaches of the fundamental rights provisions in the constitution. In addition, it might be possible to limit the types of orders that could be made on appeal—for example, allowing only a state court to send a matter back for rehearing, perhaps with some policy guidelines designed to remedy the problems that occurred in the first instance. A further possibility could be the setting up of a *kastom* court of appeal that draws its personnel, procedures and substantive laws from both systems.

In terms of supervision, it is also possible to have a structure based on a principle of minimal interference. The approach suggested by the South African Law Reform Commission of having a separate registrar outside the state court system, whose purpose is to guide and supervise the courts and transfer cases where necessary, is one that could be considered.

In addition to appeals and supervision, there are other secondary forms of regulation, such as requiring *kastom* courts to meet certain standards before the State agrees to enforce their judgments (such as the requirements of natural justice), or requiring that all sitting fees be paid into a particular account or accounted for in some other transparent way.

Kastom system regulation of the State

Regulation of the state system by the non-state justice system requires a significant amount of creative thinking, as there is little available material on where this has been tried actively in particular jurisdictions. It is unlikely that the *kastom* system would have the ability, or even the desire, to regulate the state system through appeals. There are, however, a number of *indirect* ways that the *kastom* system could regulate the state system. Such initiatives are likely to have a significant impact on enhancing the legitimacy of the state system and, hopefully, mean that it will no longer be viewed as '*kot blong waetman*'.

One indirect means is a requirement that before any significant change of legal principle or policy that will have relevant implications for the *kastom* system[25] is made by the Supreme Court or the Court of Appeal, the issues involved are discussed, and the decision concurred in, by representatives from the *kastom* system. One mechanism for doing this is for chiefs to sit as assessors in the Court of Appeal.[26]

Another approach might be the holding of a conference each year, attended by representatives of both systems and at which the judiciary is required to report to the chiefs on various matters concerning the administration of justice, and listen to their feedback and create action plans for implementing any proposed reforms that could then be reported back on the next year. Where customary leaders are dissatisfied with the quality of the listening, they could discuss pulling back certain kinds of cases from the police, the courts and the prison system.

A final idea is to include a traditional leader on the judicial appointments committee and make knowledge of customary law a factor in determining eligibility for the position of judicial officer, as has been done in Bougainville.[27]

Step 6: Develop a method of progressive implementation and evaluation of changes

This step is to develop a method of implementation of the changes that maximise the chances that the relationship between the systems is dynamic and that the links between the systems are continually reinforced. The method advocated for achieving this is an incremental one, with a method of evaluation of the changes that have occurred built into it. The method works by defining some practical initial steps for moving forward incrementally to make the changes identified, and then evaluating those changes before moving forward with further steps in light of that evaluation, and so forth. A further principle that informs this approach is Selznick's concept of responsiveness, which 'entails reconstruction of the self as well as outreach to others.[28] Established structures, rules, methods, and policies, are all open to revision, but revision takes place in a principled way, that is, while holding fast to values and purposes.' State and non-state systems are therefore viewed as existing in a dynamic relationship, which requires them to modify certain aspects of the way they relate to each other and in themselves, while retaining their own integrity.[29]

In Vanuatu, from the side of the state system, the first step that could be made could be the introduction of assessors in one level of state courts. At the end of a given period, there could be a review of how well this had worked, and if it had proved to be a success then they could be implemented at other levels. If they had not been then there could be an investigation into why not and whether it was worth trying again with a different implementation strategy, or trying one of the other mutual-adaptation possibilities set out in Chapter 7. From the side of the *kastom* system, the first step could be research into communities where the various village, area and island councils are working well and the reasons for this, and then a program devised to apply the lessons learnt from the research to another group of village, area and island councils that is not currently functioning as well. This process could then be evaluated and the lessons learnt applied to implementing the changes with a broader group of chiefly councils, and so on.

Step 7: Revise the model pluralist method

The final step is to make sure that the seven-model typology developed in Chapter 7 is continually revised in light of new empirical experiences throughout the world, by adding new models or new advantages/disadvantages of existing models that should be considered.

Conclusion: doing legal pluralism

This final chapter applies the lessons learnt through the study of plural legal orders in Vanuatu to the development of a methodology that can be used to 'do' legal pluralism in any given jurisdiction. It has shown that although today legal pluralism is not widely used by those examining customary law or engaging in practical legal reform, it has the potential to be an extremely useful tool for both. The theory of legal pluralism permits us to move from focusing all inquiries on the state system—as is required by positivism—to exploring other legal orders that exist in a given jurisdiction. Such inquiry could reveal that these systems are, in reality, performing the same work as the state system in a different, and sometimes better, way. We therefore see that in Vanuatu the *kastom* system manages more conflicts than the state system and is often preferred to the state system due to its accessibility, familiarity, efficiency and cultural relevance. Legal pluralism also provides valuable insights into the interrelationship between the various systems. It might reveal that legal orders in a society operate semi-autonomously and consequently that changes to one (through conscious reforms or societal change) will have significant consequences for the operation of the other. For example, in Vanuatu, the state system was shown to be negatively affecting the *kastom* system in a number of ways, including by undermining and destabilising the authority of the chiefs and interfering with their ability to operate their system, and vice versa. Legal pluralism thus allows us to create a complete picture of the various systems that manage conflict in a society and the ways in which these systems interact with one another.

Of course some legal theorists might argue that a situation of deep or institutional legal pluralism breaches the rule of law.[30] Although the rule of law is not a clearly defined principle,[31] there is broad agreement that it entails some requirement that human behaviour is regulated by general prescriptions, and that this is incompatible with extensive discrimination.[32] Fuller, for example, therefore argues that the rule of law requires that 'like cases must be treated alike' and that 'alternative enforcement of the rules, such as lynch mobs, street violence, and vigilantism, which create incongruence between announced legal rules and social reality must be suppressed'.[33] Such principles appear to support the universal observance of state law and to be breached by a situation in which, for example, in some areas of a country adultery is punishable but not in others, as can occur in a legally pluralist country.

Before accepting such a judgment, however, it is necessary to go behind the notion of the rule of law and investigate the principles that support it. The main rationale for the rule of law is to be a safeguard against arbitrary governance by ensuring that people are regulated by clear, known, accepted rules. In many pluralist countries, however, state law is considered by many to be foreign and arbitrary and treating everyone (for example, an educated urban dweller and an illiterate farmer) equally in reality results in substantial inequality and injustice. As Woodman comments, in 'countries where state law is largely a foreign implanted law, but customary law [is] an effective factor of local social cohesion, any additional empowerment of the state may result in a diminuition in the totality of the rule of law'.[34] If, therefore, we really wish to embrace the true basis of the rule of law, it might be more just to allow people to be regulated by their own legal orders, which are clearer and more legitimate and ensure greater equal treatment in pratice, than to attempt to impose a universal state law.[35] Various ways this could be done, together with detailed consideration of their practical and legal consequences, are set out in the typology in Chapter 7.

The limitation of legal pluralism to date has been that after helping to create a picture of the various systems that manage conflict in a society—and in doing so identifying the problematic areas in the relationships between the various legal systems—it is unable to take us further. In other words, it has not provided a normative path for reforming the various systems to allow them to work together better. Possibly, the focus that has been given to internal definitional debates in the past decade and the unwillingness to transcend normative relativism have prevented legal pluralism from continuing as the vital force it was in the 1970s and 1980s.

The major theoretical contribution of this book is therefore to move beyond this current limitation by devising a seven-step methodology that can be used to take the recognition of a situation of legal pluralism to the next step, by reforming the relationship between legal systems to allow them to work together better. It has shown that questions concerning which normative orders should be termed 'legal' and the differences between 'weak' and 'deep' legal pluralism are not as significant as confronting highly specific questions about relationships between state and non-state justice systems. The emphasis of the new method is on developing practical responsiveness to the realities of the relationship between state and non-state legal systems in a particular jurisdiction.[36] Whether what is achieved in a particular jurisdiction is weak or deep pluralism is not a preoccupation; what is important is that a way has been found for the legal systems to work together in a more supportive and mutually accountable manner than previously.

The keys to successful implementation of this method are a refusal to privilege the state over non-state systems without a good reason, creative thinking about possible relationships for the systems and mutual-adaptation possibilities, the need for continual empirical research using a participatory method, the adoption of an incremental approach and the desirability of robust public debates and participation throughout the implementation process. Further, in addition to employing a pluralist theory that pays equal attention to state and non-state systems, it is important to use a pluralist or grassroots *methodology* such as has been adopted in this study. A pluralist methodology takes as its field of inquiry all legal orders and investigates them using whatever avenues for research are available: documentary analysis, interviews, observations, conferences, and so on. The aim is to creatively blend different research techniques so as to discover, as well as possible, all of the factors affecting the management of conflict in a particular jurisdiction.

It is hoped that combining such a pluralist theory and methodology will assist any jurisdiction's justice system to become one that, in the words of one respondent, is 'a bird that flies with two wings'.

ENDNOTES

[1] For example, Johnston and Shearing, *Governing Security*, p. 145.

[2] For example, Dinnen, 'Violence and governance in Melanesia', p. 70.

[3] For example, Corrin Care ('A green stick or a fresh stick?', p. 59) states that there is a 'lack of any proved theory or methodology to guide any unification project in this field'.

[4] Braithwaite, John 2003, 'Principles of restorative justice', in A. von Hirsch et al. (eds), *Restorative Justice and Criminal Justice: Competing or reconcilable paradigms?*, p. 4.

[5] Galanter and Krishnan, '"Bread for the poor"', p. 833.

[6] Johnston and Shearing, *Governing Security*, p. 158.

[7] Government of the United Kingdom, *Non-State Justice and Security Systems*.

[8] Braithwaite, 'Principles of restorative justice', p. 18.

[9] A female respondent once told me that she accepted her husband beating her because 'otherwise how will I learn?'.

[10] Such as the *Convention on the Elimination of All Forms of Discrimination Against Women*.

[11] It might be more advantageous in some situations to reverse the order of Steps 2 and 3 as sometimes the precise nature of the challenges posed—and therefore the way in which principles should be framed—is clear only once the interaction between the two systems has been examined.

[12] Putnam, Robert 2000, *Bowling Alone: The collapse and revival of American community*.

[13] Granovetter, Mark 1973, 'The strength of weak ties', *The American Journal of Sociology*, vol. 78, no. 6, p. 1360.

[14] For example, in South Africa and some other African countries, the use that was made of the chiefs by the colonial governments made their acceptance by the community after independence difficult, which in turn affected the role they could play in the justice system. For example, Santos referred to the fact that after independence in Mozambique, traditional authorities were '[s]een as obscurantist remnants of colonialism'. Santos, 'The heterogeneous state and legal pluralism in Mozambique', p. 64.

[15] Forsyth, *Report on the Vanuatu Judiciary Conference 2006*.

[16] Discussed in detail in Chapter 1 under 'Religion and denomination'.

[17] Forsyth, *Report on the Vanuatu Judiciary Conference 2006*, p. 16.

[18] It should be noted that steps have already been taken towards achieving some of these adaptations. As already discussed, the Vanuatu Judiciary Conference in 2006 took the *kastom* system and its relationship with the state system as its theme and involved two days of discussion between the chiefs and the judiciary. In addition, the introduction of new legislation governing correctional services (discussed in Chapter 5 under 'The relationship between the prisons and the *kastom* system') is moving towards facilitating a greater relationship between the two systems.

[19] Some steps are also currently being taken in implementing some of these ideas. I am involved in a project that is a joint initiative of the University of Queensland's Australian Centre for Peace and Conflict Studies and the Malvatumauri that involves, in part, providing training to chiefs throughout Vanuatu on the functioning of the state system of governance and law and the role of the chiefs in it.

[20] Braithwaite, John, Healy, Judith and Dwan, Kathryn 2005, *The Governance of Health and Australia, The Commonwealth of Australia*, p. 31; Parker, Christine 2002, *The Open Corporation*, pp. xi, 251, 278.

[21] Woodman makes a similar suggestion when searching for 'the possibilities of activism in customary law'. He therefore states, 'A starting point might be found in the studies of ways in which some categories of subjects of customary law have manipulated and eventually changed the law to their advantage, either as individuals or as communities.' Woodman, 'Legal pluralism and the search for justice', p. 152.

[22] Discussed in Chapter 7, Model 7.

[23] Discussed in Chapter 7, Model 6.

[24] Blagg, *A New Way of Doing Business?*, p. 332.

[25] Obviously, this would not include matters such as customs duty or foreign relations.

[26] There might be a requirement that the judges and a majority of the assessors agree on the new principle or that if the judges and assessors cannot agree the judges must provide written reasons justifying their decision not to follow the assessors, as is the case in Fiji (*Criminal Procedure Code* [Fiji]:s 299).

[27] Bougainville Constitutional Commission, *Report on the Third and Final Draft of the Bougainville Constitution*, p. 197.

[28] Selznick, Philip 1992, *The Moral Commonwealth: Social theory and the promise of community*, p. 338.

[29] Selznick (ibid., p. 322) states, 'The chief virtue of integrity is fidelity to self-defining principles. To strive for integrity is to ask: What is our direction? What are our unifying principles? And how do these square with the claims of morality?'

[30] This issue was discussed in more detail in the context of Model 5 in Chapter 7.

[31] Walker, David 1980, *The Oxford Companion to Law*, p. 1093.

[32] Woodman, 'Customary law in common law systems', p. 31.

[33] West, Robin 2003, *Re-Imagining Justice*, p. 64.

[34] Woodman, 'Customary law in common law systems', p. 31.

[35] See the discussion about Model 5 in Chapter 7, where this issue is examined.

[36] Selznick, *The Moral Commonwealth*, p. 338.

Bibliography

Aboriginal and Torres Strait Islander Social Justice Commissioner 2003, Submission to the Expert Seminar on Indigenous Peoples and the Administration of Justice, Paper presented at the Expert Seminar on Indigenous Peoples and the Administration of Justice, Madrid, Spain, 2003.

Aleck, Jonathan 1992, 'The village court system of Papua New Guinea', *Research in Melanesia*, vol. 16, p. 101.

Aleck, Jonathan 1997, 'Beyond recognition: contemporary jurisprudence in the Pacific islands and the common law tradition', *Queensland University of Technology Law Journal*, vol. 7, p. 137.

Aleck, Jonathan and Rannells, Jackson 1995, *Custom at the Crossroads*.

Allen, Michael 1981, 'Innovation, inversion and revolution', in Michael Allen (ed.), *Vanuatu: Politics, economics and ritual in island Melanesia*, p. 105.

Allen, Michael (ed.) 1981, *Vanuatu: Politics, economics and ritual in island Melanesia*.

Allott, Anthony and Woodman, Gordon (eds) 1985, *People's Law and State Law: The Bellagio papers*.

Ambrose, David 1997, 'Vanuatu politics—two into one won't go', *Pacific Economic Bulletin*, vol. 12, no. 2, p. 121.

Amnesty International 1998, *No Safe Place for Prisoners*.

Anaya, James 2003, Indigenous justice systems and customary law in the United States: between colonization and self-determination, Paper presented at the Expert Seminar on Indigenous Peoples and the Administration of Justice, Madrid, Spain, 2003.

Arendell, Terry 1997, 'Reflections on the researcher–researched relationship: a woman interviewing men', *Qualitative Sociology*, vol. 20, no. 3, p. 341.

Assies, Willem 1999, 'Multi-ethnicity, the State and the law in Latin America', *Journal of Legal Pluralism*, vol. 43, p. 145.

Australian Broadcasting Corporation (ABC) 2007, 'Time to talk', *ABC Radio Australia*, viewed 27 April 2007, <http://www.abc.net.au/timetotalk/english/radio/stories/TimeToTalkTranscript_418691.htm>

Australian Law Reform Commission 1986, *The recognition of Aboriginal customary laws*, Report No. 31.

Baker, Therese 1999, *Doing Social Research*, 3rd edn.

Banakar, Reza 2000, 'Reflections on the methodological issues of the sociology of law', *Journal of Law and Society*, vol. 27, no. 2, p. 273.

Barcham, Manuhuia 2003, 'South–south policy transfer: the case of the Vanuatu Ombudman's Office', *Pacific Economic Bulletin*, vol. 18, no. 2, p. 108.

Beasant, John 1984, *The Santo Rebellion: An imperial reckoning*.

Bedford, Stuart 1996, *Pieces of the Vanuatu Puzzle*.

Bennett, T. W. 1991, *A Sourcebook of African Customary Law for Southern Africa*.

Benton, Richard 2004, Lexicography, law and the transformation of New Zealand jurisprudence, Paper presented at the Symposium on Concepts in Polynesian Customary Law, Auckland, 2004.

Berman, Paul 2007, 'Global legal pluralism', *Southern California Law Review*, vol. 80, p. 1155.

Binihi, Ricky 2005, 'All runaway prisoners behind bars', *Vanuatu Daily Post* (Port Vila), 4 August 2005, p. 5.

Binihi, Ricky 2006, 'NGO wants government to inject more funds into Public Solicitor's Office', *Vanuatu Daily Post* (Port Vila), 13 June 2006, p. 6.

Binihi, Ricky 2006, 'Family Ulas prepared to leave Luganville', *Vanuatu Daily Post* (Port Vila), 3 August 2006, p. 6.

Blackwood, Peter 1981, 'Rank, exchange and leadership in four Vanuatu societies', in Michael Allen (ed.), *Vanuatu: Politics, economics and ritual in island Melanesia*, p. 35.

Blagg, Harry 2005, *A New Way of Doing Business? Community Justice Mechanisms and Sustainable Governance in Western Australia*, Law Reform Commission of Western Australia, Project No. 94.

Blakie, Norman 1991, 'A critique of the use of triangulation in social research', *Quality & Quantity*, vol. 25, p. 115.

Boe, Jerry 2001, *A Review of Cases Relating to the Customary Law of Vanuatu*.

Boege, Volker et al. 2008, *States emerging from hybrid political orders—Pacific experiences*, The Australian Centre for Peace and Conflict Studies Online Occasional Papers Series, vol. 11, viewed 12 November 2008, <http://www.uq.edu.au/acpacs/publications>

Bohane, Ben 2002, 'The boxer: Barak Sope, ex Prime Minister and political maverick', *Pacific Weekly Review*, 25 November – 1 December 2002, p. 6.

Bohannan, Paul 1957, *Justice and Judgment Among the Tiv*.

Boko, Gideon 2000, 'Fair trial and the customary courts in Botswana: questions on legal representation', *Criminal Law Forum*, vol. 11, no. 4, p. 445.

Bolton, Lissant 1993, Dancing in mats: extending *kastom* to women in Vanuatu, PhD thesis, University of Manchester.

Bolton, Lissant 1998, 'Chief Willie Bongmatur Maldo and the role of chiefs in Vanuatu', *Journal of Pacific History*, vol. 33, no. 2, p. 179.

Bolton, Lissant 1998, Praying for the revival of *kastom*: women and Christianity in the Vanuatu cultural centre, Paper presented at the Women, Christians, Citizens: Being female in Melanesia today conference, Sorrento, Victoria, 1998.

Bolton, Lissant 1999, 'Introduction', *Canberra Anthropology*, vol. 22, no. 2, p. 1.

Bolton, Lissant 1999, 'Introduction', *Oceania*, vol. 70, no. 1, p. 1.

Bolton, Lissant 1999, 'Women, place and practice in Vanuatu: a view from Ambae', *Oceania*, vol. 70, no. 1, p. 43.

Bolton, Lissant 2005, Respect in Vanuatu, Paper presented at the Friends of the Vanuatu Museum Talks Series, Port Vila, Vanuatu, 22 November 2005.

Bonnemaison, Joel 1994, *The Tree and the Canoe: History and ethnogeography of Tanna*.

Bonnemaison, Joel 1996, 'Graded societies and societies based on title: forms and rites of traditional political power in Vanuatu', in Joel Bonnemaison et al. (eds), *Arts of Vanuatu*, p. 201.

Bougainville Constitutional Commission 2004, *Report on the Third and Final Draft of the Bougainville Constitution*.

Bouman, Marlies 1987, 'A note on chiefly and national policing in Botswana', *Journal of Legal Pluralism*, vols 25–6, p. 275.

Bourdieu, Pierre and Wacquant, Loic 1992, *An Invitation to Reflexive Sociology*.

Boyd, Marion 2004, *Dispute Resolution in Family Law: Protecting choice, promoting inclusion*, Ministry of the Attorney-General, Ontario, Canada.

Bragg, Harry 2005, *A New Way of Doing Justice Business? Community Justice Mechanisms and Sustainable Governance in Western Australia*.

Braithwaite, John 1999, 'Restorative justice: assessing optimistic and pessimistic accounts', *Crime and Justice*, vol. 25, p. 1.

Braithwaite, John 2003, 'Principles of restorative justice', in A. von Hirsch et al. (eds), *Restorative Justice and Criminal Justice: Competing or reconcilable paradigms?*, p. 1.

Braithwaite, John, Healy, Judith and Dwan, Kathryn 2005, *The Governance of Health and Australia*, Commonwealth of Australia.

Bresnihan, Brian and Woodward, Keith 2002, *Tufala Gavman: Reminiscences from the Anglo-French condominium of the New Hebrides*.

Brown, Ken 1986, 'Criminal law and custom in Solomon Islands', *Queensland Institute of Technology Law Journal*, vol. 2, p. 135.

Brown, Ken 2000, 'Indigenous forums: laughed out of court?', *Alternative Law Journal*, vol. 25, no. 5, p. 216.

Brown, Ken and Corrin Care, Jennifer 1998, 'Conflict in Melanesia: customary law and the rights of women', *Commonwealth Law Bulletin*, p. 1334.

Carter, Richard 2006, *In Search of the Lost*.

Chanock, Martin 1978, 'Neo-traditionalism and the customary law in Malawi', *Journal of African Legal Studies*, vol. 16, p. 80.

Chanock, Martin 2000, 'Introduction', in Sally Moore (ed.), *Law as Process*.

Chanock, Martin 2005, 'Customary law, sustainable development and the failing state', in Peter Orebech et al. (eds), *The Role of Customary Law in Sustainable Development*, p. 338.

Charpentier, Jean-Michel 1996, 'Bislama: origins and functions', in Joel Bonnemaison et al. (eds), *Arts of Vanuatu*, p. 296.

Charpentier, Jean-Michel 2002, *Jan Borrie JB* in Brian Bresnihan and Keith Woodward (eds), *Tufala Gavman: Reminiscences from the Anglo-French condominium of the New Hebrides*, p. 155.

Chiba, Masaji 1985, 'The channel of official law to unofficial law in Japan', in Anthony Allott and Elizabeth Minchin (eds), *People's Law and State Law: The Bellagio papers*, p. 207.

Chiba, Masaji 1986, 'The identity postulate of indigenous law and its function in legal transplantation', in Peter Sack and Elizabeth Minchin (eds), *Legal Pluralism: Proceedings of the Canberra Law Workshop VII*, p. 33.

Chiba, Masaji (ed.) 1986, *Asian Indigenous Law: In interaction with received law*.

Chiba, Masaji 1989, *Legal Pluralism: Towards a general theory through Japanese legal culture*.

Conley, M. and O'Barr, W. 1993, 'Legal anthropology comes home: a brief history of the ethnographic study of law', *Loyola of Los Angeles Law Review*, vol. 27, p. 41.

Cornwall, Andrea and Jewkes, Rachel 1995, 'What is participatory research?', *Social Science and Medicine*, vol. 41, no. 12, p. 1667.

Corrin Care, Jennifer 1999, 'Customary law and human rights in Solomon Islands: a commentary on *Remisio Pusi v James Leni and Others* (cc 218/1995, unreported [High Ct., Solom. Is.])', *Journal of Legal Pluralism and Unofficial Law*, vol. 43, p. 135.

Corrin Care, Jennifer 2001, 'Customary law in conflict: the status of customary law and introduced law in post-colonial Solomon Islands', *University of Queensland Law Journal*, vol. 21, no. 2, p. 167.

Corrin Care, Jennifer 2002, 'Off the peg', *Alternative Law Journal*, vol. 27, no. 5, p. 207.

Corrin Care, Jennifer 2002, 'Wisdom and worthy customs: customary law in the South Pacific', *Reform*, vol. 80, p. 31.

Corrin Care, Jennifer 2003, 'Reconciling customary law and human rights in Melanesia', *Hiberian Law Journal*, vol. 4, p. 53.

Corrin Care, Jennifer 2006, 'A green stick or a fresh stick?: locating customary penalties in the post-colonial era', *Oxford University Commonwealth Law Journal*, vol. 6, no. 1, p. 27.

Corrin Care, Jennifer and Zorn, Jean 2001, 'Legislating pluralism: statutory "developments" in Melanesian customary law', *Journal of Legal Pluralism*, vol. 46, p. 49.

Cotterell, Roger 1992, *The Sociology of Law*, 2nd edn.

Crawford, James, Hennesy, Peter and Fisher, Mary 1988, 'Aboriginal customary laws: proposals for recognition', in Bradford Morse and Gordon Woodman (eds), *Indigenous Law and the State*, p. 27.

Crnkovich, Mary 1996, 'A sentencing circle', *Journal of Legal Pluralism*, vol. 36, p. 159.

Crowley, Terry 1990, *Beach-la-Mar to Bislama: The emergence of a national language in Vanuatu*.

Crowley, Terry 2004, *Bislama Reference Grammar*.

Culliwick, Jonas 2007, 'Sessivi Vila burns', *Vanuatu Daily Post* (Port Vila), 11 March 2007, p. 1.

Curtis, Tim 2002, Talking about place, PhD thesis, The Australian National University.

de Deckker, Paul and Faberon, Jean-Yves 2001, *Custom and the Law*.

Deacon, Bernard 1934, *Malekula: A vanishing people in the New Hebrides*.

Demian, Melissa 2003, 'Custom in the courtroom, law in the village: legal transformations in Papua New Guinea', *Journal of the Royal Anthropological Institute*, vol. 9, p. 97.

Denzin, Norman 1989, *The Research Act: A theoretical introduction to sociological methods*, 3rd edn.

Dewhurst, Dale 2004, 'Parallel justice systems, or a tale of two spiders', in Catherine Bell and David Kahane (eds), *Intercultural Dispute Resolution in Aboriginal Contexts*, p. 213.

Dinnen, Sinclair 1995, 'Custom, community and criminal justice in Papua New Guinea', in Jonathan Aleck and Jackson Rannells (eds), *Custom at the Crossroads*, p. 148.

Dinnen, Sinclair 1999, 'Violence and governance in Melanesia', *Pacific Economic Bulletin*, vol. 14, no. 1, p. 63.

Dinnen, Sinclair 2001, *Law and Order in a Weak State*.

Dinnen, Sinclair 2002, *Building bridges: law and justice reform in Papua New Guinea*, Discussion Paper 2002/2, State, Society and Governance in Melanesia Research Paper Series, The Australian National University, viewed 31 May 2007, <http://rspas.anu.edu.au/melanesia/discussion.php>

Dinnen, Sinclair and Jowitt, Anita (eds) 2003, *A Kind of Mending: Restorative justice in the Pacific islands*.

Douglas, Bronwen 1998, *Across the Great Divide: Journeys in history and anthropology*.

Douglas, Bronwen 2002, 'Christian citizens: women and negotiations of modernity in Vanuatu', *The Contemporary Pacific*, vol. 14, no. 1, p. 1.

Douglas, Bronwen 2005, Christian custom and the Church as structures in 'weak states' in Melanesia, Paper presented at the Civil Society, Religion and Global Governance: Paradigms of power and persuasion Conference, Canberra, Australia, 2005.

Ehrlich, Eugen 1936, *Fundamental Principles of the Sociology of Law*.

Elechi, Ogbonnaya Oko 1996, 'Doing justice without the State: the Afikpo (Ehugbo) Nigeria model of conflict resolution', *International Journal of Comparative and Applied Criminal Justice*, vol. 20, no. 2, p. 337.

Elechi, Oko 2004, Human rights and the African indigenous justice system, Paper presented at the Eighteenth International Conference of the International Society for the Reform of Criminal Law, Montreal, Quebec, Canada, 2004.

Erzberger, Christian and Prein, Gerald 1997, 'Triangulation: validity and empirically based hypothesis construction', *Quality & Quantity*, vol. 31, p. 141.

Facey, Ellen 1983, Ideology and identity: social construction of reality on Nguna, Vanuatu, PhD thesis, University of Sydney.

Farran, Sue 1997, 'Custom and constitutionally protected fundamental rights in the South Pacific region—the approach of the courts to potential conflicts', *The Journal of Pacific Studies*, vol. 21, p. 103.

Farran, Sue 2002, 'Land in Vanuatu: moving forwards looking backwards', *Revue Juridique Polynesienne*, vol. 2, p. 213.

Faundez, Julio 2003, Non-state justice systems in Latin America—case studies: Peru and Colombia, Paper presented at the Workshop on Working with Non-State Justice Systems, UK Department for International Development, 6–7 March 2003.

Fetterman, David 1998, *Ethnography: Step by step*, 2nd edn.

Filimone, Ratu Ralogaivau 2005, *Problem Solving—Community Based Courts Across the Fiji Islands*, Fiji Law Reform Commission.

Findlay, Mark 1997, 'Crime, community penalty and integration with legal formalism in the South Pacific', *The Journal of Pacific Studies*, vol. 21, p. 145.

Fitzgerald, T. 2001, *The Cape York Justice Study Report*, Government of Queensland.

Fitzpatrick, Peter 1984, 'Law and societies', *Osgoode Hall Law Journal*, vol. 22, no. 1, p. 115.

Fitzpatrick, Peter 1985, 'Underdevelopment and the plurality of law', in Anthony Allott and Gordon R. Woodman (eds), *People's Law and State Law: The Bellagio papers*, p. 249.

Fitzpatrick, Peter 1986, 'Custom, law and resistance', in Peter Sack and Elizabeth Minchin (eds), *Legal Pluralism: Proceedings of the Canberra Law Workshop VII*, p. 63.

Fombad, Charles 2004, 'Customary courts and traditional justice in Botswana: present challenges and future perspectives', *Stellenbosch Law Review*, vol. 15, no. 1, p. 166.

Forsyth, Miranda 2003, 'Determining chiefly title: from courts to custom and back again', *Alternative Law Journal*, vol. 28, no. 4, p. 193.

Forsyth, Miranda 2004, 'Banishment and freedom of movement in Samoa', *Journal of South Pacific Law*, vol. 8, no. 2, <http://paclii.org.vu/journals/fJSPL/index.shtml>

Forsyth, Miranda 2004, 'Beyond case law: kastom and courts in Vanuatu', *Victoria University of Wellington Law Review*, vol. 35, no. 2, p. 427.

Forsyth, Miranda 2005, 'Is there horizontal or vertical enforcement of constitutional rights in Vanuatu? *Family Kalontano v Duruaki Council of Chiefs*', *Journal of South Pacific Law*, vol. 9, no. 2, <http://paclii.org.vu/journals/fJSPL/index.shtml>

Forsyth, Miranda 2006, *Report on the Vanuatu Judiciary Conference 2006: The relationship between the* kastom *and state justice systems*, University of the South Pacific, <http://paclii.org.vu/vu/2006_jud_conf_report.html>

Forsyth, Miranda 2006, 'Sorcery and the criminal law in Vanuatu', *LawAsia*, p. 1.

Fraser, Ian 1999, 'Legal theory in Melanesia: pluralism? Dualism? Pluralism long dualism?', *Journal of South Pacific Law*, vol. 3, <http://paclii.org.vu/journals/fJSPL/index.shtml>

Galanter, Marc and Krishnan, Jayanth 2004, '"Bread for the poor": access to justice and the rights of the needy in India', *Hastings Law Journal*, vol. 55, p. 789.

Garae, Len 2003, 'Where custom seems to lack value', *Trading Post* (Port Vila), 15 May 2003, p. 4.

Garae, Len 2003, 'Chiefs urge investigation before reconciliation', *Vanuatu Daily Post* (Port Vila), 20 August 2003, p. 4.

Garae, Len 2004, 'Vaturisu says Ambae chiefs set example', *Vanuatu Daily Post* (Port Vila), 7 October 2004, p. 3.

Garae, Len 2004, 'Police want unemployed sent home', *Vanuatu Daily Post* (Port Vila), 25 November 2004, p. 3.

Garae, Len 2005, 'North Efate chiefs in prison after losing court case', *Vanuatu Daily Post* (Port Vila), 9 May 2005, p. 6.

Garae, Len 2005, 'Chiefs diffuse Tanna fight', *Vanuatu Daily Post* (Port Vila), 8 August 2005, p. 1.

Garae, Len 2005, 'Tension high after Ambrym killing', *Vanuatu Daily Post* (Port Vila), 11 October 2005, p. 3.

Garae, Len 2005, 'Ligo cautions Ambae chiefs not to interfere in alleged rape case', *Vanuatu Daily Post* (Port Vila), 27 October 2005, p. 3.

Garae, Len 2005, 'Court proceeds with rape case despite chief's appeal', *Vanuatu Daily Post* (Port Vila), 2 November 2005, p. 1.

Garae, Len 2005, 'Lakalakabulu allowed to punish Ambaeans', *Vanuatu Daily Post* (Port Vila), 21 November 2005, p. 2.

Garae, Len 2006, 'Police arrest five in tense Luganville', *Vanuatu Daily Post* (Port Vila), 4 August 2006, p. 1.

Garae, Len 2006, 'Pais hits out at police over arrests', *Vanutau Daily Post* (Port Vila), 26 October 2006, p. 3.

Garae, Len 2007, 'Chief Justice opens courts', *Vanuatu Daily Post* (Port Vila), 10 February 2007, p. 1.

Garae, Len 2007, 'Chief Justice makes new appointments', *Vanuatu Daily Post* (Port Vila), 14 February 2007, p. 2.

Garae, Len 2007, 'Chief Tarilama says chiefs, police to be blamed', *Vanuatu Daily Post* (Port Vila), 13 March 2007, p. 3.

Garae, Len and Jerety, Johnety 2007, 'Walkout offenders to be prosecuted', *Vanuatu Daily Post* (Port Vila), 31 May 2007, p. 1.

Gardiner, Margaret 1987, *Footprints on Malekula: A memoir of Bernard Deacon*.

Garu, Selwyn and Yaken, Jack 2001, *Chiefs' Legislation Project Report*, Ministry of Internal Affairs.

Ghai, Yash 1985, 'Vanuatu', in Peter Larmour and R. Qalo (eds), *Decentralisation in the South Pacific*.

Glaser, Barney and Strauss, Anslem 1967, *The Discovery of Grounded Theory: Strategies for qualitative research*.

Gluckman, Max 1955, *The Judicial Process Amongst the Barotse of Northern Rhodesia (Zambia)*.

Goddard, Michael 2004, *Women in Papua New Guinea's village courts*, Discussion Paper 2004/3, State, Society and Governance in Melanesia Research Paper Series, The Australian National University, viewed 31 May 2007, <http://rspas.anu.edu.au/melanesia/discussion.php>

Golub, Stephen 2003, Non-state justice systems in Bangladesh and the Philippines, Paper presented at the Workshop on Working with Non-State Justice Systems, UK Department for International Development, 6–7 March 2003.

Gordon, Robert and Meggitt, Mervyn 1985, *Law and Order in the New Guinea Highlands*.

Gorecki, Paul 1996, 'The original colonisation of Vanuatu', in Joel Bonnemaison et al. (eds), *Arts of Vanuatu*.

Government of Autonomous Region of Bougainville 2004, *The Constitution*.

Government of Botswana n.d., *Customary Courts Act*.

Government of Fiji n.d., *Criminal Procedure Code*.

Government of New South Wales 2002, *Report of the Review of the Legislation Affecting the Vanuatu Legal Sector*, NSW Attorney-General's Department.

Government of Papua New Guinea 2000, *Underlying Law Act 2000*.

Government of Samoa n.d., *Criminal Procedure Act*.

Government of Samoa n.d., *Village Fono Act*.

Government of Solomon Islands 2000, *Customs Recognition Act 2000*, no. 7.

Government of South Africa 2008, *Policy Framework on the Traditional Justice System Under the Constitution*, Department of Justice and Constitutional Development, South Africa.

Government of the United Kingdom 2003, *Safety, Security and Access to Justice*, GRC Exchange, Department for International Development, viewed 2 February 2005, <http://www.grc-exchange.org./g_themes/ssaj_workshop0303.html>

Government of the United Kingdom 2004, *Non-State Justice and Security Systems*, Department for International Development, United Kingdom.

Government of Tokelau 1986, *Taupulega Act 1986*.

Government of Tuvalu 1997, *Falekaupule Act 1997*.

Government of Vanuatu 1914, *The Protocol Respecting the New Hebrides (1914)*.

Government of Vanuatu 1962, *New Hebrides Condominium*, Joint Regulation 12 of 1962.

Government of Vanuatu 1997, *Initial Report to the Committee on the Rights of the Child*, State Party Report, CRC/C/28/Add.8, <http://www.unhchr.ch/tbs/doc.nsf/(Symbol)/ d29c5df777ac4b59802565240055b862?Opendocument>

Government of Vanuatu 2006, *Correctional Services Act 2006*.

Government of Vanuatu 2006, *Criminal Procedure Code (Amendment) Act 2006*.

Government of Vanuatu 2006, *Island Courts (Amendment) Act 2006*.

Government of Vanuatu 2006, *National Council of Chiefs Act 2006*.

Government of Vanuatu 2006, *Penal Code (Amendment) Act 2006*.

Government of Vanuatu n.d., *Constitution of the Republic of Vanuatu*.

Government of Vanuatu n.d., *Criminal Procedure Code*, Cap 136.

Government of Vanuatu n.d., *Decentralisation Act*, Cap 127.

Government of Vanuatu n.d., *Island Courts Act*, Cap 167.

Government of Vanuatu n.d., *Law Commission Act*, Cap 115.

Government of Vanuatu n.d., *National Council of Chiefs (Organisation) Act*, Cap 183.

Government of Vanuatu n.d., *Penal Code*, Cap 135.

Granovetter, Mark 1973, 'The strength of weak ties', *The American Journal of Sociology*, vol. 78, no. 6, p. 1360.

Gray, Ian 1971, The emergence of leaders in the New Hebrides, MA thesis, University of Auckland.

Greenhouse, Carol 1985, 'Mediation: a comparative approach', *Man (N.S.)*, vol. 20, p. 90.

Greenhouse, Carol 1998, 'Legal pluralism and cultural difference: what is the difference? A response to Professor Woodman', *Journal of Legal Pluralism*, vol. 42, p. 61.

Griffiths, Anne 1996, 'Between paradigms: differing perspectives on justice in Molepolole Botswana', *Journal of Legal Pluralism and Unofficial Law*, vol. 36, p. 195.

Griffiths, Anne 1998, 'Legal pluralism in Botswana: women's access to law', *Journal of Legal Pluralism and Unofficial Law*, vol. 42, p. 123.

Griffiths, Anne 2004, Customary law in a transnational world: legal pluralism revisited, Paper presented at the Customary Law in Polynesia Conference, Auckland, 12 October 2004.

Griffiths, John 1985, 'Four laws of interaction in circumstances of legal pluralism: first steps towards an explanatory theory', in Anthony Allott and E. Minchin (eds), *People's Law and State Law: The Bellagio papers*, p. 217.

Griffiths, John 1985, 'Introduction', in Anthony Allott and Gordon R. Woodman (eds), *People's Law and State Law: The Bellagio papers*, p. 13.

Griffiths, John 1986, 'What is legal pluralism?', *Journal of Legal Pluralism*, vol. 24, p. 1.

Griffiths, John 1995, 'Legal pluralism and the theory of legislation—with special reference to the regulation of euthanasia', in Hanne Petersen and Henrik Zahle (eds), *Legal Polycentricity: Consequences of pluralism in law*, p. 201.

Grills, Scott (ed.) 1998, *Doing Ethnographic Research: Fieldwork settings*.

Guiart, Jean 1996, 'Land tenure and hierarchies in Eastern Melanesia', *Pacific Studies*, vol. 19, no. 1, p. 1.

Gulliver, Paul 1963, *Social Control in an African Society*.

Gupta, Akhil and Ferguson, James 1997, 'Discipline and practice: "the field" as site, method and location in anthropology', in Akhil Gupta and James Ferguson (eds), *Anthropological Locations: Boundaries and grounds of a field science*, p. 1.

Hammersley, Martyn and Atkinson, Paul 1995, *Ethnography: Principles in practice*, 2nd edn.

Harrington, C. B. and Yngvesson, B. 1990, 'Interpretive sociolegal research', *Law & Social Inquiry*, vol. 15, no. 1, p. 135.

Harris, Olivia (ed.) 1996, *Inside and Outside the Law: Anthropological studies of authority and ambiguity*.

Hart, H. L. A. 1961, *The Concept of Law*, 2nd edn.

Henckel, Timo 2006, 'Vanuatu's economy: is the glass half empty or half full?', *Pacific Economic Bulletin*, vol. 21, no. 3, p. 1.

Hess, Sabine 2005, Person and place on Vanua Lava, Vanuatu, PhD thesis, The Australian National University.

Hess, Sabine 2006, 'Strathern's Melanesian "dividual" and the Christian "individual": a perspective from Vanua Lava, Vanuatu', *Oceania*, vol. 76, no. 3, p. 285.

Hoebel, Adamson 1954, *The Law of Primitive Man*.

Hoebel, Adamson and Llewellyn, K. 1941, *The Cheyenne Way: Conflict and case law in primitive jurisprudence*.

Hohe, Tanja and Nixon, Rod 2003, *Reconciling Justice: 'Traditional' law and state judiciary in East Timor*, United States Institute of Peace.

Holmes, Patricia 1996, Land tenure in Vanuatu: custom, culture, tradition…and development?, Masters in Arts (Foreign Affairs and Trade) thesis.

Horton, Lynn 2006, 'Contesting state multiculturalisms: indigenous land struggles in Eastern Panama', *Journal of Latin American Studies*, vol. 38, p. 829.

Huffer, Elise 2005, 'Governance, corruption and ethics in the Pacific', *The Contemporary Pacific*, vol. 17, no. 1, p. 118

Huffer, Elise and So'o, Asofou (eds) 2000, *Governance in Samoa*.

Hughes, Desma 2004, *Masculinity, Mental Health and Violence in Vanuatu Youth*, University of the South Pacific.

Hughes, Robert 2003, 'Legal pluralism and the problem of identity', in Anita Jowitt and Tess Newton Cain (eds), *Passage of Change*, p. 329.

Human Rights and Equal Opportunity Commission 2003, Submission to the Northern Territory Law Reform Committee Inquiry into Aboriginal Customary Law in the Northern Territory, Aboriginal and Torres Strait Social Justice Commissioner of the Human Rights and Equal Opportunity Commission.

Hume, Lynne 1986, 'Church and custom on Maewo, Vanuatu', *Oceania*, vol. 56, p. 304.

Humphreys, C. B. 1926, *The Southern New Hebrides: An ethnological record*.

Humphreys, Sally 1985, 'Law as discourse', in Sally Humphreys (ed), *The Discourse of Law: History and anthropology*, p. 241.

Ibhawoh, Bonny 2001, 'Cultural tradition and national human rights standards in conflict', in K. Hastrup (ed.), *Legal Cultures and Human Rights: The challenges of diversity*, p. 85.

International Centre for Criminal Law Reform and Criminal Justice Policy, School of Criminology and Simon Fraser University 1995, *Putting Aboriginal Justice Devolution into Practice: The Canadian and international experience*, Workshop report, viewed 16 November 2006, <http://www.icclr.law.ubc.ca/Publications/Reports/Aboriginal.PDF>

Jackson, Moana n.d., *The Maori and the criminal justice system He Whaipaanga Hou—a new perspective. Part 2*, Study Series 18, Department of Justice, New Zealand.

Jacomb, Edward 1914, *France and England in the New Hebrides: The Anglo French condominium.*

James, R. 1992, 'A comparative view of the underlying law', in R. James and I. Fraser (eds), *Legal Issues in Developing Society*, p. 146.

Jessep, O. and Reagan, A. 2001, 'Developing a coherent underlying law—interpreting custom and common law', *Twenty Years of the Papua New Guinea Constitution.*

Jick, Todd 1979, 'Mixing qualitative and quantitative methods: triangulation in action', *Administrative Science Quarterly*, vol. 24, no. 4, p. 602.

Johnston, Les and Shearing, Clifford 2003, *Governing Security: Explorations in policing and justice.*

Jolly, Margaret 1979, Men, women and rank in South Pentecost, PhD thesis, The University of Sydney.

Jolly, Margaret 1992, 'Custom and the way of the land: past and present in Vanuatu and Fiji', *Oceania*, vol. 62, p. 330.

Jolly, Margaret 1992, 'Spectres of inauthenticity', *The Contemporary Pacific*, vol. 4, no. 1, p. 49.

Jolly, Margaret 1994, *Women of the Place: Kastom, colonialism and gender in Vanuatu.*

Jolly, Margaret 1996, 'Woman ikat raet long human raet o no?', *Feminist Review*, vol. 52, Spring, p. 169.

Jolly, Margaret 1997, 'Woman–nation–state in Vanuatu: women as signs and subjects in the discourses of *kastom*, modernity and Christianity', in Ton Otto and Nicholas Thomas (eds), *Narratives of Nation in the South Pacific.*

Joseph, Robert 2007, The interface between Maori custom and state regulatory systems—Tikanga Maori consultation under the *Resource Management Act 1991*, Paper presented at the Tuhonohono Symposium: State and Custom, Waikato Endowed College, New Zealand.

Jowitt, Anita 1999, 'Island courts in Vanuatu', *Journal of South Pacific Law*, vol. 3, <http://paclii.org.vu/journals/fJSPL/index.shtml>

Jowitt, Anita 2002, 'Melanesia in review: issues and events, 2002: Vanuatu', *The Contemporary Pacific*, vol. 15, no. 2, p. 463, <http://archives.pireport.org/archive/2003/October/10-02-tcp1.htm>

Jowitt, Anita 2004, 'Indigenous land grievances, customary land disputes and restorative justice', *Journal of South Pacific Law*, vol. 8, no. 2, <http://paclii.org.vu/journals/fJSPL/index.shtml>

Jowitt, Anita 2005, 'Vanuatu', in Transparency International, *Global Corruption Report*, <http://www.transparency.org/publications/gcr/download_gcr/download_gcr_2005>

Joy, Shirley 2003, 'Police plead for government support to fight crime', *Vanuatu Daily Post* (Port Vila), 22 October 2003.

Judicial Commission of New South Wales and Aboriginal Justice Advisory Council 2003, *Circle Sentencing in New South Wales: A review and evaluation*.

Jupp, James and Sawer, Marian 1982, 'Colonial and post-independence politics: Vanuatu', in R. J. May and Hank Nelson (eds), *Melanesia: Beyond diversity*, p. 549.

Kalontano, Alice, Vatu, Charles and Whyte, Jenny 2003, *Assessing Community Perspectives on Governance in Vanuatu*, Foundation of the Peoples of the South Pacific International.

Kaloran, Morris 2007, 'Correctional services ensure rehabilitation and reintegration', *Vanuatu Daily Post* (Port Vila), 14 March 2007, p. 4.

Keesing, Roger 1982, 'Kastom in Melanesia: an overview', *Mankind*, vol. 13, no. 4, p. 297.

Keesing, Roger 1989, 'Creating the past: custom and identity in the contemporary Pacific', *The Contemporary Pacific*, vol. 1, nos 1–2, p. 19.

Keesing, Roger and Tonkinson, Robert (eds) 1982, 'Reinventing traditional culture: the politics of *kastom* in island Melanesia', *Mankind* Special Issue, vol. 13, no. 4.

Kelly, Susanna 1999, Unwrapping mats: people, land and material culture in Tongoa, Central Vanuatu, PhD thesis, University College London.

Knut, Mikjel Rio 2002, The third man: manifestations of agency on Ambrym Island, Vanuatu, PhD thesis, University of Bergen.

Kolig, Eric 1981, 'Custom or foreign influence: the paradox of Santo, Vanuatu', *Pacific Perspective*, vol. 10, no. 1, p. 57.

Kopinak, Janice 1999, 'The use of triangulation in a study of refugee well-being', *Quality & Quantity*, vol. 33, p. 169.

Kwa, E. L. 2001, *Constitutional Law of Papua New Guinea*.

Lakalakabulu Council 1996, *1996 Annual Report*.

Lakalakabulu Council 1997, *Constitution of Lakalakabulu Area Council of Chiefs*.

Larcom, Joan 1982, 'The invention of convention', *Mankind*, vol. 13, no. 4, p. 330.

Larcom, Joan 1990, 'Custom by decree: legitimation crisis in Vanuatu', in J. Linnekin and L. Poyer (eds), *Cultural Identity and Ethnicity in the Pacific*, p. 175.

Law Reform Commission of Western Australia 2006, *Aboriginal customary laws*, Report Project No. 94.

Law Reform Commission of Western Australia 2006, *Aboriginal customary laws*, Discussion Paper Project No. 94.

Lawrence, Peter 1969, 'The state versus stateless societies in Papua New Guinea', in B. J. Brown and Geoffrey Sawer (eds), *Fashion of Law in New Guinea: Being an account of the past, present and developing system of laws in Papua and New Guinea*, p. 15.

Lawson, Stephanie 1996, *Tradition Versus Democracy in the South Pacific: Fiji, Tonga and Western Samoa*.

Layard, John 1942, *Stone Men of Malekula: Vao*.

Leo, Colin 2001, The Heren Hala Council of Chiefs: a dispute resolution mechanism in North Pentecost—chief's powers and limitations, Unpublished ms.

Lindstrom, Lamont 1981, Achieving wisdom: knowledge and politics on Tanna (Vanuatu), PhD thesis, University of California, Berkeley.

Lindstrom, Lamont 1981, 'Speech and kava on Tanna', in Michael Allen (ed.), *Vanuatu: Politics, economics and ritual in island Melanesia*, p. 379.

Lindstrom, Lamont 1984, 'Doctor, lawyer, wise man, priest: big-men and knowledge in Melanesia', *Man*, vol. 19, no. 2, p. 291.

Lindstrom, Lamont 1990, 'Straight talk on Tanna', in K. A. Watson-Gegeo and G. M. White (eds), *Disentangling Conflict Discourse*, p. 373.

Lindstrom, Lamont 1994, 'Traditional cultural policy in Melanesia', in Lamont Lindstrom and Geoffrey M. White (eds), *Culture, Kastom, Tradition: Developing cultural policy in Melanesia.*

Lindstrom, Lamont 1997, 'Chiefs in Vanuatu today', in Geoffrey White and Lamont Lindstrom (eds), *Chiefs Today: Traditional Pacific leadership and the postcolonial state*, p. 211.

Lini, Hilda Motarilavoa 2006, Indigenous laws and *kastom* system, Paper presented at the Vanuatu Judiciary Law Conference, Port Vila, 2006.

Lini, Lora 2006, 'Escapees seek chiefs' help', *Vanuatu Daily Post* (Port Vila), 8 May 2006, p. 1.

Lini, Lora 2006, 'A clash of power: chiefs help prisoners return to Jail', *Vanuatu Daily Post* (Port Vila), 10 May 2006, p. 2.

Lini, Lora 2006, 'Law and order situation in Luganville questioned', *Vanuatu Daily Post* (Port Vila), 22 August 2006, p. 6.

Lini, Lora 2007, 'MP Kalsakau condemns black magic', *Vanuatu Daily Post* (Port Vila), 8 March 2007, p. 1.

Lini, Walter 1980, *Beyond Pandemonium: From the New Hebrides to Vanuatu.*

Lunabek, Vincent 2003, Developing culturally appropriate dispute resolution procedures: the Vanuatu experience, Paper presented at the fifteenth Pacific Judicial Conference, Madang, Papua New Guinea, 2003.

Lunabek, Vincent 2004, 'Adjudication of customary law in the Pacific', *Commonwealth Judicial Journal*, vol. 15, no. 4, p. 25.

Lynch, John 1998, *Pacific Languages: An introduction.*

Lynch, John and Crowley, Terry 2001, *Languages of Vanuatu: A new survey and bibliography.*

MacClancy, Jeremy 1978, Issues in the analysis of ethnography of the New Hebrides, Bachelor of Letters thesis, Oxford University.

MacClancy, Jeremy 1983, Vanuatu and kastom: a study of cultural symbols in the inception of a nation state in the South Pacific, PhD thesis, Oxford University.

MacClancy, Jeremy 2002, *To Kill a Bird with Two Stones: A short history of Vanuatu.*

MacKenzie, Melody 2007, Hawaiian values in state legislation, Paper presented at the Tuhonohono Symposium: State and Custom, Waikato Endowed College, New Zealand.

MacLachlan, Campbell 1988, 'The recognition of Aboriginal customary law: pluralism beyond the colonial paradigm—a review article', *International and Comparative Law Quarterly*, vol. 37, no. 2, p. 368.

Maine, Henry 1861, *Ancient Law*.

Makin, Bob 2005, 'Lissant Bolton on women and trade in Vanuatu', *The Independent* (Port Vila), 27 November 2005, p. 18.

Malinowski, Bronislaw 1967, *Crime and Custom in Savage Society*.

Malloch, Margaret and Kaloran, Morris 2006, A report on equity and women in Vanuatu, Paper presented at the Conference After 26 Years: Collaborative research in Vanuatu since independence, Port Vila, Vanuatu, 2006.

Malvatumauri 1994, 'Kastom polisi blong Malvatumauri', in Geoffrey M. White and Lamont Lindstrom (eds), *Culture, Kastom, Tradition: Developing cultural policy in Melanesia*, p. 229.

Malvatumauri 2004, *Corporate Plan 2004–2008*.

Marcus, George 1995, 'Ethnography in/of the world system: the emergence of multi-sited ethnography', *Annual Review of Anthropology*, vol. 24, p. 95.

Marcus, George 1999, 'What is at stake—and what is not—in the idea and practice of multi-sited ethnography', *Canberra Anthropology*, vol. 22, no. 2, p. 6.

Masing, Helen 1991, 'Braed praes', in Vanuatu National Council of Women (ed.), *Who Will Carry the Bag?*.

Mason, Merrin 2000, 'Domestic violence in Vanuatu', in Sinclair Dinnen and Ley Allison (eds), *Reflections on Violence in Melanesia*, p. 119.

Mavromatis, Geoff et al. 2005, *Implementation of the* Customary Land Tribunal Act No 7, 2001.

McLeod, Abby 2004, *Women, Peace and Security: An examination of the role of women in the prevention and resolution of conflict in Vanuatu*, UNIFEM.

Mearns, David 2002, *Looking Both Ways: Models for justice in East Timor*, Australian Legal Resources International.

Meleisea, M. 2000, 'Governance, development and leadership in Polynesia', in E. Huffer and A. So'o (eds), *Governance in Samoa*, p. 197.

Merry, Sally 1988, 'Legal pluralism', *Law & Society*, vol. 22, no. 5, p. 869.

Miles, William 1998, *Bridging Mental Boundaries in a Postcolonial Microcosm: Identity and development in Vanuatu*.

Mitchell, Jean 1998, *Young People Speak: A report on the Vanuatu Young Peoples' Project—April 1997 to June 1998*, Vanuatu Cultural Centre.

Mitchell, Jean 2000, 'Violence as continuity: violence as rupture—narratives from an urban settlement in Vanuatu', in Sinclair Dinnen and Allison Ley (eds), *Reflections on Violence in Melanesia*, p. 189.

Mitchell, Kirsty 2001, Custom in New Caledonia: its interaction with French law and prospects for survival, Masters in Foreign Affairs and Trade thesis, Monash University.

Moldofsky, L. 2001, *A Place in the Sun*, Time International, viewed 12 March 2007, <http://www.time.com/time/pacific/magazine/20010820/woman.html>

Moore, Sally Falk 1978, 'Law and social change: the semi-autonomous social field as an appropriate subject of study', *Law as Process: An anthropological approach*, p. 54.

Moore, Sally Falk 1978, *Law as Process: An anthropological approach*.

Moore, Sally Falk 1992, 'Treating law and knowledge: telling colonial officers what to say to Africans about running "their own" native courts', *Law and Society Review*, vol. 26, p. 11.

Morgan, Michael 2001, *Conference Report of the Governance for the Future: Young people and Vanuatu's governance agenda conference*.

Morgan, Michael 2004, 'Political fragmentation and the policy environment in Vanuatu, 1980–2004', *Pacific Economic Bulletin*, vol. 19, no. 3, p. 40.

Morgan, Michael 2005, *Cultures of dominance: institutional and cultural influences on parliamentary politics in Melanesia*, Discussion Paper 2005/2, State, Society and Governance in Melanesia Research Paper Series, The Australian National University, <http://rspas.anu.edu.au/melanesia/research.php>

Morgan, Michael 2006, 'Vanuatu 2001–2004: political will and the containment of unrest', in Chris Griffin and Dennis Rumley (eds), *Australia's Arc of Instability*, p. 215.

Morgan, Michael and McLeod, Abby 2007, 'An incomplete arc: analysing the potential for violent conflict in the Republic of Vanuatu', *Pacific Affairs*, vol. 80, no. 1.

Morse, Bradford and Woodman, Gordon (eds) 1988, *Indigenous Law and the State*.

Mortensen, Reid 2001, 'A voyage in God's canoe: law and religion in Melanesia', *Current Legal Issues*, vol. 4, p. 509.

Muller, Kal 1972, 'Field notes on the small Nambas', *Journal de la Société Des Oceanistes*, vol. 28, no. 35, p. 153.

Mundy, Martha and Kelly, Tobias 2002, 'Introduction', in Martha Mundy (ed.), *Law and Anthropology*, p. xv.

Murray, Christina 2003, South Africa's troubled royalty: traditional leaders after democracy, Paper presented at the Geoffrey Sawyer Lecture Series, Canberra, 2003.

Narokobi, Bernard 1986, 'In search of a Melanesian jurisprudence', in Peter Sack and E. Minchin (eds), *Legal Pluralism: Proceedings of the Canberra Law Workshop VII*, p. 215.

Narokobi, Bernard 1989, 'Law and custom in Melanesia', *Pacific Perspectives*, vol. 14, no. 1, p. 17.

Narokobi, Bernard 1989, *Lo Blong Yumi Yet*.

National Statistics Office 2000, *The 1999 Vanuatu National Population and Housing Census*.

National Statistics Office 2002, *Statistical Yearbook of Vanuatu*.

Nelson, Hank 2006, *Governments, states and labels*, Discussion Paper 2006/1, State, Society and Governance in Melanesia Research Paper Series, The Australian National University, viewed 10 March 2007, <http://rspas.anu.edu.au/melanesia/research.php>

New Zealand Law Commission 2006, *Converging currents: custom and human rights in the Pacific*, Study Paper 17.

New Zealand Law Reform Commission 2006, *Report of Proceedings*, New Zealand Law Commission Workshop on Custom and Human Rights in the Pacific, Nadi, Fiji, 2006.

Newton Cain, Tess 2001, 'Convergence or clash? The recognition of customary law and practice in sentencing decisions of the courts of the Pacific island region', *Melbourne Journal of International Law*, vol. 2, no. 1.

Newton Cain, Tess 2003, *Final Report Base Line Survey Organisational Climate Survey*, AusAID.

Nielsen, Marianne 1994, 'Criminal justice and native self-government in Canada: is the incorporation of traditional justice practices feasible?', *Law & Anthropology*, vol. 6, p. 7.

Nikoletan 1994, *Tanna Island Kastom Law*.

Northern Territory Law Reform Commission 2003, *Report of the Committee of Inquiry into Aboriginal customary law*, Report No. 8.

Ntumy, M. 1995, 'The dream of a Melanesian jurisprudence: the purpose and limits of law reform', in Jonathan Aleck and Jackson Rannells (eds), *Custom at the Crossroads*, p. 7.

NZAID 2005, *Proposed Vanuatu Community Probation Service: Summary report*.

Oba, Abdulmumini 2004, 'Lawyers, legal education and the Shari'ah courts in Nigeria', *Journal of Legal Pluralism*, vol. 49, p. 113.

Oba, Abdulmumini 2004, 'The Shariah court of appeal in Northern Nigeria: the continuing crisis of jurisdiction', *American Journal of Comparative Law*, vol. 52, p. 859.

Olson, M. D. 2000, 'Articulating custom: the politics and poetics of social transformation in Samoa', *Journal of Legal Pluralism*, vol. 45, p. 19.

Ombudsman of Vanuatu 1999, *Granting of leases by the former Minister of Lands Mr Paul Telukluk to himself, family members and wantoks*, VUOM 6, <http://www.paclii.org.vu>

Ombudsman of Vanuatu 1999, *Public report on prison conditions and mismanagement of the prison budget*, VUOM 15, <http://www.paclii.org.vu>

Ombudsman of Vanuatu 2002, *Public report on the unlawful arrest and detention of Mrs Aspin Jack*, VUOM 11, <http://www.paclii.org.vu>

Ombudsman of Vanuatu 2003, *Detention of a 12 year old child in Santo Prison*, VUOM 2, <http://www.paclii.org.vu>

Ombudsman of Vanuatu 2003, *Public report on police brutality during operation on Central Pentecost*, VUOM 16, <http://www.paclii.org.vu>

Otlhogile, Bojosi 1993, 'Criminal justice and the problems of a dual legal system in Botswana', *Criminal Law Forum*, vol. 4, p. 521.

Ottley, B. 1992, 'Custom and introduced criminal justice', in R. James and I. Fraser (eds), *Legal Issues in Developing Society*, p. 128.

Ottley, Brian 2002, 'Reconciling modernity and tradition: PNG's underlying law act', *Reform*, vol. 80, p. 22.

Ottley, Brian and Zorn, Jean 1983, 'Criminal law in Papua New Guinea: code, custom and courts in conflict', *American Journal of Comparative Law*, p. 251.

Parker, Christine 1999, *Just Lawyers: Regulation and access to justice*.

Parker, Christine 2002, *The Open Corporation*.

Paterson, Don 1995, 'South Pacific customary law and common law: their interrelationship', *Commonwealth Law Bulletin*, vol. 21, no. 2, p. 660.

Paterson, Don 2003, *A Report on Penama Provincial Government (Penama System)*.

Paterson, Don 2004, *Report on Customary Law Research Project*, AusAID.

Paterson, Don 2006, 'Customary reconciliation in sentencing for sexual offences: a review of *Public Prosecutor v Ben and Others* and *Public Prosecutor v*

Tarilingi and Gamma', *Journal of South Pacific Law*, vol. 10, no. 1, <http://paclii.org.vu/journals/fJSPL/index.shtml>

Patterson, Mary 2002, 'Leading lights in the "Mother of Darkness": perspectives on leadership and value in North Ambrym, Vanuatu', *Oceania*, vol. 73, p. 126.

Patterson, Mary 2002, 'Moving histories: an analysis of the dynamics of place in North Ambrym, Vanuatu', *The Australian Journal of Anthropology*, vol. 13, no. 2, p. 200.

Pedersen, Mille S. 2003, The historical development of the Greenlandic judicial system, Paper presented at the Expert Seminar on Indigenous Peoples and the Administration of Justice, Madrid, Spain, 2003.

Penal Reform International 2000, *Access to Justice in Sub-Saharan Africa: The role of traditional and informal justice systems*.

Penama Province 1994, *Penama Social Development Plan*.

Philibert, Jean-Marc 1981, 'Living under two flags', in Michael Allen (ed.), *Vanuatu: Politics, economics and ritual in island Melanesia*, p. 315.

Philibert, Jean-Marc 1986, 'The politics of tradition: toward a generic culture in Vanuatu', *Mankind*, vol. 16, no. 1, p. 1.

Pospisil, Leopold 1958, *Kapauku Papuans and Their Law*.

Pospisil, Leopold 1974, *Anthropology of Law: A comparative theory*.

Potas, Ivan et al. 2003, 'Circle sentencing in New South Wales: a review and evaluation', *Australian Indigenous Law Reporter*, vol. 2004, p. 16, <http://www.austlii.edu.au/au/journals/AILR/2004/16.html>

Powles, Guy 1997, 'The common law at bay? The scope and status of customary law regimes in the Pacific', *Journal of Pacific Studies*, vol. 21, p. 61.

Powles, Guy 2004, Some thoughts on the future of customary law in Pacific island states, Paper presented at the Australasian Law Teachers Association Conference, Darwin, July 2004.

Premdas, Ralph and Steeves, Jeff 1984, *Decentralisation and political change in Melanesia: Papua New Guinea, the Solomon Islands, and Vanuatu*, Working Paper No. 3, South Pacific Forum Working Papers Series.

Proctor, J. H. 1999, 'Scottish missionaries and the governance of the New Hebrides', *Journal of Church and State*, vol. 41, no. 2, p. 349.

Putnam, Robert 2000, *Bowling Alone: The collapse and revival of American community*.

Ragin, Charles C. 1994, *Constructing Social Research*.

Rawlings, Gregory 1995, *Urbanisation, Kastom, Economic Practice and the Dynamics of Social Change in a Vanuatu Peri-Urban Community: The case of Pango Village, South Efate—a field report.*

Rawlings, Gregory 1999, 'Foundations of urbanisation: Port Vila Town and Pango Village, Vanuatu', *Oceania*, vol. 70, no. 1, p. 72.

Reagan, A. 1992, 'Constitutionalism, legitimacy and the judiciary', in R. James and I. Fraser (eds), *Legal Issues in Developing Society.*

Regenvanu, Ralph 1999, 'Afterword: Vanuatu perspectives on research', *Oceania*, vol. 70, no. 1, p. 98.

Regenvanu, Ralph 2007, State of emergency, Posting to the Vanuatu Research Interest Group, 5 March 2007.

Richardson, David 1987, Roots of unrest: decolonization in Vanuatu with particular reference to Tanna, Masters of Arts thesis, University of Hawai'i.

Riles, Annelise 1994, 'Representing in-between: law, anthropology, and the rhetoric of interdisciplinarity', *University of Illinois Law Review*, no. 3, p. 597.

Rio, Knut 2002, 'The sorcerer as an absented third person: formation of fear and anger in Vanuatu', *Social Analysis*, vol. 46, no. 3, p. 129.

Ritchie, Jane and Lewis, Jane (eds) 2003, *Qualitative Research Practice: A guide for social scientists and researchers.*

Roberts, Simon 1972, 'The survival of the traditional Tswana courts in the national legal system of Botswana', *Journal of African Law*, vol. 16, p. 103.

Roberts, Simon 1979, *Order and Dispute: An introduction to legal anthropology.*

Roberts, Simon 2005, 'After government? On representing law without the State', *The Modern Law Review*, vol. 68, no. 1, p. 1.

Rodman, Margaret 1976, Spheres of exchange in a northern New Hebridean society, Masters of Arts thesis, McMaster University.

Rodman, Margaret 1981, 'A boundary and a bridge: women's pig killing as a border-crossing between spheres of exchange in East Aoba', in Michael Allen (ed.), *Vanuatu: Politics, economics and ritual in island Melanesia*, p. 85.

Rodman, Margaret 1981, Customary illusions: land and copra in Longana, Vanuatu, PhD thesis, McMaster University.

Rodman, Margaret 1987, *Masters of Tradition.*

Rodman, Margaret 2001, *Houses Far From Home: British colonial space in the New Hebrides*.

Rodman, William 1973, Men of influence men of rank: leadership and the graded society on Aoba, New Hebrides, PhD thesis, University of Chicago.

Rodman, William 1977, 'Big men and middlemen: the politics of law in Longana', *American Ethnologist*, vol. 4, p. 525.

Rodman, William 1983, 'Gaps, bridges and levels of law: middlemen as mediators in a Vanuatu society', in William Rodman and Dorothy Ayers Counts (eds), *Middlemen and Brokers in Oceania*, p. 69.

Rodman, William 1985, 'A law unto themselves: legal innovation in Ambae, Vanuatu', *American Ethnologist*, vol. 12, p. 603.

Rodman, William 1993, 'The law of the State and the state of the law in Vanuatu', in Virginia Lockwood et al. (eds), *Contemporary Pacific Societies: Studies in development and change*, p. 55.

Roebuck, D. 1985, 'Custom, common law and constructive judicial lawmaking', in R. De Vere, D. Colqhoun-Kerr and J. Kaburise, *Essays on the Constitution of Papua New Guinea*, Tenth Anniversary Advisory Committee, Port Moresby.

Rouland, Norbert 1994, *Legal Anthropology*.

Rousseau, Benedicta 2003, *The Report of the Juvenile Justice Project: A resource on juvenile justice and kastom law in Vanuatu*, Vanuatu Cultural Centre.

Rousseau, Benedicta 2004, The achievement of simultaneity: kastom in contemporary Vanuatu, PhD thesis, University of Cambridge.

Roy, Raja 2004, 'Challenges for juridical pluralism and customary laws of indigenous peoples: the case of Chittagong hill tracts, Bangladesh', *Arizona Journal of International & Comparative Law*, vol. 21, no. 1, p. 113.

Rubenstein, Robert 1978, Placing the self on Malo: an account of the culture on Malo Island, New Hebrides, PhD thesis, Bryn Mawr College.

Sack, Peter 1985, 'Bobotoi and Pulu Melanesian law: normative order or way of life?', *Journal de la Societe des Oceanistes*, vol. 41, p. 15.

Sack, Peter and Aleck, Jonathan (eds) 1992, *Law and Anthropology*.

Sack, Peter and Minchin, Elizabeth (eds) 1986, *Legal Pluralism: Proceedings of the Canberra Law Workshop VII*.

Sahlins, Marshall 1963, 'Poor man, rich man, big man, chief: political types in Melanesia and Polynesia', *Comparative Studies in Society and History*, vol. 5, p. 285.

Santos, Boaventura de Sousa 2002, *Toward a New Legal Common Sense*, 2nd edn.

Santos, Boaventura de Sousa 2006, 'The heterogeneous state and legal pluralism in Mozambique', *Law and Society Review*, vol. 40, p. 39.

Scaglion, R. 1983, *Customary Law in Papua New Guinea: A Melanesian view*, Law Reform Commission of Papua New Guinea.

Scarr, Deryck 1967, *Fragments of Empire: A history of the Western Pacific High Commission 1877–1914*.

Schärf, Wilfried 2001, 'Policy options on community justice', in Wilfried Schärf and Daniel Nina (eds), *The Other Law: Non-state ordering in South Africa*.

Schärf, Wilfried 2003, Non-state justice systems in southern Africa: how should governments respond?, Paper presented at the Workshop on Working with Non-State Justice Systems, UK Department for International Development, 6–7 March 2003.

Schärf, Wilfried et al. 2003, *Access to Justice for the Poor of Malawi? An appraisal of access to justice provided to the poor of Malawi by the lower subordinate courts and the customary justice forums*, Malawi Law Commission.

Selznick, Philip 1992, *The Moral Commonwealth: Social theory and the promise of community*.

Seymour-Smith, Charlotte 1986, *The Macmillan Dictionary of Anthropology*.

Shaffir, William 1998, 'Doing ethnographic research in Jewish orthodox communities', in Scott Grills (ed.), *Doing Ethnographic Research: Fieldwork settings*.

Shah, Prakash 2005, *Legal Pluralism in Conflict: Coping with cultural diversity in law*.

Shears, Richard 1980, *The Coconut War: The crisis on Espiritu Santo*.

Sheridan, Greg 2006, 'Melanesia a huge disaster', *The Australian* (Sydney, Australia), 20 April 2006, viewed 20 April 2006 <http://www.theaustralian.com.au>

Sherkin, Samantha 1999, Forever united: identity construction across the rural–urban divide, PhD thesis, University of Adelaide.

Shineberg, D. 1966, 'The sandalwood trade in Melanesian economics, 1841–65', *Journal of Pacific History*, vol. 1, p. 129.

Sillitoe, Paul 1998, *An Introduction to the Anthropology of Melanesia: Culture and tradition*.

Simo, Joel 2005, *Report of the National Review of the Customary Land Tribunal Program in Vanuatu*, Vanuatu Cultural Centre.

Sinclair, James 1981, *Kiap: Australia's patrol officers in Papua New Guinea*.

Slatter, Claire 2007, Gender and custom in the South Pacific, Paper presented at the Tuhonohono Symposium: State and Custom, Waikato Endowed College, New Zealand.

Snyder, Francis 1981, 'Anthropology, dispute processes and law: a critical introduction', *British Journal of Law & Society*, vol. 8, no. 2, p. 141.

South African Law Commission (SALC) 2003, *Report on traditional courts and the judicial function of traditional leaders*, Project No. 90.

Speiser, Felix 1923, *Ethnology of Vanuatu: An early twentieth century study*.

Spriggs, Matthew 1981, *Vegetable Kingdoms: Taro irrigation and Pacific prehistory*.

Stavenhagen, Rodolfo 2004, *Report of the Special Rapporteur on the Situation of Human Rights and Fundamental Freedoms of Indigenous Peoples*, United Nations Commission on Human Rights.

Steiner, Henry 1991, 'Ideals and counter-ideals in the struggle over autonomy regimes for minorities', *Notre Dame Law Review*, vol. 66, p. 1539.

Stewart, A. 2000, 'The contribution of feminist legal scholarship', in A. Stewart (ed.), *Gender Law and Social Justice*, p. 3.

Storey, Donovan 2005, *Urban governance in Pacific island countries: advancing an overdue agenda*, Discussion Paper 2005/7, State, Society and Governance in Melanesia Discussion Paper Series, The Australian National University, <http://rspas.anu.edu.au/melanesia/discussion.php>

Strathern, Marilyn 1988, *The Gender of the Gift*.

Super, Gail 2000, *A Needs Assessment of Juvenile Justice Issues in Fiji and Vanuatu*, UNICEF.

Supreme Court of Vanuatu 2002, *Island Court Review*.

Svesson, Tom 2005, 'Interlegality, a process for strengthening indigenous peoples' autonomy: the case of the Sami in Norway', *Journal of Legal Pluralism*, vol. 51, p. 51.

Tamanaha, Brian 1993, 'The folly of the "social scientific" concept of legal pluralism', *Journal of Law and Society*, vol. 20, p. 192.

Tamanaha, Brian 2001, *A General Jurisprudence of Law and Society*.

Tamanaha, Brian 2007, *Understanding legal pluralism: past to present, local to global*, St John's University School of Law Legal Studies Research Paper Series, no. 07-0080.

Taurakoto, Michael 2005, *Good Governance, Education, Advocacy and Training Project Report*, Wan Smol Bag Theatre.

Taylor, Steven and Bogdan, Robert 1998, *Introduction to Qualitative Research Methods: A guidebook and resource*, 3rd edn.

Te Matahauriki Research Institute 2007, *Te Matapunenga: A compendium of references to the concepts and institutions of Maori customary law*, Te Matahauriki Research Institute, University of Waikato, New Zealand.

Tepahae, Chief Philip 1997, *Chiefly power in Southern Vanuatu*, Discussion Paper 1997/9, State, Society and Governance in Melanesia Research Paper Series, The Australian National University, <http://rspas.anu.edu.au/melanesia/research.php>

Tie, Warwick 1999, *Legal Pluralism: Toward a multicultural conception of law*.

Tinning, Esther 2004, 'Court sentences brothers and sister for assault', *Vanuatu Daily Post* (Port Vila), 11 September 2004, p. 8.

Toa, Evelyn 2005, 'Hundreds of summons stranded with Public Prosecutor', *The Independent* (Port Vila), 8 March 2005, <http://www.news.vu/en/news/judicial/050308-summons-stranded.shtml>

Tomaino, John 2006, *Aboriginal (Nunga) courts*, Information Bulletin No. 39, Government of South Australia, viewed 20 July 2006, <http://www.ocsar.sa.gov.au/docs/information_bulletins/IB39.pdf>

Tong, Maureen 2003, Indigenous peoples and the administration of justice: the South African case study, Paper presented at the Expert Seminar on Indigenous Peoples and the Administration of Justice, Madrid, Spain, 2003.

Tonkinson, Robert 1968, *Maat Village Efate: A relocated community in the New Hebrides*.

Tonkinson, Robert 1981, 'Church and kastom in Southeast Ambrym', in Michael Allen (ed.), *Vanuatu: Politics, economics and ritual in island Melanesia*, p. 237.

Tonkinson, Robert 1982, 'National identity and the problem of kastom in Vanuatu', *Mankind*, vol. 13, no. 4, p. 306.

Tonkinson, Robert 1982, 'Vanuatu values: a changing symbiosis', in R. J. May and Hank Nelson (eds), *Melanesia: Beyond diversity*, p. 73.

Tor, Roselyn and Toka, Anthea 2004, *Gender, Kastom and Domestic Violence: A research on the historical trend, extent and impact of domestic violence in Vanuatu*, Department of Women's Affairs.

Tryon, Darrell 1996, 'Dialect chaining and the use of geographical space', in Joel Bonnemaison et al. (eds), *Arts of Vanuatu*, p. 170.

Tryon, Darrell 2000, 'Identity and power in Vanuatu', *The New Pacific Review*, vol. 1, no. 1, p. 32.

Twining, William 2003, 'A post-Westphalian conception of law', *Law and Society Review*, vol. 37, p. 199.

United Nations 2002, *Vanuatu: United Nations Development Assistance Framework (2003–2007)*, Office of the United Nations Resident Coordinator.

United Nations 2006, *Human Development Report 2006*, United Nations Development Program, <http://hdr.undp.org/hdr2006/ statistics/countries/data_sheets/cty_ds_VUT.html>

Va'a, U. 2000, 'Local government in Samoa and the search for balance', in Elise Huffer and A. So'o (eds), *Governance in Samoa*.

Vaai, Saleimoa 1995, The rule of law and the Faamatai: legal pluralism in Western Samoa, PhD thesis, The Australian National University.

Vaai, Saleimoa 1997, 'The idea of law: a Pacific perspective', *The Journal of Pacific Studies*, vol. 21, p. 225.

Vaai, Saleimoa 1999, *Samoa Faamatai and the Rule of Law*.

Van Trease, Howard 1995, *Melanesian Politics: Stael blong Vanuatu*.

Vanuatu Electoral Commission 2002, *Sixth General Election Report*.

von Benda-Beckmann, Franz 1981, 'Some comments on the problems of comparing the relationship between traditional and state systems of administration of justice in Africa and Indonesia', *Journal of Legal Pluralism*, vol. 19, p. 165.

von Benda-Beckmann, Franz 1985, 'Some comparative generalizations about the differential use of state and folk institutions of dispute settlement', in Anthony Allott and Gordon R. Woodman (eds), *People's Law and State Law: The Bellagio papers*, p. 187.

von Benda-Beckmann, Franz 1986, 'Anthropology and comparative law', in Keebet von Benda-Beckmann and Fons Strijbosch (eds), *Anthropology of Law in the Netherlands: Essays on legal pluralism*, p. 90.

von Benda-Beckmann, Franz 1988, 'Comment on Merry', *Law and Society Review*, vol. 22, no. 5, p. 897.

von Benda-Beckmann, Franz 2001, 'Legal pluralism and social justice in economic and political development', *IDS Bulletin*, vol. 32, no. 1, p. 46.

von Benda-Beckmann, Franz 2002, 'Who's afraid of legal pluralism?', in *Legal Pluralism and Unofficial Law in Social, Economic and Political Development: Papers of the XIIIth International Congress of the Commission on Folk Law and Legal Pluralism, 7–10 April, 2002, Chiangmai, Thailand*.

von Benda-Beckmann, Franz and von Benda-Beckmann, Keebet 2006, 'Changing one is changing all: dynamics in the Adat-Islam-state triangle', *Journal of Legal Pluralism*, vols 53–4, p. 239.

von Benda-Beckmann, Franz and von Benda-Beckmann, Keebet 2006, 'The dynamics of change and continuity in plural legal orders', *Journal of Legal Pluralism*, vols 53–4, p. 1.

von Benda-Beckmann, Keebet 2002, 'The contexts of law', *Legal Pluralism and Unofficial Law in Social, Economic and Political Development: Papers of the XIIIth International Congress of the Commission on Folk Law and Legal Pluralism, 7–10 April, 2002, Chiangmai, Thailand*, p. 299.

Vurobaravu, Fred 2005, 'VP given mayor in new arrangement', *Vanuatu Daily Post* (Port Vila), 11 November 2005, p. 1.

Wai, Isaac and Maia, Paul 2005, 'What we do in Saraga: building community peace and harmony', *Development Bulletin*, vol. 67.

Waiwo, Elenor 2005, 'Than receives new chiefly title', *Vanuatu Daily Post* (Port Vila), 25 October 2005, p. 6.

Waiwo, Elenor 2007, 'Father accepts sorry for son's death', *Vanuatu Daily Post* (Port Vila), 10 March 2007, p. 6.

Walker, David 1980, *The Oxford Companion to Law*.

Walter, Matthew 2004, 'Luganville judiciary team to visit Gaua', *Vanuatu Daily Post* (Port Vila), 22 September 2004, p. 6.

Walter, Matthew 2004, 'Forty suspects netted in Malekula operation', *Vanuatu Daily Post* (Port Vila), 26 November 2004, p. 2.

Walter, Matthew 2005, 'Financial difficulties delay hearing of criminal cases', *Vanuatu Daily Post* (Port Vila), 3 August 2005, p. 4.

Wawn, William 1973, *The South Sea Islanders and the Queensland Labour Trade*.

Webber, Jeremy 1993, 'Individuality, equality and difference: justifications for a parallel system of Aboriginal justice', in Royal Commission on Aboriginal Peoples (ed.), *Aboriginal Peoples and the Justice System: Report of the National Round Table on Aboriginal Justice Issues*, p. 133.

Webber, Jeremy 1994, *Reimagining Canada: Language, culture, community and the Canadian constitution*.

Webber, Jeremy 1995, 'Relations of force and relations of justice: the emergence of normative community between colonists and aboriginal peoples', *Osgoode Hall Law Journal*, vol. 33, p. 623.

Weisbrot, David 1988, 'Law and native custom in Vanuatu', *Law and Anthropology*, vol. 3, p. 103.

Weisbrot, David 1989, 'Custom, pluralism and realism in Vanuatu: legal development and the role of customary law', *Pacific Studies*, vol. 13, no. 1, p. 65.

West, Robin 2003, *Re-Imagining Justice*.

Westermark, George 1978, 'Village courts in question: the nature of court procedure', *Melanesian Law Journal*, vol. 6, nos 1–2, p. 79.

Westermark, George 1981, Legal pluralism and village courts in Agarabi, PhD thesis, The University of Washington.

Westermark, George 1986, 'Court is an arrow: legal pluralism in Papua New Guinea', *Ethnology*, vol. 25, no. 2, p. 131.

White, Geoffrey 2006, *Indigenous governance in Melanesia*, Research Paper, State, Society and Governance in Melanesia Research Paper Series, The Australian National University, <http://rspas.anu.edu.au/melanesia/research.php>

White, Geoffrey M. 1993, 'Three discourses of custom', *Anthropological Forum*, vol. 6, no. 4, p. 475.

White, Geoffrey M. 1997, 'The discourse of chiefs', in Lamont Lindstrom and Geoffrey White (eds), *Chiefs Today: Traditional Pacific leadership and the postcolonial state*, p. 229.

Willie, Royson 2005, 'Inmates remind president of deteriorating prisons', *Vanuatu Daily Post* (Port Vila), 29 October 2005, p. 2.

Willie, Royson 2007, 'Armed police arrest over 100', *Vanuatu Daily Post* (Port Vila), 6 March 2007, p. 1.

Willie, Royson 2007, 'Vt77m worth of Melip marijuana finally destroyed', *Vanuatu Daily Post* (Port Vila), 9 May 2007, p. 1.

Wirrick, Parkinson 2008, 'Restricting the freedom of movement in Vanuatu: custom in conflict with human rights', *Journal of South Pacific Law*, vol. 12, no. 1, viewed 12 November 2008, <http://paclii.org.vu/journals/fJSPL/vol1no1/>

Wittersheim, Eric 2005, *Melanesian elites and modern politics in New Caledonia and Vanuatu*, Discussion Paper 1998/3, State, Society and Governance in Melanesia Discussion Paper Series, The Australian National University, <http://rspas.anu.edu.au/melanesia/discussion.php>

Woodman, Gordon 1996, 'Legal pluralism and the search for justice', *Journal of African Law*, vol. 40, p. 152.

Woodman, Gordon 1998, 'Ideological combat and social observation: recent debate about legal pluralism', *Journal of Legal Pluralism*, vol. 42, p. 21.

Woodman, Gordon 1999, 'Legal theory, anthropology and planned legal pluralism', in Keebet von Benda-Beckmann and Harald Finkler (eds), *Papers of the XIth International Congress Folk Law and Legal Pluralism: Societies in transformation*, p. 30.

Woodman, Gordon 2001, 'Customary law in common law systems', *IDS Bulletin*, vol. 32, no. 1, p. 28.

Woodman, Gordon 2002, 'Why there can be no map of law', *Legal Pluralism and Unofficial Law in Social, Economic and Political Development: Papers of the XIIIth International Congress of the Commission on Folk Law and Legal Pluralism, 7–10 April, 2002, Chiangmai, Thailand*, p. 383.

Woodman, Gordon 2007, 'The possibilities of co-existence of religious laws with other laws', in Erik Sand et al. (eds), *Religion and Law in Multicultural Societies*.

Zorn, Jean 1990, 'Lawyers, anthropologists and the study of law: encounters in the New Guinea Highlands', *Law and Social Inquiry*, p. 271.

Zorn, Jean 1991, 'Making law in Papua New Guinea: the influence of customary law on common law', *Journal of Pacific Studies*, vol. 14, no. 4, p. 1.

Zorn, Jean and Corrin Care, Jennifer 2002, '"Barava tru": judicial approaches to the pleading and proof of custom in the South Pacific', *The International and Comparative Law Quarterly*, vol. 51, no. 3, p. 612.

Legal cases

Vanuatu

Banga vs Waiwo, 1996, VUSC 5, <http://www.paclii.org.vu>

Boe & Taga vs Thomas, 1980–94, Van LR 293.

M vs P, Re the child G, 1980–94, Van LR 333.

Marango vs Chief Natmatsaru and Maraki Navata Council of Chiefs, 2002, VUSC 33, <http://www.paclii.org.vu>

Public Prosecutor vs Atis Willie, 2004, VUCA 4, <http://www.paclii.org.vu>

Public Prosecutor vs Ben and Others, 2005, VUSC 108, <http://www.paclii.org.vu>

Public Prosecutor vs Gideon, 2002, VUCA 7, <http://www.paclii.org.vu>

Public Prosecutor vs Kota and Others, 1989–94, 2 VLR 661.

Public Prosecutor vs Munrel, 2005, VUSC 75, <http://www.paclii.org.vu>

Public Prosecutor vs Niala, 2004, VUCA 25, <http://www.paclii.org.vu>

Tenene vs Nmak, 2003, VUSC 2, <http://www.paclii.org.vu>

Waiwo vs Waiwo and Banga, 1996, VUMC 1, <http://www.paclii.org.vu>

Working Group for Justice vs Government of the Republic of Vanuatu, 2002,
VUSC 55, <http://www.paclii.org.vu>

Other jurisdictions

Leituala vs Mauga, 2004, WSSC 9, <http://www.paclii.org.vu>

Police vs Afoa, 1994, WSSC 3, <http://www.paclii.org.vu>

Sefo vs Attorney-General, 2000, WSSC 18, <http://www.paclii.org.vu>

Teonea vs Kaupule and Falekaupule, Unreported, High Court of Tuvalu, October
2005.

Newspaper articles

'Something must be done', Editorial, *The Independent* (Port Vila), 28 February
2004, p. 2.

'No faen i go long PVTCC—kot i mas harem Apil: bong i talem', *The Independent*
(Port Vila), 14 August 2005, p. 4.

'Municipal elections: from chiefly to municipal council?', *The Independent* (Port
Vila), 30 October 2005, p. 1.

'Transparency International raises concerns over public prosecution handling
of Ambae rape case', *Vanuatu Daily Post* (Port Vila), 5 December 2005.

'Police breakout: chiefs maintain peace', *The Independent* (Port Vila), 14 May
2006, p. 2.

'Twenty escape from inhuman treatment', *The Independent* (Port Vila), 14 May
2006, p. 3.

'Correctional reform bills', *Vanuatu Daily Post* (Port Vila), 15 May 2006, p. 4.

'Protest over human rights of prisoners', *Vanuatu Daily Post* (Port Vila), 16 May
2006, p. 4.

'Re: protest over human rights of prisoners', *Vanuatu Daily Post* (Port Vila),
22 May 2006, p. 7.

'Confrontation religieuse a Atchin', *The Independent* (Port Vila), 5 November
2006, p. 3.

'Repeated Theft Victim' 2007, 'Have you been offered a "great deal" for
electronics?', *Your Letters, Vanuatu Daily Post* (Port Vila), 3 March 2007,
p. 7.

'Two confirmed dead in Ambrym and Tanna clash', *Vanuatu Daily Post* (Port
Vila), 5 March 2007, p. 1.

'Efate MP Sope deplores killings', *Vanuatu Daily Post* (Port Vila), 7 March 2007,
p. 1.

'Malvatumauri to meet over riots', *Vanuatu Daily Post* (Port Vila), 9 March 2007, p. 3.

'West Ambrym chiefs willing to supply local food to victims', *Vanuatu Daily Post* (Port Vila), 10 March 2007, p. 3.

'The roots of the man Tanna/man Ambrym row', *The Independent* (Port Vila), 11 March 2007, p. 3.

'Vieroroa' 2007, 'Freedom of movement clause', *Your Letters, Vanuatu Daily Post* (Port Vila), 26 March 2007, p. 7.

'Police Concern Officer' 2007, 'Complaint against Correctional Services Management', *Your Letters, Vanuatu Daily Post* (Port Vila), 20 April 2007, p. 5.

'Three VRP members assaulted by UMP leaders', *Vanuatu Daily Post* (Port Vila), 21 April 2007, p. 8.

'Ol Jif blong Ambrym oli askem kompensesen mo depotsesen blong Franco long gavman', *The Independent* (Port Vila), 22 April 2007, p. 5.

'Kranki Kona', *Vanuatu Daily Post* (Port Vila), 26 April 2007, p. 5.

'Premiers contacts entre Les Iles Banks/Torres et le ministere du culte "Terre Promise"', *The Vanuatu Independent* (Port Vila), 3–9 June 2007, p. 11.

www.ingramcontent.com/pod-product-compliance
Lightning Source LLC
Chambersburg PA
CBHW061227270326
41928CB00025B/3376